NEGOTIATING GOVERNANCE ON
NON-TRADITIONAL SECURITY IN
SOUTHEAST ASIA AND BEYOND

Negotiating Governance on Non-Traditional Security in Southeast Asia and Beyond

Mely Caballero-Anthony

Columbia University Press

New York

Columbia University Press
Publishers Since 1893
New York   Chichester, West Sussex
cup.columbia.edu

Library of Congress Cataloging-in-Publication Data
Names: Anthony, Mely Caballero, author.
Title: Negotiating governance on non-traditional security in Southeast
Asia and beyond / Mely Caballero-Anthony.
Description: New York : Columbia University Press, 2018. | Includes
bibliographical references and index.
Identifiers: LCCN 2018019513 | ISBN 9780231183000 (cloth : alk. paper) |
ISBN 9780231182997 (pbk. : alk. paper) | ISBN 9780231544498 (e-book)
Subjects: LCSH: Human security—Southeast Asia. |
Human security—East Asia. | Security, International—Southeast
Asia—International cooperation. | Security, International—
East Asia—International cooperation. | Emergency management—
Southeast Asia—International cooperation. | Emergency
management—East Asia—International cooperation. |
Non-state actors (International relations)—Southeast Asia. |
Non-state actors (International relations)—East Asia.
Classification: LCC JZ6009.S644 A57 2018 | DDC 355/.033559—dc23
LC record available at https://lccn.loc.gov/2018019513

Columbia University Press books are printed on permanent and durable acid-free paper.
Printed in the United States of America

Cover art: Irny Volina © Alamy

Contents

Preface   vii
List of Abbreviations   xiii

I   Security Governance in Southeast Asia and Beyond   1

II   State and Non-State Actors and NTS Governance
in Southeast Asia and Beyond   26

III   Governance of Health Security   52

IV   Governance of Environmental Security   85

V   Governance of Migration   113

VI   Governance of Humanitarian Assistance and
Disaster Relief Operations   141

VII   Governance of Nuclear Energy   171

VIII   Governance of Food Security   196

[v]

Conclusion: Building Security Governance in Times
of Turbulence and Uncertainty   218

Notes   237
Bibliography   275
Index   305

Preface

There is a "new security consensus" where "the biggest security threats we face now, and in the decades ahead, go far beyond States waging aggressive war. They extend to poverty, infectious disease and environmental degradation; war and violence within States; the spread and possible use of nuclear, radiological, chemical and biological weapons; terrorism; and transnational organized crime. The threats are from non-State actors as well as States, and to human security as well as State security."

—UN HIGH-LEVEL PANEL ON THREATS, CHALLENGES AND CHANGES, 2004

In my years working on non-traditional security (NTS) challenges, I have always wanted to write about my experience of how these threats were being dealt with by states and non-state actors in the region. My journey began in 2003 when a novel virus hit East Asia. Severe acute respiratory syndrome (SARS) caught the region by surprise, causing widespread fear and uncertainty as it spread across and beyond the region. That experience to me was most instructive.

While governments grappled with controlling an international health crisis from escalating further, the realities of responding to the transboundary security threats posed by SARS were unfolding. The crisis exposed limitations in the ability and capacity of states to effectively address this kind of challenge. And, given that the crisis was caused by a novel virus that transcended borders, the power of states to secure their borders was also called into question. States were also faced with the emergence of other actors—international organizations, transnational networks, local and international nongovernmental organizations, grassroots movements—that wanted to have say on how the threats were addressed. The array of actors competed with states and even among themselves in claiming a space in the governance arena, actively redefining security, setting the agenda for security policies, and transforming security practices.

As the different actors negotiated their roles within the governance space, I began to observe the beginnings of a new mode of security governance where both state and non-state actors can be "security actors," with the latter providing security where there had been none and filling in the gaps in security provision when states' responses are lacking. From the health crisis in 2003 to the many other types of NTS threats that are confronting the region, we are seeing civil society organizations and the private sector getting involved and working with governments, regional institutions like the Association of Southeast Asian Nations (ASEAN), and international organizations like the World Health Organization and the United Nations Office for the Coordination of Humanitarian Affairs, in helping address a range of NTS threats affecting the region, from pandemics to transboundary pollution, irregular migration, and humanitarian disasters.

The proliferation of actors in the region's security space has led me to question how much has changed in regional security practices and to reexamine the nature of security governance in Southeast Asia and the wider East Asian region. In the first place, can security governance even exist in a region of Westphalian states known to be overly zealous about protecting their sovereignty? If yes, how can security governance be described and operationalized within the context of the region? In writing this book, I started with the premise that in an increasingly complex global environment, security governance is no longer just be about governments and their policies alone. Security governance is now about how state and non-state actors across multiple levels and across tracks work together to pursue shared goals of peace, security, and development.

In capturing the complexities of NTS threats and the developments in security governance, I argue that East Asia, and particularly the ASEAN region, presents a mosaic of security governors representing multiple sites of governance that are shaping the nature of regional security governance. Knowledge of who these security governors are and how they carry out their security roles allows us to appreciate the thick web of multilayered security processes that have evolved and are continuing to do so in the region. In doing so, we move beyond state-centric analyses of security governance, delve deeper into the complexities of how new security challenges affect our security, and explore new approaches in addressing the different kinds of twenty-first century problems.

The book sets out to answer the following questions:

- How have NTS threats changed state behavior and security practices in East Asia, particularly Southeast Asia?

- How has the involvement of different security actors and security governors changed the nature of security governance in the region?
- To what extent has the emergence of different security governors effected normative change in security governance in Southeast Asia?
- What explains the success or failure to institute change?
- What are the implications of the dynamic processes of security governance on the future of East Asia's regional security architecture?

In addressing these questions, the book provides a new perspective on the dynamic intersections between security, regionalism, and governance in Southeast Asia and the wider East Asian region. Why is this important? East Asia, broadly understood as comprising the ten member states of ASEAN plus China, Japan, and South Korea, is where we have seen some of the most robust developments in building multilateral security institutions, from regional bodies like ASEAN, to wider security frameworks like ASEAN Plus Three, the ASEAN Regional Forum, and the East Asia Summit. These also make East Asia the only region in the world with multilateral security institutions that facilitate active engagement between the major powers (United States, China, Japan, India) and small- and medium-sized powers (i.e., the countries of Southeast Asia). Yet multilateral security cooperation, impressive as it has been, is not the culmination of the security governance story in Southeast Asia and the broader East Asian region. I argue that the emergence of a multiplicity of security actors in response to NTS threats is transforming the nature of security governance in the region. Security practices are moving from regional multilateral cooperation to a more complex mode of security governance where states are no longer the main security actors.

The new modes of security governance are explained in chapters 1 and 2 of the book, followed by six case studies on security governance focused respectively on health, the environment, migration, humanitarian crises, nuclear energy, and food security. Through the analyses of the six NTS challenges, the book aims to provide insights on variations in security governance that are both bottom-up and top-down and involve different actors and institutions in East Asia. Arguably, these processes can be regarded as constitutive processes that redefine regional norms in managing security threats. As the cases show, there have been tensions and conflicts among the different security actors, but nonetheless the processes continue to evolve. It is therefore important to capture these multiple processes in order to better shape the future of the region's security landscape.

My experience in examining the dynamics of security governance continues after having written this book. I have been fortunate to have been involved in the multilayered governance processes that I have described in this book. As head of the Centre for Non-Traditional Security Studies (NTS Centre) at the S. Rajaratnam School of International Studies (RSIS), I have benefited from being part of the think tank community engaged in the region's work on health governance, humanitarian assistance and disaster relief, nuclear energy governance, and food security. Having had the opportunity to serve as director of external relations at the ASEAN Secretariat in 2011–2012, and as member and most recently chair of the UN Secretary-General's Advisory Board on Disarmament Matters, I am able to appreciate the many challenges, opportunities, and rewards of bringing state and non-state actors together in addressing the NTS challenges facing the region and the global community today. This book therefore is also a journal of the many journeys that people have taken in ensuring the human security of the peoples in the region. I salute their dedication and commitment to their work and advocacy.

I am deeply grateful for all those who have helped me in many ways in writing this book. My sincere thanks to Ong Keng Yong, executive deputy chair of RSIS, for his valuable support and encouragement as I worked on this book during and after my sabbatical. My thanks also to my dear colleagues at the RSIS NTS Centre, whose boundless energy in working on numerous NTS research projects is uplifting. My special thanks to Lina Gong, Julius Trajano, Jose Ma Luis Montesclaros, and Beatrice Bernardino for their research support. I am also most grateful to Yen Ong, who deserves major credit for her excellent editorial skills and thoughtful comments. My thanks to Paul Teng, Alistair Cook, and Jonatan Lassa, whose insights on NTS governance in the region have been both congenial and stimulating. I also wish to thank the anonymous reviewers of my book whose constructive comments helped me to flesh out the major arguments of this book.

I am grateful to friends and colleagues in ASEAN and beyond whose leadership and commitment to work on human security and NTS in the region have been a constant inspiration, including the late Surin Pitsuwan, Noeleen Heyzer, Carolina Hernandez, Soedrajat Djiwandono, Makarim Wibisono, Adelina Kamal, Syed Faisal, Rahmawati Husein, Ton Nu Thi Ninh, and ANM Muniruzzaman. My thanks also to many friends in various parts of the region who shared their views on the many human security challenges and policies we face today. I cannot name all of them, but among them are Simon Tay, Amitav Acharya, Rizal Sukma, Dan Smith, Zha Daojiong, Yanzhong Huang, Miki Honda, Leena Gosh, Rahimah Abdulrahim, Noel Morada, Sara Davies, Alex Bellamy, and Trevor Findlay.

Finally, to dearest Denis and Jeremy, whose love, support, patience, and humor have sustained me throughout the writing of this book, making the journey a more enjoyable experience than it would otherwise have been.

Abbreviations

AADMER	ASEAN Agreement on Disaster Management and Emergency Response
ACSC	ASEAN Civil Society Conference
ADInet	ASEAN Disaster Information Network
ADMM	ASEAN Defence Ministers Meeting
AERR	ASEAN Emergency Rice Reserve
AFSIS	ASEAN Plus Three Food Security Information System
AHA Centre	ASEAN Coordinating Centre for Humanitarian Assistance on Disaster Management
AMMDM	ASEAN Ministerial Meeting on Disaster Management
APA	ASEAN Peoples' Assembly
APEC	Asia-Pacific Economic Cooperation
APLN	Asia-Pacific Leadership Network for Nuclear Non-Proliferation and Disarmament
APTERR	ASEAN Plus Three Emergency Rice Reserve
ASEAN	Association of Southeast Asian Nations
ASEAN-ERAT	ASEAN Emergency Rapid Assessment Team
ASEAN Plus Three	ASEAN plus China, Japan, and South Korea

ASEAN-ISIS	ASEAN-Institutes of Strategic and International Studies
ASEANTOM	ASEAN Network of Regulatory Bodies on Atomic Energy
AusAID	Australian Agency for International Development
BATAN	National Nuclear Energy Agency of Indonesia
BIG	Geospatial Information Agency (Indonesia)
COMMIT	Coordinated Mekong Ministerial Initiative against Trafficking
CSCAP	Council for Security Cooperation in the Asia Pacific
DELSA	Disaster Emergency Logistics System for ASEAN
ECPAT	End Child Prostitution, Child Pornography and Trafficking of Children for Sexual Purposes
FAO	Food and Agriculture Organization of the United Nations
FSC	Forest Stewardship Council
Gavi	Global Alliance for Vaccines and Immunization
GDP	gross domestic product
GF-TAD	Global Framework for Progressive Control of Transboundary Animal Diseases
HADR	humanitarian assistance and disaster relief
IAEA	International Atomic Energy Agency
ICRC	International Committee of the Red Cross
IOM	International Organization for Migration
MERS	Middle East respiratory syndrome
NADI	Track 2 Network of ASEAN Defense and Security Institutions
NGO	nongovernmental organization
NTS	non-traditional security
NTS Centre	Centre for Non-Traditional Security Studies
OCHA	United Nations Office for the Coordination of Humanitarian Affairs

OECD	Organization for Economic Cooperation and Development
PEPFAR	President's Emergency Plan for AIDS Relief (US)
RSIS	S. Rajaratnam School of International Studies
RSPO	Roundtable on Sustainable Palm Oil
SAPA	Solidarity for Asian People's Advocacy
SARS	severe acute respiratory syndrome
SEARCA	Southeast Asian Regional Center for Graduate Study and Research in Agriculture
TEPCO	Tokyo Electric Power Company
UNDP	United Nations Development Programme
UNHCR	United Nations High Commissioner for Refugees
WFP	World Food Programme
WHO	World Health Organization
WWF	World Wide Fund for Nature

CHAPTER I

Security Governance in Southeast Asia and Beyond

It is the best of times, and the worst of times. We have everything before us, we have nothing before us.

—BASED ON CHARLES DICKENS, *A TALE OF TWO CITIES*, 1859

These are interesting times for Asia, with dramatic transformations occurring in its economic, political, and strategic landscapes. The region is experiencing rapid economic growth, one of the fastest in the world; and it has proven remarkably resilient in the aftermath of the 2007 global financial crisis. Even as many parts of North America and Europe are still reeling from the destructive impact of the crisis, the region has largely bounced back, with many countries posting positive economic growth over the last several years. This upward trajectory has been most visible in Southeast Asia and the wider East Asian region. (East Asia is often understood to encompass the ten countries of Southeast Asia—namely, Brunei, Cambodia, Indonesia, Laos, Malaysia, Myanmar, the Philippines, Singapore, Thailand, and Vietnam—and the three Northeast Asian states of China, Japan, and South Korea. For the purposes of this book, I will be using this designation for this region.)

This economic vibrancy has changed the face of the region. Home to more than half of the world's population of 7.5 billion, East Asia is rapidly urbanizing. The region's major capitals and megacities boast teeming skylines and extensive infrastructure development, with mass transportation systems that promise faster and more efficient trains, new ports and airports, and new airlines with modern fleets that have significantly expanded regional and international travel. The economic buzz is further fueled by an increasingly affluent and mobile population flocking to shopping and tourist destinations in the region and beyond.

East Asia's dazzling economic prospects are tempered, however, by gnawing unease over the security outlook for the region. Security analysts warn of the risks of escalating territorial disputes in the South China Sea and the growing precariousness of an unstable North Korea with increasing nuclear capabilities. Threats of terrorism and violent extremism have plagued the region over the last decade or so. The paradox is that while East Asia is and continues to be a significant engine of global economic growth, it is also a region where security challenges abound.

The Case for a Security Governance Analysis

The Changing Security Landscape

Discussions of Southeast Asian security cannot be confined to nor divorced from the wider region that it is highly integrated with—East Asia. But what is East Asia? How big is its geographical footprint? These questions remain the subject of intense debate among scholars and analysts. For many scholars of Asian regionalism, East Asia is essentially about the deeply embedded interactions between the ten Southeast Asian states, which are also members of the Association of Southeast Asian Nations (ASEAN), and the three Northeast Asian states of China, Japan, and South Korea.[1] With ASEAN as the institutional hub, East Asia is generally taken to refer to the ASEAN Plus Three configuration. But the idea of East Asian security has a wider geographical footprint. It brings into the fold the states to the south of ASEAN, namely, Australia and New Zealand, and it stretches northward to India and westward to Russia, the United States, and Canada. This is reflected in the configuration of an important institution in the region called the East Asia Summit, a regional body established in 2005 that brings the thirteen states of the ASEAN Plus Three together with India, Australia, New Zealand, and, since 2001, the United States and Russia.

What is less contested is that East Asia articulates more than a geographical space. It could be understood as a constructed "region," defined by the dynamism and strength of the ties that bind the states and the societies of this region. Although the region is marked by great diversity of countries and cultures, the ties that exist and bind these countries together extend beyond the political and economic spheres to span the sociocultural and emotional links made possible by an increasingly hyperconnected world. Given this, the discussion of security governance in Southeast Asia necessarily goes beyond the geographic space of ASEAN and into the interlocking processes generated within the broad landscape of the ASEAN states and their engagement with the three Northeast Asian states. Thus, while the examples of security governance covered in this book focus largely on security challenges found in Southeast Asia, within the context of multilevel and multi-actor governance processes, the repeated reference to East Asia as the regional arena underscores the interconnectedness among actors and institutional frameworks that are constantly engaged in the dynamic processes of governance.

The increased, and increasingly multiplex, connectivities in the region are indeed significant. While we celebrate the revolutionary advances in information technology that have made ASEAN Plus Three and the rest of the world one global village, these interlinkages have also made us more sensitive, exposed, and vulnerable to the different security challenges confronting the region. And it is increasingly difficult to remain insulated from the problems affecting humanity. Whether you are from Indonesia or China, or from Japan, Russia, or the United States, an insecurity in one state could become everyone else's insecurity. We have seen how terrorism and religious extremism, pandemics, and financial crises have translated into far-reaching transborder security implications for states and societies.

The breadth of the security threats that can reach one's border and the speed at which they may arrive underscore how deeply interconnected and interdependent the world is. Addressing the UN General Assembly at the 2005 World Summit Meeting, then UN secretary-general Kofi Annan remarked that "in today's world, no State, however powerful, can protect itself on its own. Likewise, no country, weak or strong, can realize prosperity in a vacuum."[2] He highlighted that the security challenges of the twenty-first century range from climate change, infectious diseases, and migration to terrorism, mass atrocity crimes, and nuclear proliferation. Annan implored the international community to act urgently to find common solutions to the shared problems described in his report entitled "In Larger Freedom."

A decade later, East Asia finds itself confronting many of the security issues first raised by Annan in his 2005 report. But even as the region deals with the new security challenges, old problems persist and have become more complex. We only have to think about how the nature of the security equation in the Korean peninsula has dramatically changed. The defense postures and military deterrence calculus of ideologically opposed parties, once largely defined by the use of conventional arms and ammunitions, have now shifted to nuclear deterrence and weapons capability, given that the North Korean regime continues to develop nuclear warheads and more advanced intercontinental ballistic missiles.

To say that Asia's security landscape has changed is thus an understatement. The speed of the change has been breathtaking and its impact more readily felt because of the increasing connectedness of people across the globe. Against such dynamics, how do we assess the security outlook in Southeast Asia and the wider East Asian region? And how do we deal with the security challenges?

This book approaches these questions from the perspective of security *governance*, broadly defined here as the structures and processes that enable public and private actors to cooperate, collaborate, and collectively respond to security challenges. In doing so, it brings to light the multiplicity of actors and processes involved in managing security in Southeast Asia and beyond. Understanding security governance in the region therefore must begin with having a broader perspective of what security is, how this is defined by multiple actors in the region, and how they regard certain issues as affecting and threatening their well-being and security.

This book therefore explicates how security actors respond to and address the myriad security challenges facing the region today. It captures the multiple processes that have emerged and that continue to evolve as different actors engage in the governance of security. These security actors may be termed security *governors*, following Deborah Avant, Martha Finnemore, and Susan Sell, who define governors as "actors who exercise powers across borders with some degree of legitimacy and continuity for the purposes of affecting policy in an issue area"; they say that these actors "create issues, set agendas, establish and implement rules or programs and evaluate and/or adjudicate outcomes."[3] This book highlights how governance is contested and negotiated among different security governors at different levels, from the national to the regional, and how these multiple processes might contribute to and influence the way security challenges are governed at the international level.

This book examines an area that often falls under the radar of many security analysts—the governance of non-traditional security (NTS) threats, or nonmilitary issues that threaten the well-being and security of states and societies. Within the context of the wider East Asian region, NTS threats include public health emergencies (such as pandemics), irregular migration, environmental pollution, climate change, and natural disasters. Crucially for the region, many states simply do not have sufficient capacity to deal with the scale or frequency of the threats they face. Several states in the region are also extremely vulnerable to certain NTS threats—sea-level rise, typhoons, or earthquakes, for example—due to their geography. The impact of NTS threats on human and state security in the region is grave, yet many security analysts focus mainly on military threats, with discussions about security responses remaining limited to postures like deterrence, sanctions, and containment. Also, the debates in the international security and international relations literature are predicated on an international system portrayed as either an anarchic, self-help system (defined by the power-balancing strategies of states) or a cooperative system (defined by the building of cooperative security frameworks). The injection of NTS issues into the security analysis paves the way for more nuanced understandings.

This book thus focuses on the dynamics of security governance within the context of a vibrant region where different actors are actively engaged in the governance of security and where these actors often work with and negotiate with state actors in crafting strategies and mechanisms that fall outside the usual classification of balancing and competition.

Beyond Current Security Lenses

Analyses of East Asian security are often informed by two opposing views and through the prism of two broad security lenses. A realist perspective of East Asia's regional order is one of uncertainty and instability, riven by major power competition, territorial conflicts, and maritime disputes. The uncertainties are fueled by power asymmetry among the major powers in the region and characterized by rivalry and competition between the United States and China and the impact of their relations on medium- and small-sized states in the region. Complicating this rivalry are the historical tensions between Japan and China and South Korea that are intermittently rekindled, disrupting current relations. These tensions are usually triggered through actions by Japan that remind China and South Korea of

Japan's atrocities during the Second World War. More recently, there is also the heightened instability in the Korean peninsula due to the rising intransigence of a North Korean regime bent on demonstrating its nuclear capabilities toward its avowed enemies.

The realist view is that, unless guaranteed by a strong military alliance (led by the United States and including Japan, South Korea, and Australia) and a powerful military capability to deter rogue states, the prospects of escalating bilateral tensions between states with a history of war and an arms race are high. The risks of nuclear proliferation and war cannot also be dismissed. From this perspective, Asia and particularly East Asia is now at a critical juncture in history where it is most insecure.

The liberal-institutionalist perspective is more sanguine. It argues that institutions matter in maintaining stability amid uncertainties. So, while there are real threats and tensions affecting East Asian security, these can be regarded with equanimity rather than alarm given the multiplicity of institutions and processes that have evolved over decades to manage the host of threats and challenges to regional security. An eminent international relations scholar, Robert Keohane, once referred to these institutions as the "persistent and connected set of rules (formal and informal) that prescribe behavioral roles, constrain activities and shape expectations."[4]

Following these perspectives, how states respond to their security environment, whether through confrontation or cooperation, is shaped largely by their ability to construct multilateral institutions and mechanisms for cooperation and even integration. Security analysts with a realist lens would tend to downplay the importance of actors and institutions and argue that the overlay of the balance-of-power politics leads states to either "initiate or manipulate institutions."[5] Those from a liberal-institutionalist and constructivist perspective, on the other hand, argue that institutions matter for security in East Asia. They observe that the institutions in the region have put in place a set of norms that have significantly defined regional relations and set in motion different types of mechanisms and processes geared toward addressing and managing a range of regional security challenges, including NTS threats.

There are, however, security analysts who prefer a nonbinary view of state behavior. Scholars of Asian security like Muthiah Alagappa contend that Asia's regional order can be depicted as somewhere between one based on balance of power and a regional community with the relevant institutional and normative attributes.[6] He argues that it is not often easy to pin down which of the two strategies is the one preferred by states as both balancing and engagement behavior can and have coexisted. The behavior of states in East Asia straddles power-balancing strategies through memberships in U.S.-led alliances, and security cooperation strategies through engagement in multilateral security frameworks. In Southeast Asia, for instance, states that are not members of U.S.-led military alliances have not objected to the U.S. hub-and-spokes security arrangements in the region. Non-U.S. allies have allowed port calls by U.S. ships at their naval facilities and have often participated in military training exercises related to counterterrorism, humanitarian assistance and disaster relief (HADR), and piracy, which are jointly conducted by the United States and its allies in the region.

Meanwhile, with ASEAN as the core institution and initiator of ASEAN-led multilateral institutions, states in wider East Asia have been part of and contributed to the building of multilateral security frameworks since the mid-1990s. The region's turn to multilateralism—translated into policies of engagement rather than containment, inclusiveness rather than exclusivity—and its promotion of trust and confidence building had been considered the more realistic approach for small- and medium-sized states in dealing with security challenges in a constant state of flux. Hence, since the establishment of the ASEAN Regional Forum in 1995 paved the way for the formation of other similar frameworks, multilateral security cooperation has served as the leitmotif and foundation for security governance in the region.

Notwithstanding the respective merits of these two opposing perspectives, there is a major shortcoming in the analyses of the regional order: the prevailing paradigms of security and security approaches are still stuck in state-centricity. This ignores the fundamental transformation in the way security is conceptualized as a result of the emergence and escalation of new security challenges and the shift in the global threat environment. In the face of the rapid changes in the global security environment, the region's security dynamics present a much more complex picture than the kind of regional order envisioned by the realist or the institutionalist. For one thing, the security actors are no longer just limited to states. Part of the dramatic transformation in the global security landscape is the fact that security challenges such as terrorism and violent extremism, pandemics, and climate change threaten not only the security of the state but also that of its people, to varying degrees. Most significantly, many of these NTS challenges are also transnational in nature, transcending borders in their reach and impact. Responding to threats of this nature would stretch or be beyond the capacity of states and existing institutions involved in providing security. The implications of these changes to regional and global security are compelling arguments for reexamining how we view security governance in the twenty-first century and the impact on East Asia. Only then are we able to chart the way ahead for a new vision of security governance.

Beyond Security Governance by the State

The idea that governance traverses multiple layers of actors helps us to situate this study on security governance in Southeast Asia and the wider East Asian region and highlights the emergence of multiple actors and networks that desire to participate in the regional and global system. These actors aim to set the security agenda and influence the way complex transnational security challenges are addressed and managed by the regional community. That this generates contestations in security practices is particularly useful in analyses of not only Southeast Asian security but also that of the broader region, in that it helps us understand how the contested security practices deal with transborder non-traditional threats, what their impact is on different people, and the extent to which these contestations may or may not effect normative change.

We see that, given the complexity of NTS threats, East Asia presents multiple sites of governance that shape the nature of security governance in the region. These sites of governance are not only limited to regional organizations like ASEAN but are also found within and across state borders. More importantly, in examining the dynamic nature of regional security governance, we open the once "closed" state-centric analyses to identify who else are the security governors. Where do these security governors come from and how do they influence the way security challenges are addressed? The multiplicity of security governors and their role and influence within multitrack processes are discussed further in chapter 2.

Before proceeding further, we also need to be mindful of two distinct trends that have influenced the current state of global security governance and how this affects East Asia. One is the changing nature of the security challenges that have emerged in tandem with the changes in international politics with the end of the Cold War. The other relates to questions of who provides security and who has had the monopoly on the legitimate use of force for security.

Security is no longer just about protecting state borders from military threats. The traditional approach that strictly defined security in military terms came under challenge in the early 1990s as countries began to realize that nonmilitary problems like energy shortages, environmental pollution, global warming, and food insecurity have the potential to threaten the existence of states and people.[7] Scholars like Barry Buzan pointed out that the destruction caused by natural disasters might be equivalent to that inflicted by wars.[8] As the hegemonic confrontation between the United States and the Soviet Union ended in 1989 and as the risk of large-scale armed conflict declined, many states began to adjust their threat assessments to examine other causes of state insecurity. This in turn led to more resources being made available to address security threats that are nonmilitary in nature yet threaten the well-being of states and people.

Across the globe, different regions have had their own distinct experiences of this strategic transformation, and this is reflected in their regional security discourses. In East Asia, a string of crises and emergencies in finance, public health, disaster relief, and communal violence has shaped the evolution of the regional security discourse.[9] The Asian financial crisis in 1997 was a watershed event that triggered a host of socioeconomic and political consequences that altered the security environment in the region. What started as a financial crisis in one state turned into a contagious, transnational crisis of magnified proportions, resulting in the rapid deterioration of economies in the region and sparking societal tensions, racial riots, and political instability within a very short period.[10] The sheer scale of the impact on political stability and economic prosperity, two pillars of state legitimacy, proved a potent wake-up call.[11] In the wake of the crisis, the ASEAN Plus Three countries felt compelled to assess the effectiveness of existing frameworks and to step up financial, monetary, and economic cooperation to address sudden economic downturns and future financial crises. They established regional arrangements like the East Asia Summit, the Chiang Mai Initiative (an expansion of the ASEAN Swap Arrangement), and a network of bilateral swap arrangements.[12] These arrangements have altered the nature of security governance in the region through introducing regional mechanisms that would once have been considered intrusive of the domestic affairs of states, such as an economic surveillance system.

East Asia has also faced a number of public health emergencies. The outbreak of severe acute respiratory syndrome (SARS) in 2002 and 2003 caught the region by surprise and severely tested its public health systems (see chapter 3).[13] The SARS crisis extended beyond the region to parts of North America and Europe. There have also been outbreaks of variants of avian influenza since 2006 and the Zika virus became a concern in 2016. These public health emergencies underscored the importance of regional information sharing, disease surveillance systems, and coordination of responses to such challenges.

Natural disasters are another major source of insecurity in Asia, with countries such as China, Indonesia, and the Philippines prone to them (see chapter 6). The 2004 Indian Ocean tsunami claimed the lives of 230,000 people and affected fourteen countries in Asia and Africa. China, Japan, and Nepal were hit by major earthquakes (magnitude over 8) in 2008, 2011, and 2015, respectively. Apart from heavy loss of lives and property, natural disasters could potentially deteriorate into complex emergencies that severely affect all sectors of societies. The nuclear meltdown at the Fukushima nuclear power plant after the Great East Japan Earthquake in 2011 drew international attention to the issue of nuclear safety and security (see chapter 7).

The nature of the security threats has made it imperative to rethink how security is managed and delivered. In Europe, where regional integration has reached its highest level, there exists a regional authority that acts on behalf of the national government on certain issues. For instance, the European Union negotiated the Paris Agreement on climate change as a single party based on the consensus of all of its members. Asia's different level of regional integration presents dynamics notably different from Europe. While cooperation and coordination on common security challenges have been increasingly emphasized, a supranational arrangement as in the European Union is absent in the region, and countries manage NTS issues based on their national assessments and standards. Underlying this is the preference of the ASEAN Plus Three states to adhere strictly to the principles of sovereignty and noninterference, and to uphold the primacy of the state in managing security issues.

In a region that places a premium on sovereignty and noninterference, could multilevel security governance take place? What has been observed is that while states remain the central actor in the provision of security, the region has seen a proliferation of security governors who play an increasingly prominent role in identifying, managing, and addressing NTS challenges.[14] It is important to analyze how the various actors influence the formulation and implementation of policies in the state-dominated societies of the region. The examination contributes to the understanding of how the security transformation in Asia has unfolded and where it is leading to. It also provides insights on the relationship between state and non-state actors in governing NTS issues. Moreover, as a region that hosts several major powers and an influential group of countries, the Asian perspective on security and its experience in security governance make up the essential constituents of the security discourse and security studies at the global level.

Following the discussion on the changed security environment and the need to examine security governance, the rest of this chapter proceeds as follows. The next section reviews changes in the conceptualization of security, including the inclusion of "new" referent objects of security and the expansion of global and regional security agendas. Then it moves on to an introduction of NTS with a focus on the NTS challenges facing the countries of Southeast Asia and the wider East Asian region. This is followed by a review of how governance, global governance, and security governance have been defined. These definitions form the bases for developing an understanding of NTS governance and examining the actors involved in this process. A key argument here is that the attention given to new referent objects of security and to broadening the scope of security has catalyzed changes in how security issues are managed and addressed.

So what is new about security governance processes in Southeast Asia and beyond? With NTS issues looming large in the security agenda of states, we are now witnessing the evolution of what I call "state-plus" processes, which bring states (within the frameworks of regional organizations like ASEAN and ASEAN Plus Three) together with a host of non-state actors, including civil society organizations, nongovernmental organizations (NGOs), and international foundations that are actively engaged in regional governance processes, to address problems like infectious diseases/pandemics, transborder pollution, humanitarian crises, and migration, among others. Unlike many other analyses of how security threats are dealt with that proceed from a state-centric perspective, the security governance approach used in this study includes critical contributions and interventions by regional organizations and non-state actors. By drawing on the theory of securitization by Waever and Buzan and the governance framework advanced by Avant, Finnemore, and Sell, I refer to these multiple actors as "security governors"—actors that create issues, set agendas, and influence the way security challenges are governed at the national, regional, and international level.[15]

While not dismissing the role of the state as a security actor or governor, I give attention to the proliferation of actors that engage, challenge, and negotiate with states on how NTS issues should be addressed. And, while the engagement of these actors inadvertently brings about tensions and conflicts, it is important to see how this interaction in turn changes the dynamics of security governance in the region where attempts at introducing new norms like the "responsibility to protect" and "preparedness" necessitate multisectoral and multistakeholder collaboration in dealing with complex, twenty-first century challenges.

Revisiting Security

Expanding the Scope of Security

Security is a contested concept with varied interpretations by different schools of security studies. Arnold Wolfers described security as the "absence of threats to acquired values," including the most basic value, which is the physical safety of individuals.[16] Defining what the other values are, however, is contingent on whose security we are dealing with or the security referent. There can be multiple or competing referents of security—the state, the individual, the environment, the planet—but the bottom line for all referents is survival, and the way to ensure this is not limited to military means. Following this logic, the scope of security can therefore be broadened.

Buzan's work on securitization defines security as essentially survival from an "existential threat to a designated referent object," for which exceptional and extraordinary measures are justified.[17] According to this definition, the identification of the referent object of security is a precondition for broadening the scope of security as existential threats are subject to who the referent object is.

The military used to be the only security sector, as security is strictly conceived as national sovereignty and territorial integrity. However, this is insufficient for the contemporary security challenges we face. The inclusion of people and communities as referent objects of security justifies the identification of issues like extreme poverty, climate change, and resource depletion as existential threats, or potentially at least. Attempts to broaden the scope of security have been seen in both the research and policy communities. In addition to the military sector, Buzan, in his 1983 broadening of security agendas, included the political, economic, societal, and ecological security sectors.[18] The notion of human security, which is discussed later in this chapter, consists of seven components: economic security, food security, health security, environmental security, personal security, community security, and political security.[19]

It is increasingly evident that potential threats can now emanate from within the state or through non-state actors rather than from another state, as was largely the case in the past. Today security, international legitimacy, and sovereignty rest not only on territorial control but also the ability of the state to guarantee the rights of its citizens and provide for their basic needs.[20] In this context, issues like internal conflicts, pandemics, hunger, and transnational crime pose a more imminent threat to people as they could be triggers for armed conflict and war. Energy security and water security could also threaten the survival of the state and the well-being of people. For instance, Japan, which depends heavily on energy imports, has long made energy security a component of its security agenda.[21] Water security used to be a top priority of the Singaporean government, given its reliance on neighboring Malaysia for much of its freshwater supply. Such challenges have increasingly become major work agendas for governments and policy communities around the world.

Non-Traditional Security

Against this background, NTS has been brought forward to broaden the notion of security and increase the appreciation of the NTS challenges we face. According to the Consortium of Non-Traditional Security Studies in Asia (also known as the NTS-Asia Consortium), NTS issues refer to nonmilitary challenges to the survival and well-being of people and states, which include climate change, resource scarcity, infectious diseases, natural disasters, irregular migration, food shortages, and transnational crimes.[22] This definition identifies two referent objects of NTS: people and the state. These two referent objects are not mutually exclusive but mutually reinforcing. On the one hand, state security is built on the security of individuals within the society. Social tensions accumulating from individual insecurities could escalate into political instability and violence that threaten state security, as illustrated by the Arab Spring uprisings between 2010 and 2012. On the other hand, the state is the primary provider of security for its population, and the insecurity of the state threatens the well-being of individuals.

Transnationality is another prominent feature of NTS issues, a characteristic that entails substantive changes in how security is governed. As demonstrated by the natural disasters, public health emergencies, and humanitarian crises over the years, the impacts of NTS issues often go beyond national borders. The subprime mortgage crisis that unfolded in the United States between 2007 and 2009 turned into a global financial crisis. Forest fires in Indonesia had a severe impact on air quality in Singapore and Malaysia, threatening the health of the people in the two countries. Radioactive particles from the nuclear meltdown in 2011 at the Fukushima nuclear power plant in Japan reached as far as the west coast of the United States. The Zika virus disease broke out in South America in 2015, but infections have been reported in Southeast Asia. Globalization and technological advances in communication and transportation have increased countries' vulnerability to external threats and made it extremely difficult for individual countries to control and manage NTS challenges alone. The transnationality of NTS issues poses a challenge to the conventional approach to security that places the government, the representative of the state, as the sole provider of security.

The magnitude of NTS threats in some cases far outstrips the capacity of the countries affected by the threats to deal with them, particularly in the case of developing countries. Typhoon Haiyan, one of the most intense tropical cyclones on record, devastated the infrastructure in affected areas, which meant that the delivery of humanitarian resources and personnel relied heavily on airlifts. The Filipino government however was under-resourced for HADR operations of this scale. Its armed forces, for instance, had only three functioning C130 aircrafts, which was below the transportation capacity needed for the relief efforts.[23] Another example is the Ebola crisis between 2014 and 2015, the largest such outbreak on record. Developing countries such as Liberia, Sierra Leone, and Guinea were among the worst affected as they had limited capacity in conducting independent pharmaceutical responses to the epidemic.[24]

Sources of insecurity therefore are no longer limited to balance-of-power politics. When the source of insecurity is nonmilitary—arising from human activities or changes in nature, for example—the use of force becomes irrelevant in most cases. While the military remains a key actor in dealing with NTS challenges, it is mostly mobilized for civilian purposes, such as providing logistical support for HADR or enforcing quarantines during outbreaks of infectious diseases. The nonmilitary nature of NTS issues also requires other actors—international organizations, civil society groups, businesses, and NGOs—to become involved in governing NTS issues.

With the reframing of security as both the survival of the state and the well-being of people, security governance also needs to shift from the conventional government-led approach. Governments in many cases do not have sufficient resources and capacity to effectively manage NTS issues. New approaches are needed for mobilizing resources and manpower from as many sources as possible. Given the complexity, magnitude, and urgency of many NTS problems, cooperation and coordination among different actors are essential.

Framing Security Governance

From Government to Governance

The broadening scope of security and the recognition of more sources of insecurity have created the space for the proliferation of actors in the field of security. With the rise of these new actors, *governance* and how it differs from *government* has become salient. The frequency of "governance" appearing in policy and academic discussions began to increase in the 1980s.[25] The meaning of the concept varies according to the context and the level of analysis. In the domestic realm, governance is often conceived as an alternative to government in terms of delivering public services. Government has been defined in terms of "the activity or process of governance," "a condition of ordered rule," "those people charged with the duty of governing," and "the manner, method or system by which a particular society is governed."[26] Governance implies changes in these characteristics of government. It is defined as "the pattern or structure that emerges in a socio-political system as [a] 'common' result or outcome of the interacting intervention efforts of all involved actors. This pattern cannot be reduced to one actor or group of actors in particular."[27] Governance thus denotes multiple actors and levels in managing public issues.

Government and governance represent different approaches to managing issues and challenges of common concern, with the former state-centric and hierarchical while the latter is society-centric and nonhierarchical. Governance is more encompassing than the government-led model as it also includes activities through informal channels.[28] A key difference between the two is that there is no central authority in the governance model. Without negating the role of government, governance gives more weight to the role of other societal actors, as political authorities have fragmented among state and non-state actors in the post–Cold War global politics.

Given that many contemporary challenges are of regional and global concern, effective governance needs to be multilevel and multi-actor in nature (figure 1.1). The notion of governance has been used more frequently in the global discourse since the early 1990s, when NTS issues like humanitarian emergencies, civil conflicts, natural disasters, and financial crises began to be perceived as threats to the well-being of people and their communities.[29] As with many other important concepts in international studies, there is no unified definition of global governance. What could be said is that it is essentially focused on the provision of global public goods. As such, global governance could be seen as the collective effort to address social, economic, political, cultural, and security issues of common interest to the world. The purpose is to form effective responses to these issues, the scale of which is usually beyond the capacity of individual states. It is a process that consists of identifying problems, setting goals, exploring directions, and formulating and implementing policies. This process is built on the participation and contribution of various actors, mechanisms, arrangements, and structures. The expected outcome is to bring control and order back to problems and crises, but this is shaped by a range of variables, from power and resources to leadership and mobilization.[30]

Security Governance

Security governance aims to provide security for referent objects through structures and processes that allow state and non-state security actors at various levels to coordinate their needs and responses and to formulate

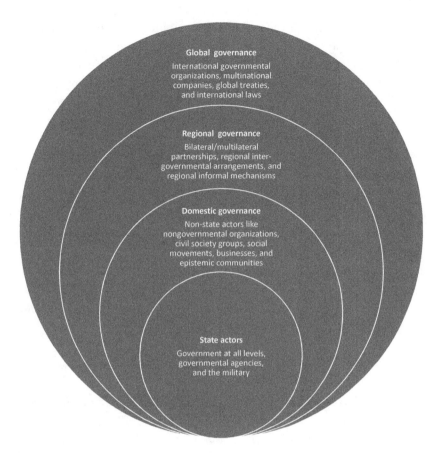

Figure 1.1 Governance

policy.[31] At the state level, this involves governance of the security sector.[32] At the regional level, security governance is performed through the regional security architecture established to organize orderly, collective response to a region's security challenges. These challenges span both traditional security and NTS threats, including interstate wars, territorial disputes, domestic crises with regional repercussion, and transnational problems. Without proper control and management, these issues could threaten the security and well-being of individual states, their populations, and the region as a whole.

The flows of governance come from both formal and informal structures of authority that coordinate and cooperate with each other. Regional security governance is thus a sum of unilateral, bilateral, and multilateral institutional actions.[33] It is based on treaties, binding agreements, norms, and regionally accepted practices. For instance, the "ASEAN way" that emphasizes mutual respect for sovereignty and noninterference in the affairs of other states guides countries in Southeast Asia in addressing security issues of regional concern, as seen in the 1976 Treaty of Amity and Cooperation in Southeast Asia and the 2002 Declaration on the Conduct of Parties in the South China Sea.

NTS Governance

NTS governance is an increasingly important component of security governance as NTS issues are interlocking and have repercussions across borders. Building on the definitions of global governance and security governance outlined above, NTS governance refers to the collective effort to address NTS challenges through arrangements at multiple levels with the participation of security actors.

FOUR DIMENSIONS OF NTS GOVERNANCE

In their work on global governance and governors, Avant, Finnemore, and Sell describe the general process of governance as agenda setting, negotiation, decision making, implementation, monitoring, and enforcement.[34] NTS governance requires that securitization also be emphasized. As NTS issues are not within the purview of traditional security agendas, securitization is crucial for ensuring that NTS threats, both imminent and potential, receive sufficient attention and resources. Securitization also serves as the starting point in the continuum of security processes. Thus, this book discusses NTS governance as a four-phase process (see figure 1.2): (1) identifying, assessing, and understanding the threat, and securitizing the threat; (2) setting goals and directions for responding to the threat; (3) seeking solutions; and (4) implementation.

Identifying the threat and securitization. The identification of threats is the basis for the following phases to take place, and securitization is an important step in this phase.[35] Whether an issue is a security threat or public emergency leads to notable differences in the response since securitization allows exceptional and extraordinary measures. Amid the Ebola outbreak in West Africa, the United States, China, France, and the United

Figure 1.2 Dimensions of NTS governance

Kingdom sent military personnel and equipment to the areas affected by the disease, and NGOs like Médecins Sans Frontières and Oxfam, which had earlier opposed such intervention, accepted the military deployment. Securitization also leads to more attention and resources being devoted to addressing the threat, or potential threat. The United States and the United Kingdom mobilized financial resources exceptionally quickly to support the research and development of drugs and vaccines for Ebola.[36]

Agenda setting. The setting of the agenda and goals for addressing a problem follows securitization. This is illustrated by the case of the Responsibility to Protect, a concept first put forward in 2001.[37] The securitization of the four mass atrocities of genocide, war crime, crimes against humanity, and ethnic cleansing through the Responsibility to Protect mobilized international support and attention to the need for all actors in the international community to prevent and stop the atrocities. The UN General Assembly has held annual meetings on implementing the Responsibility to Protect since 2009. The agenda themes have included implementation (2009); early warning (2010); the role of regional actors (2011); timely and decisive response (2012); the role of national actors (2013); and the role of international actors (2014).

Policy solutions. Within the scope of the agenda, policy solutions are formulated to achieve the set goals, including the introduction of emergency measures. For instance, in response to the high death rate and fast transmission of Ebola, the World Health Organization decided that experimental drugs that have not undergone human testing could be used to treat Ebola patients as the campaign to address the issue was involved in a race against time.[38]

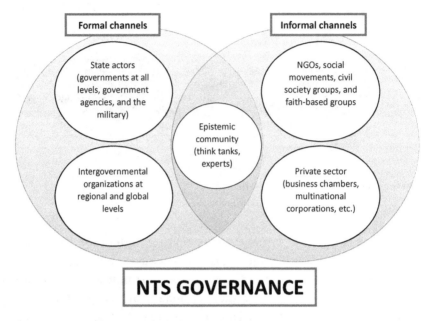

| Formal channels | Informal channels |

State actors (governments at all levels, government agencies, and the military)

NGOs, social movements, civil society groups, and faith-based groups

Epistemic community (think tanks, experts)

Intergovernmental organizations at regional and global levels

Private sector (business chambers, multinational corporations, etc.)

NTS GOVERNANCE

Figure 1.3 Security actors and NTS governance

Implementation, monitoring, and institutionalization. Given that some NTS threats are persistent and recurrent—natural disasters and climate change, for instance—the institutionalization of the responses to the threats effectively reduces transaction costs and improves the speed and effectiveness of mobilization and coordination.[39] It is important to have designated government agencies or departments, established procedures, and instruments like regulations and laws to deal with NTS issue areas.[40] With the institutionalization of the domestic response to public health emergencies in China following the SARS outbreak—through the Regulations on Public Health Emergencies (2003), and the Regulations on the Release of Government Information (2007) and related procedures and systems—China has become notably more timely and effective in dealing with public health emergencies. When Ebola broke out in West Africa in 2014, China's foreign ministry issued travel alerts to Chinese citizens; its immigration authorities tightened monitoring over passengers arriving in China from Ebola-affected countries; and the central government set up a cross-ministerial mechanism to deal with the threat.[41]

IDENTIFYING A NEW REFERENT OBJECT
OF SECURITY

In the traditional security paradigm that defines security solely in military terms, the state is the referent object of security. Existential threats therefore include interstate war, foreign invasion, and encroachment on sovereignty and territorial integrity. This state-centric approach has been problematized as narrow and lacking explanatory power for the security challenges we face today. The civil war that has been going on in Syria since 2011 is a case in point. Its impact on regional and international security is illustrated by the influx of millions of refugees into Europe and the adoption of the New York Declaration for Refugees and Migrants in 2016. Similarly, the unanimous adoption of the principle of the Responsibility to Protect by global leaders at the 2005 World Summit indicates that mass atrocities are a threat to international security. When Typhoon Haiyan swept across the Philippines in 2013, killing over ten thousand people and displacing hundreds of thousands, the government declared that it was not only a national calamity but also a national emergency, in other words, a matter of national security.[42]

The notion of human security complements the policy and academic discussions on security by presenting a referent object of security other than the state.[43] The first official articulation of this notion was in the 1994 Human Development Report by the United Nations Development Programme. According to the report, security is more than absence of war with other states and the securing of borders. There are common chronic and complex insecurities affecting individuals and societies, and it is always people—vulnerable groups and communities in particular—who bear the brunt of the suffering. For instance, undernourishment is widespread in some developing countries, with children being worst affected. According to the United Nations, malnutrition takes the life of 3.1 million children every year, and a quarter of the world's children suffer stunted growth.[44] As such, human security needs to mean freedom from fear and freedom from want.[45] In the framework of human security, the well-being of people and communities are relevant and important to international politics and security.

Scale and significance are important considerations in whether an issue is treated as a security issue, and there is the concern that individual-based security concerns are too broad and diverse to generate sufficient interest from relevant security actors.[46] Some scholars argue that human security is too vague and expansive to be a viable framework for academic research and policymaking.[47] Buzan, for example, recognized the relevance of individuals for discussions on security, but the state remains the referent in his analysis of international security.[48] Despite the criticism and skepticism, human security, which calls for more attention to the insecurities facing people and communities, provides an important platform for underprivileged communities to raise their security concerns and engage with the efforts to redefine security.

The Evolving Role of State Security Actors

Security actors can be broadly grouped into state/governmental and non-state actors. State and governmental actors form the traditional security sector and usually operate in formal arrangements. Examples are government agencies, the military, and intergovernmental organizations. These security actors have seen their roles and responsibilities evolve as new threats are identified and with the increasing recognition of people and communities as a referent object of security.

Security sector reform and other developments within the security sector illustrate such shifts in roles and responsibilities. Security sector reform refers to "a process of assessment, review and implementation as well as monitoring and evaluation led by national authorities that has as its goal the enhancement of effective and accountable security for the State and its peoples without discrimination and with full respect for human rights and the rule of law."[49] It aims to address problems endemic in the security sector of many developing countries, such as corruption, abuse of power, and violations of human rights. The end of the Cold War also saw the outbreak of civil war in many countries and struggles associated with the transition from authoritarian regimes to democracies. Security sector reform is therefore often associated with post–conflict societies or democratic transition.

The ultimate goal of security sector reform is to contribute to lasting peace and security. Specifically, the military and other law enforcement agencies should be able to carry out their tasks effectively and be sensitized to issues like human rights and the rule of law. An incompetent and corrupt security sector is a source of public discontent that fuels social tensions and increases the risk of political instability and violence. It is thus critical for countries to improve the capabilities and discipline of their state security apparatus.[50]

Security sector reform affects conventional security actors—the armed and police forces—that belong to the category of state actors. It is a state-centric approach with the reform implemented in a top-down manner. Thus, while it is a major element of the effort to ensure the security and well-being of the state and its people, security in the context of security sector reform mainly refers to physical security.

In the NTS discourse, the role of the armed forces is broader than the provision of physical security. In Indonesia and Thailand, the military has been involved in development programs such as the building of roads and schools. Increasingly also, the militaries of East Asia have taken on HADR roles. Following the 2008 Sichuan earthquake, the armed forces of China began to list nonmilitary operations as a component of its use of military power. In response to the need to strengthen military cooperation in the area of rapid assistance and response, Singapore set up a regional disaster relief coordination center in 2014 to organize the activities of militaries from different countries during a natural disaster in the region. Such developments reflect the transformation of the military's role in the face of growing security threats from NTS issues. This extends to such areas as countering transnational organized crimes (which includes drug trafficking and human smuggling) and terrorism.

The Rise of Non-State Security Actors

Given the nonmilitary and transboundary nature of NTS, there are limits to how effective conventional security actors can be in addressing threats such as large-scale outbreaks of pandemics and the incidence of complex humanitarian crises brought on by natural disasters or conflicts. Non-state actors are thus playing more significant roles in various dimensions of NTS governance. For example, the World Health Organization securitized SARS in 2003 after receiving information on the breakout from non-state sources.[51] In the wake of the 2015 Nepal earthquake, agencies involved in international HADR demonstrated that insufficient communication and coordination with local entities led to instances of relief materials not matching local needs. Given their familiarity with the situation on the ground, local entities play a critical role in identifying and assessing the needs and challenges in relief and recovery.[52] During the Ebola outbreak in West Africa in 2014, effective containment of the disease relied heavily on efforts at the community level, which included surveillance and education campaigns.[53] The private sector has also been seen to step in to meet resource needs. For example, in the aftermath of Typhoon Haiyan, businesses contributed to HADR activities by offering the use of their vehicles.[54]

In their engagement with NTS governance processes, non-state actors rely on various sources of authority (see chapter 2 for a more detailed discussion). For example, think tanks and epistemic communities draw on their knowledge and expertise to influence NTS-related policies. Expert authority is an important element in efforts by think tanks to promote the NTS agenda they are interested in, particularly for issues that require specialized knowledge like public health and nuclear safety and security. In an earlier work on epistemic communities, Peter Haas describes the members of this community as having common characteristics that include a shared set of normative and principled beliefs and a common enterprise.[55] This allows them to take on roles such as "communicating and translating global values and agreements to regional and local audiences"; "reviewing international agreements and recommending the formulation of national and regional policy options"; "convening and building alliances among NGOs and civil society"; and "training and teaching fledgling NGOs on organizational management planning and advocacy."[56]

The input of knowledge and expertise into securitization and other dimensions of security governance is represented in but not limited to processes within Track 2 (networks of policy institutes and knowledge elites with access to policymaking). With their access to decision making and their non-official status, these actors have the flexibility and privilege to facilitate cross-level dialogues. In East Asia, think tank networks like the Council for Security Cooperation in the Asia Pacific have been active in bringing attention to NTS issues like the need for preparedness to meet the threats of natural disasters and nuclear accidents.

Conclusion

This chapter has highlighted how the changes in the global and regional security environment and the emergence of new security challenges have given rise to new security actors or governors. By revisiting how these changes have helped transform the dynamics of governance, we have examined how the concept of security governance is operationalized within the context of East Asia.

The multilayering of governance through the involvement of a dense web of networks comprising state actors and non-state actors (the epistemic community, think tanks, NGOs, intergovernmental organizations, and business groups) has become the site for the formulation and implementation of governance. The proliferation of security issues and the fragmentation of authority have created new spheres for governance where problems and issues are shaped, defined, and contested, and where they are securitized and framed to allow for regulations, policies, and norms to be generated to manage security outcomes. Chapter 2 provides a more comprehensive discussion of these different actors and how they engage in security governance, and the dynamics of security governance is illustrated further in the subsequent chapters that present case studies of NTS challenges.

To help in understanding the dynamics of security governance in the region, this chapter also revisited the changing conceptualization of security. The move to expand the referents of security beyond the state, with the attendant recognition that people are and should in fact be the main referents of security, is integral to the understanding and analyses of the different NTS challenges that have emerged and that occupy the security agenda of states. More importantly, the notions of human security and NTS have problematized the state-centric approach to security.

While remaining a central actor, governments in many cases do not have sufficient resources and capacity to effectively respond to growing security challenges such as irregular migration, transnational crimes, food insecurity, or natural disasters. The expanding variety of security threats to states and people gives rise to the need for a more encompassing approach that involves a greater variety of actors to govern NTS issues. In this regard, multilayered governance that incorporates both formal and informal mechanisms and that complements state-led approaches is critical. The engagement of a wide range of non-state actors therefore not only provides alternative ideas and modes of governance but, more importantly, also contributes to the different dimensions of NTS governance, from securitization to agenda setting and policy implementation.

CHAPTER II

State and Non–State Actors and NTS Governance in Southeast Asia and Beyond

The expansion of security agendas in the post–Cold War era has led to a transformation in how security is governed. The complex, uncertain, and transboundary nature of non-traditional security (NTS) issues has seriously challenged the capacity of states to effectively deal with them and exposed the weakness, even failure, of existing security architecture. This has created space for an array of non-state actors to step in to play a role in managing security challenges, eroding state monopoly over the provision of security. Scholars noting this trend, as we discussed in chapter 1, describe a transition from *government* as the central or sole security actor to that of *governance* by a range of state and non-state actors. Associated with this is the fragmentation of political authority among public and private actors as well as subnational, national, regional, and international actors.[1] These changes in governance patterns can be observed in many areas, from the geographical to the functional and normative, as well as in governance processes such as agenda setting, solution formulation, policymaking, service delivery, regulation, and oversight.[2] Such shifts have been most pronounced in the multiple roles that non-state actors carry out as they work separately or with state actors on NTS challenges such as humanitarian emergencies, public health crises, or environmental threats, as illustrated in the cases in the subsequent chapters of this book.

But under whose authority do these non-state actors work? To be part of the governance process requires legitimacy derived from authority, which in turn constitutes the foundation of governance.[3] In the traditional security framework, the state, represented by its security apparatus, which includes its military forces, defense officials, and intelligence personnel, has been the main actor in charge of security governance. Its agencies monopolize the legitimate use of force to defend against existential threats, based on the authority bestowed by sovereignty.[4] Non-state actors, on the other hand, come from diverse backgrounds and are organized differently. Their functions are less structured than state security agencies and not designated clearly. Their legitimacy and authority are derived from the support provided by their respective bases. Given these differences, what is notable behind the growing role of non-state security actors is the emergence of different sites of authority that define the nature of the evolving processes of security governance and security architecture. These sites in turn shed light on how non-state actors contribute to governance.

Security governance is a multilevel process that spans from the subnational to the global, with regional governance having a critical place in this spectrum.[5] While the greater involvement of non-state security actors is a global trend, the various regions have their own distinctive dynamics and the mode of regional security governance is very much informed by the regional security environment. For instance, while European security is characterized by high-level institutionalization, with the European Union and the North Atlantic Treaty Organization at the center of various security arrangements and mechanisms, there are many non-state actors committed to interdependency of openness, welfare maximization, and democratic principles that have made their presence felt in the regional governance processes.[6] Europe has also seen the transformation of security governance with the privatization of the armaments industry and the proliferation of private security companies. This has caught the attention of researchers examining security governance in the Euro-Atlantic region. Their studies show how various non-state actors—international NGOs, multinational corporations, private security firms—have assumed a greater role in providing security and influenced transnational and global policymaking and implementation.[7]

Asia presents a different picture, but the study of security governance still largely approaches the region through a Eurocentric lens; great power rivalry and the rise of China are seen as key security concerns, with discussions mainly focused on issues of maintaining regional order like preventing interstate conflict.[8] Also, while NTS threats like pandemic outbreaks, climate change, and migration have already become part of the region's security agenda, the language of "governance" rather than "security governance" predominates in the discourse.[9] Arguably then, the conceptual and theoretical dimensions of security governance have been underexamined in East Asia. Yet, regardless of the context in which they operate, the engagement of non-state actors in security governance is undoubtedly significant and merits more attention.

This chapter examines the place of non-state actors on the continuum of NTS governance primarily in Southeast Asia but also in the wider East Asian region by identifying who they are and how they have also assumed the role of non-state security actors. This chapter argues that how non-state actors engage in governance processes is significant, whether they are involved in agenda setting through securitization, policymaking by generating policy recommendations, providing services, or participating in oversight functions. Mindful of the expanse that a discussion of governance by non-state actors can lead to and to put this within the context of East Asia, this chapter begins by revisiting the conceptual definitions and typology of non-state actors to provide clarity on the kinds of security actors and governors we are dealing with. This is followed by a discussion of how non-state actors have evolved into non-state security actors by being part of the multilayered processes of security governance. The last section examines the dynamics of NTS governance in East Asia that is characterized as multitrack and multilevel.

Defining Non-State Actors

Competing definitions of non-state actor exist, with the broadest being "all entities different from the state."[10] A much narrower definition includes just international NGOs and transnational corporations.[11] In the context of global governance, non-state actors have been defined as

> organizations that are largely or entirely autonomous from central government funding and control: emanating from civil society, or from the market economy, or from political impulses beyond state

control and direction; operating as or participating in networks which extend across the boundaries of two or more states—thus engaging in "transnational" relations, linking political systems, economies, societies; and acting in ways which affect political outcomes, either within one or more states or within international institutions—either purposefully or semi-purposefully, either as their primary objective or as one aspect of their activities.[12]

Some scholars describe actors participating in global governance as "governors," noting that these actors seek to address issues of global concern, influence the making and implementation of related policies, and even transform governing norms and institutions.[13] Non-state actors are members of this collectivity of governors. They are active in the political spaces outside the state system that have opened up as a result of the surge in demand for governance and the need to fill gaps in security provision.

Independence and Influence

Non-state actors display distinctive features that help inform global governance, including independence and influence. Independence is a key feature distinguishing non-state actors from state actors and also a source of their unique contribution to governance. Non-state actors hold their own positions on issues, which may or may not align with those held by their host governments, and they generate their own funds. Theoretically, such autonomy allows them to think outside the "box" of the statecentric approach to examine emerging challenges from different perspectives and come up with solutions that complement or even challenge established state-led efforts. In practice, however, it is difficult to neatly delineate the boundary between state and non-state domains because cooperation and collaboration between, on the one hand, governmental and formal institutions, and, on the other, nongovernmental and informal institutions is the essence of governance.

Governmental and transgovernmental actors have been known to subcontract projects to non-state actors, which opens up spaces for cross-domain collaboration to address issues of common concern. For instance, the Global Fund to Fight AIDS, Tuberculosis and Malaria, a partnership between governments, civil society, and the private sector, represents a new scheme for raising funds to combat against threats to human health security.[14] Also, the

United Nations, through the UN Global Compact framework, has been cooperating with the business sector in addressing issues related to poverty and the rights of vulnerable groups like women and children.[15] Good working relationships with the state provide a key channel for non-state actors to influence and change policymaking and outcomes.

The independence of non-state actors from the state is therefore a relative notion that is contingent on specific contexts. In East Asia, where a majority of countries hold a traditional understanding of sovereignty, many governments closely monitor the activities of non-state actors.[16] China's Foreign NGO Management Law, passed in 2016, requires foreign NGOs to register with public security authorities and subjects NGOs to tighter financial scrutiny.[17] Similar laws and regulations have been enacted in Cambodia, Laos, and Indonesia.[18] Nevertheless, there are still spaces and channels for NGOs to help improve people's security. For instance, in China, Save the Children made important contributions to service delivery, policy development, and advocacy through its Integrated Management of Childhood Illness project, doing so by engaging in cooperation with relevant government departments and agencies at local and national levels. This initiative, piloted in Cangyuan County in Yunnan Province in 2011, laid the foundation for the production of relevant documents by the county government and was recognized by China's National Health and Family Planning Commission.[19]

The other important feature of non-state actors is their influence, particularly transnational influence, which contributes significantly to governance.[20] However, the notion of transnational influence and its trajectory, whether from global to local or vice versa, needs to be nuanced, particularly in the context of Asia. There is sufficient evidence that local non-state actors are important stakeholders of subnational and national governance and have become the building blocks of transnational governance.[21] An example is Grameen Bank, a microfinancing NGO helping the rural poor, which was established in Bangladesh in 1976 by Muhammad Yunus.[22] The organization has expanded into a global network, but not before first becoming an influential actor in Bangladesh. Another way non-state actors play a role in transnational governance is to shape the preferences and interests of a state and change its international behavior. For instance, Greenpeace and the World Wide Fund for Nature, through their monitoring of forest fires and their involvement in setting standards in palm oil production, aim to make states assume responsibility for dealing with incidents of transboundary pollution.[23]

The influence exercised by non-state actors does not have to be transnational in scope for their contribution to governance to matter. In the case of the National Disaster Risk Reduction and Management Council of the Philippines, representatives from civil society organizations and private businesses have become key stakeholders in policy formulation and implementation.[24] In examining security governance in Southeast Asia and beyond, this book covers those non-state actors at subnational, national, and regional levels that are independent from the ambit of state control and can influence policy. Even without a global presence, these non-state actors can, for all intents and purposes, also be considered security governors, given their role in and engagement with governance at multiple levels.

Market-Based Actors and Civil Society

The concept of non-state actors is a broad one that represents a diverse group of entities engaging in political, security, economic, and civil affairs at all levels of human society. Their multi-engagement forms an integral part of governance as they interact with other actors. In Kenneth Abbott and Duncan Snidal's conception of governance, transnational regulation is viewed as a triangular space with participation from three major types of actors, namely, states, firms, and NGOs (figure 2.1).[25] In a previous work, I make a similar observation in the context of Asia, describing the state, the market, and civil society as three major forces in the sphere of contemporary transnational governance.[26] Due to the complexity of current global challenges, the actors are often unable to govern alone.[27] Instead, they form policy networks encompassing a variety of actors, both state and non-state. A policy network may be defined as a set of informal and formal interactions between a variety of usually collective public (state) and private (non-state) actors who have different but interdependent interests.[28]

Economic globalization has opened up the space for the market to influence policymaking and outcomes, especially on but not restricted to economic issues, as economic development is often interlocked with other problems like environmental pollution and inequality.[29] This has facilitated the entry of market-based actors such as companies, industry associations, credit rating agencies, trade unions, and other corporate actors.[30] Apart from their involvement in the regulation of economic and financial issues, many corporate actors are also stakeholders in the management of social,

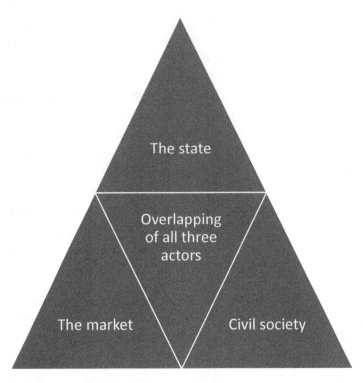

Figure 2.1 Governance Triangle

cultural, and security issues within the framework of corporate social responsibility, which is increasingly gaining traction in global governance. Companies not only promote accountability but are also held accountable and adopt standards of socially responsible practices in such areas as labor, the environment, human rights, and gender equality.[31]

Private military and security companies and contractors are a special type of market-based actor that operates in issue areas related to high politics, which is more sensitive than ordinary business. They provide services to governments, businesses, and increasingly, intergovernmental organizations and NGOs.[32] Private military and security companies offer services such as military training, security assessments, consulting, physical protection, and intelligence.[33] Armaments companies also become stakeholders, given their involvement in the production of weapons and small arms, which has bearing on conflict prevention and civilian protection.

Civil society occupies the intermediate space between the state and the market.[34] Given the breadth of the roles played by civil society organizations, who exactly belongs to this group is a matter of debate. Some scholars equate civil society with NGOs only, while others also include social movements, faith-based organizations, epistemic communities, lobbyist groups, and philanthropic associations.[35] NGOs are familiar to the public as they are often at the forefront of delivering services and protection to people in need. The big international NGOs include Save the Children and Médecins Sans Frontières. Regional NGOs include the Asia Pacific Refugee Rights Network, the Asia Migrants Network, and the ASEAN Civil Society Conference (ACSC).

Faith-based organizations refer to a variety of congregational groups, civil society bodies, and national religious representative groups. Their engagement in governance focuses on human well-being in areas such as education, health, and development. They provide an estimated 50 percent of education and health services globally.[36] While some have questioned the relevance of the role of faith-based organizations in a world experiencing rapid technological advancement, this concern has largely been laid to rest. Since religion remains prominent in social life at all levels, the religious affiliation of faith-based organizations—their most distinctive feature—places them in a good position to mobilize social resources and reach their audience.[37]

Philanthropic groups like the Rockefeller Foundation, the Bill & Melinda Gates Foundation, and the Chan Zuckerberg Initiative are a growing force in governance, both transnationally and nationally. These private foundations are non-state, exempted from taxation, and funded from a single source. They are overseen by a board of trustees and provide financial support for social improvement and charitable causes.[38]

Epistemic communities are networks of "professionals with recognized expertise and competence in a particular domain and an authoritative claim to policy-relevant knowledge within that domain or issue-area."[39] These communities have become more valuable as the security challenges that emerge have become not only more complex but also more technical in nature. Through diffusion of new ideas and thinking, members of epistemic communities may redefine security and national interests and thus influence or even transform policymaking. They may work in the research arms of government agencies, in think tanks, or at university research institutes. Think tanks in particular provide a good space for ideas to be generated and channeled to the policy community.[40] As non-profit and financially independent entities, think tanks are less driven by their own interests than multinational or transnational corporations and have more autonomy in research agendas. Compared with academic institutions, they are more policy relevant and less theoretical.

Epistemic communities are increasingly becoming important sources of knowledge for policymaking. For instance, China's central leadership, the Politburo, invites scholars and experts from across China to share their insights and provide recommendations at seminars attended by its top leaders. These seminars cover an array of domestic and international topics, including NTS issues such as global warming, carbon emissions, energy security, environmental protection, public health emergencies, financial stability, and economic security.

The role of epistemic communities has also been recognized by private foundations. These foundations channel funds toward these communities for research and for capacity-building programs in underdeveloped communities and countries. Through providing financial support, the private foundations are able to influence security discourses and consequently policies and practices. For instance, the financial support of a number of foundations was instrumental to the production of an influential report in 2001 titled *The Responsibility to Protect*, which highlighted the imminent threat of four mass atrocities and introduced the Responsibility to Protect norm.[41] The MacArthur Foundation provided US$68 million over a seven-year period (from 2009) for a project, the Asia Security Initiative, focused on examining the security challenges facing Asia. The grant went to twenty-seven research institutions, including the Centre for Non-Traditional Security Studies at the S. Rajaratnam School of International Studies in Singapore. The Chan Zuckerberg Initiative announced an investment of US$3 billion to develop technologies that can facilitate research on disease.[42] The Bill & Melinda Gates Foundation has committed more money to global health than the World Health Organization (WHO), a development regarded by some scholars as a game changer in the global governance of health issues.[43]

The expertise and knowledge of the various non-state actors often complement each other: private foundations usually have stable and reliable funding sources; faith-based groups and social movements are often moral authorities and thus good at mobilization; the knowledge elites, think tanks, and research institutes provide intellectual support for decision making; the private sector has access to resources, technology, and expertise; and grassroots organizations have good access to people. While competition does occur among non-state actors, they recognize that partnerships and networks are more effective in dealing with the mounting challenges facing individual countries and the globe as a whole.

Security Governors and NTS Governance

In its broadest conception, global governance is seen as the aggregate of governance across different sectors, from economic to environmental and from political to security, all sharing similar elements of being nonhierarchical, multilevel, cross-sectoral, and multi-actor. Part of this broad canvas of governance is security governance, which deals with threats and challenges to the security and well-being of states and societies. Unlike other sectors of governance, security threats often entail urgent response and exceptional measures, such as the allocation and mobilization of certain resources on a priority basis. Emergency measures may also be called for. This distinctive feature of security governance leads to certain processes of security governance that are not seen in the governance of non–security issues. It also entails certain tasks specifically for actors engaging in this process. Before discussing these processes, we will first examine how the configuration of actors in the security sector has shifted and expanded as the security landscape changed.

Broadening of the Security Sector

The nature of security governance is often analyzed based on the interactions of the constituent units of the security sector. Existing studies of the security sector at the national level have emphasized a traditional understanding of security. Heiner Hänggi defines the security sector as including "all the bodies whose main responsibilities [are] the protection of the state and its constituent communities—ranging from the core structures such as [the] armed forces, police and intelligence agencies to those institutions that formulate, implement and oversee internal and external security policy."[44] According to the United Nations, the security sector refers to "the structures, institutions and personnel responsible for the management, provision and oversight of security in a country," taking these to include the armed forces; law enforcement; the intelligence services; institutions responsible for border management, customs, and civil emergencies; and some elements of the judicial sector.[45] The security sector at the national level is the most important constituent in the multilevel spectrum of security governance.

As the notion of security and its challenges have changed, however, the understanding of the security sector has also expanded accordingly. Civil society groups, non-state actors such as faith-based organizations, and private security services have increasingly come to be considered part of the security sector.[46] Nevertheless, in definitions of the security sector, the state security apparatus is still listed first. This reflects the continued primacy of traditional security concerns and conventional security actors in this sector. There is, however, some space given to nonmilitary issues. The United Nations definition mentions civil emergencies and Hänggi also recognizes the broadening of the notion of security.[47] Apart from the military sector, other security-related sectors may include the economic, societal, environmental, health, political, energy, food, and climate sectors.[48] In brief, the "new" notion of what constitutes the security sector can be understood as the sum of interactions between and among state and non-state actors as well as formal and informal arrangements on different security issues at multiple levels. Security-sector dynamics at the regional and subnational levels are also getting more attention in view of the transnational nature of many of the challenges confronting the international community.

Securitizing Actors and Functional Actors

NTS governance could be understood as occurring in four phases or dimensions, beginning with identifying and securitizing the threat, followed by agenda setting, policy formulation, and policy implementation, which includes monitoring and institutionalization (see chapter 1, figure 1.2). By using these four dimensions, we can examine how non-state actors and non-state security actors engage in the NTS governance process and come to assume the role of security governors.

As governance actors, security governors can be categorized differently according to what they do and where they fall in continuum of the NTS governance process. In terms of function, they can be divided into two groups: securitizing actors and functional actors. Securitizing actors are those that "securitize issues by declaring something—a referent object—existentially threatened."[49] They can be national governments (representing states), governmental agencies, intergovernmental organizations, political leaders, lobbyists, and pressure groups. Pressure groups may include those entities whose opinions policymakers pay heed to, like NGOs, transnational corporations, and faith-based organizations. A well-known case of an NGO as a securitizing actor is the International Campaign to Ban Landmines, whose securitizing efforts played a significant role in the eventual passage of the 1997 Ottawa Treaty banning antipersonnel mines.[50]

Current and former political leaders as well as eminent personalities can be securitizing actors, but their placement in the state/non-state dichotomy depends on whether they are acting in an official or private capacity. The speech acts of political leaders are often automatically tied to their official affiliations, which imparts authority to their claims and arguments (see also the next section on the bases of authority and the legitimacy of security governors). In her address to the UN Security Council on the Ebola disease in 2014, Dr. Margaret Chan, then director-general of WHO, warned that the disease constituted "a threat to national security well beyond the outbreak zones."[51] Her assessment was taken seriously by officials of different countries and the NGO community.[52]

Former leaders, politicians, and eminent personalities derive authority from their respective expertise or the values that they represent. For instance, Dr. Surin Pitsuwan, former Thai foreign minister and former secretary-general of ASEAN, has been a patron of the regional effort to mainstream the Responsibility to Protect in Southeast Asia. He led the production of a regional report in 2014 that outlined how ASEAN can promote the Responsibility to Protect. The report was forwarded to the United Nations, where it was received by the officials in charge of genocide prevention and the Responsibility to Protect.[53] Following the launch of the report in New York in September 2014, he participated in a series of outreach activities across the region to disseminate the findings in the report.

Functional actors differ from securitizing actors in that they may not have the interest or incentive to securitize a particular issue, but their behaviors and opinions affect the dynamics of a sector and they are thus able to influence policy decisions.[54] For instance, the business community is an influential actor in the environmental sector. Nike, the well-known athletic footwear company, has led in promoting environmental sustainability; part of its mission is to "reduce energy use, carbon emissions, water use and waste throughout [its] value chain."[55] Temasek, a Singapore-based investment company, has established foundations to support programs focused on, for example, sustainable ecosystems and innovative solutions for livable cities.[56] On the flip side are those businesses whose activities pose a threat to the environment, such as the multinational palm oil and paper and pulp companies in Indonesia blamed for the hazardous level of air pollution in some parts of Southeast Asia.[57] In China, the information technology industry has been responsible for heavy-metal pollution in several provinces, and the textile industry is a major polluter of water resources.[58]

Consent, Legitimacy, and Sources of Authority

Security governors are able to act based on consent and legitimacy, which constitutes the normative component of governance.[59] The security governor gains access to consent and legitimacy through authority. A range of sources of authority have been identified: sovereign authority, institutional authority, delegated authority, expert authority, principled authority, and capacity-based authority.[60]

Sovereignty is the most important source of authority for state actors such as national governments because it bestows them with absolute jurisdiction in the domestic domain, despite the post-Westphalian trend. Institutional authority originates from affiliation with established multilateral institutions, which derive their authority from legal agreements, rules, procedures, and norms.[61] International and regional organizations and their officials usually draw from this form of authority. Delegated authority refers to the situation where state actors authorize intergovernmental institutions and non-state actors to lead the management of particular security issues. The UN Security Council, WHO, and the International Organization for Migration are examples of institutions that draw on delegated authority.

Expert authority is based on knowledge and expertise in a given area. The role of knowledge elites, think tanks, and epistemic communities in security governance is legitimized by their claim to authoritative knowledge. Principled authority originates from the altruistic motive behind the actor's service to the public. NGOs, faith-based organizations, and philanthropic groups often draw on such authority. Capacity and competence are also a source of authority. This source of authority has become more important with the expansion of security agendas, creating and widening capacity gaps in security provision.[62] For instance, gaps in provision of basic health care in underdeveloped countries and regions are filled by NGOs such as Save the Children.

Security governors often draw authority from multiple sources. For instance, the activities of NGOs and charity groups are justified by both moral authority and capacity. In the case of NTS threats, the securitization phase of NTS governance is particularly critical for security governors. NTS threats such as climate change and infectious diseases often do not appear to be as threatening as traditional security problems, which means that effective use of authority is even more critical in convincing relevant audiences that an issue is an existential threat.[63] At the policy formulation, enforcement, and institutionalization phase, security governors also need authority to assure their constituencies that the policies are suitable and necessary and that they are able to deliver the desired outcomes.

Non-State Actors as Security Governors

Apart from the function-based categorization, the state/non-state distinction is another angle of study. Non-state security governors can be the armaments industry, private security and military companies, transnational corporations, NGOs, faith-based organizations, advocacy groups, private foundations, grassroots organizations, think tanks, and knowledge elites. They bring their respective strengths to the different phases of security governance. Some take the lead in advocating the securitization of a particular issue, as in the case of Greenpeace and environmental security; others may support the governance process by contributing material resources, financial aid, knowledge, and expertise; while still others criticize or oppose existing policies and push for change.[64]

Epistemic communities can influence security governance by providing authoritative assessments and recommendations.[65] Scientific evidence is crucial for securitizing an issue and identifying policy solutions.[66] Evidence-based medicine, developed in Canada in the early 1990s, shaped the emphasis on drug-based interventions in responding to pandemic influenza in Asia at the turn of the twenty-first century.[67] In addition to the natural sciences, social science studies that draw a nexus between different issues also play an important role in shaping policies. For instance, the research of the Council for Security Cooperation in the Asia Pacific (CSCAP) study group on climate change in 2010 demonstrated the implications of climate change for other NTS issues such as public health, food, energy, and movement of people.[68] The interlocking nature of the challenges suggests the need to adopt an integrated and institutionalized approach to address the problems arising from climate change.

The protection of migrant workers in Southeast Asia has seen civil society organizations actively engage in developing regional governance frameworks (chapter 5). The Declaration on the Protection and Promotion of the Rights of Migrant Workers adopted by ASEAN leaders in 2007 benefited from input by civil society, with the key platform for consultation with civil society being the Task Force on ASEAN Migrant Workers. At the behest of ASEAN, the task force was established at the Singapore regional consultation process in 2005. The task force is composed of major regional civil society organizations and trade unions engaged in the protection of migrant workers like Migrant Forum in Asia and the Mekong Migration Network. The work of the task force was welcomed in 2007 by then-ASEAN secretary-general Ong Keng Yong, who encouraged close engagement between the task force and the related ASEAN unit.[69]

The task force was responsible for the "Civil Society Position Paper on an ASEAN Instrument on the Promotion and Protection of the Rights of Migrant Workers," which was presented at the ACSC in 2006.[70] This was followed by further rounds of national and regional consultations from 2007 to 2008 to develop the "Civil Society Proposal for an ASEAN Framework Instrument on the Protection and Promotion of the Rights of Migrant Workers." The final proposal was submitted to the ASEAN Secretariat and the ASEAN Senior Labour Officials Meeting in May 2009. It was later adopted by the Thai Ministry of Labor at the second ASEAN Forum on Migrant Labor in July 2009.[71]

The task force also compiled a set of recommendations on protecting migrant rights at the Civil Society Organizations–Trade Unions Consultation on Protection and Promotion of the Rights of Migrant Workers held in Indonesia in 2007.[72] The recommendations focused on the ratification and adoption of international and national legal instruments for migrant protection; the establishment of national and regional arrangements for reporting and coordination; actions against discrimination; health and educational assistance; gender; and the role of civil society. The workshop also resulted in a set of recommendations specifically for Indonesia, which was submitted to the 2007 ASEAN Senior Labour Officials Meeting.[73]

The Philippines is a major source country of migrant labor in Asia, with over 8.5 million Filipinos working and living abroad.[74] As foreign remittance constitutes an important component of the country's gross domestic product, the regulation of migrant-related issues has been institutionalized since the 1970s and the relatively open and free domestic environment has allowed civil society to play an active role in this process. In fact, the Migrant Workers and Overseas Filipinos Act of 1995 recognized the importance of NGOs in protecting the rights of migrant workers. And the United Filipinos in Hong Kong, an alliance of Filipino migrant organizations, successfully campaigned for the revocation of an executive order by the government of the Philippines that required migrant workers to remit at least half of their salaries back home.[75]

At the implementation end, the role of non-state security governors is more visible and substantive. The disaster response to the 2004 Indian Ocean tsunami again proved the importance of local groups in assistance and relief operations. Insufficient communication between international actors and local organizations resulted in imbalances in the distribution of aid among the various affected communities.[76] In Aceh, one of the hardest-hit regions, many people were traumatized by the disaster as well as the protracted armed conflict there. The Pulih Foundation, a national NGO based in Jakarta, responded by expanding its psychological services. As funding drained gradually after the crisis, the organization had to significantly downsize its office in Aceh. But because it had trained local staff and volunteers through capacity-building programs, the Aceh office could continue to offer support to local communities. The Crisis Center of the Faculty of Psychology at the University of Indonesia also established a school-based psychological program. Faculty members, students, and alumni of the school trained teachers to provide psychological support for the students. They also trained midwives and cadres to provide basic health services to local communities.[77]

Market-based actors can also be sites of governance for noneconomic issues. During disasters, the resources and capabilities of corporate actors, particularly transnational corporations, can contribute greatly to relief operations. In addition to financial support, access to their equipment and technologies is also useful. After Typhoon Haiyan, the Philippine Disaster

Resilience Foundation, comprising large businesses in the Philippines, offered to provide vehicles and other facilities. Similarly, after the 2004 Indian Ocean tsunami, companies like UPS and Dow Chemical contributed to relief efforts according to their respective strengths.[78]

NTS Governance in Southeast Asia and the Wider East Asian Region

Southeast Asia, and the three neighboring Northeast Asian states, is one of the regions most affected by NTS problems, from natural disasters to public health emergencies, from sudden economic downturns and irregular migration to environmental pollution. These grave challenges have sensitized leaders in the region to the risks posed by NTS threats to state and human security. This has led to the establishment of regional mechanisms to address the range of NTS challenges confronting the region. The transnational and interlocking nature of these NTS problems has compelled different security actors and governors to adopt an integrated, inclusive, and coordinated regional approach to governance. This section briefly outlines the ongoing processes of NTS governance in East Asia by highlighting examples of how governance has evolved.[79] A more detailed discussion of these processes based on selected case studies of NTS issues follows in the next chapters.

Multitrack Processes in NTS Governance

East Asia's governance environment remains largely influenced by the state-centric political culture. National governments are still the primary provider of security, particularly in policymaking, despite the development of regional institutions in recent years. Intergovernmental institutions (such as ASEAN, ASEAN Plus Three, the ASEAN Regional Forum, and the East Asia Summit) and regional mechanisms (such as the ASEAN Plus Three Health Ministers Meeting, the Chiang Mai Initiative, and the ASEAN Surveillance Process) have been the loci of regional decision making on security and security-related issues. Interactions on policy through these channels are known as Track 1 processes.

Nonetheless, spaces are being created for non-state actors to engage on security issues, particularly in addressing NTS threats. Nonmilitary threats to security have become increasingly complex, and leaders and state actors have to turn to technical advice from experts. Addressing security threats like financial crises, health emergencies, and climate change requires specialized knowledge. Epistemic communities are thus formed to provide intellectual support for policymaking. This is labeled a Track 2 process. Track 2 refers to networks of policy institutes and knowledge elites that have good access to policymaking.[80] Track 2 activities usually involve influential academics/scholars, domain experts, and leaders of civil society organizations that interact more freely with officials. Some analysts use the term Track 1.5 where official and nonofficial actors dialogue to analyze and come up with ideas to manage and resolve conflict.[81] Track 2 actors influence policy through diffusion of ideas to the policy community in both formal and informal settings. Many Track 1 arrangements in East Asia have their own Track 2 mechanisms. Examples include CSCAP to the ASEAN Regional Forum; the Network of East Asian Think Tanks to the ASEAN Plus Three Summit; and the Track 2 Network of ASEAN Defense and Security Institutions (NADI) to the ASEAN Defence Ministers Meeting. Considering the historical and current problems in some bilateral relationships in the region, Track 2 networks provide an alternative site for dialogue on sensitive issues like maritime disputes and conflict resolution. Moreover, with a bottom-up model of policymaking and governance gaining traction in line with the commitment of ASEAN to a people-centered community, Track 2 networks also serve as a bridge between Track 1 and Track 3.[82]

The Track 3 space is filled by those civil society actors that are less associated with governments than Track 2 actors are. Just as there are semiofficial research institutions in Track 2, there are think tanks in Track 3 committed to conceptual and empirical research on security issues in Asia. The Centre for Non-Traditional Security Studies at the S. Rajaratnam School of International Studies in Singapore, which was established in 2008, is one of the more prominent institutions involved in research on NTS issues. Its initiatives in the areas of health security, food security, and humanitarian assistance and disaster relief (HADR) have been recognized by the region's policy and academic communities as pioneering. For instance, after the SARS outbreak in 2003, the center convened a regional conference on pandemic preparedness and argued that public health crises should be securitized. These engagements with policy and academic circles have led to policy papers and journal articles.[83] The center has also been active in institutionalizing the Responsibility to Protect in Asia, serving as one of the secretariats of Southeast Asia's high-level advisory panel on the Responsibility to Protect and producing the report of the panel under the leadership of Dr. Surin Pitsuwan, as mentioned earlier in this chapter. It was also instrumental in establishing the Consortium of Non-Traditional Security Studies in Asia, also known as the NTS-Asia Consortium, which brings together thirty-one research institutes from across Asia and the Pacific.

Track 3 circles also include civil society actors such as international and local NGOs, faith-based organizations, and social movements. They contribute to NTS governance through complementing state capacity in service delivery and advocating for changes in governance. The developing countries of East Asia, particularly Southeast Asia, have wide capacity gaps in the provision of security, and these have largely been filled by non-state security governors. Muhammadiyah, a faith-based organization in Indonesia, has helped boost the country's capacity to manage complex health emergencies. Similarly, community-based organizations and local NGOs have played a critical role in AIDS treatment in areas lacking trained health care personnel. For instance, AIDS Care China provides medication to fifteen thousand AIDS patients, about a quarter of the patients being treated in China.[84] Through providing on-the-ground information and data, they have also been able to influence policymaking at the national level.

To reach policy processes at the transnational level, civil society actors often form networks to give a stronger voice to their proposals and recommendations. End Child Prostitution, Child Pornography and Trafficking of Children for Sexual Purposes (ECPAT) is a global network committed to fighting the commercial sexual exploitation of children. ECPAT originated in Thailand in 1990 and grew into an NGO network with global influence by the mid-1990s. It has helped organize the World Conference Against Commercial Sexual Exploitation of Children since 1996.[85] The most prominent Track 3 networks involved in addressing aspects of NTS concerns in East Asia are the ASEAN Peoples' Assembly (APA) and the ACSC, both of which are described further in the next section.

Dynamics of Security Governance

Against the brief examples in the previous section are the interesting dynamics unfolding in regional security governance featuring interactions between formal and informal mechanisms, as illustrated in figure 2.2. Track 2 and Track 3 actors support policy deliberation and development at Track 1 by providing knowledge, policy ideas, and information. And feedback and critiques from non-state security governors on existing policies and practices help in the implementation and institutionalization of new policies and security practices. Their respective inputs complement and supplement the shortcomings in state capacity. These dynamics are illustrated below in the examples of the workings and interactions of Tracks 2 and 3 security governors with Track 1 processes.

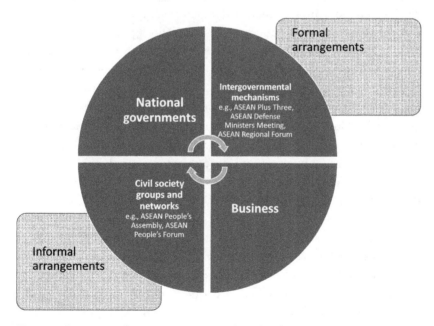

Figure 2.2 Dynamics of security governance: formal and informal mechanisms

CSCAP is one of the most prominent and institutionalized Track 2 networks in the Asia-Pacific, with a membership of twenty research institutes across the region and the European Union. It was initiated in Kuala Lumpur, Malaysia, in 1993 to examine emerging regional security issues. The scope of CSCAP activity ranges from conceptual studies of security to research on specific security issues in the region, such as maritime environmental protection and the contributions of Asia-Pacific countries to UN peacekeeping operations. CSCAP activities are guided by a steering committee cochaired by two representatives respectively from ASEAN and non-ASEAN members. Study groups are formed to bring together experts to build consensus and identify solutions. A study group has a two-year term, during which participants meet twice a year and produce meeting reports accordingly. At the end of the term, the study group delivers a memorandum and puts forward recommendations for Track 1 deliberation.

CSCAP influences the policy process by defining concepts and identifying and framing issues, either at the behest of the ASEAN Regional Forum or by proposing issues that could emerge as threats to regional security. A good example is its work on the topic of preventive diplomacy at the request of the ASEAN Regional Forum.[86] Its Confidence- and Security-Building Measures Working Group organized a workshop in 1999 on the definition and principles of preventive diplomacy, which was attended by CSCAP members and representatives of the ASEAN Regional Forum. The Australian government noted that CSCAP's research formed the base for the ASEAN Regional Forum's work on conflict management and resolution the next year.[87] Another example is its Transnational Crime Working Group, set up in 1996, which generated regional interest in transnational crime as a security concern.[88] Of note also is the Maritime Environmental Protection Working Group, established in 2015 amid escalating tensions between claimants of the South China Sea. Given the sensitive nature of maritime disputes and the ASEAN Regional Forum's practice of not getting involved in security concerns between members, maritime environmental protection is a good entry point for enhancing mutual understanding and building consensus.

As noted earlier, NADI is to the ASEAN Defence Ministers Meeting what CSCAP is to the ASEAN Regional Forum. NADI was initiated by a Singapore-based think tank, the S. Rajaratnam School of International Studies, in 2007 to explore military cooperation among ASEAN countries on defense and security issues, particularly NTS issues. Compared with CSCAP, NADI has a smaller and narrower membership, with participating think tanks coming strictly from the ten ASEAN countries. It engages in regional policy processes through recommendations in the NADI Chairman's Report to the ASEAN Defense Senior Officials Meeting. At NADI annual meetings, time is allocated for discussing issues that could emerge as security concerns or even threats. Among such emerging security issues that NADI has proposed to the ASEAN Defence Ministers Meeting is capacity building and coordination on HADR at national and regional levels. The inputs and recommendations of NADI on this issue were recognized in the joint declarations of the ASEAN Defence Ministers Meeting in 2015 and 2016.[89]

Despite achieving progress in a few areas, concerns remain regarding the role and effectiveness of Track 2 networks like CSCAP and NADI within the statecentric culture in East Asia. Their close ties to governments call into question the autonomy and independence of their activities.[90] As the representative of their respective countries, Track 2 think tanks need to align themselves with their governments, particularly on sensitive issues. For instance, in 2015, NADI fielded a request from one delegation for the network to discuss the South China Sea issue. NADI members, however, decided against pursuing the issue out of respect for the official stance of the ASEAN Summit and its ministerial meetings.[91] Nevertheless, CSCAP and NADI still represent the existing institutionalized channels for the translation of knowledge and ideas into policies.

TRACK 3: APA AND ACSC

The APA was launched in 2000 in Batam, Indonesia. Motivated by the idea of a people-driven mechanism, the ASEAN-Institutes of Strategic and International Studies (ASEAN-ISIS), a Track 2 network, spearheaded efforts leading to the creation of the APA. Held in parallel with the ASEAN Summit, the APA was to be a platform for Track 1 and Track 3 to engage and seek mutual understanding and consensus, given that civil society actors are often critical of state-led governance of some issues. The first APA had three hundred participants, including NGOs, grassroots leaders, activists, think tanks, business representatives, and government officials in their private capacity. NTS-related items on the APA agenda included environmental management and poverty. The participation of a wide range of civil society actors and positive feedback from participants marked the event as a success, a substantive step forward for a region where many countries had just recently emerged from authoritarian rule.[92]

The APA held six forums until its conclusion in 2009. While ASEAN-ISIS had been instrumental in creating the forum, its close ties with governments created tensions, particularly given that APA official statements to ASEAN leaders had to go through ASEAN-ISIS. This arrangement led to complaints of lack of freedom and independence in the activities of the APA.[93] Rules of participation also meant that APA meetings were open only to selected or preferred civil society organizations. The dissatisfaction was intensified by differences in how ASEAN-ISIS and civil society viewed issues such as regional integration.[94]

The discontent and distrust drove some civil society organizations to turn to the ACSC as the forum to advocate for their agendas. The first ACSC was organized in conjunction with the 11th ASEAN Summit in Malaysia in 2005 and was initiated by then Malaysian prime minister Abdullah Badawi. It was even included in the official proceedings of the summit, setting the precedent that civil-society-organization activity is recognized as part of the ASEAN Summit.[95] The notable difference between the APA and the ACSC is the existence of a channel for direct engagement between civil society organizations, the people, and government leaders. Statements of the ACSC were submitted to ASEAN leaders directly, and representatives of civil society organizations from member countries can meet heads of government through informal dialogues or presentations to the ASEAN Summit.[96] The ACSC was designated the ASEAN People's Forum at the ASEAN Summit in 2009.

The Solidarity for Asian People's Advocacy (SAPA), a regional network established in February 2005, had been the lead organizer of the ACSC since 2005. SAPA members work on a range of issues concerning people's rights and well-being, some of which are within the scope of NTS, like migrant rights, sustainable farming, and human trafficking.[97] SAPA aims to enhance communication and coordination among civil society organizations in the region to achieve better effects in policy advocacy. By organizing the ACSC and establishing a direct link between Track 1 and Track 3, it has taken that aim a step further. With a membership of over one hundred local and regional NGOs, the network has strong research capacity to support its advocacy. The aforementioned Task Force on ASEAN Migrant Workers includes SAPA members and is a subgroup of the SAPA Working Group on ASEAN.

TRACK 3: CIVIL SOCIETY

(FAITH-BASED ORGANIZATIONS)

Muhammadiyah is one of the largest faith-based organizations in Indonesia. It is engaged in providing a range of welfare services from education to health and has been an active actor in humanitarian aid since 2004. During the response to the Indian Ocean tsunami, Muhammadiyah's strengths in mobilization and access were displayed. The tsunami caused massive damage to infrastructure, making it difficult for aid to reach victims. Muhammadiyah helped mitigate this to a certain extent, collaborating with international organizations and international NGOs to distribute humanitarian aid through its members across the country. It also organized its own relief operation, deploying doctors from its hospitals to the affected communities. Muhammadiyah teachers and volunteers were also sent to help children and young people.[98] Muhammadiyah has continued to expand its role as a humanitarian actor, helping out in the Yogyakarta earthquake in 2006, the Sumatra earthquake in 2009, and the Mount Merapi eruption in 2010.[99] To improve their response to natural disasters, Muhammadiyah hospitals have collaborated with foreign actors to implement programs to train medical staff to provide health services during large-scale natural disasters.[100] It is now one of the most influential HADR actors in Indonesia and a representative of Indonesia in the international arena in this issue area.[101]

Another example of faith-based organizations making important contributions to HADR is during Typhoon Haiyan, which hit the Philippines in 2013. Organizations such as the Taiwan Buddhist Tzu Chi Foundation Philippines, the U.K. Christian Aid, the U.S. Catholic Relief Services, and the U.S. Catholic Medical Mission Board carried out extensive HADR operations to help affected communities. Tzu Chi provided cash and goods to over sixty-four thousand families. Its volunteers and medical professionals went to affected areas just days after the disaster to deliver health services. Tzu Chi also implemented a cash-for-work program to remove the debris and prepare for rebuilding, which has benefited tens of thousands of people.[102]

These cases demonstrate the ways that non-state security governors have contributed to NTS governance in East Asia through the diffusion of ideas, bottom-up advocacy, and service delivery. The role of these security governors in service delivery has a long history and is less contested. However, the space for non-state security governors to influence policies is limited given the adherence to Westphalian sovereignty by a majority of countries in the region. Nevertheless, because NTS issues are less sensitive, and with the pressure on leaders to effectively deal with NTS challenges mounting, channels have been created and progress has been made.

Conclusion

This chapter examined the role of state and non-state actors in the governance of NTS issues in Southeast Asia and the wider region. The discussion began by laying out the conceptual and empirical perspectives to support the argument that NTS governance in East Asia is no longer the monopoly of state actors. Non-state actors have made use of the spaces that have opened for them to take on the role of security governors in managing issues close to their domain expertise. Expert authority legitimizes the role of epistemic communities in shaping NTS-related policies. Moral authority and capacity have enabled civil society actors to participate in NTS governance processes, from securitization to agenda setting and delivery of services.

Moreover, civil society organizations and other non-state actors are able to govern and make their impact felt by forming networks to enhance their capacity and enable them to work along with other actors. Like other non-state actors, private actors assert their influence and complement efforts by other actors to help manage NTS challenges by capitalizing on their resources and drawing on expertise and capacity as bases for their governance authority.

The engagement of multiple actors in crosscutting NTS issues at multiple levels of governance is not often smooth. In this book, the processes of multilevel governance by state and non-state actors in a number of NTS challenges present alternative sites of governance and can generate conflicts. As will be shown, the challenge for most actors is to navigate the complexities of working together and finding ways to work through different interests while trying to address a health crisis, transboundary pollution, and concerns about threats of food, nuclear energy security, and people's movements.

The following chapters introduce empirical cases of how NTS governance takes place in Southeast Asia and beyond, illustrating the processes generated by the engagement among state and non-state actors working as security governors at multiple levels and on multiple tracks.

CHAPTER III

Governance of Health Security

ealth governance is an important security agenda for Southeast
Asia and the three Northeast Asian states (China, Japan, South
Korea) given the region's exposure to infectious disease risks.
Public health crises caused by outbreaks of infectious diseases present multiple consequences that cut across other non-traditional security (NTS)
challenges, such as economic and political security. The transnational reach
of the crises and the severity of their impact on the well-being of peoples
and states give impetus to a multilateral approach that involves states and
other actors in the international community. In dealing with emerging
threats to global health security, current emphases go beyond international
cooperation and coordination to include approaches that bring together
multiple actors at different levels in order to comprehensively address an
increasingly complex area of concern. In this chapter, the term "East Asia"
is consistently used to denote the breadth of networks and extent of activities that work on health governance in the region.

East Asia's story in regional health governance began after the outbreak
of severe acute respiratory syndrome (SARS) in 2003. The SARS crisis was
a watershed in the region's path toward a more coordinated and effective
regional response to emerging infectious diseases. The crisis also opened
the way to a rethinking of how other health insecurities are to be addressed,
particularly the kind of regional policies to be adopted to promote and
institutionalize health governance in East Asia. Fourteen years on, it is

timely to review the evolution of regional governance of health security in East Asia, assess the progress of regional frameworks that were developed, and identify the gaps.

It should be noted at the start that the breadth of the topic of health security governance can make for an unwieldy analysis. Yet it is useful at the outset to have a brief overview of the strong linkages between health and human security. This would not only help contextualize why health governance has become a critical security agenda in the region; it would also show how health security, historically regarded as falling mainly in the medical domain, became part of the regional security discourse. This is important because, unlike other areas of security cooperation in East Asia, there had been no significant history of cooperation on health security. Until the outbreak of SARS, there had been almost no mention of health in the regional security cooperation agenda. But given the interconnectedness of health threats with other NTS challenges in the region, the outbreaks of new types of infectious diseases led governments and other actors to push for the development of regional frameworks to address the complex challenges to health security. Thus, health governance in the region actually started with the securitization of health by states, and this in turn provided the pathways for multiple sites of governance on health security.

Following the health and human security overview, the rest of the chapter is organized as follows. It reviews the securitization of threats to public health in the international and regional security discourses through the case of the HIV/AIDS epidemic as well as that of emerging infectious diseases. This is followed by an analysis of the East Asian response to health insecurities, including examining the types of actors, mechanisms, and institutions that are involved in the multiple processes of health security governance. I assess how governance processes have evolved since the SARS outbreak and some of the governance issues that have emerged, and I argue that efforts among actors across different levels to cooperate and coordinate laid the foundation for effective regional health governance, particularly for those health threats that are transboundary in nature.

Health and Human Security: Iterating Linkages

It is a sobering reality that, despite the Alma-Ata Declaration of 1978, which affirmed health as a fundamental human right and called for the attainment of the highest possible level of health care for all, the global community is still addressing the same goal forty years later.[1] This lack of progress, particularly in the context of a developing Asia, could be attributed to the low recognition of the security ramifications of health issues. At least until the region's frightening experience with SARS in 2003, there had been limited investment in public health systems.

Health is an integral part of human security. At the very heart of the notion of human security is the protection of human lives from "critical pervasive threats," including illness and disability.[2] As a security framework, human security, by its comprehensive nature, captures the importance of addressing the complex health issues affecting populations. Health is a fundamental right of every human being, and improving health is a key element of any strategy aimed at combating poverty and promoting development. Indeed, health was a key focus identified in the Millennium Development Goals.[3] Achieving health security featured again in the Sustainable Development Goals, ranking third out of the seventeen global goals outlined and broadly framed as good health and well-being.[4] Health is also instrumental in achieving human security by enabling a fuller range of human functioning, choice, freedom, and equitable development.

Health and human security therefore are mutually constitutive concepts. From this perspective, health issues must be seen as not just a "medical" concern but also a human security one, and the artificial distinctions between health and security must be overcome. Moreover, given the different but interconnected NTS challenges facing East Asia and the wider global community today, it is arguably important to emphasize the highly interdependent relationship between health and human security.[5]

Being able to appreciate the intricate linkages between health and human security also makes for a better understanding of the nature of the global health threats today. At the turn of the millennium, the World Health Organization (WHO) began warning about the emerging threat of influenza pandemics. Their studies had identified the rise of significant drivers of global health threats, including international travel, urbanization, changing sexual habits, misuse of antibiotics, poor water and air quality, and the resettlement of humans into natural areas containing lethal pathogens. These drivers have facilitated the emergence and spread of infectious diseases and changed the patterns and determinants of health worldwide.

However, until the mid-2000s, health security was not a priority for most states in the region. While the ASEAN countries were actively promoting a more "comprehensive" concept of security that included economic and political threats, the notion of health security did not feature at all. It was not therefore surprising that the ASEAN states were caught totally unprepared by SARS. At that time, there were no regional frameworks for dealing with pandemic outbreaks and pandemic preparedness.[6]

The region's experience with SARS, followed by H5N1 (avian influenza virus, commonly known as bird flu) in 2005–2006, and H1N1 (pandemic influenza A, or swine flu) in 2009, brought home the point that infectious diseases pose a clear and present danger to the security and well-being of societies and states. A full-scale influenza pandemic could cost the global economy over US$800 billion within a year, with approximately 2 million casualties worldwide, according to the most conservative estimates.[7] Other contagious diseases like AIDS, tuberculosis, malaria, and the West Nile virus also present grave consequences to peoples and states. Also posing significant risks are a number of emerging and reemerging infectious diseases that often contribute to far greater morbidity and mortality. In nations with poor public health systems, the operational challenges in containing the outbreaks of any one of these infectious diseases could be daunting. These risks were instrumental in the securitization of health in the region and beyond.

It should be noted that while health may have been securitized, the focus has fallen mainly on acute, transboundary public health emergencies rather than problems associated with chronic diseases or social determinants of health.[8] This is evident with the 2007 World Health Report entitled *A Safer Future: Global Public Health Security in the 21st Century*. The report focuses on minimizing vulnerability to "public health emergencies of international concern" that threaten the collective health of populations across geographic regions and political boundaries.[9] This privileging of public health emergencies caused by highly pathogenic diseases like SARS has, it is argued, led to many of the other health challenges faced by more vulnerable groups being overlooked. This skewed priority goes against the global development goal of advancing a more human-centered approach to health security. Thus, in the wider scheme of global health governance, there are important issues of inequities and exclusions that cannot be ignored and would need to be addressed if health security were to be comprehensively achieved.[10] This chapter does not delve into this aspect of the health security discussion, choosing instead to focus on how rising awareness of the risks that new kinds of highly infectious diseases pose to the security of states and peoples has compelled governments and other actors in the region to securitize the issues, and beyond that, to institutionalize health governance by developing regional processes and mechanisms for health security.

The State of East Asia's Health Security

The people of Asia suffer a disproportionate burden of communicable diseases compared to the rest of the world. Of the 14 million deaths that occur annually in the region, 40 percent are due to communicable diseases, compared with the global average of 28 percent.[11] HIV/AIDS, tuberculosis, and malaria are among the major infectious diseases that threaten people's health and life in the region. In 2015, 4.47 million new tuberculosis cases were seen in the WHO South-East Asia Region, about half of the world's total.[12] Nearly 5 million people in the region were living with HIV/AIDS in 2015, with India, Thailand, Myanmar, Indonesia, and Nepal among the high-burden countries.[13]

The impacts of health insecurity have been further demonstrated by the outbreaks of a string of emerging infectious diseases since the early 2000s, from SARS to the Middle East respiratory syndrome (MERS) and the Zika virus disease. At the height of the SARS outbreak in 2003, figures show that China and the countries of Southeast Asia were the most affected, with 7,760 cases out of the world's total of 8,096 cases.[14] In 2015 South Korea saw the biggest outbreak of MERS outside of Saudi Arabia, where the disease was first diagnosed in 2012. It had 186 infections, with 36 deaths associated with the disease.[15] In 2016 Zika emerged as the most recent infectious disease to be declared by WHO as a "public health emergency of international concern." Southeast Asia was not spared, with cases reported in Malaysia, Singapore, and Thailand. These health emergencies underscore how difficult it is within the context of globalization and a connected world to contain infectious diseases within national borders.

Epidemics and emerging infectious diseases have an array of negative impacts on countries and their populations, with economic disruption as the most direct and visible consequence. The SARS health crisis resulted in the loss of an estimated US$30 billion in the gross domestic product (GDP) of the East and Southeast Asian economies in 2003.[16] Vietnam saw its economic growth slide 1.1 percent while Singapore's GDP growth was reduced by 0.5 to 1 percent.[17] As many countries in the region are popular tourist destinations, tourism was among the most affected sectors. Tourist data from Hong Kong indicated that inbound tourist figures fell by 70 to 80 percent, while outbound tourists were down 20 percent. In Singapore, tourist arrivals fell to 70 percent of previous levels. The decline of tourist arrivals also affected other tourist-related sectors such as air travel, hotel, and retail.[18]

There are also the more indirect economic impacts. Zika, for example, is known to cause microcephaly among babies and neurological disorders like Guillain-Barré syndrome, which require longer-term medical and other support. While the short-term economic costs of Zika are relatively low compared to SARS—the World Bank estimates that Zika cost Latin America and the Caribbean, which saw the biggest outbreak, 0.06 percent of the region's GDP—it is the longer-term financial impact of caring for, for instance, those with microcephaly, that poses greater concern, particularly among the poorer communities in developing countries. These communities are often at greatest risk, as they live in densely populated areas with poor sanitation and where the risks of zoonotic transmissions are highest. It is also in these areas that health systems are weak.

Social well-being also could be affected by health crises. People living with HIV/AIDS, for example, face stigma and discrimination, which may deter them from seeking antiretroviral treatment and leading a normal life. During the SARS outbreak, people tried to avoid going to public spaces and coming into contact with others to reduce the chance of infection. Health crises that result from unknown pathogenic viruses could further create political instability and even affect relations among states. In Hong Kong, when mandatory quarantine was required for people suspected of being exposed to the SARS virus, the order was met with resistance and was criticized as a violation of people's rights. In 2009, to prevent the spread of the H1N1 influenza in the country, Beijing put in place an array of measures like border control, quarantine of foreign visitors, and trade restrictions. This heavy-handed approach strained China's relations with other countries affected by H1N1, such as Mexico and Canada.[19] Governments could also lose credibility. In China, the central government had to replace the health minister and the mayor of Beijing in April 2003 due to their mismanagement of the SARS epidemic in the initial phase of the crisis.

The potential spread of disease across borders, the rapidity with which that can happen, and the tremendous strain on existing health governance systems as a result have convinced states to look for new regional solutions. Beyond that, and perhaps more significantly, the intersections with serious economic, social, and political security risks have driven health up the regional and international agenda. The next sections look at how health became increasingly securitized and the implications of that for health governance.

The Dynamics of Securitizing Health: Regional Characteristics

Broadly, health governance refers to the management of all public health problems ranging from chronic diseases like diabetes and hypertension, to heart conditions and cancers, and malnutrition and maternal mortality. Yet not all these diseases are viewed as threats to security and thus included in the security agenda defined by states. To understand how certain health issues have been securitized in East Asia, it is useful to discuss briefly what the process of securitizing health entails. In the traditional understanding of international politics and security, the management of public health belongs to the realm of ordinary domestic public policy and the low politics of international relations. But, as mentioned earlier, this began to be challenged in the 1990s as the international community began to see and consider the link between certain infectious diseases and peace and security. Therefore, the elevation of health issues to the domain of high politics coincided with the beginning of health evolving into a security agenda.

For this to happen, securitizing actors had to first convince their audience that an existential threat was looming.[20] The securitization of HIV/AIDS since the late 1990s illustrates this process. HIV/AIDS, believed to originate from Africa, was first diagnosed in the United States in 1981 and spread rapidly across the world, leading some scholars to declare it "the first modern pandemic."[21] In addition to studies on its health, demographic, and socioeconomic consequences, extensive research was conducted on HIV/AIDS as a risk factor to peace and security.[22]

The U.S. government also played an active role in securitizing HIV/AIDS at the turn of the twenty-first century, with its government officials and agencies using the language of security to refer to HIV/AIDS on different occasions.[23] The U.S. intelligence agencies were among the first within the U.S. government system to draw the link between HIV/AIDS and national and international security.[24] Proponents of securitizing the disease argued that the high prevalence of HIV/AIDS in countries emerging from armed conflict could cause state failure and, consequently, regional instability. The high prevalence of HIV/AIDS would also jeopardize the health of the soldiers deployed to those countries by countries outside the region. U.S. president Bill Clinton and vice president Al Gore both referred to the disease as a threat to security.

This is not to say that the securitization of HIV/AIDS was uncontroversial. Some feared that the inclusion of health issues into the security domain would dilute the concept while others were concerned about the militarization of health.[25] Nevertheless, AIDS eventually became an agenda of the UN Security Council, the body tasked with maintaining international peace and security by the United Nations Charter. The United States made use of its turn at the presidency of the Security Council in January 2000 to insert the issue into the council's deliberations. Security Council Resolution 1308 was adopted on July 17, 2000, to express the concern that the spread of HIV/AIDS constituted a potential risk to the health of UN peacekeepers and support personnel.

The securitization of HIV/AIDS had its own dynamics in East Asia. The securitization of the disease in several Asian countries occurred later than the global campaign led by some Western countries. While Vietnam, for instance, was listed as one of fifteen states benefiting from the U.S. President's Emergency Plan for AIDS Relief (PEPFAR), its government had initially regarded the disease as a social problem, calling it a "social evil" in 2002.[26] The prevalence of HIV/AIDS in Vietnam was between 0.3 to 0.4 percent in the early 2000s, very low compared with many African countries like Botswana, whose numbers were as high as over 30 percent. The Vietnamese government later strengthened its effort to deal with the disease, but this was primarily the result of the influence of donor countries like the United States.[27] China, on the other hand, started to securitize HIV/AIDS after the UN declared it a threat to international security. The Chinese leader first admitted that HIV/AIDS was more than a health problem in 2001.[28] The language of security was explicitly used in 2003. In November that year, a few months after the end of the campaign against SARS was declared, China's Foreign Ministry listed HIV/AIDS as one of the six non-traditional threats to China's security.[29] The executive vice minister of health for China, Gao Qiang, declared:

HIV/AIDS is a common enemy of the whole mankind as it seriously threatens public health and safety. The Chinese government has attached great importance to HIV/AIDS prevention and treatment and has treated it as a strategic issue for social stability, economic development, national prosperity and security, making it a first priority of the government work.[30]

While Asia has been identified in some research as the region where the next wave of high HIV/AIDS prevalence will occur, the threat of the disease to people's health and regional security is seemingly not as imminent as emerging infectious diseases. Influenza pandemics present as being more acute and the negative socioeconomic impacts more immediate and visible. Nonetheless, the spread of HIV/AIDS globally had set the precedent of linking health with security and to some extent had prepared the ground for the securitization of other health problems.

The prevalence in some Asian countries of some emerging infectious diseases and their fast spread due to globalization have made them the more urgent agenda in health security in East Asia. This is reflected in a report from the ASEAN Secretariat in 2006 titled "ASEAN Regional Security: The Threats Facing It and the Way Forward."[31] Figure 3.1 depicts the relative weight given to different types of diseases by the governments of ASEAN and other countries in East Asia. At the apex are the most securitized health threats such as SARS; strains of avian and human influenza, including H1N1, H5N1, and MERS; and Zika. The lowest layer includes a whole swathe of health concerns: noncommunicable diseases, primary health care, health systems strengthening, and universal health coverage. There is a valid argument to be made that the health issues in the bottom layer deserve greater attention as they intersect with poverty, humanitarian emergencies (such as famine, flooding, natural disasters), illiteracy, and environmental degradation. But as the pyramid of priorities shows, such social, political, and economic determinants of health are often ranked below the health threats that are deemed to have transnational security impact.

This brings us to the analytical focus of this chapter. While all diseases affect the health and well-being of individuals and communities and are integral to human security, this chapter's analysis of the governance of health security in East Asia deals mainly with how states and other actors have dealt with diseases that have had transnational impact and been accorded higher political priority due to their immediacy and the urgency of crafting a collective response. These are the infectious diseases that have

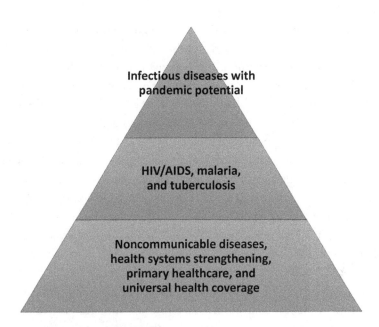

Figure 3.1 Prioritization of health security issues in Asia
Source: Based on World Bank data.

been categorized by WHO as public health emergencies of international concern, examples of which include pandemic influenza like SARS and H1N1 as well as Ebola and Zika. Health governance is therefore addressed here in a narrow sense and specifically refers to the processes through which coordinated policies and actions are generated by a multiplicity of actors to deal with urgent health crises.

Securitizing SARS and the Impact on Regional Health Governance

The first case of SARS infection is believed to have appeared in China's Guangdong Province in November 2002. WHO played a key role in securitizing SARS after receiving information from non-state sources about the outbreak.[32] It issued a global health alert on March 12, 2003, followed three days later by an emergency travel advisory. "This syndrome, SARS, is now a worldwide health threat," said Dr. Gro Harlem Brundtland, WHO's director general at the time.[33]

The outbreak of SARS took the Chinese government by surprise. The denial and attempts to cover up the outbreak in the first few months led to strong international criticism of Beijing's management of the crisis. Eventually Premier Wen Jiabao openly admitted on April 20 that the situation in China remained "grave." He noted that "the health and security of the people, overall state of reform, development, and stability, and China's national interest and international image are at stake."[34] The Chinese foreign minister made a similar reference to the epidemic as an NTS factor when discussing the crisis.[35] Under heavy international pressure, the Chinese government reached out to its neighbors in Southeast Asia for understanding and support. Meanwhile, Singapore prime minister Goh Chok Tong and Thai prime minister Thaksin Shinawatra led initiatives to gather together their regional counterparts to address the crisis under the aegis of ASEAN.[36]

The crisis generated unprecedented coordination among the member countries of ASEAN and China, Japan, and South Korea, collectively known as ASEAN Plus Three. Various multilateral mechanisms were used as platforms for the securitization of the health threat in the region. The ASEAN Plus Three countries held successive meetings of heads of government and top officials to discuss the SARS epidemic. Following the ASEAN Plus Three Health Ministers Meeting in Kuala Lumpur, Malaysia, on April 26, 2003, the Special ASEAN Summit on SARS and the Special ASEAN–China Leaders' Meeting were held back to back in Bangkok, Thailand, on April 29. The Special ASEAN–China Leaders' Meeting resulted in a pledge to undertake joint efforts to cope with the epidemic. Security was mentioned in the point about assessing the impacts of SARS on different sectors.[37] In June 2003 the health ministers of the Asia-Pacific Economic Cooperation (APEC) forum issued a statement recognizing that "infectious diseases can have a deleterious impact on trade and regional security."[38]

Apart from the official discourses, academic circles in Asia also started to associate infectious disease and public health with security following the SARS outbreak. In December 2003, shortly after the epidemic was contained, a national symposium on NTS in China was convened in Beijing, with the participation of more than 150 top scholars and experts from across the country. At the meeting, the conceptualization of security and China's national security was debated, and public health was recognized as a major NTS threat in China as it can cause social instability.[39] In Southeast Asia, where the discussion on expanding the security agenda dates back to the late 1980s, scholars have argued that infectious disease, particularly influenza pandemics, should be treated within a security framework.[40]

The Institute of Defense and Strategic Studies in Singapore, the predecessor of the S. Rajaratnam School of International Studies (RSIS), a major think tank in Asia, hosted a workshop on the dynamics of securitization of NTS in Asia in September 2004, which devoted one session to health and infectious disease.[41] In 2009 RSIS convened an international conference on pandemic preparedness in Asia, a topic that was seeing increased interest in the region. The conference, which brought together some of the best medical experts and security analysts from the region, identified gaps in preparedness planning and discussed the roles that different societal actors can play in formulating operational pandemic preparedness frameworks to strengthen regional cooperation.[42]

Securitizing Actors

Different security governors have engaged with the process of securitizing infectious diseases and the broader health agenda. The state, represented by national governments, leaders, and top officials, has been the leading actor, as in the example of Washington's role in the case of HIV/AIDS and that of Beijing and ASEAN states like Singapore, Thailand, and Vietnam in the case of SARS. As discussed in chapter 2, states possess sovereign authority in their governance of issues of public concern, which gives them absolute authority over the domestic jurisdiction. In most cases, the national government also dominates social resources like material capacity, public information, intelligence, and the media. National governments are therefore usually better positioned to assess an emerging situation and make informed decisions—although there are cases where decision making is hampered by other considerations like domestic stability and international image, as we saw from China's initial instinct to deny that it had a SARS crisis on its hands.

Regional organizations, like ASEAN, ASEAN Plus Three, and the East Asia Summit, have provided critical platforms for securitization to take place at the regional level and for the subsequent crafting of regional governance policies. Intergovernmental organizations have also played an important role in elevating health issues to the high political domain. As mentioned earlier, the UN Security Council, the representative forum for discussing traditional security issues, rendered its support for the effort to link infectious diseases with security by adopting Resolution 1308 (2000). The legitimacy of the Security Council derives from its institutional and delegated authority as it is mandated by the member states to deal with issues related to international security. The resolution represented the shared recognition in the United Nations of the grave threat to international security posed by HIV/AIDS.

WHO, a specialized health agency in the UN system, exercises two types of authority as a governor of global health: delegated and capacity-based authorities. Its delegated authority derives from its broad representation (194 member countries), its constitution, and legal instruments like the International Health Regulations. Before the outbreak of SARS, the International Health Regulations covered only three communicable diseases (cholera, plague, yellow fever), and WHO was considered toothless. However, it was this powerless bureaucracy that had made the aforementioned decisive securitizing moves. The impressive performance of the organization led to the revision of the International Health Regulations in 2005, strengthening its authority and power during epidemics. WHO also drew its authority from its capacity, which included its global surveillance networks (such as the Global Outbreak Alert and Response Network and the Global Influenza Surveillance and Response System), its work on global health statistics and a database, and its laboratories.

Epistemic communities are another group of actors that has contributed to the securitization of infectious disease in the region. Scholars of regional security studies identified the emerging nonmilitary issues and their security impacts on the countries affected. They also analyzed the similarities among these new challenges, highlighting the new trends in the security environment in East Asia. Such research formed a more holistic understanding of regional security by connecting points and events occurring in different sectors. Epistemic communities provided the securitization process with a scientific and conceptual basis.

HIV/AIDS and emerging infectious diseases are among the most pressing health problems in East Asia. The securitization of these two health threats legitimizes the use of extraordinary measures in responding to health emergencies, such as quarantine, border control, regulation of domestic travel, and mobilization of military forces for noncombat purposes. Moreover, this development has deeper meaning for the broader health agenda in that it has strengthened the recognition that health problems can have implications beyond the ordinary socioeconomic areas and that an integrated and coordinated approach is needed to address health insecurities.

Governing Health Security in East Asia

Governance of health security consists of different components, including prevention, control, treatment, capacity training, and institutionalization. Moreover, in view of the transboundary effects of many infectious diseases, coordination in areas like reporting and information sharing is crucial for timely and effective response, as proved by China's failure in containing SARS in the initial phase of the outbreak. Cooperation is also essential for effective health governance at both national and regional levels because countries in East Asia vary in the capacity of their health systems, as reflected in the share of public health in each country's government expenditure and the health expenditure per capita (see tables 3.1 and 3.2).

TABLE 3.1
Public Health Expenditure (Percentage of Government Expenditure), 2004–2014

Country	2004	2009	2014
China	9.99	10.31	10.43
Japan	17.90	18.52	20.28
South Korea	8.79	10.77	12.28
Cambodia	17.25	6.55	6.13
Indonesia	4.82	5.58	5.73
Brunei	6.87	6.70	6.47
Laos	5.42	8.79	3.44
Malaysia	6.37	5.89	6.45
Myanmar	1.89	1.49	3.59
Singapore	7.44	10.20	14.15
Thailand	11.33	12.99	13.28
Vietnam	5.64	8.13	14.22
Philippines	7.47	8.74	10.01

Source: World Bank data.

TABLE 3.2
Health Expenditure per Capita (in Current US$), 2004–2014

Country	2004	2009	2014
China	70.62	192.52	419.73
Brunei	665.22	789.85	957.61
Cambodia	26.18	46.74	61.28
Indonesia	27.24	63.93	99.41
South Korea	789.63	1220.65	2060.25
Malaysia	184.42	290.62	455.83
Laos	19.08	34.22	32.57
Myanmar	4.57	13.20	20.29
Singapore	828.28	1655.89	2752.32
Thailand	86.68	162.97	227.52
Vietnam	30.14	73.22	142.37
Philippines	34.87	81.01	135.20
Japan	2927.44	3741.59	3702.95

Source: World Bank data.

Since the transboundary nature of infectious diseases means that health insecurities in one country can affect the rest of the region, countries need to cooperate to compensate for each other's weaknesses and so generate effective regional governance. In addition, coordination and cooperation is necessary not only among governments of the countries concerned but also among different actors, like WHO, pharmaceutical companies, NGOs, and epistemic communities.

Processes of Health Governance

EMERGING INFECTIOUS DISEASES

Governance of health security varies with type of disease. Emerging infectious diseases like SARS, pandemic influenza A (H1N1), and the Nipah virus usually have acute symptoms and are caused by unknown or novel pathogens, and the response to this type of insecurity should be tailored according to their features. The Asia-Pacific strategy for emerging infectious diseases focuses on five priorities: surveillance and response, laboratory, zoonoses, infection control, and risk communications.[43] Surveillance constitutes a critical phase of the governing process as effective surveillance enables early response. It is built on extensive networks at the grassroots level to monitor unusual signs, and on a set of indicators.[44]

Early response is needed, which consists of investigation of the problems, assessment of the risks, and reporting of the situation on the ground to local and national governments. Laboratory services are critical for timely and effective response as accurate diagnosis is the foundation for appropriate medical and clinical solutions. However, laboratory capacity requires financial investment, and this varies across the region (see tables 3.1 and 3.2). The director of the National Center for Laboratory and Epidemiology in Laos acknowledged at a WHO regional meeting on laboratory services in Kuala Lumpur, Malaysia, in 2011 that their capacity to deal with emerging infectious diseases is limited.[45] The gaps in capacity and resources have given rise to the need for cooperation between different countries and actors.

The importance of zoonoses is grounded in the fact that 60 percent of all known human pathogens originate from animals.[46] Moreover, animal health is linked with food security as there have been cases of disease transmission through food contamination. This connection makes the agricultural sector relevant to the governance of human health security. Between February and March 2017, China reported fifty-eight cases of human infection of avian influenza A (H7N9) in the mainland and Hong Kong. In response, they strengthened supervision and control of live poultry markets and cross-regional transportation. Live poultry markets in several Chinese provinces were closed.[47] To prevent and control human infections of threatening pathogens, it is necessary to implement surveillance of animal health and institute timely response to zoonotic emergencies so as to reduce the risk of transmission at the animal–human interface.

Infection prevention and control is key to stopping the spread of infectious diseases. In urgent situations like SARS, extraordinary measures are justified, like travel restrictions and quarantine of people having physical contact with confirmed cases of infection. During the SARS outbreak, students in many Chinese universities were ordered to stay on campus to reduce the risk of infection. Such forceful measures are an essential component of effective response to health crises like SARS, and only the state has the authority and power to impose them. Coordination plays a key role,

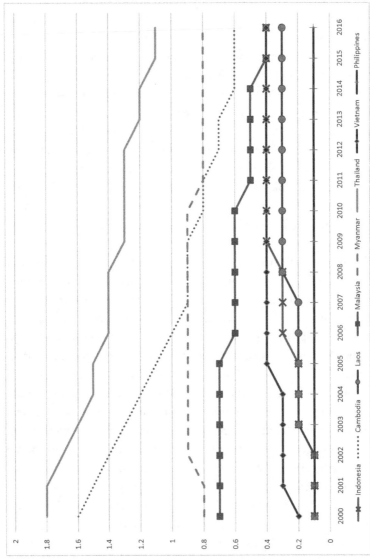

Figure 3.2 Prevalence of HIV by total percentage of population ages 15–49

Source: Based on World Bank data.

as shown by the more effective control of transboundary transmission of SARS after Beijing started reporting to WHO and sharing information with countries in the region.

HIV/AIDS

The priorities in the governance of HIV/AIDS differ from that of infectious diseases as these two types of health insecurities have different features. The governance of HIV/AIDS consists of three major components: prevention, treatment, and care.[48] Prevention aims to interrupt the HIV transmission; specific prevention measures include "testing and counselling for HIV and other sexually transmitted infections, condom use, communication and behavioural interventions, voluntary medical male circumcision, pre- and post-exposure prophylaxis, harm reduction among drug users, universal screening of blood donations and the elimination of mother-to-child transmission."[49] The development of HIV symptoms usually takes years, progressing from acute infection to chronic infection and eventually AIDS. In this process, care and support from the outside contribute to a healthier and longer life for people living with HIV/AIDS.

Antiretroviral therapy is now the most widely adopted treatment for HIV infection. The effectiveness of this intervention has been seen in the decline or stabilization of HIV prevalence in Asia, as indicated in figures 3.2 and 3.3. Cambodia and Thailand have the highest coverage rate of antiretroviral therapy among ASEAN countries, increasing from around 30 percent in 2007, to 80 percent and 69 percent, respectively, in 2016; correspondingly, the prevalence in the two countries has dropped noticeably, from 1.6 and 1.8 percent, respectively, in 2000, to 0.6 and 1.1 percent in 2016. Myanmar, listed as an HIV high-burden country by WHO, has seen its coverage of antiretroviral therapy increase from 5 percent in 2007 to 55 percent in 2016.[50] While the prevalence rate in the country has stayed stable at 0.8 to 0.9 percent over the period, the number of AIDS-related deaths dropped by 10 percent from 2014 to 2015. In Indonesia, on the other hand, coverage of antiretroviral therapy has been minimal, only 13 percent in 2016, making it the lowest among ASEAN countries. Its prevalence rate, meanwhile, has gone up from 0.3 percent in 2007 to 0.4 percent in 2016.

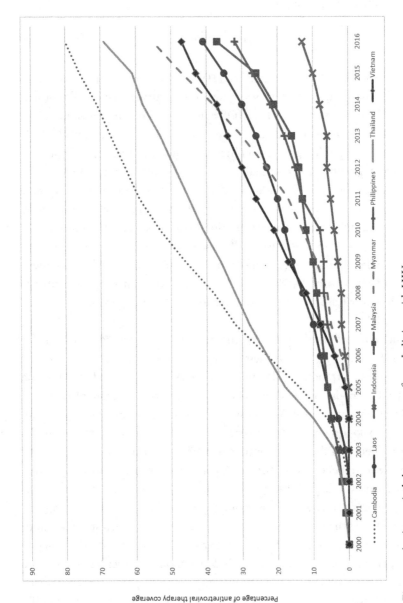

Figure 3.3 Antiretroviral therapy coverage of people living with HIV
Source: Based on World Bank data.

Structures at the National and Regional Level

In line with the aforementioned priorities, East Asia has seen the establishment and development of a two-level structure of governance—national and regional—that involves multiple actors including regional and foreign governments and agencies, international organizations, local and international NGOs, private foundations, and epistemic communities. Lessons from the outbreak of SARS in 2003 have culminated in and accelerated the formation of a variety of networks and mechanisms to deal with health insecurities threatening the region. Areas of focus include promotion of good practices, institutionalization of response, and capacity building at both national and regional levels.

NATIONAL EFFORTS

Effective preparedness and response at the national level can significantly reduce the risk of transboundary spread of infectious diseases. Countries have made efforts to improve the different components of domestic health governance such as surveillance and laboratory services. China's Ministry of Health, in cooperation with its Ministry of Science and Technology, set up a national platform for infectious disease surveillance in 2009. This network consists of 91 surveillance laboratories and 240 designated hospitals across the country. The focus is on five clinical syndromes: febrile respiratory disease, fever with rash, meningitis/encephalitis, hemorrhagic fever, and bloody and watery diarrhea.[51] Laos established its National Influenza Center in 2010 to provide laboratory services to support surveillance.

In Singapore, the National Public Health Laboratory is tasked to track and detect new and reemerging infectious diseases. Singapore's response to the spread of the Zika virus in 2016 was recognized by WHO as a model in dealing with the disease.[52] After Zika spread widely in several countries in South America in 2015, the Singapore government instituted precautionary measures to reduce the risk of a Zika outbreak in the country, including vector control, quarantine of confirmed cases, screening of people with close contact with a case, and testing of the blood samples of suspected cases; these measures were communicated through two public statements, among others.[53]

TABLE 3.3
Regional Health Frameworks and Areas of Cooperation

Regional frameworks	Areas of health security cooperation			
	Emerging infectious diseases with pandemic potential	Infectious diseases: HIV/AIDS, malaria, and tuberculosis	Noncommunicable diseases	Health systems strengthening
ASEAN–China	X		X	
ASEAN–Japan	X		X	X
ASEAN–Korea	X	X	X	X
ASEAN Plus Three Health Cooperation Framework	X	X		
East Asia Summit	X	X		

In the developing countries of East Asia, health governance capacity is constrained by limitations in material and human resources, and collaboration with foreign donors is an important driver of progress and improvement. Indonesia is among the countries with the highest number of human cases and has one of the highest fatality rates from avian influenza virus (H5N1) in the world, with 113 deaths out of the total of 247 worldwide as of December 2008.[54] During the crisis from 2005 to 2010, the Indonesian government collaborated with international organizations such as the Food and Agriculture Organization of the United Nations (FAO), WHO, and foreign donors in responding to the outbreaks. The U.S. Agency for International Development, the Australian Agency for International Development, and the Japan International Cooperation Agency funded the Participatory Disease Surveillance and Response project to monitor poultry health.[55] Under the program, 2,123 officers were trained to collect samples from backyard village poultry in twenty thousand villages across Indonesia. The United States, as noted earlier, supports AIDS relief in Vietnam under the PEPFAR program. PEPFAR funding in 2006 and 2007 amounted to US$1 billion, far exceeding the spending by the Vietnamese government of US$14.4 million in the same period.[56]

REGIONAL COOPERATION AND COORDINATION

At the regional level, there are a variety of mechanisms and networks to address different aspects of health governance, from regional surveillance and risk communication to capacity building, as summarized in table 3.3 and mapped out in figure 3.4.

Most of the current regional health security initiatives started off as responses to the SARS and avian influenza outbreaks during their course from 2003 to 2009, which explains the high number of frameworks addressing emerging and reemerging infectious diseases with pandemic potential, including but not limited to SARS (2003), H5N1 (2005–2006), H1N1 (2009), and H7N9 (2013).[57] Many of these initiatives have been implemented through technical and financial support from the developed countries of East Asia and are concentrated in the developing ASEAN countries. Table 3.3 shows that priorities other than pandemics have at least appeared on the agenda of many regional cooperative frameworks, though at a lower priority level than would be preferred.

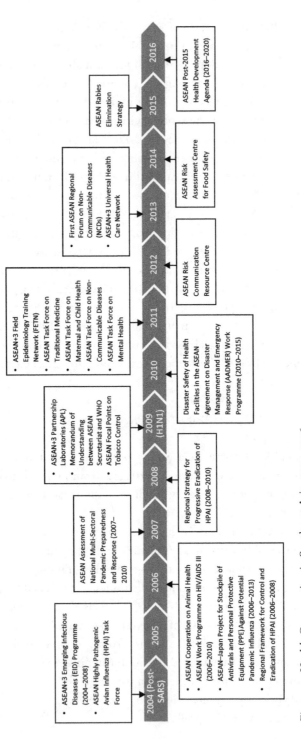

Figure 3.4 Health Cooperation in Southeast Asia, 2004–2016

2004 (Post-SARS)
- ASEAN+3 Emerging Infectious Diseases (EID) Programme (2004–2008)
- ASEAN Highly Pathogenic Avian Influenza (HPAI) Task Force

2005
- ASEAN Cooperation on Animal Health
- ASEAN Work Programme on HIV/AIDS III (2006–2010)
- ASEAN–Japan Project for Stockpile of Antivirals and Personal Protective Equipment (PPE) Against Potential Pandemic Influenza (2006–2013)
- Regional Framework for Control and Eradication of HPAI (2006–2008)

2007
- ASEAN Assessment of National Multi-Sectoral Pandemic Preparedness and Response (2007–2010)

2008
- Regional Strategy for Progressive Eradication of HPAI (2008–2010)

2009 (H1N1)
- ASEAN+3 Partnership Laboratories (APL)
- Memorandum of Understanding between ASEAN Secretariat and WHO
- ASEAN Focal Points on Tobacco Control

2010
- Disaster Safety of Health Facilities in the ASEAN Agreement on Disaster Management and Emergency Response (AADMER) Work Programme (2010–2015)

2011
- ASEAN+3 Field Epidemiology Training Network (FETN)
- ASEAN Task Force on Traditional Medicine
- ASEAN Task Force on Maternal and Child Health
- ASEAN Task Force on Non-Communicable Diseases
- ASEAN Task Force on Mental Health

2012
- ASEAN Risk Communication Resource Centre

2013
- First ASEAN Regional Forum on Non-Communicable Diseases (NCDs)
- ASEAN+3 Universal Health Care Network

2014
- ASEAN Risk Assessment Centre for Food Safety

2015
- ASEAN Rabies Elimination Strategy

2016
- ASEAN Post-2015 Health Development Agenda (2016–2020)

WHO AND FAO

WHO presence in the region is spearheaded by its regional offices: the Western Pacific Regional Office and the Southeast Asia Regional Office. These offices have initiatives spanning communicable diseases, family health and research, health systems development, and sustainable development and healthy environment. East Asia also houses 137 WHO collaborating centers, the majority of which are based in China and Australia, with others based in Japan, South Korea, Singapore, Malaysia, New Zealand, the Philippines, and Vietnam.[58]

WHO initiated the Asia Pacific Strategy for Emerging Diseases in 2005 and revised it in 2010. A technical advisory group provides advice on the development and implementation of the strategy. A range of collaborative mechanisms has also been set up for laboratory services and technical matters. WHO and ASEAN adopted a five-year laboratory work plan for emerging infectious diseases at a meeting in May 2010 in Manila, Philippines.

With regard to governance of animal health, the FAO is a key collaborating party for countries in East Asia. The Global Framework for Progressive Control of Transboundary Animal Diseases (GF-TAD) constitutes a platform for coordination on matters related to diseases threatening human and animal health. The Emergency Center for Transboundary Animal Diseases is the implementation arm of the GF-TAD, helping states respond to transboundary animal health threats. These dense networks fulfilling different functions have formed the system of health governance in East Asia, creating channels and providing support for coordination and cooperation.

DEVELOPMENT ASSISTANCE FOR HEALTH INITIATIVES

China, Japan, and South Korea have been supportive in terms of development assistance for health to developing countries, but it was only in the last decade that cooperation on regional health matters materialized in East Asia.[59] The trilateral cooperation arrangement between China, Japan, and

South Korea extended its areas of cooperation to health only in 2007. In 2009 they committed to strengthening communication and consultation on public health as a regional and international concern.[60] In 2012 the Trilateral Summit recognized the importance of regular meeting mechanisms and cooperation between their health ministries on various health issues.[61]

The three countries also cooperate with ASEAN on a range of health-related issues. Examples include the ASEAN–Japan High Level Officials Meeting on Caring Societies, which has met annually since 2003, and initiatives to prevent communicable diseases under the ASEAN–Japan Plan of Action (2011–2015).[62] The ASEAN–China Health Ministers Meeting has met every two years since 2006. In 2012 the level of engagement was strengthened through the ASEAN–China Memorandum of Understanding on Health Cooperation. The ASEAN–Korea Plan of Action (2011–2015) also includes cooperation on health.[63]

ASEAN AND ASEAN PLUS THREE

ASEAN and the biannual meetings of the ASEAN Plus Three health ministers and their special meetings on urgent issues are also venues for setting regional health agenda and deliberating and determining regional health policies. The ASEAN Senior Officials' Meeting on Health Development is responsible for strategic management and laying the groundwork for the ministers' meetings.

In response to the avian influenza crisis, the 26th Meeting of the ASEAN Ministers on Agriculture and Forestry in 2004 set up the ASEAN Highly Pathogenic Avian Influenza Task Force to formulate and recommend solutions as well as promote and supervise implementation. The task force presented the Regional Framework for Control and Eradication of Highly Pathogenic Avian Influenza to the 27th Meeting of the ASEAN Ministers on Agriculture and Forestry in September 2005 in Tagaytay City, Philippines. The framework prioritized eight focus areas to cope with the outbreaks, and each area was assigned to a member state for coordination. The ASEAN Animal Health Trust Fund was set up to fund projects within the framework.[64]

ASEAN Plus Three has also strongly supported a framework for emerging infectious diseases, a legacy of the urgency of developing effective responses after the region's experience with SARS. In parallel with the Highly Pathogenic Avian Influenza Task Force, the ASEAN Plus Three Emerging Infectious Diseases Program was initiated in 2004. WHO provided inputs on program design; a few research centers in Australia contributed to the implementation of Phase I; and China, Japan, and South Korea provided expertise. As with the initiative on highly pathogenic avian influenza, the Emerging Infectious Diseases Program designated one coordinating party for each of the areas of collaboration. In addition, the Asian Development Bank, the Japanese government, and the Australian Agency for International Development have provided financial assistance to the efforts to end the avian influenza crisis.[65]

Examples of ASEAN Plus Three initiatives on emerging infectious diseases include the ASEAN Plus Three Partnership Laboratories established in 2005, with Malaysia as the coordinating country for efforts to strengthen the capacity of regional laboratories and the quality of their services. ASEAN Plus Three also established a Field Epidemiology Training Network in 2011. And it has been involved in specific disease interventions (including malaria, rabies, and dengue) and in collaborations on animal–human health issues related to influenza virus spread. Figure 3.4 summarizes the many initiatives that have been launched in the post-SARS period.

EAST ASIA SUMMIT

Another forum for health security, though a relatively young one, is the East Asia Summit. Health was an agenda right from the first East Asia Summit in 2005, where the Declaration on Avian Influenza Prevention, Control and Response acknowledged the impact of the avian influenza outbreak not only on the regional poultry industry but also on public health, livestock production, trade, tourism, and economic and social development. It aimed to enhance the capacity to tackle avian influenza and potential transformation into human influenza, through collaboration and coordination among governments, communities and businesses, and regional and international organizations and mechanisms.[66] In 2012 the East Asia Summit expanded its areas of focus to malaria through the Declaration on Regional Responses to Malaria Control and Addressing Resistance to Antimalarial Medicines.[67]

Cooperation on specific measures to cope with health insecurities encompass regional and subregional surveillance networks, laboratory collaboration, communication, and capacity building. In the Greater Mekong Subregion, where the risk of avian influenza outbreak is high, several surveillance networks have been established to monitor human and animal health, share information, and build local and national capacity.

The Mekong Basin Disease Surveillance Project, funded by the Rockefeller Foundation, covers two provinces in China (Yunnan and Guangxi) and the five continental ASEAN members (Cambodia, Laos, Myanmar, Thailand, and Vietnam). The project completed three phases between 1999 and 2011, and the decision was made at the health ministers' meeting of the six participating countries in May 2007 that the cooperation would continue indefinitely.[68]

The project has contributed to the surveillance of infectious disease in the Greater Mekong Subregion in several ways. The number of surveillance sites in the border areas between the six members has been increased, from four to twenty-four, covering most of the important junctures.[69] Each of the six members is responsible for one component of the surveillance. For instance, Vietnam oversees the human–animal sector interface and community-based surveillance, China provides laboratory services, and Myanmar coordinates risk communication. The project also set up a practice of periodic reports and meetings to facilitate information sharing and trust building.[70]

The six countries have also carried out other bilateral and multilateral cooperation to deal with health threats. For instance, programs on HIV/AIDS prevention and control were implemented in China's border areas with Myanmar, Vietnam, and Laos in 2012. China also launched a pilot cooperation program to jointly prevent and control malaria/dengue fever in the border areas between China's Yunnan Province and the Greater Mekong Subregion.

Other surveillance projects include the Greater Mekong Subregion Communicable Disease Control Project and the Surveillance and Investigation of Epidemic Situations in Southeast Asia initiative.[71] Countries in the region have also cooperated on research networks to provide scientific support and develop policy recommendations on the governance of infectious diseases. Examples include the Southeast Asia Infectious Disease Clinical Research Network, the Asian Partnership on Emerging Infectious Disease Research, and the Asia Pacific Emerging Infectious Diseases Research Network.[72]

Security Governors: Non-State Actors and Networks

DONORS AND FINANCIAL INSTITUTIONS

Most regional WHO bodies are dependent on donor contributions from developed member countries, foundations, and dedicated multilateral funds such as the Global Alliance for Vaccines and Immunization (Gavi) and the Global Fund to Fight AIDS, Tuberculosis and Malaria. Gavi has disbursed approximately US$1.6 billion while the Global Fund to Fight AIDS, Tuberculosis and Malaria has committed approximately US$2.97 billion to the developing countries of East Asia.[73]

Aside from WHO and United Nations bodies with specific health agendas, a few other major organizations are involved in securing health as part of their other priorities—for example, the World Bank, through its poverty reduction, human development and social protection, and risk management projects, and the World Trade Organization because of its interest in intellectual property and public health.[74] From 1986 to 2013, 128 of the World Bank's projects were focused on the health sector in East Asia and the Pacific (particularly in Indonesia, Vietnam, China, the Philippines, and Laos), amounting to US$7.24 billion.[75]

At the regional level, the Asian Development Bank supports various projects with health implications. They include: (1) infrastructure development, particularly water supply and sanitation and transportation; (2) economic governance and public expenditure management for the cost-effective delivery of health programs and services, which includes health care financing; (3) regional public goods, including the prevention and control of HIV/AIDS (through the Cooperation Fund for Fighting HIV/AIDS) and other communicable diseases (avian influenza), regional communicable disease control (Greater Mekong Subregion projects), and a regional health observatory (Asia Pacific Observatory on Health Systems and Policies); (4) knowledge management and knowledge products; and (5) its health community of practice for health sector development and advocacy in the region.[76] From 2003 to 2012 the Asian Development Bank financed health projects amounting to US$718 million.

RESEARCH ENTITIES

Research communities, including think tanks and non-state organizations involved in research and advocacy on public health, health governance, health diplomacy, "health as foreign policy," and health security, are also part of the whole spectrum of actors involved in developing and supporting regional health security frameworks in East Asia.

The tropical medicine network of the Southeast Asian Ministers of Education Organization has, since 1993, expanded its scope from research, education, and training on tropical medicine to include health and development, with increasing collaborations with other institutions in developed countries as well as the developing countries of the Asia-Pacific.[77] One of the byproducts of the avian influenza outbreak in 2005, for example, was the establishment of the Asia Partnership on Emerging Infectious Diseases Research made up of more than thirty partner institutions from Cambodia, China, Laos, Indonesia, Thailand, and Vietnam. By 2009 its agenda had expanded to include all emerging infectious diseases.[78]

Another regional health research initiative is the Asia Pacific Observatory on Health Systems and Policies established in 2011 and supported by the World Bank, the WHO Western Pacific Region, and the Asian Development Bank, which can be considered as part of a trend toward increased multisectoral and interagency collaboration on health security. Described as a partnership of governments, development agencies, and the research community, it involves over thirty-five institutions across the Asia-Pacific and aims to bring researchers and policymakers together to advance "evidence-informed health system policy" in the region.[79] Another example is the ASEAN Non-Communicable Diseases Network established in 2013, an informal network of health care experts and thought leaders. Interestingly, this is supported by Philips, a multinational company, reflecting the involvement of the private sector.[80]

These regional non-state networks, despite not being able to outweigh official regional health security frameworks, have the potential to advance a human security approach to health security by virtue of their role in widening the spectrum of actors engaged in advancing health security, even in fragments.

Civil society organizations in the region have been increasingly instrumental in complementing and supporting if not substituting for (the lack of) state-driven health security activities. Civil society organizations driven by health agendas are considerable contributors to human security at the individual, regional, and global levels as direct service providers, as alternative sources of information, as providers of material and human resources for mobilization, and as transnational networks to combat common health threats.[81]

Most of the health-promoting civil society organizations in East Asia work on HIV/AIDS prevention and control. There are some working on infectious diseases and health system capacity building, and a relatively few working on noncommunicable diseases. In terms of development and engagement, which are dependent on the political opportunity structures for civil society organizations to operate in, they have more clout in health security promotion in Japan, Thailand, and Indonesia, where interest in HIV/AIDS is high, than in China, Vietnam, and Laos.[82]

International NGOs have been critical in building networks that bring together different sectors, policy actors, and stakeholders on health issues. Health Action International Asia-Pacific and the AIDS Society of Asia and the Pacific, which focus on increasing access to essential medicines, are examples of such collaborative networks. Some of the regional cooperative networks focus on a specific policy intervention to address noncommunicable diseases, such as the Southeast Asia Tobacco Control Alliance, a multisectoral alliance comprising representatives from government, WHO, and leading tobacco control NGOs from across Southeast Asia. There are also networks focused on women's sexual and reproductive rights, including the Asian-Pacific Resource and Research Centre for Women and the Asia Pacific Alliance for Sexual and Reproductive Health and Rights.

Local civil society organizations and community-based actors have also made important contributions. Their extensive presence at the grassroot level places them in a good position to carry out campaigns to disseminate information and raise awareness. During the avian influenza crisis in Indonesia, Muhammadiyah, together with other civil society organizations, participated in a network of twenty-seven thousand volunteers in West Indonesia to disseminate information on avian influenza

MUHAMMADIYAH AND ITS ROLE IN COMBATING
AVIAN INFLUENZA

Muhammadiyah is one of the oldest faith-based organizations in Indonesia. Part of its mission is to uplift the health and living situations of the people it serves. At the height of the avian influenza pandemic prevention efforts in Indonesia in 2006, Muhammadiyah played a big role.

For example, in Manis Jaya, one of the communities near Jakarta, Muhammadiyah was able to promote knowledge and awareness of the disease and assist locals in coming up with a pandemic contingency plan. As a result, the community was better prepared to detect whether someone in their neighborhood was showing symptoms of influenza.

The strength of Muhammadiyah lies in its ability to bridge the gap between the government and local communities when it comes to human security issues. Noteworthy as well is the organization's ability to reach out to the key decision-makers and stakeholders, whether in the government or those at the grassroots level. The result of this is none other than increased capacity and resilience for communities in dealing with the threat to their health.[1]

1. Siti Masyitah Rama, "The Role of NGOs in Combating Avian Influenza in Indonesia: A Muhammadiyah Case Study" (Singapore: S. Rajaratnam School of International Studies, 2010).

and raise awareness on hygienic practices (see box 3.1). This campaign contributed to reducing human infections of H5N1.[83]

The role of civil society organizations in governing HIV/AIDS has been even more essential. Discrimination and social stigma often discourage people living with HIV/AIDS and high-risk populations like drug addicts and sex workers from seeking help and support.[84] The Radanar Ayar Rural Development Association in Yangon, Myanmar, provides a range of services and support to hundreds of people, including counseling, referral for HIV testing, antiretroviral therapy, home-based care, and prevention activities. In many developing countries with limited health capacities, civil society organizations fill a substantive share of the gaps in governance.

Conclusion

This chapter has reviewed how health issues have been securitized through the two cases of HIV/AIDS and emerging infectious diseases, and it has examined the development of the governance of the two health threats in the region. Overall, the governance of health security in East Asia involves a variety of actors that undertake different responsibilities in the process. National governments set the agenda and direction, impose extraordinary measures whenever necessary, and establish domestic procedures and institutions for prevention of and response to infectious diseases. International organizations like WHO and FAO, which have specific expertise and capacities, provide advice. Foreign donors contribute to the process by providing financial support and are thus able to set the priorities in the health sector. The strength of civil society is in implementing education and awareness campaigns. From the analyses of both HIV/AIDS and emerging infectious diseases, it is clear that coordination and cooperation are essential for effective governance because infectious diseases can spread across borders, and countries in the region vary in terms of their health governance capacity.

Responses to health insecurities differ according to the specific health threat as distinctive features of the diseases require different approaches; consequently, the configuration of the governance structure required also varies between different insecurities. In the face of a health crisis like SARS, the role of the state appears to be more prominent as it is the only actor that holds the authority to implement forceful measures like quarantining and travel restrictions. But in the case of HIV/AIDS, where the governance cycle is long and social discrimination is a major factor discouraging people from seeking appropriate treatment, the role of civil society is crucial.

Finally, the various regional frameworks and the proliferation of non-state regional health security actors have provided more multilevel channels for advancing health governance in the region. To the extent possible, these different actors pushing for health governance also help advance the human security agenda, given that they have increasingly adopted principles of inclusive participation and cooperation among diverse actors at different levels of health governance.

Despite the engagement of different actors working to improve governance of health issues in the region, major challenges remain—not least is the fact that public health systems remain weak in the less developed countries in the region. Health systems are at the heart of how each country and the regional and international community as a whole respond to emerging or reemerging infectious diseases like SARS and avian influenza, as well as to a host of existing communicable diseases, including HIV/AIDS, malaria, tuberculosis, and the neglected tropical diseases. The agenda for strengthening health systems in Asia is therefore critical, if one looks at the key issues that affect the health security of states and societies in the region.

But with these different avenues for multisectoral collaboration increasing, opportunities for deeper and expanded cooperation for a health and human security agenda can also be harnessed. Hence, while progress in practice is slower and can be seen to be more reactive than preventive, the increasing number of official regional bodies engaged in health security is a positive step in the right direction. And, while the approach that informs these official frameworks is observed to still be largely confined to the securitization of infectious diseases, the rising number of non-state actors that focus on health and human security issues would hopefully tip the balance in favor of a broader approach to health and human security.

CHAPTER IV

Governance of Environmental Security

The notion of environmental security has had a long history in the reconceptualization of security in the post–Cold War era. It was one of the first nonmilitary threats to national security identified by scholars and policy analysts in the pioneering efforts to expand the meaning of security.[1] Since then, the importance of environmental security has only increased. Environmental insecurity, in its many forms, is a shared threat to humanity. The list of environmental challenges seems almost infinite, from pollution of many kinds to degradation of land and marine ecosystems, deforestation, loss of habitat, ozone depletion, decline of biodiversity, desertification, and climate change. An estimated 24 billion tons of fertile soils are affected by erosion on a yearly basis; biodiversity in more than half of the world's lands is declining at an alarming rate; and degradation and unsustainable exploitation of resources are affecting over 60 percent of the world's marine ecosystems.[2]

Developing countries have found themselves more severely affected by environmental stresses compared to developed countries due to the gaps in capacity, technology, institutions, and awareness. For instance, indoor air pollution results in 3.5 million deaths every year, and wood and waste fires are a major cause of this type of pollution.[3] Air pollution also causes over US$5 trillion worth of losses in social welfare annually, 60 percent of which are borne by developing countries.

The importance of environmental insecurity for a developing Asia cannot be overstated. East Asia is home to the world's most populous developing countries. China, Indonesia, and the Philippines each have well over 100 million people, many of whom are concentrated in the megacities of Beijing, Shanghai, Jakarta, and Manila. Vietnam and Thailand have more than 50 million people.[4] In addition, this region has maintained steady economic growth in the past two decades and is expected to continue to do so despite economic headwinds in the short- to midterm.[5] With rapid growth, the pressure on the environment is mounting as countries in East Asia struggle to support the livelihoods of almost 2 billion people and maintain strong economic growth. We can only imagine how this pressure will be magnified in years ahead, with the world's population expected to reach 9 billion by 2050, more than half of that in Asia.[6]

The impact of environmental degradation is increasingly felt in the region, from severe air pollution in China and Indonesia to the depleting fish stocks in the seas of East Asia and the threatened ecosystems in the Mekong Delta. Although it has long been recognized that environmental concerns have serious socioeconomic and security consequences and extensive efforts have been taken to address such issues, environmental stresses continue to weigh on the region. The share of arable land in China's total land area shrank from 13.1 percent in 1990 to 11.2 percent in 2014; the forest coverage in Indonesia declined from 65.4 percent of its terrestrial area in 1990 to 50.2 percent in 2015; and the average carbon dioxide emission per capita in ASEAN Plus Three countries increased from 4.8 metric tons in 1990 to 5.8 metric tons in 2013.[7]

From a governance perspective, understanding the nature of the environmental challenges is a critical step toward identifying effective measures to curb environmental degradation. In this regard, it has been argued that the current model of economic development is unsustainable and places major stress on the environment, with the impacts magnified by the world's growing population. The 2015 Sustainable Development Goals have pushed for a "transformative" agenda, urging the international community to seriously consider changes in economic growth patterns and lifestyle changes that would mitigate the impact of climate change and lead to more sustainable growth. A major thrust of goal number 12 encourages responsible consumption and production. The call for transformative action has become an important component of environmental governance. This is particularly salient for East Asia, home to more than a quarter of the world's population and a region undergoing rapid economic development and urbanization. The transformative agenda gains further urgency when we factor in the projection that by 2050, nearly 70 percent of the world's population will live in urban areas.[8]

Against these global trends, this chapter examines the nature of regional environmental governance with a focus on how different security actors are addressing the challenges of environmental security and sustainable development in Southeast Asia and the wider East Asian region. At the outset, it is important to note that environmental security is based on a symbiotic relationship between the environment and human beings, and building such a relationship rests on the joint efforts of all stakeholders. Given the breadth of what constitutes an agenda for environmental security and the complexities involved, it becomes even more important for states to engage with different security actors across the range of environmental concerns. The need for multisectoral and multilevel engagement forges critical partnerships, promotes closer cooperation among different actors, and manages competing interests. This in turn helps to mitigate the serious contestations on how to best protect the environment and how the human insecurities arising from environmental degradation can be addressed.

This chapter begins with an overview of environmental security in East Asia, looking at the evolution of the discourse and the implications of environmental stresses for human security and regional security. This is followed by a discussion of the complexities of environmental governance, which looks at the relationship between the referents of environmental security and transboundary environmental governance. The next section examines existing efforts to address environmental threats and how different actors contribute to environmental governance, starting with how state actors promote sustainable development, institute environmental regulations at the national and regional level, and promote regional cooperation and institution building. The section then looks at parallel efforts taken by non-state actors who engage in the different processes of environmental governance, noting in particular their role in setting the agenda, monitoring activities that contribute to the degradation of the environment, and setting environmental protection standards and norms.

Overview of Environmental Security in East Asia

Defining Environmental Security

Understanding the different ways in which environmental security has been defined helps us chart out what different actors see as environmental threats and priorities, and what their ideas are for dealing with these threats. It also lets us examine how different actors—state and non-state—engage in the multiple processes of environmental governance.

One of the earliest definitions of environmental security came in 1986 from Lester Brown, who was concerned with the economic implications of "new sources of danger [arising] from oil depletion, soil erosion, land degradation, shrinking forests, deteriorating grasslands, and climate alteration."[9] He warned that "these developments, affecting the natural resources and systems on which the economy depends, threaten not only national economic and political security, but the stability of the international economy itself."[10] Other definitions have focused on human well-being, such as when environmental security is defined as "relative public safety from environmental dangers caused by natural or human processes due to ignorance, accident, mismanagement or design and originating within or across national borders."[11]

A more recent study on environmental challenges provides an all-encompassing meaning of environmental security, referring to it as a term that includes

> a range of concerns that can be organized into three general categories:
>
> i. Concerns about the adverse impact of human activities on the environment—the emphasis here is on the security of the *environment as a good in itself*, for the sake of future generations, as the context for human life.
>
> ii. Concerns about the direct and indirect effects of *various forms of environmental change* (especially scarcity and degradation) which may be natural or human-generated on national and regional security. Here the focus is on environmental change *triggering, intensifying or generating the forms of conflict and instability* relevant to conventional security thinking. . . .

iii. Concerns about *the insecurity individuals and groups* (from small communities to humankind) *experience due to environmental change* such as water scarcity, air pollution, global warming, and so on. Here the focus is on the material well-being of individuals and there is no presumption that this is a traditional security issue or that traditional security assets will be useful.[12]

Taken together, we can conclude that "the condition of environmental security is one in which social systems interact with ecological systems in sustainable ways, all individuals have fair and reasonable access to environmental goods, and mechanisms exist to address environmental crises and conflicts."[13]

Evolution of the Environmental Security Discourse

The various definitions of environmental security reflect how the concept has evolved over the years. The concept of environmental security not only has a long history but has also had significant influence on the efforts to expand the concept of security to include nonmilitary issues. The first UN Conference on the Human Environment in 1972 saw the beginning of the international discourse on the environment.[14] The securitization of environmental concerns was marked by the 1987 Brundtland Report, entitled *Our Common Future*, which explicitly used the language of security to refer to the threats to the environment and their impact on state security. The report stated that "the deepening and widening environmental crisis presents a threat to national security—and even survival—that may be greater than well-armed, ill-disposed neighbours and unfriendly alliances."[15] A chapter on peace, security, and development and the environment called for "a comprehensive approach to international and national security [that] must transcend the traditional emphasis on military power and armed competition."[16]

The Brundtland Report informed to a significant extent the convening of the UN Conference on Environment and Development in 1992, also known as the Earth Summit, which lifted the environmental discourse to a higher level by bringing it to a more influential audience, with global media coverage and the participation of state leaders, government officials, industry leaders, and representatives from NGOs. The report also found traction at the national level. The 1991 National Security Strategy of the United States mentioned the link between environmental stresses and political conflict.[17] The German defense white paper in 1994 noted the necessity of broadening the scope of security to include ecological issues.[18]

The securitization of the environment found a bigger voice in 1992 with the release of the Agenda for Peace by UN secretary-general Boutros Boutros-Ghali. Ecological damage was recognized as a new risk to stability: "a porous ozone shield could pose a greater threat to an exposed population than a hostile army."[19] Environmental issues made further inroads into the international security agenda when the UN Security Council convened meetings in 2007 and 2011 to discuss the implications of climate change for international peace and security.

Climate change as a major cause of environmental insecurity has received particular attention from Western countries. The two Security Council meetings on climate change in 2007 and 2011 were initiated by the United Kingdom and Germany, respectively. The United Kingdom identified climate change as the greatest challenge to security and stability at both the national and global levels in its 2008 National Security Strategy. Susan Rice, then the U.S. ambassador to the United Nations, declared in a speech to the Security Council in 2011 that climate change jeopardized the security and stability of all nations and threatened peacebuilding efforts in countries emerging from armed conflicts.[20] She argued that the Security Council had an essential role to play in tackling climate change, considering the "clear-cut" impacts on peace and security. Such sentiments were nevertheless still very much informed by a view of security that focused on the survival of the state. If there was a non-traditional aspect that could be gleaned from the discourse, it was that climate change and other environmental insecurities were considered as great a threat to the security of the state as military threats such as foreign invasion and interstate wars.

While environmental security had come to be part of the agenda for international security, there was still a lack of consensus on how environmental security should be framed and addressed. Who should be the referent of security? Should it be the environment, the state, or the people? While earlier iterations of environmental security had focused largely on how ecological degradation impacts state security, the UN Human Development Report of 1994 brought an additional dimension to the meaning of environmental security. The report identified the environment as one of the seven constituent elements of human security.[21] This framing brought attention to the kinds of insecurities faced by peoples and communities encountering environmental harms caused by environmental degradation, resource scarcity, loss of livelihood, diseases, and health burdens.[22] (These human insecurities are discussed in more detail later in this chapter in the discussion on the complexities of environmental governance.)

While many states agreed that environmental challenges could exacerbate the risk of conflict, they differed in their approach to dealing with the issue. Despite the securitization of the environment and climate change, one of the recurring points of contention was whether to treat climate change as a security or a development issue. This was reflected in the deliberations at the Security Council where some delegates insisted that the issue should be dealt with by other bodies and not the Security Council. For instance, in a 2007 meeting the Indonesian representative argued that climate change "is being addressed, and should be addressed more effectively, in other forums of the United Nations system, including the Commission on Sustainable Development."[23] China and India held similar views. The Chinese ambassador to the United Nations stated in 2011 that climate change is "fundamentally a sustainable development issue."[24] The representative from India placed climate change in the same category as threats to people's well-being such as poverty, food security, and underdevelopment.[25] He also argued that further evidence was needed on the link between climate change and violent conflict. The statements of the three Asian countries echoed some of the concerns raised in earlier debates on the concept of human security. Is human security more about freedom from want (development issues) or freedom from fear (violence and conflict)? The responses in the Security Council suggest that certain Asian states remain uncomfortable with the approach of securitizing the environment and climate change, despite the tacit recognition that environmental challenges and the impact of a changing climate threaten state and peoples' security. One of the best examples to illustrate the preference of certain states for a development-oriented approach is the way in which environmental security has been framed within the context of an ASEAN political and security community. The blueprint for the community states that it "subscribes to a comprehensive approach to security, which acknowledges the interwoven relationships of political, economic, social-cultural and environmental dimensions of development."[26]

Such differences are not limited to states alone but are found between states and non-state actors, and even among non-state actors. It is therefore useful to flesh out the differences in the framing of what environmental security is and whether the referent of security is the environment, the state, or the people and communities. Doing so allows us to better examine how different actors address different kinds of environmental challenges and, more importantly, how these actors take on their respective roles as security governors within the multitrack, multilevel processes of environmental governance.

Environmental Insecurities in East Asia

What is the state of environmental security in East Asia? The large population base, the high growth rate, and rapid urbanization and industrialization have placed the environment under increasing stress. Environmental security encompasses diverse components, including biodiversity conservation and natural heritage, freshwater resources and forests, the marine environment, human settlements, and the atmosphere.[27] Some issues within those categories are considered more challenging and more urgent for the region.

Countries in the region also vary in their priorities depending on their respective situations. In China's 2015 State of the Environment Report, the atmosphere, fresh water, and the marine environment are the first three issues examined. For states in ASEAN, deforestation (due to the conversion of land for economic development) ranks high on the list of environmental issues that impact regional security. The annual deforestation rate in ASEAN is 1 percent, three times higher than the global average.[28] This is followed by the overexploitation of natural resources such as fresh water, timber, and fish stocks. Pollution from industrialization and urbanization is another major threat.[29]

Transboundary Air Pollution in East Asia

Air pollution is a serious environmental security concern for China. In December 2016 more than twenty cities in northern China were affected by three waves of severe smoggy days, and the first-ever red alert for heavy air pollution was issued.[30] And the pollution may be affecting other countries. Some have suggested that the pollutants from the coal-fired power plants and the residential biomass and coal-burning ovens of China are responsible for the significant air pollution in South Korea.[31] The average annual population-weighted $PM_{2.5}$ (fine particulate matter less than 2.5 micrometers in size) in South Korea is 29 micrograms per cubic meter in 2015, almost double the 15 micrograms average for the countries of the Organization for Economic Cooperation and Development.[32] It is not easy to assign blame, however. While China has admitted that its air pollutants have transboundary impacts, there is a lack of credible data to determine the extent and nature of the pollutants.[33] Moreover, South Korea has its own sources of pollution, including diesel vehicles and coal-fired power plants.[34]

Meanwhile, compared to neighboring South Korea and China, Japan has a relatively low average annual population-weighted $PM_{2.5}$, at 13 micrograms per cubic meter.[35] It remains vulnerable, however, to a natural phenomenon known as Asian Dust. In the spring, large amounts of dust particles would be blown eastward from Mongolia, (northern) China, and parts of Central Asia toward the Korean peninsula, Japan, and the northern and eastern parts of China.[36] These dust storms disrupt daily activities, cause economic damage, and pose serious health risks. Overgrazing, deforestation, soil degradation, and desertification in the source countries have aggravated the intensity of the storms. And changes in the chemical makeup of the dust have made it an even more serious threat to human health; ammonium, sulfate, and nitrate ions have been detected in Japan, and these are believed to have come from the factories in China.[37]

The experience of China, South Korea, and Japan suggests that air pollution in one country could have serious transboundary implications for neighboring countries. This is also seen in Southeast Asia, where the haze problem has plagued some countries for decades (box 4.1).

Implications for Regional Security

Health risks are the most worrying consequence of air pollution.[38] According to the Health Effects Institute, ambient (outdoor) particulate matter is the fifth-leading risk factor for total deaths from all causes for all ages and sexes in 2015.[39] Long-term exposure to fine particulates is implicated in diseases that lead to premature deaths, such as ischemic heart disease, stroke, lung cancer, and acute lower respiratory infections in children. Smog and

BOX 4.1

TRANSBOUNDARY HAZE IN SOUTHEAST ASIA

The haze problem has been a long-standing case of environmental governance for ASEAN states. The first major regional haze event occurred in 1997, caused mainly by large-scale forest fires in the Indonesian provinces of Kalimantan and Sumatra and in some parts of Malaysia.[1] Unregulated slash-and-burn farming was a major factor in the fires, with dry weather conditions making the situation worse.

The haze inflicted considerable damage on neighboring Singapore, Malaysia, and Brunei. Malaysia and Singapore suffered an estimated US$1 billion losses in economic activities such as tourism and air travel, as well as immediate health costs.[2] The pollution in parts of Malaysia and Brunei reached alarming levels, forcing people to leave their homes until the haze abated.

The haze returned in 2013 and again in 2015. The El Niño phenomenon had led to prolonged dry spells in the region, which made the forest fires last longer than usual. This in turn intensified the severity of the haze. The problem had also increased in scale over the years with the expansion of oil palm plantations in Indonesia. Large areas of land were being cleared using the slash-and-burn techniques previously used by smallholders. In 2015 the pollutant standards index in parts of the Indonesian provinces of Kalimantan and Sumatra reached above 1,000, with Central Kalimantan hitting a record high of 1,995 in September 2015. Over in Singapore, the pollutant reading reached a record high of 401.

1. Euston Quah, "Transboundary Pollution in Southeast Asia—The Indonesian Fires," *World Development* 30, no. 3 (2002): 429.
2. Simon Tay, "The Environment and Security in Southeast Asia," in *Beyond the Crisis: Challenges and Opportunities*, ed. Mely Caballero-Anthony and Jawhar Hassan (Kuala Lumpur, Malaysia: Institute of Security and International Studies, 2000), 149–60.

haze are also associated with acute upper respiratory tract infections, allergies, worsening of asthma and bronchitis, acute conjunctivitis, and eczema. As an example, fine particulates are estimated to have contributed to over 1 million deaths in 2015 in China.[40] During the haze event in 2015, Indonesia saw a massive rise in cases of respiratory infection: 53,428 in South Kalimantan, 34,846 in Pekanbaru, 22,855 in South Sumatra, 21,130 in West Kalimantan, and 4,121 in Central Kalimantan.[41] Meanwhile, the number of asthma cases in some areas of Malaysia doubled.[42]

Air pollution also has significant economic impacts. The 2015 haze cost Indonesia an estimated US$16 billion.[43] Absenteeism and closures disrupted businesses, with tourism, the hospitality industry, and air travel among the hardest hit sectors. At least twenty airports in Indonesia were closed, and some countries warned against traveling to Singapore.[44] Air pollution causes trillions of dollars in economic losses every year. According to a World Bank study, the cost of air pollution runs to 10 percent of China's gross domestic product (GDP) and 8 percent of Cambodia's in 2013.[45] The study concludes that air pollution severely impedes economic development as it poses major health risks to people, leads to high foregone labor output, and reduces productivity.

Apart from the health and economic consequences, environmental issues also affect social stability and interstate relations. The 2013 and 2015 haze outbreaks saw blame being passed around among affected states. At one point, the vice president of Indonesia, Jusuf Kalla, criticized Singapore and Malaysia for complaining about the haze. He said: "For 11 months, they enjoyed clean air from Indonesia and they never thanked us . . . They have suffered because of the haze for one month and they get upset."[46] This not only dismayed his counterparts in the region but also embarrassed his own officials. Meanwhile, several protests broke out in Indonesia's Riau Province, which was badly affected by the haze. In China, environmental concerns have taken over from land disputes and other social tensions as a major cause of mass protests in China. The number of environment-related protests increased by 29 percent annually between 1996 and 2011, particularly since 2010.[47]

There are therefore at least two ways to analyze the security implications of environmental issues, either through the lens of environmental degradation leading to instability and violence or along the lines of environmental insecurity hampering economic development and threatening human security. The developing states of East Asia have, understandably, been more concerned with the economic implications of the various environmental threats and the impact on sustainable development.

Complexities in the Governance of Environmental Security

The state of environmental security in East Asia is indeed alarming, with environmental threats increasing in frequency and severity. Issues like transboundary haze have led to calls for urgent action at the regional level. Governments have been urged to raise awareness, improve capacity, and take decisive actions. But dealing with environmental challenges brings out distinctive dynamics in governance that are not often found with other types of non-traditional security threats. One of these is the dilemma of responding to the issue of a security referent.

Whose Security?

Security governance is about providing security for referent objects of security through coordinating public and private actors to formulate and implement related policies. The traditional security paradigm focuses on the state as the sole referent object of security. In contrast, the human security paradigm puts people—their survival and their well-being—as the main security referent. The non-traditional security framework, meanwhile, adopts a more inclusive approach, seeing both the state and the people as referents of security. Environmental security, however, is not just about the security of states and peoples. It is also about the security of the environment itself.[48] Further complicating the analysis is the fact that the environment is one big ecosystem that consists of diverse components, from the atmosphere to the marine and terrestrial ecosystems that in effect also become referents of security.

Since environmental security can be conceived as the relationship between human society and the environment or a set of interactions between human activities and the environmental dynamics, this other security referent adds another layer or dimension to the nature of the governance of environmental threats. The explosive population growth, the depletion of resources, the excessive emission of pollutants, and other unsustainable aspects of human development have exceeded the limits of environmental sustainability and threatened its existence. Environmental degradation in turn threatens the peace and stability of countries and the survival and well-being of people. Climate change further aggravates the threat and strains the relationship between people and the environment.

Thus, governance of environmental security needs to be seen holistically, bringing together the concerns of the state, human beings, and the environment. All three are not mutually exclusive. An imbalance in one affects all three. When the ecological balance is disrupted, either by human activities such as unsustainable development or man-made accidents, or by natural causes such as climate change and natural disasters, the security of all referent objects is at risk. Therefore, the balanced relationship between the environment and humanity constitutes the foundation of environmental security.[49]

Interestingly, this idea has been embedded in China's development outlook since the 1990s, when the state of its environment began to deteriorate. China's national development strategy unveiled in 2012 incorporates an ecological dimension: a harmonious relationship between human activities and nature is seen as a critical component in its vision for development. China's commitment to balancing development with environmental protection is supported by the United Nations Environment Programme.[50] This thinking is informed by the logic that the respective security concerns of the three referent objects are mutually reinforcing.

Actors in Environmental Security Governance

Environmental security governance brings a similar configuration of actors as in other non-traditional security issues, like health security. It draws multiple actors: national and local governments and intergovernmental organizations, non-state actors such as NGOs, epistemic communities, and private companies. Governments and international organizations have better access to resources, but the role of non-state actors in the environmental sector is particularly significant. Environmental NGOs such as Greenpeace and the World Wide Fund for Nature (WWF) play an important role in securitizing environmental issues in national and global discourses. Epistemic communities contribute to the securitization and the management of environmental concerns by providing expert advice, while business corporations contribute to the instituting of standards and best practices that advance environmental protection.[51]

Since the tension between economic development and environmental sustainability is a major driver behind environmental insecurity, economic actors like corporations are more influential in the environmental sector than in some other non-traditional security sectors. Seen in terms of the securitization framework described in chapter 2 of this book, they may play the role of powerful functional actors with the ability to affect the dynamics of the sector. Put another way, whether corporations comply with related regulations and fulfill their social responsibilities make a substantive difference to the outcome of environmental governance. For instance, the surge in sulfur dioxide emissions by industry led to China's failure to meet its target for air pollution control in 2005.[52] Discharge of untreated wastewater by pharmaceutical companies in China and India leads to rivers and the soil being contaminated by antibiotics, resulting in widespread antibiotic resistance as the substance enters the food chain.[53] And transboundary haze in Southeast Asia is the result of the unregulated conversion of peatlands to oil palm plantations in Indonesia and Malaysia. Given that corporate activities have important environmental implications, it is imperative that economic actors are involved in the governance process.

In terms of policy approaches, the major components of environmental governance in East Asia are pollution control, prevention, and rehabilitation; sustainable development; and responsible consumption. A multitrack, multipronged approach toward environmental governance is essential given the many factors underlying a host of environmental challenges. The measures required—legislation, market regulation, institution building—can no longer be national in scope. It has become necessary to enhance collaboration and cooperation, education, and awareness raising at the regional level. Importantly, as credible implementation rests on different commitments of actors and stakeholders, the participation of non-state actors has also become imperative.

The State of Environmental Governance in Southeast Asia and Beyond

The different kinds of environmental challenges and their impact on human, state, and regional security are crosscutting and have become a common concern among states. The case of severe transboundary haze in Southeast Asia best illustrates this shared vulnerability and risk, underlining the argument that success in addressing the multidimensional challenges can only be achieved if environmental governance is inclusive. In East Asia, ASEAN's efforts at managing the haze problem can shed light on the challenges of environmental governance in the region.

REGIONAL-LEVEL RESPONSES

As we saw earlier, transboundary haze has been a serious and ongoing problem for Southeast Asia. ASEAN has seen diverse efforts to address the issue, from bilateral cooperation to regional agreements. The 1995 ASEAN Cooperation Plan and the 1997 Regional Haze Action Plan established the initial mechanisms for surveillance, reporting, and capacity building.[54] The 1997 plan evolved to become the 2002 Agreement on Transboundary Haze Pollution, the first legally binding agreement adopted by ASEAN. The agreement entered into force just a year after its signing. By 2015 all ASEAN members had ratified the agreement and deposited their instrument of ratification with the ASEAN secretary-general.

Under the agreement, ASEAN members agreed to cooperate and coordinate on the following measures: (1) monitoring and assessment; (2) prevention; (3) preparedness; (4) national and joint emergency response; (5) procedures for deployment of people, materials, and equipment across borders; and (6) technical cooperation and scientific research. The agreement also created an integrated web of institutions and supporting mechanisms to implement those measures (figure 4.1).

The agreement established a framework made up of a conference of the parties to the agreement, consisting of ASEAN environmental ministers, and a committee under it, whose role is to assist the conference (figure 4.2). Together, they deal with the implementation of the agreement. The framework also includes two subregional arrangements, each dealing with specific haze-related concerns taking place within their respective areas: (1) the Subregional Ministerial Steering Committee on Transboundary Haze Pollution, comprising Brunei, Indonesia, Malaysia, Singapore, and Thailand; and (2) the Subregional Ministerial Steering Committee on Transboundary Haze Pollution in the Mekong Subregion, comprising Cambodia, Laos, Myanmar, Thailand, and Vietnam.

Although the agreement came into force in 2003, its implementation has been problematic. It took Indonesia twelve years to ratify the agreement, finally doing so in 2014. This delay is highly significant as most of the transboundary haze originates from Indonesia's provinces. This lack of

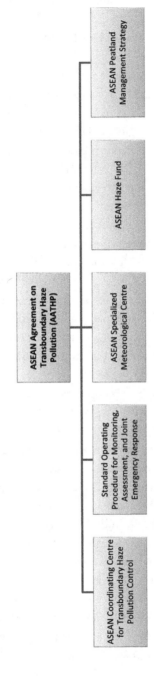

Figure 4.1 ASEAN Agreement on Transboundary Haze Pollution and its supporting mechanisms

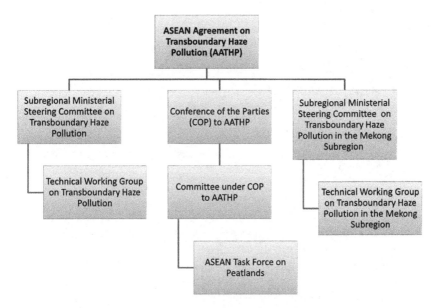

Figure 4.2 ASEAN Agreement on Transboundary Haze Pollution and its institutional mechanisms

action from one party is also indicative of the difficulties faced by ASEAN in generating collective action and commitment to address a shared regional problem. As noted by one analyst, the time it took Indonesia to finally ratify the agreement reflects the view from within that Indonesia is doing "nothing more than signing a non-enforceable agreement."[55]

The agreement also did not do much to prevent transboundary haze from occurring again in 2013 and 2015, with even more severe impacts seen compared to 1997. The lack of progress, particularly on the part of Indonesia with respect to controlling the forest fires in its territory, ruffled regional relations and tested ASEAN's credibility as an effective organization. Nevertheless, despite the slow progress and occasional hiccups in interstate relations, the agreement has its merits. It set in motion a series of regional cooperative measures aimed at improving capacity in preventing and monitoring forest fires, including the ASEAN Peatland Management Strategy (see box 4.2).

Also within the framework of the ASEAN Agreement on Transboundary Haze Pollution, ASEAN has established the ASEAN Specialized Meteorological Centre. This provides satellite information on hotspots—the

BOX 4.2
ASEAN PEATLAND MANAGEMENT STRATEGY

Dry peatlands burn easily, and because of their depth, putting out peatland fires takes a long time. It is therefore important to manage the peatlands properly, maintaining the appropriate moisture level to prevent them from drying and combusting. In response to this issue, the ASEAN Peatland Management Strategy (2006–2020) was developed under the framework of the ASEAN Peatland Management Initiative (2003–2005) and the ASEAN Agreement on Transboundary Haze Pollution.

STRATEGIC GOALS

- Promote sustainable management of peatlands in the ASEAN region.
- Encourage collective actions and enhanced cooperation among the member countries.
- Foster such cooperation in order to support and sustain local livelihoods, reduce risk of fire and associated haze, and contribute to global environmental management.

actual locations and origins of the fires—as well as weather and climate forecasts for the region. The agreement has also helped put in place a mechanism for joint emergency response to deal with forest fires. Under Article 12 of the agreement, an affected party can request assistance or accept assistance offered. Over the years, standard operating procedures have been developed, and during the major outbreaks in Indonesia, neighboring countries have responded with assistance in different forms within the ASEAN frameworks.[56] Malaysia deployed firefighters to Indonesia in at least four instances; Singapore and Thailand dispatched helicopters to help with firefighting at the request of the Indonesian government; and the ASEAN panel of experts was deployed to Indonesia several times. The ASEAN Social Forestry Network, the ASEAN Expert Group on International Forest Policy Processes, and the ASEAN Knowledge Networks on Forest Law Enforcement and Governance and Climate Change led the technical aspect of haze governance by crafting related guidelines.[57] More recently, ASEAN adopted the haze monitoring system, which monitors the perpetrators of fires for enforcement purposes. These regional mechanisms and frameworks have laid the foundation for cooperation and coordination among countries on different aspects of haze governance.

Northeast Asia also has its own subregional arrangements on transboundary air pollution. Unlike ASEAN however, Northeast Asia tends to deal with common environmental concerns through bilateral and multilateral arrangements. China, Japan, and South Korea began to ink agreements on environmental protection in the early 1990s, with bilateral cooperation in areas such as data sharing and technology transfer.[58] Mechanisms like the Tripartite Environment Ministers' Meeting and the Senior Officials Meeting on Environmental Cooperation in Northeast Asia have regularized intergovernmental dialogues on environmental issues.[59] While there are diverse regional arrangements for environmental cooperation, the level of institutionalization in Northeast Asia is low and a legally binding arrangement is still absent.

That said, while regional mechanisms in ASEAN are better and more developed, regional collective actions remain limited in scope. Regional efforts need domestic support; and credible actions at the national level are critical for effective implementation of the programs in the regional agreement. These include instituting appropriate laws to stop forest fires, followed by strict enforcement and more concerted efforts to stop corruption and collusion between local officials and the plantation companies responsible for the forest fires. Equally important is the prosecution of the companies or individuals responsible for illegal forest fires.

In this regard, a study by Nazia Nazeer and Fumitaka Furuoka on the governance of the haze issue in Indonesia is instructive.[60] They identify key issues that hinder effective management. Lack of institutional capacity and a workforce large enough to deal with fire-related forest protection and management is one factor. Issues related to the judicial process are another factor. For example, local courts in Indonesia are not well informed about the regulations and laws needed to deter and punish those who set fire to the forests. There is also a lack of effective oversight, which applies particularly to the problem of endemic corruption among lower-level officials. Thus, despite official pronouncements that the haze has to be seriously addressed, these structural problems have impeded national efforts to prevent fires or prosecute those who break the law.[61]

STATE-LEVEL RESPONSES

The severity of the 2013 haze compelled governments in Southeast Asia to institute immediate actions to address what was perceived as an annual problem for the region. The Indonesian government merged its environment and forestry ministries to improve speed and efficiency in responding to incidents like forest fires and dealing with consequences like transboundary pollution. Also, since Indonesia's overlapping concession maps are often cited as one of the main hindrances to law enforcement efforts in affected areas, the Geospatial Information Agency (BIG) was established as part of the country's "one-map policy." BIG launched a basic geospatial information map and several thematic maps to provide standard geospatial data for government use. The aim of the one-map policy is to create a unified authority for information, data, standards, and reference for government actions in order to effect better cooperation and coordination among relevant agencies.[62]

In line with ASEAN's Peatland Management Strategy, the Indonesian government established the Peatland Restoration Agency in 2016. Its objective is to restore about 2 million hectares of peatlands within five years. The government also enhanced disaster preparedness in case of forest fires by increasing patrols and implementing measures to reduce the firefighting response time, particularly in remote areas more susceptible to fires.[63] In addition, Indonesia hosts the ASEAN Coordinating Centre for Transboundary Haze Pollution Control.[64]

Given its proximity to the Indonesian provinces experiencing forest fires, Singapore has been severely affected by the transboundary haze. To mitigate this situation, Singapore passed the Transboundary Haze Pollution Act in 2014, which allows the Singapore government to take action against companies deemed responsible for unhealthy levels of haze in Singapore. In 2015 the Singaporean government launched legal action against five Indonesian companies involved in setting forest fires in Indonesia that had caused hazardous levels of haze.[65] If found guilty, these companies could face massive fines. This was followed by the issuance of notices to six companies requesting information on their plans to extinguish and prevent fires on their land. If the companies failed to comply with the terms of the notice, the Singaporean government could arrest the companies' representatives upon their next entry into Singapore.[66]

While efforts taken by Indonesia and other states to address the haze have become more visible, doubts remain as to whether these policies are enough to achieve a haze-free region. Since land and forest fires can flare up anytime, and with such fires occurring mostly in remote areas, prevention and preparedness must go hand in hand with monitoring and surveillance of fire outbreaks. The extent of the work involved in monitoring and surveillance requires massive manpower, and this is where the participation and contribution of non-state actors become essential.

ROLE OF NON-STATE ACTORS

State-led actions constitute the backbone of environmental governance. Legislation, regulation, environmental policy, and a national development strategy are essential instruments to control pollution and transform patterns of economic development. However, with environmental challenges escalating in scale and scope, state actors can no longer effectively address them acting alone. A number of non-state actors have stepped in, working with national and regional officials to address the environmental challenges and promote environmental governance. These non-state actors have mainly focused on information gathering and monitoring the activities of farmers and businesses that contribute to forest fires. There are also private non-state actors that contribute to governance by helping to set environmental standards and good practices. The activities of Greenpeace, Aidenvironment, and the WWF illustrate these processes.

Greenpeace

Greenpeace Indonesia is active in environmental advocacy, especially in promoting awareness of the haze problem in Indonesia. Its 2015 report, *Indonesia's Forests: Under Fire*, makes the case that "Indonesia's fire crisis is a test of corporate commitment to forest protection."[67] The report provides analyses of palm oil companies operating in Indonesia that have been complicit in the forest fires in the country. This report, together with other information on their website, helps public and private actors monitor unsustainable and even criminal activities related to forest fires.

The resources initiated by Greenpeace Indonesia include a digital map of the country's forests created using satellite images and data from various sources. This map includes information useful for identifying the owners of the plantations responsible for the forest fires and could potentially serve also as legal evidence against violators since the data come from official/ government sources.[68] To raise awareness of the impact of unsustainable forest practices, Greenpeace Indonesia also produces documentaries featuring stories of people who have lost their livelihoods or become sick, and of animals whose habitats have been lost.

The information gathered by non-state actors could serve as a form of public pressure on companies engaged in harmful practices. For instance, in 2017 Greenpeace released a report on the role of financial institutions in providing credit facilities to the palm oil industry entitled *Dirty Bankers*, which focused on HSBC, a British multinational banking and financial holdings company.[69] The bank had introduced an agricultural commodities policy in 2014, which stated that the bank had no interest in financing illegal operations such as clearance by burning or the destruction of rainforests, and which required its customers to have the necessary certification that they were operating sustainably.[70] Greenpeace called out the effectiveness of this policy by examining the companies financed by the bank, and by compiling information on whether they were engaged in unsustainable practices or involved in uncontrollable fires.[71] As a result of the report, the bank's policy was revised in 2017 to ensure greater consistency with the "no deforestation, no peat, and no exploitation" standard, and the bank extended its policy to include refiners, traders, growers, and millers.[72]

Aidenvironment Asia

Aidenvironment Asia provides services and research on sustainable production and trade. It helps make sure that the "no deforestation, no peat, and no exploitation" policy is observed by palm oil companies by monitoring the actions of the third-party suppliers of the major palm oil refining and trading groups in Southeast Asia. The organization begins by identifying the subsidiaries of the palm oil companies and the social and environmental risks, and by mapping out their oil palm concessions. It then verifies compliance with buyer and investor policies, paying particular attention to activity in undeveloped land as this is where noncompliance of suppliers usually takes place. It makes use of satellite images and drones to obtain information on deforestation and peatland development, supplementing these efforts with field investigations.[73] It then submits its findings to buyers of crude palm oil and palm kernel oil to help them in their purchasing decisions.

WWF

The WWF has been active in increasing awareness of the environmental destruction brought about by the palm oil industry. The palm oil industry is a key source of revenue for Indonesia, which is the world's largest palm oil producer and accounts for 88 percent of the world's production. Indonesia's exports of crude palm oil in 2010 represented 9.3 percent of the country's total exports. The palm oil sectors are also major employers in Indonesia, creating 8 million employment opportunities.[74] Given the economic importance of palm oil to Indonesia, the WWF has taken a market-based approach and actively encourages the growth and use of certified sustainable palm oil through the Roundtable on Sustainable Palm Oil, or RSPO (see box 4.3).

The WWF also helps promote the Forest Stewardship Council (FSC), which is an international certification and labeling system that is dedicated to responsible forest management. It does this by reminding consumers to buy wood-based products that are FSC certified. Another significant WWF initiative is its 2016 Palm Oil Buyers Scorecard, which shows how committed companies are to procuring palm oils that are sustainable and haze-free.[75] It also teams up with think tanks like the Singapore Institute of International Affairs to increase awareness of the perils of unsustainable land use. In 2015 the WWF launched the *We Breathe What We Buy* campaign to inform consumers about their responsibility in environmental governance, stressing their role in promoting sustainable development practices. The public was also encouraged to buy FSC-certified products and to pledge to demand for more companies to be certified.[76]

Local Groups

Activities related to environmental governance—such as promoting education, raising awareness, engaging in monitoring and oversight, and improving transparency in enforcement—involve more than the big non-state actors. Local groups and communities not only support such work but have also been involved in many of the governance processes. For example, to help state authorities and local communities put a stop to forest fires in the districts of Siak, Pelalawan, and Kampar in Indonesia's Riau Province, more than twenty-one civil society organizations and individuals came together to form an alliance to bring companies suspected of being responsible for fires to court.[77] Scale Up, an organization promoting sustainable development that monitors the impact of land and forest fires on the rights and welfare of the people living in the three districts, also joined the alliance. By organizing meetings and providing opportunities for local

BOX 4.3
ROUNDTABLE ON SUSTAINABLE PALM OIL

The RSPO is a certification scheme initiated by the WWF that aims to set and implement global standards for sustainable palm oil. Established in 2004, the RSPO brings together stakeholders from the seven sectors of the palm oil industry: oil palm producers, processors or traders, consumer goods manufacturers, retailers, banks/investors, environmental NGOs, and social NGOs. It has 3,413 members from ninety countries.

The scheme consists of a set of environmental and social criteria to minimize the environmental and social costs of palm oil production. Some of ASEAN's policies and standards like the zero-burning policy are incorporated into the assessment.[1] Companies need to comply with the criteria to have their palm oil products certified. For markets like the European Union that set high environmental standards, certification facilitates market access.

The main purpose of the RSPO is to deter multinational companies from clearing forests through industrial-scale burning, which carries high risk of large-scale fires and subsequent major haze episodes.[2] Moreover, the RSPO has served as a comprehensive and progressive socioenvironmental regulating instrument that has enhanced sustainable production practices in the palm oil industry, particularly among the large transnational plantation companies that have become mindful of their reputation among consumers.[3]

As far as protection of land rights is concerned, the RSPO is far more responsive than governments and may be a "valuable governance alternative to state-based mechanisms" when it comes to the land rights of rural and indigenous communities by providing due process for land claimants and by recognizing that these communities may have legitimate rights to land even if the companies had been awarded legal title by governments.[4]

1. Shahar Hameiri and Lee Jones, *Governing Borderless Threats: Non-Traditional Security and the Politics of State Transformation* (Cambridge: Cambridge University Press, 2015), 104.
2. Hameiri and Lee Jones, *Governing Borderless Threats.*
3. Helen E. S. Nesadurai, "Food Security, the Palm Oil–Land Conflict Nexus, and Sustainability: A Governance Role for a Private Multi-Stakeholder Regime like the RSPO?," *Pacific Review* 26, no. 5 (2013): 505.
4. Nesadurai, "Food Security," 523.

villages to participate in the process, Scale Up helped raise awareness of people in the affected areas about their rights and put pressure on businesses in the region to comply with regulations, including the obligation to share 5 percent of their profit with the people in the area.[78]

Environmental Governance Beyond Southeast Asia

Many of the same processes seen in the case of transboundary haze in Southeast Asia are echoed in developments in the rest of East Asia. In China, for example, the scale of the pollution, particularly in its megacities, has made the need to limit emissions of pollutants, optimize energy use, and upgrade technologies used to fight air pollution more urgent. Measures to achieve these goals include replacing vehicles and machinery that do not meet the emissions standards, transforming industrial production, and promoting clean energy sources.

To respond to and control pollution, governments at various levels in China have put in place a set of measures and institutionalized several mechanisms. Beijing launched the Air Pollution Prevention and Control Action Plan in 2013, amended the Environmental Protection Law in 2014, and is drafting its first soil pollution law. The Ministry of Environmental Protection was restructured in 2016 to give more attention to the different environmental concerns that have emerged in China. The Beijing municipal government set up a comprehensive emergency response system to deal with public emergencies like severe air pollution. Hubei Province passed the Soil Pollution Prevention and Control Regulation of Hubei Province in 2016, the first local regulations on soil pollution in China.

Striking a balance between economic development and environmental protection is a major challenge given the pressures that economic growth has on domestic politics. The transformation toward more sustainable growth and development is a long process that generates conflict when different interests from different stakeholders compete. For provinces such as Shanxi and Hebei, whose economic pillars are polluting industries like coal mining and steel production, any economic transformation is likely to affect their GDP, at least in the short term, which could make governments reluctant to effect the needed measures. In other cases, powerful interest groups in the economic sector have been able to influence the formulation and implementation of environmental policies.[79]

It is therefore necessary to tap the regulating power of other actors like the market to promote shifts in production patterns. The Corporate Information Transparency Index, a quantitative evaluation system to measure the environmental supply-chain performance of various brands in China, is one such innovation along these lines. The index was developed through the collaborative efforts of China's environmental NGOs, the Institute of Public and Environmental Affairs, and the Natural Resources Defense Council. The index uses a weighted scoring system that consists of nine indicators in five categories, including public engagement, data disclosure, transparency, wastewater treatment, and recycling.[80] It targets more than one hundred large companies, primarily those from polluting industries like the textile, leather, information technology, and automobile industries. The annual evaluation reports have been released since 2014. These evaluations put pressure indirectly on the supply chains of these big companies, for which corporate social responsibility is a critical component of their public image.

Like the RSPO, the index reflects efforts by non-state actors to monitor and even regulate the environmental performance of big companies by resorting to the force of the market. Although the companies covered in the report account for only a tiny share of the pollution discharged into China's environment every year, these efforts raise awareness about green production and consumption both in policy circles as well as in the public domain. This higher profile has borne fruit. The green supply chain was incorporated into the declaration released at the 2014 meeting of the leaders of the Asia-Pacific Economic Cooperation (APEC) forum in Beijing.[81] This was followed by the establishment of a pilot center for the APEC Green Supply Chain Cooperation Network in Tianjin, China, in 2015.[82]

NGOs have also begun to make their presence felt in environmental governance in China. Over the past two decades there has been an increase in environmental NGOs in the country.[83] Among the more prominent is the China Environmental Protection Foundation, which is involved in reforestation efforts.[84] Another is Friends of Nature, founded in 1994 and considered the country's first legal NGO. Friends of Nature has brought attention to the pollution of rivers by industry. It successfully prevented the destruction of a virgin forest in Yunnan Province and stopped the building of huge dams along the Salween River and one of the gorges along the Yangtze River.[85]

But while environmental NGOs have been given the space to engage and contribute to environmental governance processes, their actions remain constrained by several factors. These include the need to maintain a good relationship with the local and central government in China and wariness about being used by international NGOs to pursue certain political agenda.[86] Also, as media censorship exists on many issues, they have to rely on social media if they want to bring attention to an issue. Limitations in the litigation process in China also make it difficult to have environmental offenders punished.

Conclusion

Environmental problems present existential threats to the security of the state and its people. The deteriorating state of the environment in East Asia is alarming; so is the increasing frequency of incidences of severe environmental problems. Environmental security cannot be ignored as it has a critical bearing on the state of other non-traditional security issues, like food security, energy security, health security, and peace and stability.

Against these developments, it has become more urgent for countries in the region to take effective actions on a collective basis. The growing severity, complexity, and transboundary nature of environmental insecurities have underscored the reality that no country can go it alone. The ASEAN experience in dealing with transboundary pollution is a case in point. Regional initiatives like peatland management are important in that they not only foster deeper regional cooperation but also help to build capacity for communities that are directly affected by forest fires. Regional programs also provide incentives for local governments to work with experts in land use and with NGOs who work directly with communities. At the same time, much of the success and effectiveness of regional efforts is also highly dependent on national efforts and national support for regional initiatives. Environmental security governance then is very much the sum of all the efforts and processes geared toward managing environmental challenges by different actors at multiple levels. As the experience of ASEAN and the wider East Asian region has shown, regardless of the impediments and challenges that present themselves, environmental governance exists.

Given the complex relationship between environmental security and economic growth, we are reminded that sustainable development is the path to ensure long-term environmental security. Transforming production and consumption patterns is essential if security and development were to be achieved. This would require the participation, engagement, and cooperation of all relevant security actors. While state actors will continue to take the lead in instituting effective governance practices with their access to policymaking and resources, the challenges of balancing the different interests of stakeholders and the issue of transnationality in impact and legal jurisdiction can affect the level and effectiveness of governance. For instance, while Singapore's Transboundary Haze Pollution Act 2014 is a significant development, the effectiveness of the law depends on the ability to accurately identify errant companies or entities operating in Indonesia. The Indonesian government itself has previously filed suit against Indonesian companies, but the rulings and implementation have been complicated by the aforementioned reasons.[87] However, as shown by the experience of the RSPO and China's Corporate Information Transparency Index, innovative responses by non-state actors in the areas of standard setting and best practices could help promote sustainable patterns of production by making use of the power of the market. Environmental security therefore hinges on all stakeholders fulfilling their responsibilities, not just governments but also enterprises and individuals.

CHAPTER V

Governance of Migration

G lobalization has, more than ever, increased the interconnectedness of people, goods, and services. With the exponential growth in communication and technology, the movements of people within and especially across states have been made easier, making state borders more porous and the management of migration flows more complex. This is compounded by the new phenomenon of mixed migration, which sees people on the move, driven by different root causes and insecurities, which in turn suggests having to deal with and respond to a range of needs. These emerging features of migration need to be understood, considered, and managed properly or, as we have seen in some parts of the world already, humanitarian crises could ensue. The migration crisis in Europe that unfolded in 2015 illustrates the immensity of the challenges faced by affected states in stemming the flow of thousands of people wanting to cross into their territories. The global humanitarian community has found itself totally unprepared for the daunting task of dealing with the sudden influx of millions of people attempting to cross borders despite the risks to their lives. As Europe grapples with how to control the massive inflow of people into its territories, the ongoing crisis is forcing a reevaluation of global norms in managing the movement of people.

Europe's ongoing migration crisis is instructive in analyzing the trends of mixed migration found in Asia and their implications for state and human security and migration governance. The kinds of challenges confronting affected European states are relevant to and resonate with some of the challenges facing states in the region. While not to the scale of the problem faced in Europe, the issues of human rights and protection for vulnerable populations, on the one hand, and the security and stability of receiving states, on the other, present dilemmas in normative practices and policy. These interwoven challenges are particularly salient in East Asia, a region comprising states that are the source or recipient of different forms of people movements.

The movement of people or migration is not a new phenomenon in Asia, where hundreds of thousands of people have always been on the move. In 2015 alone, Asia hosted about a third of the 244 million international migrants.[1] What has changed in the region is the scope of the flows of people and their complexity. The region is no longer one that mostly sends migrants but is emerging as a destination for different forms of migration. Irregular migration is also increasingly mixed in nature. Such trends have made the situation even more challenging for states.

This chapter begins with an analysis of current migration flows in East Asia and distills from these trends the types of policy challenges facing the region. It looks at how state actors have dealt with the new patterns of migration in the region and the ways in which state and non-state actors securitize issues of migration. It goes on to examine the migration regimes found in the region and how different actors have become part of the governance processes that have evolved to manage the complex challenges that come with the new faces of migration.

This chapter suggests that the existing migration regimes in East Asia are largely inadequate for addressing the protection needs and rights of migrants, reflecting the wider failures of the international community in responding to emerging and complex movements of people globally. The complexities of current migration trends in turn bring about new humanitarian challenges that exacerbate the insecurities and threats already faced by vulnerable communities while creating tensions between the imperatives of protecting the population and that of protecting state or regime security. Against such a backdrop and because of constraints faced by state actors in addressing the new complexities of migration, the role of non-state actors has become very important. Equally vital in the governance of migration is how non-state actors are part of the rethinking of normative practices and policies to manage a rapidly changing phenomenon.

The Many Faces of Migration in East Asia

Before discussing the migration trends in East Asia, it is useful to revisit our understanding of migration. One general observation is how broadly migration has been defined by the International Organization for Migration (IOM). It defines migration as

> the movement of a person or a group of persons, either across an international border, or within a State. It is a population movement, encompassing any kind of movement of people, whatever its length, composition and causes; it includes migration of refugees, displaced persons, economic migrants, and persons moving for other purposes, including family reunification.[2]

Accordingly, a "migrant" is

> any person who is moving or has moved across an international border or within a State away from his/her habitual place of residence, regardless of (1) the person's legal status; (2) whether the movement is voluntary or involuntary; (3) what the causes for the movement are; or (4) what the length of the stay is.[3]

Notwithstanding the nuances offered by such definitions, in practice states tend to frame migration or movements of peoples in terms of legal status—that is, whether the migration is regular (documented) or irregular (undocumented). Regular migration could include "labor migration," the movement of people for the purpose of employment, usually for a limited or specified period of time.[4] Discussions of labor migration usually focus on the significant flows of usually low-skilled workers from developing countries who have been contracted to work in mid- to high-income countries. Irregular migration is defined by the IOM as "movement that takes place outside the regulatory norms of the sending, transit and receiving countries."[5] It may involve people on the move in search of jobs or economic opportunities, but this category also includes refugees and asylum seekers, victims of human trafficking, and those forced to move due to reasons such as natural disasters, environmental crises, or development projects.

Regular Labor Migrants

Cross-border migration in Asia from the mid-1980s to the early 1990s has mostly involved labor migration. In the 2000s regular labor migration grew in importance for several reasons, one of which is the change in the demographic profile of the receiving countries in the region as their population growth slows and their people age. As of 2010 Asia is home to about 13 percent of the world's migrant population. Increasingly, the region has both sending and receiving countries. The IOM estimates that 43 percent of Asian migrants move to other countries within the region. As intra- and interregional migration flows have significantly increased over the years, so have their spatial complexity.[6] Labor-sending countries are themselves facing labor shortages and aging populations. As a result, countries have to confront the challenges that come from labor migration across a broad spectrum of skills.[7]

Asia is the world's largest source of international migration. In 2013, 79.5 million migrants were from Asia, with South Asia being the largest source, contributing 44 percent of the Asian total, followed by Southeast Asia.[8] There have been many studies on migration that identify the push and pull factors of cross-border migration. They mostly cite economic factors. Many sending countries promote labor migration as a means of relieving domestic pressures of unemployment while also generating income to boost economic growth through the remittances of their migrant workers. Southeast Asia received about US$51 billion in remittance flows in 2014, one-fifth of the Asian total.[9]

Given the economic importance of migrant workers to both sending and receiving countries, there appears to be no doubt that international labor migration is set to continue being a part of the regional migration picture. This makes it even more important for the region to address reports of labor and human rights abuses and to ensure that these workers are accorded the rights and protections they need and deserve.

Irregular and Forced Migration

Irregular migration is a feature of migration flows in East Asia. What is more significant, though, is the nature of these irregular flows, which has been characterized as "mixed." Both the IOM and the Office of the United Nations High Commissioner for Refugees (UNHCR) have been concerned with the issue of mixed migration, with the IOM observing that mixed migration is characterized by "the irregular nature of and the multiplicity of factors driving such movements, and the differentiated needs and profiles of the persons involved," and the UNHCR focusing on the mixed nature of the flows, where we see different types of migrants and people on the move "using the same routes and means of transport or engaging the services of the same smugglers."[10] Such definitions highlight the increasing complexity of regional and global migration patterns.

This is being compounded by a discernible rising trend in the number of refugees and migrants since 2014. The UNHCR's 2015 Global Trends report is sobering, as it notes that the number of people displaced from their homes due to conflict and persecution reached 65.3 million in 2015. This is more than 5 million higher than the 2014 figure of 59.5 million.[11] This record of displacement is unprecedented in human history and more than exceeds the number of people displaced during the Second World War.[12]

Another key feature of the region is the significance of statelessness and its nexus with migration. Aside from ethnic groups that are not recognized as citizens in their countries of residence, there is the issue of second-generation migrants, who are at risk of statelessness because their parents, in an irregular situation, did not register them at birth. Stateless persons—in the absence of a national identity document—often have no access to international travel documents and therefore have no option but to resort to irregular migration channels. Their status often limits their social and economic opportunities and makes them more vulnerable to being targeted by traffickers.[13]

Irregular migration routes are not only intraregional but also extend beyond the region. Some of these movements are supported by smugglers. The increased security concerns associated with such movements, combined with the negative perception of migration and migrants among host populations, have led many countries to take a stronger stand against irregular movements. The following briefly discusses the kinds of security threats posed by irregular migration from the perspective of state and human security.

The UN Protocol to Prevent, Suppress and Punish Trafficking in Persons, Especially Women and Children, supplementing the UN Convention Against Transnational Organized Crime, defines trafficking in persons as

> the recruitment, transportation, transfer, harboring or receipt of persons, by means of the threat or use of force or other forms of coercion, of abduction, of fraud, of deception, of the abuse of power or of a position of vulnerability or of the giving or receiving of payments or benefits to achieve the consent of a person having control over another person, for the purpose of exploitation.[14]

The act of human trafficking may occur either across borders or within a country, and any person from any country can be a victim of human trafficking. Human trafficking can take place with or without the involvement of organized crime groups.[15] Globally, trafficking crimes are estimated to be 80 percent for sexual exploitation and 20 percent for forced labor. The International Labour Office estimates the illegal profit from forced labor to be US$150.2 billion per year.[16]

The countries of East Asia are sources, transit points, and destinations for trafficking victims. In fact, East Asia and the Pacific ranks second-highest globally in the number of trafficking victims, after sub-Saharan Africa.[17] Children and both men and women are vulnerable to trafficking (women, 51 percent; men, 21 percent; underage girls, 20 percent; underage boys, 8 percent).[18] Based on available data, women and children are still considered the most vulnerable group.[19] However, the number of men who are trafficking victims is increasing, with most of them being trafficked into forced labor.[20] Table 5.1 suggests that trafficking and forced labor remains a significant issue in East Asia, with the countries of the region being among the top third of the 167 countries covered in terms of estimated proportion of the population in modern slavery.

While sexual exploitation and forced labor are the most common types of trafficking globally as well as a trend in East Asia, other forms exist, such as forced and sham marriages, removal of organs, selling of children, forced begging, and the use of child soldiers. Traffickers and their victims

TABLE 5.1

2016 Global Slavery Index: Ranking of Countries in East Asia

Estimated proportion of population in modern slavery, by country	Absolute number of people in modern slavery, by country
3 — Cambodia	2 — China
9 — Myanmar	10 — Indonesia
14 — Brunei	12 — Myanmar
20 — Thailand	16 — Thailand
29 — Malaysia	19 — Philippines
32 — South Korea	25 — Japan
33 — Philippines	27 — Cambodia
37 — Laos	34 — South Korea
39 — Indonesia	47 — Vietnam
40 — China	50 — Malaysia
41 — Japan	106 — Laos
45 — Singapore	130 — Singapore
47 — Vietnam	151 — Brunei

Note: The index measures the prevalence of modern slavery, with total number of countries ranked being 167. Rank 1 represents the country with the highest prevalence of modern slavery among those studied.
Source: Global Slavery Index 2016.

usually have something in common—nationality, place of origin, language, or gender—which makes it easier for traffickers to find their victims and gain their trust. Box 5.1 highlights some of the observable trends of human trafficking in East Asia.

REFUGEES

As noted earlier, the UNHCR reports an unprecedented number of displaced in 2015, of which 21.3 million are refugees, 3.2 million are asylum seekers, and 40.8 million are those internally displaced within their own countries.[21] The total number of 65.3 million, when measured against the world's population of 7.4 billion people, means that 1 in every 113 people around the world is now either a refugee, an asylum seeker, or internally displaced. While half

BOX 5.1
HUMAN TRAFFICKING IN EAST ASIA

Human trafficking takes many forms in East Asia, as these examples show.[1]

Filipino Sex Workers in South Korea
Many of those recruited into South Korea enter using the E-6-2 visa, one of the entertainment visas offered by South Korea. The majority of these E-6-2 visa holders are women from the Philippines. By means of fraud, deception, and abuse, these women are trafficked for the purpose of working in the sex industry. Bars and clubs are the most common workplaces for these women, and they serve as prostitutes and sell drinks to customers. They usually work overtime, have no days off, and are not paid on time. Moreover, they are often subjected to sexual violence and find it hard to seek help from the authorities.

Trafficking of Children in Cambodia
Cambodia is notorious for the trafficking of children. These children are transported to different cities in Cambodia by means of abduction, force, coercion, and fraud. They are trafficked for the purpose of commercial sexual exploitation, forced labor such as begging, and orphanage tourism. Many sex offenders are foreign nationals who knowingly visit the country to engage in such acts. Since the victims are children, it is more difficult for them to seek help from the authorities. What makes the situation even worse is when their own family members are complicit in the forms of slavery the children are being subjected to, in exchange for money.

Vietnamese Bride Trafficking in China
Bride trafficking has been a problem in China, with most of the victims being from Vietnam. While there are cases of matches being made through legitimate channels (and the brides in such cases are not facing abuse), some women are being transported to China by means of fraud under the pretext that there is a job waiting for them. Some are abducted or tricked and sold by relatives and friends. These trafficked girls eventually end up in brothels as sex workers or are forced into marriage. The supply and demand of Vietnamese brides in China could be attributed to a variety of factors: Vietnamese women looking for better jobs to improve their lives; Chinese men, especially those from impoverished rural areas who do not want to pay or cannot afford the dowry for a Chinese bride; and the impact of China's one-child policy, which has resulted in men outnumbering women.

1. U.S. Department of State, *2016 Trafficking in Persons Report* (Washington, D.C.: U.S. Department of State, 2016); and Pamela Boykoff and Alexandra Field, "Vietnamese Girls Smuggled into China and Sold as Child Brides," *CNN*, updated April 19, 2016, http://edition.cnn.com/2016/04/17/asia/vietnamese-girls-child-brides-china/index.html.

of these refugees come from war-torn countries like Syria, Afghanistan, and Somalia, the other half are from developing countries in the Global South that experience a range of conflicts and humanitarian disasters.

Asia has its share of refugees, despite the absence of major wars in the region. The 2015 figures from the UNHCR show that Southeast Asia is home to more than 500,000 refugees and asylum seekers who are from within the region and beyond. While international attention is focused on the plight of the Rohingyas, the problems extend beyond that group. Refugees in the region include the Kachins, Shans, and Chins in Myanmar and groups such as the Karens of northern Thailand.

Asylum seekers in Southeast Asia generally come from outside the region, with refugees arriving in cities across the region from distant lands such as Bangladesh, China, Pakistan, Sri Lanka, North Korea, Syria, Somalia, and the Balkans. The deportation of 109 Uyghurs, part of the Muslim minority group in China seeking refuge in Thailand, reflects the serious and systemic nature of the refugee crisis in the region, which is not often known or captured in regional discourses.[22]

In many countries in the region, refugees are categorized under the political euphemism "irregular migration," a designation that includes both economic and political migrants. The recognition that these two categories are intertwined is helpful to the extent that it shows that a political solution to the refugee question cannot be understood when divorced from the larger issue of migration flows, including the flows of economic migrants whose experiences are marked by severe exploitation and personal risk. However, in practice, combining the political and the economic has become a way for countries to ignore the urgent humanitarian needs of refugees fleeing conflict and persecution as opposed to those who have migrated to seek economic opportunity.

Securitization of Migration: Whose Security?

Both regular and irregular (or forced) migration pose major challenges to both state and human security. State actors and agencies securitize migration from the perspective of threats to state security. For regular migration, particularly labor migration, state security is linked to economic security: how does labor migration enhance or threaten economic security? For irregular migration, state security concerns are often linked to criminal activities associated with human trafficking, forced labor, and sexual exploitation, and even threats of terrorism.

A further complication in dealing with mixed flows of migrants is the difficulty of distinguishing between an economic migrant and a refugee, or a documented migrant from one that is trafficked or smuggled. The process of distinguishing an economic migrant from a refugee and asylum seeker has also become more difficult as these persons often engage the services of organized smugglers and use the same routes and means of transport. Hence, as far as state security is concerned, preventing the entry of irregular migrants rather than providing protection for these migrants is the main concern. Efforts therefore focus on establishing robust prevention regimes. For both sending and receiving countries, the security agenda includes addressing the lack of resources and capacity to monitor different types of irregular migration, particularly human trafficking and human smuggling, and the lack of stricter laws and regulatory frameworks to fight criminal activities such as drug trafficking, human trafficking, illegal trade of small arms and light weapons, terrorism, and extremism. Irregular migration could also lead to societal conflicts brought on by local populations who feel threatened by the competition from migrants for resources and opportunities, so the security agenda might also have to include the need to maintain societal cohesion.

From the perspective of human security, the securitization of migration is predicated on the threats posed to affected individuals and communities. Securitization is therefore framed along protection issues that individuals and communities face in their respective conditions of being considered regular and irregular migrants. For regular labor migrants, issues of concern include protection from exploitative labor practices (long working hours, no pay or being underpaid, high recruitment cost, etc.); physical, sexual, and psychological abuse; access to medical and legal care; and discrimination. For irregular migrants, the issues vary depending on their status and can include protection from extortion by criminal networks, protection from physical abuse, access to legal protection, access to health care, and assistance in repatriation or integration.

Regional Migration Regimes

Since migration deals with movements of people, often from one state to another, state actors become the main security governors of different types of migration issues. The relevant state-led regional frameworks that have been developed to address the issue of regular as well as irregular migration are examined here. They include the 2007 ASEAN Declaration on the Protection and Promotion of the Rights of Migrant Workers; the 2015 ASEAN Convention Against Trafficking in Persons, Especially Women and Children; the Coordinated Mekong Ministerial Initiative Against Trafficking (COMMIT); and the Bali Process on People Smuggling, Trafficking in Persons and Related Transnational Crime.

ASEAN Declaration on the Protection and Promotion of the Rights of Migrant Workers

In addressing the protection needs of irregular labor migrants and trafficked victims, it is important to note that there is an international mechanism in place. The International Convention on the Protection of the Rights of All Migrant Workers and Members of Their Families, which entered into force in 2003, spells out the rights of migrants in three sections: the rights held by all persons; the rights of all migrant workers, regular and irregular; and other rights specifically reserved for documented migrant workers. However, the application of the convention is limited both on a global and regional level, as many states have not ratified or acceded to it, including many in Asia.

Southeast Asia does, however, have a regional regime in place. The ASEAN Declaration on the Protection and Promotion of the Rights of Migrant Workers, adopted in 2007, calls on countries of origin and destination to ensure the dignity of migrant workers. It outlines states' obligations in the areas of protection from exploitation, discrimination, and violence, among others. This framework establishes a set of international and regional (ASEAN) standards proclaiming the aspirations for and the right to greater access to social protection by all workers across the region. The declaration does not, however, recognize the rights of undocumented migrant laborers.

While a step in the right direction, implementation has been weak. Migrant workers coming from and moving within Southeast Asia continue to have limited access to social protection, with countries generally and to varying degrees providing only for illness and universal emergency medical access.[23] With the exception of the Philippines, which has made reasonably robust attempts to increase social protection for Filipino migrant workers overseas, many sending and receiving countries lack clear practices to guarantee wider social protection for the migrant workers in, or leaving from, their countries.

There are also increasing reports of exploitation of migrant workers in the receiving countries of Southeast Asia. These range from low pay and poor working conditions to abusive practices such as the withholding of passports and wages. Other common problems are verbal and physical abuse, long working hours, and wages being lower than promised. These issues affect migrant workers across the range of industries, from manufacturing and construction to agriculture and fishing.[24] Clearly, the regional framework has not provided adequate protection for these migrant workers, and the region needs to examine the reasons for the shortcomings in implementation.

ASEAN Convention Against Trafficking in Persons, Especially Women and Children

The 2004 ASEAN Declaration Against Trafficking in Persons was the first attempt by states in the region to securitize human trafficking at the regional level. The declaration was signed into a convention by ASEAN leaders in November 2015. The convention, which came into force in March 2017, establishes a legal framework for the region to effectively address the issue of trafficking in persons.[25] The objectives include preventing and combating human trafficking, protecting and assisting human trafficking victims with full respect for their human rights, and promoting cooperation among relevant parties. The convention also aims to strengthen enforcement and promote closer cooperation and collaboration among ASEAN member states in the fight against trafficking in persons.

Coordinated Mekong Ministerial Initiative Against Trafficking

COMMIT and the Bali Process, described in the next subsection, are institutional mechanisms that complement the ASEAN Convention Against Trafficking in Persons. COMMIT is a mechanism of the Greater Mekong Subregion, which includes Cambodia, China, Laos, Myanmar, Thailand,

and Vietnam. This initiative was born in 2004, when the six governments signed a ministerial-level memorandum of understanding that commits them to a response to human trafficking that meets international standards. The memorandum also highlights the need for multilateral and bilateral cooperation to fight human trafficking and for cooperation between governments and NGOs on this issue.

Members meet on a regular basis to advance a more comprehensive approach to trafficking in persons, with a focus on programs to reintegrate trafficked persons into society.[26] COMMIT has made major progress in the subregion. One human trafficking expert observes that its success could be attributed to its emphasis on sensitivity to the citizenship or ethnic group a trafficked person belongs to; the many interventions to protect the victims; the presence of many bilateral agreements and memoranda of understanding; and an inclusive approach that allows governments, the United Nations, and civil society to work together.[27]

Bali Process on People Smuggling, Trafficking in Persons and Related Transnational Crime

The Bali Process was formed in 2002 as a platform for dialogue among nations in the Asia-Pacific and various international organizations. It was established as a response to the securitization of human trafficking and transnational crime in the region in the late 1990s and early 2000s. Its goal is to raise awareness and build capacity in combating human smuggling, trafficking, and transnational crime. Its membership includes forty-five states and three international agencies (UNHCR, IOM, and UN Office on Drugs and Crime). All ASEAN countries as well as China, Japan, and South Korea are members of the Bali Process.

Gaps and Challenges

Regional migration frameworks could be seen to focus largely on the issue of human trafficking. A common critique of these regional antitrafficking regimes is their focus on criminalizing and prosecuting the trafficking as opposed to protecting the victims of trafficking and their rights. For example, out of the thirty articles in the ASEAN Convention Against Trafficking in Persons, Especially Women and Children, six address criminalization and prosecution while only two are dedicated to the protection of victims and only one focuses on preventing human trafficking. The convention also does not make specific mention of a plan to deal with labor trafficking and neglects the vulnerability of migrant workers to trafficking.[28]

This focus on criminalization and prosecution is reflected in how resources are allocated and where capacity-building efforts are directed. Thus, while there is increased awareness of human trafficking and smuggling, not much has gone into proactive measures to identify those who may have been trafficked and to addressing their protection needs. Apart from personal safety and security, there is a need to ensure access to legal protection, health care, and temporary shelter as well as assistance with repatriation and integration.

Non-State Actors as Security Actors in Managing Migration Challenges

Against the complexities associated with different forms of migration, non-state actors have securitized and advocated for the protection of migrant workers and their rights. The experience in Asia shows that these actors perform key functions in advocacy and in the education and training of migrant workers. These actors also facilitate migrants' integration into their host countries. NGOs and civil society organizations fill many of the protection gaps found in both sending and receiving countries and where government efforts are lacking.[29]

For sending countries, the primary concern of civil society organizations is to support and protect their citizens when they go overseas as migrant workers and to ensure that they have the information they need to safeguard their rights. In the Philippines, for example, civil society groups have played a key intermediary role in managing out-migration from the country. They have operated openly and legally since 1986 and are seen as "partners of the State in the protection of Filipino migrant workers and in the promotion of their welfare," as provided for in the Philippines' Migrant Workers and Overseas Filipinos Act of 1995. There are sixty officially recognized Philippines-based civil society organizations, including Philippine Migrants Rights Watch, which serves as a platform for the promotion and protection of the rights of workers, and the Philippine Migration Research

Network, which provides scholarly and policy research support to both the government and other NGOs.[30]

What is also significant is the way that these civil society organizations have been able to branch out and form networks and alliances with similar organizations outside the country. One of the earliest networks is the Consultative Council on Overseas Filipino Workers. It was formed in 2001 to institutionalize a dialogue process between migration NGOs and the government. Another example is Migrante International, established in 1996, a network of over ninety different migration organizations in over twenty countries.[31] The transnationalization of migration NGOs has been recognized as an important part of good migration governance, underscoring the argument that governance is a multilevel process. The involvement of NGOs in migration governance illustrates governance from below, promoting self-governance and the empowerment of migrant communities.[32]

In Indonesia, the NGOs that work with migrants operate like labor unions. They examine issues of domestic labor, collect data, advocate policies, provide training and assistance, and raise public awareness. NGOs are also becoming increasingly engaged in protecting women's rights, as seen in the work of Solidaritas Perempuan (Women's Solidarity) and Migrant Care. Much like the Philippine case, civil society organizations and interest groups have been established overseas in places like Hong Kong to provide protection for Indonesian migrant workers. However, unlike in the Philippines, the civil society organizations in Indonesia have yet to gain enough leverage to lobby the Indonesian government for better protection for their own migrant workers. According to one scholar, gradual deepening of political reforms in Indonesia would have to occur before civil society organizations are able to effectively engage with the government on advancing the protection agenda for Indonesian foreign workers.[33]

Labor-receiving countries like Malaysia and Singapore also have civil society organizations involved in promoting workers' rights and advancing the agenda of protection. Malaysia's Tenaganita assists migrant workers by providing legal aid services and helps trafficked women as well. Meanwhile, in Singapore, civil society organizations such as Aidha, 45Rice, and Transient Workers Count Too support migrants through skills training and skills-upgrading programs on topics such as computer literary and entrepreneurship as well as health care and food services.

At the regional and international levels, transnational civil society organizations are also critical actors in building and promoting international

ASIA PACIFIC REFUGEE RIGHTS NETWORK

The Asia Pacific Refugee Rights Network, established in 2008, is a network of over three hundred civil society organizations and individuals spanning twenty-six countries across the Asia-Pacific.[1] This network offers an alternative approach to the Bali Process. It runs as a transnational activist network that seeks to promote the rights of refugees and the protection of forced migrants through advocacy, capacity strengthening, and knowledge and resource sharing and outreach.

The Asia Pacific Refugee Rights Network differs from the Bali Process in that it has a strong normative agenda and it seeks to challenge the Bali Process framework, which it considers as having a predominantly statist perspective and hierarchical approach. Its engagement process is thus designed to be more inclusive, bringing in other civil society organizations to participate in agenda setting and in the decision-making process. Membership to the network is strictly limited to those civil society organizations not affiliated with any government.[2] Aside from its advocacy on refugee protection, one of its major achievements is its ability to engage with the UNHCR at multiple levels (country, regional, and international). It also serves as one of the major dialogue partners of UNHCR in its regular consultations with NGOs. Its members also engage with national legislative assemblies like in Nepal and regional organizations like ASEAN.

1. Asia Pacific Refugee Rights Network, "Who We Are," undated, accessed September 21, 2017, http://aprrn.info/about-us/who-we-are/.
2. Susan Kneebone, "The Bali Process and Global Refugee Policy in the Asia-Pacific Region," *Journal of Refugee Studies* 27, no. 4 (2014): 596–618.

norms of protection. Aside from advocacy, they help push the ratification of international conventions and monitor governments' actions through establishing transnational networks and in the process become catalysts to bridge local-level experience and migrant-oriented perspectives into higher political dialogues on managing migration flows more effectively.[34] An example is the ASEAN Civil Society Conference, which has been an important platform for discussing migrant rights issues. At its 2014 conference in Yangon, which gathered together three thousand participants, the rights of undocumented migrants and other migration-related issues often considered controversial were addressed. It is in forums like these that frank and often robust exchange about the gaps in national policies and regional regimes on protection of migrant workers takes place.[35] Another example is the Asian Regional Initiative Against Trafficking in Women and Children meeting, established in Manila in 2000. This network brings together governments, international organizations, funding agencies, and NGOs. Its action plan is anchored on preventing trafficking of people, protecting victims' welfare and legal rights, and prosecuting traffickers. The Asia Pacific Refugee Rights Network also deserves mention. It is a strong advocate of robust protection regimes for forced migrants, and it plays a prominent role in challenging the strong prevention and prosecution agenda of state-led frameworks (see box 5.2).

Engaging with the Private Sector

The Bali Process Ministerial Declaration on Human Smuggling and Trafficking of March 2016 notes the value of working with the private sector on anti–human trafficking efforts.[36] In line with this, the Bali Process has begun inviting the private sector to official dialogue events. In September 2016, it organized a forum titled the "Pathways to Employment: Expanding the Legal and Legitimate Labor Market Opportunities for Refugees" in Bangkok, Thailand.[37] Apart from the usual participation by governments, UN agencies, and civil society organizations, the forum had, for the first time, representatives from the private sector. This is significant for at least two reasons. One is the recognition that the private sector has an important role in helping refugees and facilitating their access to the labor market. Another is the notion that "corporate social responsibility" initiatives by the private sector in training, internships, and formal employment can produce in turn innovative regional policies, strategies, and solutions related to granting labor rights to refugees. The forum generated some important ideas, including a refugee entrepreneurship scheme, a skills recognition program, and a regional identity document to facilitate identity checks for refugees. There is also a plan to set up a National Organization of Migration to coordinate migration policies and services in the region.

Following that initiative, the Bali Process Government and Business Forum was announced by Indonesian president Joko Widodo and Australian prime minister Malcolm Turnbull. Held in August 2017, the forum brought together government ministers and business leaders to promote closer cooperation between the state and the market, and to send a clear signal to the corporate world that it could make an important contribution to stopping the inhumane practices that are taking place in its business supply chains.[38] This forum is also set to become a permanent track of the Bali Process.

One of the organizations supporting the Bali Process and helping to enhance the business–government partnership in fighting against human trafficking is the Walk Free Foundation. The foundation is responsible for the Global Slavery Index and has also produced a guidebook for companies to help them eradicate slavery in their businesses (see box 5.3). The involvement of its founder, Andrew Forrest, as one of the business co-chairs of the Bali Process Government and Business Forum was in line with its interest in mobilizing support from business leaders on the issue of human trafficking.[39]

Partnering with the Media

The media is an important actor in combating human trafficking as they help bring issues into the spotlight. The media also plays a role in shaming traffickers, mobilizing public support, and disseminating information (on

helplines for trafficking victims and on how and where to report suspected
cases of trafficking).[40] An Associated Press report in 2015 that uncovered
trafficked fishermen forced into slavery in Indonesia is a good example in
this regard (box 5.4).

Promoting the Norm of Protection:
The Rohingya Refugees

In Southeast Asia, the refugee situation remains critical, despite the absence
of major wars for many years. For over three decades, refugees from Myanmar have making their way to camps along the border with Thailand.
Many of them are Rohingyas, who the Myanmar government has refused
to recognize as one of the country's ethnic groups. As stateless entities, they
lack any kind of legal protection from the Myanmar government and are
vulnerable to persecution and violence. The problem has escalated in recent
years, with an estimated 168,500 Rohingyas leaving Myanmar between
2012 and 2016.[41] This sizable irregular migration has overwhelmed countries like Thailand, Malaysia, and Indonesia.[42]

Many of those fleeing have become victims of human trafficking. As the region continued to ignore their protection needs, smugglers and traffickers stepped in with promises of passage to Malaysia or Thailand. Some of them went by sea, where they were held in cramped boats with little or no food, beaten by ship crew, and held for ransom. By land, they were brought to trafficking camps in the jungle of Thailand.[43] Some ended up being abducted and sold into forced labor in Thailand's fishing industry or, in case of Rohingya children, used as drug mules, beggars, prostitutes, and child brides.[44]

Their plight came into the spotlight in 2015. In May of that year, Rohingya refugees were found stranded at sea. At the height of the crisis, at least five thousand people were stranded at sea, at least eight vessels were left by smugglers, and at least seventy deaths occurred on the boats.[45] The boat people were either turned away, given temporary shelter (by Indonesia and Malaysia), or repatriated.[46] This crisis attracted the attention of international media and world leaders. It was also around this time (May 2015) that at least two hundred graves were found in smugglers' camps near the Thai–Malaysian border.[47]

The different responses from the international community at that time reflected the challenges faced by the regional and global community in dealing with the refugee crisis in East Asia. The discourse centered on whether to securitize or desecuritize the refugees, and on why the protection and promotion of their basic rights mattered. The contrast in views could not have been starker between state and non-state actors.

ASEAN states made no visible effort to address the problem of the boat people. There was no serious collective and sustained effort to deal with the crisis. Instead, a state of denial crippled both national and regional political instruments. The result was ad hoc and temporary solutions, which allowed governments in the region to avoid collective responsibility.[48] In fact, most countries in Southeast Asia also lack the mechanisms to protect and process refugees and asylum seekers. This means that many of the refugees who travel through Southeast Asia are treated as illegal migrants rather than refugees.[49] Only Cambodia and the Philippines have ratified the UN Convention Relating to the Status of Refugees (commonly referred to as the 1951 Refugee Convention). Thailand, which receives most of the refugees from Myanmar, is not even a party to the Refugee Convention and does not have any domestic law that allows people to seek asylum there. That is why a number of refugees end up being arrested or put in detention. Malaysia and Indonesia, too, do not have strong domestic asylum systems and have yet to ratify the Refugee Convention.

Non-state actors such as Amnesty International and Human Rights Watch decried the lack of action on the part of ASEAN. In an open letter dated May 22, 2015, Amnesty International appealed not only for the protection of refugees but also for ASEAN to uphold Article 1.7 (Principles and Purposes) of the ASEAN Charter which stipulates that it should "promote and protect human rights and fundamental freedoms."[50] The letter argued for a "strong regional protection framework which is consistent with the ASEAN Charter and respects international human rights law."[51] Meanwhile, Human Rights Watch urged countries in Southeast Asia to stop the policy of turning away (pushing back) the refugees, and urged ASEAN states to pressure Myanmar to end its discriminatory policies and ensure protection for the Rohingyas so that they could return to their homelands.[52] Local NGOs, such as Tenaganita, a human rights organization based in Malaysia, joined their international counterparts in pushing for more decisive action by ASEAN states.[53]

Various UN agencies also spoke up on the plight of the refugees. In May 2015 the UN high commissioner for human rights, Zeid Ra'ad al-Hussein, urged Thailand, Malaysia, and Indonesia to stop pushing away the boats, calling the act "incomprehensible and inhumane."[54] He also encouraged ASEAN to take a leadership role. On May 19 the UN offices and agencies for refugees, migration, and human rights joined the IOM in calling for Indonesia, Malaysia, and Thailand to protect migrants and refugees stranded at sea, asking them "to facilitate safe disembarkation, and to give priority to saving lives, protecting rights, and respecting human dignity."[55]

Following the international outcry against the treatment of the boat people, a special meeting on irregular migration in the Indian Ocean was convened in Bangkok, Thailand on May 29. The meeting brought together seventeen representatives from concerned nations, including the five directly affected by the issue—Bangladesh, Indonesia, Malaysia, Myanmar, and Thailand. Representatives from the IOM, UNHCR, and the UN Office on Drugs and Crime were also present. The meeting resulted in seventeen proposals and recommendations related to protection, prevention, and addressing root causes. Indonesia and Malaysia agreed to provide humanitarian assistance and temporary shelter to the refugees, and the five directly affected countries promised to intensify their search and rescue operations. The meeting also agreed that the UNHCR and IOM will have access to the migrants.[56]

The UN offices and agencies on migration, refugees, and human rights issued another joint statement in July 2015 that highlighted the need for a comprehensive, people-oriented approach to the irregular movement of migrants and refugees in Southeast Asia. They called for avenues for safe and legal migration, including for family reunification and labor migration at all skill levels; better law enforcement, including the prosecution of individuals involved in human trafficking and migrant smuggling; and intensified efforts to identify and respond to the drivers and root causes of the irregular movements.[57]

The second Special Meeting on Irregular Migration in the Indian Ocean was convened in Bangkok in December 2015. This time, there were representatives from eighteen countries and six intergovernmental organizations (the UNHCR, IOM, United Nations Development Programme, UN Office on Drugs and Crime, European Union, and ASEAN Secretariat). The meeting agreed to draft an action agenda for the five most affected countries to address the irregular migration. It also agreed to implement a multimedia regional information campaign with the help of the IOM to increase awareness on the risks of irregular migration and to send a message to the trafficking syndicates that the region is serious about eradicating them. The meeting also reported on the progress of the establishment of the ASEAN Trust Fund, which will be used to help irregular migrants.[58] IOM Director General William Lacy Swing, who in the first meeting had stressed the fact that "migration is not a problem to be solved, but a reality to be managed," called again on states to consider measures such as short-term visas, temporary refuge, and seasonal work visas.[59]

It is interesting to note that civil society organizations were not represented in the meeting. Indeed, some were critical of the approaches being discussed by the states and the big UN agencies at the meeting. The Asia Pacific Refugee Rights Network criticized the meeting for not addressing the persecution of Rohingyas in Myanmar, which is at the root of the refugee issue.[60] It argued that the recommendations were short term in scope and that states in the region were more concerned about protecting their borders and securitizing them from the threat of refugees than protecting the people in need of help.

Intervention by Non-State Actors in Aceh, Indonesia

While the plight of the Rohingya refugees at sea was being discussed at international and regional forums, local NGOs in Aceh sprang into action and came to the rescue of the boat people, providing them with temporary shelter in camps.[61] Despite orders from the Indonesian government (military) not to help the boat people, many Acehnese still decided to help those stranded near their coast. Civil society organizations and individuals also sent donations for the migrants.

The assistance rendered by these communities reflected their empathy for the plight of the Rohingyas, given their own experience after the devastating tsunami in 2004. Moreover, Acehnese and Rohingyas have a shared cultural, religious, and culinary background. In fact, since 2009, small numbers of Rohingyas have already landed (and been stranded) in Aceh. But there are significant constraints to the Rohingyas remaining in Aceh long term. First, Indonesia is not a signatory to the 1951 Refugee Convention, and its policy has been to support only repatriation or resettlement for those seeking asylum. Second, the government's position is that the problem has to be resolved by addressing the root cause—that is, by urging the Myanmar government to put an end to the persecution of the Rohingyas. Finally, there are practical considerations related to the long-term settlement of the refugees, one of which is the capacity of local NGOs to meet the needs of the refugees. While the NGOs have access to donations to help the Rohingyas, they are not adequately equipped to run the camp based on international standards and to properly attend to the various needs of the asylum seekers and refugees without government support and the intervention of international humanitarian actors.[62]

Fixing Broken Regimes?

The plight of the Rohingya refugees is a symptom of a deeper problem faced by states and non-state actors in dealing with the complexities of irregular migration. Aside from the Rohingyas, there are other minorities, like the Uyghurs from China, the Montagnards from Vietnam, and the Hmong in Laos, who have fled their homelands for countries such as

Thailand and Malaysia. Even while addressing the plight of the Rohingyas, it is important to remember that these other refugees and asylum seekers have similar protection needs.

Also, not all refugees live in United Nations refugee camps. Many use cities, such as Bangkok, as a transit point while their refugee status is being processed, during which they lack legal protection. They are not covered by any international or regional migration regimes while waiting to be recognized as refugees. Instead of receiving protection, they are prosecuted, detained, or forcibly deported for illegally crossing state borders.[63] Many of them are also victimized by traffickers and illegal recruiters.

The labels used to describe the refugees are another issue of concern. One analyst notes that states in Southeast Asia are reluctant to label refugees as such, using instead the term "irregular migrants," a pattern of "ambiguous labeling" that has been "a recurrent theme in a region where states have been reluctant to recognize their responsibilities under international law."[64]

The general practice of states in Southeast Asia thus far is to grant temporary refuge with minimal rights protection. This contradicts the ASEAN Human Rights Declaration, which recognizes the right of every person to seek and receive asylum in another state.[65] However, ASEAN members have been reluctant to put asylum-seeker issues on ASEAN's formal agenda because of the perception that it would violate the charter principle of non-interference in the internal affairs of member states. It therefore goes without saying that the effectiveness of the international framework for both refugees and stateless people in the region and the wider Asia-Pacific region is limited by the fact that very few states have signed or ratified the 1951 Refugee Convention, the 1954 Convention on the Status of Stateless People, and the 1961 Convention on the Reduction of Statelessness.

Most of the states in Southeast Asia do not have any domestic legal framework giving legal recognition to refugees. The Asia Pacific Refugee Rights Network notes that refugees in Malaysia had been "subject to numerous and severe rights violations, including arbitrary arrest; indefinite detention; unfair trial; cruel and inhuman punishment; expulsion; and refoulement."[66] Malaysia has also not fully cooperated with the UNHCR in fulfilling its obligations to refugees under numerous labor treaties and customary international law. Their status and their rights as refugees are currently not recognized under Malaysian domestic laws, and they do not have meaningful access to domestic remedies for violations of their rights.[67]

The migration regimes in Southeast Asia are, as we have seen, woefully inadequate to the migration complexities facing the region. What needs to be done? The UNHCR had expressed its hope after the second Special Meeting on Irregular Migration in the Indian Ocean in December 2015 that ASEAN would set up a regional mechanism to coordinate efforts not just on law enforcement but also on locating and rescuing boats in distress, facilitating passengers to land, and providing reception facilities in accordance with states' international obligations. Beyond that, there is a need to consider creative solutions that uphold the human rights of refugees and the displaced and that meet their protection needs.

Other Emerging Migration Issues

Aside from the intractable problem of dealing with refugees, there are also emerging migration issues that will have a bearing on the security of states and people in East Asia. One of these is the protection of migrants caught in a crisis, since a large number of labor migrants from East Asia work in the Middle East and Africa in areas that are at risk of conflict. In previous cases, ad hoc cooperation between the UNHCR and the IOM had brought relief to many migrants displaced by crisis; but without an established international legal framework or mechanism that can fully address the situation, migrant workers remain vulnerable to heightened risk of exploitation in times of crisis.[68] A framework for international or regional cooperation in this area needs to be developed.

This issue has been discussed at the Colombo Process, a regional consultative effort on labor migration in Asia that brings together China, six South Asian countries (Afghanistan, Bangladesh, India, Nepal, Pakistan, Sri Lanka), and four Southeast Asian countries (Indonesia, the Philippines, Thailand, Vietnam). The deliberations led to the establishment of the IOM's Migration Crisis Operational Framework and an emergency fund, both important steps in addressing the needs of migrants in crisis-hit countries. Since 2013, the Philippines and Bangladesh have led a small international working group focused on developing an initiative to address the problems faced by migrants in crisis-hit countries.[69]

Mainstreaming migration into future development frameworks is yet another challenge, a critical one, given that the Asia-Pacific is still home to two-thirds of the world's poor despite experiencing rapid economic growth. A growing volume of research suggests that migrants and migrant communities could contribute to sustainable development and poverty reduction in the Asia-Pacific region.[70] However, these research findings have yet to be fully translated into national development priorities. Doing so and working out how to include migration into the Sustainable Development Goals will be key to sustainable growth in the region.

Coupled with this is the issue of how to develop and integrate gender-responsive policies and programs into migration frameworks. Migration and work experiences often vary for men and women; therefore, it is crucial to address the effects of migration by gender and on gender relations, including the effect on the children and families left behind. Within Asia, for instance, women migrant workers are especially vulnerable to exploitation and abuse, given that many have low levels of education. Female domestic workers are also highly vulnerable since they work in the home. A recent study suggests that women migrants from Indonesia and the Philippines, particularly those involved in domestic work, are more likely to have their labor rights violated by employers or recruitment agencies compared to men.[71]

Conclusion

Irregular migration comes with real security challenges for both states and societies, but managing such migration has proven to be extremely problematic for different stakeholders. The protection of all types of migrants regardless of their status often stands in tension against approaches to migration that focus on preventing irregular migration and prosecuting crimes associated with such migration. This suggests that current migration regimes and norms have to be reexamined in order to develop a more balanced and humane approach that takes into account the particular needs and insecurities faced by peoples on the move today.

States need to take the lead on such efforts, but, as we have seen, the involvement of different actors at multiple levels—local communities, civil society organizations, the private sector, regional organizations, international agencies—is not only desirable but may in fact be essential. The meaningful engagement of local communities and NGOs in providing assistance to displaced populations, victims of human trafficking, and refugees lessens the burden on state authorities and the UN agencies working on these issues. Local communities can also help mitigate security concerns related to the fear and misperception of migrant communities and engender a more positive environment to help vulnerable communities. The private sector could play a role by funding programs for different migrant groups in need of shelter, medical access, skills training, and even employment.

As discussed in this chapter, managing the different facets of migration presents multiple challenges and different interests that are bound to result in more contestation and conflicts. From the perspective of the state, protecting sovereignty must be balanced with protecting the rights of irregular migrants, while for non-state actors that represent the interests of different migrants, their human security must be ensured. This variance in interests has created different sites of governance, which nevertheless add to the dynamics of governance of migration in the region. Thus, against the multifaceted migration challenges facing the global community today, addressing the competing demands and pressures on both states and societies compels no less than multilevel and multisectoral approaches founded on the principle that today's migration is a shared responsibility.

Epilogue

The Rohingya crisis again erupted in late August 2017 after a harsh military crackdown in the northern part of Myanmar's Rakhine State in response to attacks by the Arakan Rohingya Salvation Army on military posts in Rakhine. The crackdown caused the flight of over six hundred thousand Rohingyas to refugee camps in Bangladesh. The brutality of the crackdown was described by UN High Commissioner for Human Rights Zeid Ra'ad al-Hussein as "a textbook example of ethnic cleansing."[72] On December 24, 2017, the UN General Assembly adopted a resolution to call on the government to end the military campaign against the Rohingya and it called for the appointment of a UN special envoy. So far, Myanmar has refused to cooperate.

The plight of the hundreds of thousands of Rohingya refugees once again put tremendous pressure on ASEAN to respond and call on its member, Myanmar, to act decisively to end the crisis. Thus far, while the UNHCR and other non-state actors like the International Committee of the Red Cross have provided immediate assistance to the Rohingya in refugee camps in Bangladesh, and while the Myanmar government has announced plans for an orderly return of Rohingya refugees to Myanmar through verification processes, progress is yet to be seen. Although there have been back room efforts by ASEAN officials to help seek a workable approach to deescalate the current conflict, much of the "intervention" has been limited to providing humanitarian aid to displaced communities, an effort facilitated by the ASEAN Coordinating Center for Humanitarian Assistance on disaster management. Meanwhile, hundreds of NGOs have also gone to the refugee camps in Bangladesh to deliver relief items and provide health care and education services to the displaced Rohingya communities.

CHAPTER VI

Governance of Humanitarian Assistance and Disaster Relief Operations

A s we continue to examine the many challenges dotting the security landscape in Southeast Asia and the wider region, the increasing frequency and severity of natural disasters reveal new layers of human security threats confronting the peoples and states in this region. Just within the last decade, the region has seen catastrophic disasters: the Indian Ocean tsunami in 2004 that left a trail of devastation in Indonesia's province of Aceh, parts of Thailand, Myanmar, and all the way up to Sri Lanka and India; the high-magnitude Sichuan earthquake in 2008; Cyclone Nargis, which hit Myanmar in 2008; the Great East Japan Earthquake in 2011; and Super Typhoon Haiyan, which hit the Philippines in 2013. The physical damage and lives lost have been staggering. More than 230,000 were lost in the 2004 Indian Ocean tsunami; 80,000, in the Sichuan earthquake; and around 140,000, in Myanmar.[1]

East Asia is the most natural-disaster-prone region in the world. According to the UN Office for the Coordination of Humanitarian Affairs (OCHA), half of the ten most disaster-affected countries in the world are from East Asia. They are ranked as follows: China (most affected by disasters), the Philippines (third), Indonesia (fifth), Vietnam (ninth), and Japan (tenth).[2] The number of countries goes up to seven if we include India (fourth) and Bangladesh (sixth).

In the disasters across the world from 1994 to 2013, Asia had the most people affected (3.8 billion) and killed (841,000).[3] The economic cost for the same period was staggering, with Asia suffering the most, taking up half of the economic losses globally (US$1,285 billion).[4] A study covering five Association of Southeast Asian Nations (ASEAN) countries—Indonesia, Malaysia, the Philippines, Thailand, Singapore—revealed that over the period 2001 to 2011, disasters had negative effects on gross domestic product growth, tourist arrivals, tourist receipts, and the unemployment rate.[5] For countries with a large agricultural sector, cyclones or drought can be devastating. During the El Niño season that brought prolonged drought in Vietnam in 2016, an estimated 2 million people lost their income due to damage to their harvest, and the lack of a harvest inevitably leads to food shortages.[6]

The unspeakable human suffering caused by natural disasters has changed the face of humanitarian operations in the region. With every major earthquake, cyclone, typhoon, or flood, the impacts to affected communities have become more severe and the nature of the humanitarian crisis more acute. In turn, the urgency of providing immediate assistance to minimize loss of lives and the immensity of the task involved in post-disaster relief and rebuilding have taxed the capacity of affected states and the international community to respond effectively. And the disasters are not limited to natural ones. Conflicts and protracted crises have led to loss of life, destruction of property, and massive population displacements.

In response to such trends, more responsive and effective governance of humanitarian assistance is now a key agenda for regional security cooperation in East Asia. Framed as the humanitarian assistance and disaster relief (HADR) agenda, it features prominently and frequently in the speeches of state leaders and ministers in the region and is found in official declarations of regional institutions like ASEAN, ASEAN Plus Three, the ASEAN Regional Forum, and the East Asia Summit. HADR has also generated tremendous interest among non-state actors and international organizations. It has catalyzed networks and collaborative frameworks between states and non-state actors. More platforms for advocacy and agenda setting on the many elements of HADR have also opened up. More importantly, this has provided opportunities to seriously revisit some of the principles of humanitarianism, along with the region's security practices and norms on protection, all of which have significant implications on the governance of humanitarian assistance.

Against this background, this chapter begins with a review of the securitization of natural disasters and the implications for human security. It moves on to examine the evolving platforms and regional mechanisms for

HADR operations and the governance actors that drive the different agendas related to humanitarian operations. This is followed by an assessment of the effectiveness of existing platforms and regional mechanisms for HADR operations. The key challenges that have emerged as the regional community deals with multiple HADR challenges are highlighted, with a focus on how state and non-state actors negotiate governance in advancing the agendas of disaster preparedness, risk reduction, disaster assistance and response, civilian protection, and resilience.

Why Securitize Natural Disasters?

Natural hazards have occurred since time immemorial—they become "disasters" only when they affect humans. In other words, a natural disaster is

> an act of nature of such magnitude as to create a catastrophic situation in which the day-to-day patterns of life are suddenly disrupted and people are plunged into helplessness and suffering, and, as a result, need food, clothing, shelter, medical and nursing care and other necessities of life, and protection against unfavourable environmental factors and conditions.[7]

Given that natural disasters pose an existential threat to the security and well-being of human beings and states, securitizing natural disasters would seem to be a logical security agenda. However, until the Indian Ocean tsunami, when images of the catastrophic impacts were beamed on televisions across the world, the regional approach to dealing with natural disasters has been largely from the perspective of disaster management, assistance, and relief. Many states in the region and beyond have been mostly reactive in responding to the effects of floods, earthquakes, and cyclones. Government agencies established to deal with the aftermath of disasters have also viewed their operations from the lens of disaster assistance and relief.

However, the increasing frequency of extreme weather events, and the multiple threats posed by them, has impelled a move toward dealing with natural disasters through the lens of security.[8] The securitization impulse has come not just from the heads of regional and international institutions involved in disaster relief but also, most significantly, from the leaders of states that had experienced catastrophic disasters (box 6.1).

BOX 6.1
SECURITIZATION OF NATIONAL DISASTERS
BY STATE ACTORS IN EAST ASIA

The following statements illustrate that as the region came to realize the scale and scope of the impacts of natural disasters on the security of states and their peoples, regional and national leaders began to signal the urgency of addressing the issue:

• In 2005, ASEAN Secretary-General Ong Keng Yong declared in a speech at the 2005 ASEAN Day for Disaster Management that "the tsunami disaster of December 2004 showed that our mitigation, relief and response effort pales in comparison to the devastation that nature can inflict upon us. It had exposed our weaknesses in collectively addressing such large scale calamities." He added that there was a "need to focus on preventive measures, rather than mitigation measures. Our investment should primarily target the community at large, the poor people and vulnerable groups who are most affected by disasters. We should invest to mainstream disaster management into national development initiatives. We should invest in early warning systems so that we are better prepared when disasters inevitably strike. We should make such investment a way of life to ensure a safer and resilient world."[1]

• In 2008, the next secretary-general of ASEAN, Surin Pitsuwan, stated that "we are now working and living in a world of globalisation. While we bene-fited a lot, we were also exposed to each other's problems—diseases, violence, terrorism, climate change—all these calamities are now having more severe impacts on human lives across the world because of our integration, because of our globalization. . . . Human beings are now the direct victims of such natural forces." He added, "The world is changing and evolving in its concept of coop-eration and security coordination—ASEAN can do no less. The Asia-Pacific can do no less."[2]

• In 2005 Minister Counsellor of the Permanent Mission of China to the United Nations Yao Wenlong declared at the 60th Session of the United Nations General Assembly that "in recent years, the world has been hit by frequent major natural disasters. In addition, floods, hurricanes, snowstorms, locust infestation and droughts that occurred across the globe have caused widespread devasta-tion and the loss of livelihood for hundreds of millions of people. The frequent occurrence of natural disasters has increased demands for humanitarian assis-tance provided by the international community and severely challenged the capacity of UN humanitarian assistance system."[3]

• In 2011, a few days after the Great East Japan Earthquake and tsunami in Japan, Prime Minister Naoto Kan declared, "I consider this earthquake and tsunami along with the current situation regarding the nuclear power plants to be in some regards the most severe crisis in the 65 years since the end of the Second World War."[4] At a press conference in August 2011 in which he announced his resignation as prime minister, he said, "Japan is one of the most earthquake-prone islands on this planet, and we also have many nuclear power stations. The extreme danger posed by the experience this time taught us that even one accident can threaten the future of this country and its people."[5]

• In 2012, after a massive earthquake in the Indonesian province of Yogya-karta, Indonesian president Susilo Bambang Yudhoyono, in his speech at the Asian Ministerial Conference on Disaster Risk Reduction, declared that "nat-ural disasters in all its forms—tsunamis, earthquakes, forest fires, floods, land-slides, volcanic eruptions—have been the greatest threats to our national security and public well-being. They have caused more damages to property and to citi-zens' lives than any other factors."[6]

• When Typhoon Haiyan swept across the Philippines in 2013, killing more than ten thousand people and displacing hundreds of thousands, the government declared that it was not only a national calamity but also a national emergency—in other words, a matter of national security.[7]

1. Ong Keng Yong, "Message from the Secretary-General of ASEAN on the Occasion of the 2005 ASEAN Day for Disaster Management" (speech, October 12, 2005).

2. Surin Pitsuwan, "Keynote Address by ASEAN Secretary General at the Launch of the RSIS Centre for Non-Traditional Security Studies" (speech, Singapore, May 6, 2008).

3. Yao Wenlong, "Statement by Mr. Yao Wenlong, Minister Counsellor of the Permanent Mis-sion of China to the United Nations, at the 60th Session of the UNGA under Agenda Item 73 Enti-tled 'Strengthening of the Coordination of Humanitarian and Disaster Relief Assistance of the United Nations, including Special Economic Assistance,'" *Permanent Mission of the People's Republic of China to the UN*, November 14, 2005, http://www.china-un.org/eng/xw/t221480.htm.

4. Naoto Kan, "Message from the Prime Minister," *Prime Minister of Japan and His Cabinet*, March 13, 2011, http://japan.kantei.go.jp/kan/statement/201103/13message_e.html.

5. Naoto Kan, "Press Conference by Prime Minister," *Prime Minister of Japan and His Cabinet*, August 26, 2011, http://japan.kantei.go.jp/kan/statement/201108/26kaiken_e.html.

6. Susilo Bambang Yudhoyono, "Disasters Are 'Greatest Threats to Our National Security'" (speech, Asian Ministerial Conference for Disaster Risk Reduction, Yogyakarta, Indonesia, Octo-ber 23, 2012).

7. "Typhoon Haiyan: Philippines Declares State of Calamity," *BBC News*, November 12, 2013, http://www.bbc.com/news/world-asia-24901993.

Framing the impact of disasters as threats to human and national secu-rity found traction among policymakers, practitioners, civil society actors, the private sector, and other actors across states in the region. Aside from tremendous loss to lives and property, disasters present other interconnected threats. These include health threats and psychological shock to affected populations. The risk of infectious disease outbreak goes up, particularly when basic health, water, and sanitation services collapse. Water-borne dis-eases like typhoid fever, leptospirosis, hepatitis A, and cholera can easily break out. Exposure to corpses heightens risk of infectious diseases like tuberculosis, bloodborne viruses (hepatitis B/C, HIV), and gastrointestinal infections (rotavirus diarrhea, salmonellosis, E. coli). Such threats become greater when the affected areas are also host to a large number of people displaced due to damage to their homes.[9] About 2.4 million people were internally displaced after Cyclone Nargis in 2008 and over 4.1 million people as a result of Typhoon Haiyan in 2013. In 2016 the total number of people displaced by disasters in East Asia and Pacific stood at 24.2 million.[10] Flooding, cyclones, and drought can also lead to serious food and water scarcity, and as the experience of Asia shows, the impact can be both prolonged and widespread. For instance, El Niño affected eleven states across the Asia-Pacific in 2015; in Vietnam alone, more than 2 million people did not have access to potable water.[11]

Disasters therefore heighten human insecurities and can be powerful amplifiers of existing vulnerabilities and threats. This is particularly true for less-developed countries. An analysis by the Center for Research on the Epidemiology of Disasters shows that those in the poorest countries are more than three times more likely to lose their lives in a disaster compared to those in the richest countries.[12] The level of economic development, rather than exposure to natural hazards itself, is a major factor in the mortality rate.[13] From a national security perspective, a number of studies have drawn direct and indirect linkages between persistent food shortages and famines, and greater social unrest and conflicts.[14]

With the convergence of views of how disasters affect state and human security, the securitization of natural disasters galvanized efforts to establish multiple frameworks of HADR cooperation in East Asia. The speed at which these frameworks, which bring together actors at multiple levels, have been created exemplifies how collective efforts can be achieved when risks and vulnerabilities are shared, and when there is a congruence of interests among different stakeholders. The next section highlights the kinds of mechanisms established following the Indian Ocean tsunami.

Regional Mechanisms in HADR Governance

Since 2005 ASEAN has taken the lead in initiating and coordinating regional efforts on the HADR agenda in the region. Cognizant of the need for collective action on HADR, ASEAN has established a number of mechanisms to build regional capacity in disaster management and boost regional preparedness in disaster response. In July 2005 the ASEAN Agreement on Disaster Management and Emergency Response (AADMER) was launched. It is one of only a few legally binding agreements of ASEAN and one of the first frameworks related to the Hyogo Framework for Action, an international plan to build resilience among nations and communities in the face of natural hazards.[15] With AADMER, ASEAN has a focused and dedicated regional mechanism to facilitate coordination and collaboration on disaster management and emergency responses in the region (box 6.2).

AADMER spawned a thick web of regional institutions, arrangements, and networks all geared toward facilitating and coordinating effective disaster response and relief operations (figure 6.1). The most important of these is the ASEAN Coordinating Centre for Humanitarian Assistance on Disaster Management (AHA Centre), which was established in 2011. The AHA Centre, the operational arm of AADMER, is governed by the ASEAN Committee on Disaster Management. The main responsibility of the AHA Centre is to facilitate the coordination and cooperation of ASEAN member states with the United Nations and other international organizations in the areas of disaster management and emergency response.[16] The center has worked with United Nations bodies such as OCHA, the United Nations Development Programme (UNDP), the UN Economic and Social Commission for Asia and the Pacific, and the World Food Programme (WFP) as well as the International Organization for Migration (IOM), the International Committee of the Red Cross (ICRC), the European Union, and several regional and international centers dealing with disaster management.

As the operational arm of AADMER, the AHA Centre facilitates and supports disaster relief operations in the region. It collates reports on disasters in the region and organizes regional training and executive leadership programs on disaster preparedness and cooperation. The center also runs the ASEAN Disaster Information Network (ADInet), a database of up-to-date information on the natural disasters reported in the region, and it manages the ASEAN Emergency Rapid Assessment Team (ASEAN-ERAT).

The ASEAN-ERAT concept was first proposed by the ASEAN Committee on Disaster Management following Cyclone Nargis in 2008. The team, which has over a hundred personnel, plays a key role in the initial phase of a disaster. It rapidly assesses the disaster, identifies the immediate needs of affected populations, and, coordinated by the AHA Centre, deploys regional HADR assets to affected areas.[17] ASEAN-ERAT also participates regularly in regional exercises such as the ASEAN Regional Disaster

ASEAN AGREEMENT ON DISASTER MANAGEMENT AND EMERGENCY RESPONSE

AADMER was signed by all the ministers of the ASEAN member countries in 2005 and entered into force in 2009. It addresses all aspects of disaster management by providing a regional framework for cooperation, coordination, technical assistance, and resource mobilization. Through its mechanisms, the agreement seeks to strengthen national capabilities as well as regional and international cooperation. The goal is to significantly reduce the human, economic, social, and environmental losses from disasters.

Obligations

AADMER specifies four general obligations for the parties to the agreement:

- Cooperate on developing and implementing measures to reduce disaster losses. The measures may include identification of disaster risk; development of monitoring, assessment, and early-warning systems; standby arrangements for disaster relief and emergency response; exchange of information and technology; and the provision of mutual assistance.
- Immediately respond to a disaster occurring within a member state's own territory. If a disaster is likely to have possible impacts on other member states, the state is to respond promptly to a request for relevant information by a member state or by states that are or may be affected by the disasters in order to minimize the consequences.
- Promptly respond to a request for assistance from an affected party.
- Take legislative, administrative, and other measures necessary to implement the obligations under the Agreement.

Implementation

The implementation mechanism of AADMER is its work program, which specifies important goalposts for developing regional preparedness and capacity involving the whole gamut of HADR operations. These include, among others, building capacity in regional risk assessment and setting up a regional system for early warning and monitoring; integrating disaster risk reduction into national development plans as well as urban and community action plans; and developing a more effective and timely relief and response strategy.[1]

1. Association of Southeast Asian Nations (ASEAN) Secretariat, "ASEAN Forges Stronger Multi-Stakeholder Partnership for Disaster Management Makati City, Philippines," *ASEAN*, media release, May 20, 2016, http://asean.org/asean-forges-stronger-multi-stakeholder-partnership-for-disaster-management-makati-city-philippines-20-may-2010/.

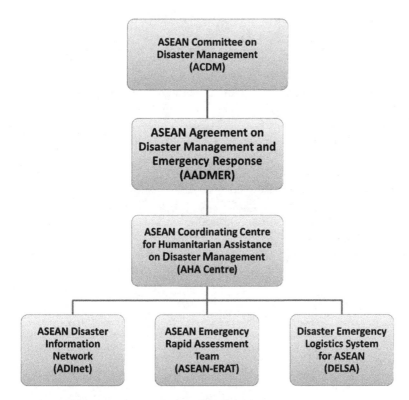

Figure 6.1 AADMER and its institutional mechanisms

Emergency Response Simulation Exercise and the ASEAN Regional Forum Disaster Relief Exercise.

While relatively young, the AHA Centre is gradually developing its capacity to mobilize resources and coordinate disaster relief assistance in times of disaster.[18] In 2012 it responded to an earthquake in the Mandalay region of Myanmar and to Typhoon Bopha in the Philippines. In 2013 it responded to earthquakes in the Indonesian province of Aceh and in Central Philippines as well as to flooding in Laos. Also in 2013 the AHA Centre responded to Typhoon Haiyan in the Philippines (see box 6.3).

Another mechanism established by ASEAN is the Disaster Emergency Logistics System for ASEAN (DELSA). Launched in 2012, DELSA serves as a logistics hub for the region's stockpile of relief supplies, with the AHA Centre coordinating delivery to ASEAN states affected by disasters.[19] The DELSA warehouse is colocated with the UN Humanitarian Response Depot in Malaysia, and the stockpile is funded by the Japan-ASEAN

BOX 6.3

AHA CENTRE AND THE RESPONSE TO TYPHOON HAIYAN

The Haiyan case illustrates how the AHA Centre and ASEAN-ERAT facilitate HADR cooperation among ASEAN member states in times of disaster:[1]

Before Landfall
- The AHA Centre monitored the movement and strength of Haiyan and sent its team from Jakarta and ASEAN-ERAT to arrive in Manila before Haiyan's landfall.
- The team from the AHA Centre met and coordinated with the head of the Philippines' National Disaster Risk Reduction and Management Council.
- An emergency specialist in information and communications technology from ASEAN-ERAT was deployed directly to Tacloban City, the center of Haiyan's destruction, to help set up and test emergency communications equipment to support the local disaster response agency.

After Landfall
- Within forty-eight hours of Haiyan's landfall, the full ASEAN-ERAT team had arrived in Tacloban to establish coordination, conduct assessments, and facilitate the arrival of incoming assistance from ASEAN member states.

1. Malyn Tumonong, "Five Years of AHA Centre: Experiences, Challenges and Future Outlook of Disaster Management in the ASEAN" (presentation at the United Nations/India Workshop on the Use of Earth Observation Data in Disaster Management and Risk Reduction: Sharing the Asian Experience, Hyderabad, India, March 8–10, 2016), http://www.unoosa.org/documents/pdf/spider /activities/2016/india/Day3/Plenary_session2/5_Years_of_AHA_Centre_mmltumonong.pdf.

Integration Fund. As we have seen, the AHA Centre has grown to become the regional nerve center for HADR response in the region, an achievement recognized by ASEAN leaders at the ASEAN Summit in Manila, the Philippines, in April 2017, where it was acknowledged that the center plays a primary role in realizing the region's vision of "One ASEAN, One Response."[20]

Key Governance Actors at the Regional Level

The AHA Centre, ASEAN-ERAT, and DELSA all serve as operational mechanisms of AADMER. But within ASEAN, there are significant bureaucratic agencies that serve as governance actors driving the agenda, policy formulation, and policy implementation for effective HADR in the region. This section maps out these actors and analyzes their respective contributions to the regional HADR agenda.

ASEAN Committee on Disaster Management

The ASEAN Committee on Disaster Management is a policymaking body for disaster management that was created in 2003 by the ASEAN Standing Committee, which is composed of senior officials from the member states' foreign affairs ministries. The committee comprises the heads of the national agencies responsible for disaster management in the respective ASEAN member states. The main objective of the committee is to "enhance cooperation in all aspects of disaster management prevention, mitigation, response, and recovery through mutual collaborative activities."[21]

The ASEAN Committee on Disaster Management was preceded by an expert working group on disaster management issues that oversaw regional cooperation as specified under the Declaration of ASEAN Concord I in 1976 and the ASEAN Declaration on Mutual Assistance on Natural Disasters of 1976. However, the working group did not have sufficient influence at the national level. The ASEAN Committee on Disaster Management has been more successful. One tangible evidence of the committee's role in agenda setting is the creation of AADMER. The seeds for that were planted in 2004 when the committee recommended that ASEAN should have an action plan to deepen regional cooperation in disaster response. The idea gained urgency when the destruction caused by the 2004 Indian Ocean tsunami affected several ASEAN members.

The ASEAN Committee on Disaster Management has important functions that make it an important HADR governance actor in the region. First, as the governing board for the AHA Centre, it outlines the center's roles and responsibilities and supervises its performance.[22] Second, the committee oversees the AADMER Work Programme.[23] The committee has crafted two AADMER Work Programmes, for 2010–2015 and 2016–2020 (see also box 6.2).

The committee has also advanced ideas to boost cross-sectoral and multistakeholder participation and collaboration, both within ASEAN and beyond.[24] It actively collaborates with ASEAN's dialogue partners, which include regional, international, and multilateral agencies, and it works with

NGOs and the private sector.[25] In all these areas, the committee has been the main security actor linking the national and regional institutions responsible for coordinating and implementing regional HADR activities. Combined with its oversight functions, the ASEAN Committee on Disaster Management significantly contributes to HADR governance in Southeast Asia.[26]

Beyond the goals of effective coordination and response, the ASEAN Committee on Disaster Management is also an advocate for social protection programs. This is reflected in the AADMER Work Programme for 2016 to 2020. While the focus remains on effective cross-sectoral coordination, the officials have also stressed the importance of developing social protection guidelines to build disaster resilience. It is envisaged that measures would be promoted that could reduce disaster risks for vulnerable communities and empower them to respond to disasters and recover from the impact of disasters.[27]

ASEAN Ministerial Meeting on Disaster Management (AMMDM)

Another key governance actor is the AMMDM, created in October 2013 when the ASEAN heads of state signed the ASEAN Declaration on Enhancing Cooperation in Disaster Management. The AMMDM serves as the ministerial body in charge of promoting cooperation in disaster management. Accordingly, it oversees the ASEAN Committee on Disaster Management.

At the AMMDM in Manado, Indonesia, in October 2016, ASEAN ministers discussed the progress and implementation of the second AADMER Work Programme and the strategies for the ASEAN Vision 2025 on Disaster Management to form a disaster-resilient and safer ASEAN community. The ministers also tackled measures to realize the objectives of the ASEAN Declaration on One ASEAN One Response, which was signed by ASEAN leaders on September 6, 2016, during the 28th and 29th ASEAN Summits in Vientiane, Laos.[28]

ASEAN Secretary-General as ASEAN Humanitarian Assistance Coordinator

One regional mechanism that often receives less attention but is equally significant is the role of the ASEAN secretary-general as the ASEAN humanitarian assistance coordinator. The genesis of this special designation could be traced to the controversial refusal by Myanmar to allow foreign assistance into the country in the immediate aftermath of Cyclone Nargis. ASEAN members were able to persuade the Myanmar government to accept outside help on condition that this be facilitated by ASEAN and the United Nations, and the ASEAN secretary-general was tasked to help coordinate and facilitate relief assistance.

Ever since then, the secretary-general has had the mandate of the ASEAN leaders to coordinate ASEAN's efforts at the highest political level during the response and recovery stages of any large-scale disaster in the region.[29] This coordinating role is particularly important in mobilizing resources and assistance from external partners such as the United States, Japan, China, Australia, and the European Union, which have huge capacity, resources, and technical expertise in disaster response.

ASEAN Militaries Ready Group on HADR

Since disaster management is a complex and multifaceted operation, the military is often deployed to assist civilian agencies. The ASEAN Militaries Ready Group on HADR was proposed by Malaysia in 2015 to foster greater cooperation among the region's militaries with the aim of preparing a regional military contingent for rapid deployment to disaster-hit areas in a coordinated and timely manner.[30]

Mindful of the sensitivities of states on the matter of external assistance, the concept paper on the ASEAN Militaries Ready Group on HADR specified that the affected state shall have "the primary responsibility to respond to a disaster occurring within its territory. External assistance or offers of assistance may only be provided upon the request or with the consent of the affected State."[31] The group shall also be constituted as a flexible, nonbinding, and voluntary arrangement, with member states retaining sole sovereign decision on whether to deploy resources.[32] Terms of reference for the group were adopted at the ASEAN Defence Ministers' Meeting in May 2016.[33] At the time of this writing, the ASEAN Militaries Ready Group on HADR is yet to be operational.[34]

Changi Regional HADR Coordination Center

Another mechanism that supports military collaboration in the region is the Changi Regional HADR Coordination Center based in Singapore.[35] Launched in 2014, the center's mission is to facilitate military-to-military coordination on HADR. It focuses on providing support to the military in a disaster-affected state by coordinating assistance provided by foreign militaries. Through its day-to-day monitoring and assessment of disasters and its capacity-building programs, the center also supports and complements other mechanisms such as OCHA and the AHA Centre.

HADR Actors in the Wider East Asia Region

The security agenda of HADR has drawn the attention and cooperation of other formal institutions in the wider East Asian region. They are described in the following sections.

ASEAN DEFENCE MINISTERS' MEETING AND ADMM-PLUS

The ASEAN Defence Ministers' Meeting (ADMM) and ADMM-Plus are security-oriented, defense-led meetings that substantially reinforce regional efforts on HADR in Southeast Asia. The ADMM is made up of the defense ministers of the ten ASEAN member states and is considered the highest defense policy platform for Southeast Asia. The ADMM has been contributing to HADR in the region since its inception in 2006. It has generated various concept papers to advance cooperation on HADR. Its 2009 concept paper, "The Use of ASEAN Military Assets and Capacities in Humanitarian Assistance and Disaster Relief," sets forth an early framework for cooperation between the militaries of the member states. The ADMM has also organized workshops to follow its concept papers, including one based on the aforementioned concept paper and another on ASEAN defense establishments and civil society organizations' cooperation in non-traditional security.[36]

ADMM created ADMM-Plus as a platform "to strengthen security and defence cooperation for peace, stability, and development in the region" between ASEAN and its eight dialogue partners (Australia, China, India, Japan, New Zealand, Russia, South Korea, and the United States).[37] ADMM-Plus has established an experts' working group on HADR to generate ideas on deepening multilateral military cooperation. The working group has already proposed several initiatives for the consideration of the ADMM-Plus ministers, including a legal mechanism for cooperation on HADR operations, the setting of criteria for defining a common understanding of issues among member countries, and joint exercises to strengthen multilateral relationships.[38]

To improve interoperability in HADR operations, joint military exercises have been organized to facilitate multinational military collaboration and create synergy among ADMM-Plus militaries in joint response to disasters. The first ADMM-Plus HADR and military medicine exercise, hosted by Brunei in 2013, allowed troops from ASEAN, the United States, China, Japan, India, Australia, and South Korea to work side by side.[39] This type of joint exercise was also recognized as a best practice and a model for future ADMM-Plus cooperation.[40]

ASEAN REGIONAL FORUM

Wider forums like the ASEAN Regional Forum also contribute actively to the multiple aspects of disaster management. Established in 1994 as the primary platform for security dialogue between the ten ASEAN member states and their seventeen dialogue partners, the ASEAN Regional Forum, through its regular meetings on HADR and its multinational exercises, is developing and shaping a common understanding of cooperation and coordination procedures among military and civilian actors. It focuses on the response aspect of HADR and not the rehabilitation and reconstruction phase.[41] The agenda-setting function of the ASEAN Regional Forum's HADR efforts is structured to feed into the AADMER Work Programme 2010–2015, particularly the strategic component on preparedness and response.

The biannual ASEAN Regional Forum disaster relief exercise, which brings together ASEAN's ten member states and its seventeen dialogue partners, plays a significant role in enhancing confidence and mutual under-standing among participants within the context of multinational disaster relief operations. Such exercises also encourage collaboration among a wide range of actors and help improve civil–military coordination at the opera-tional and tactical level.[42]

TRACK 2 NETWORK OF ASEAN DEFENSE AND SECURITY INSTITUTIONS

The work of ADMM and ADMM-Plus is supported by their counterpart, the Track 2 Network of ASEAN Defense and Security Institutions (NADI). NADI aims to strengthen cooperation and build confidence and familiarity among policy analysts, academics, and security and defense officials partici-pating in their private capacity. Their deliberations and policy recommen-dations are submitted to ASEAN defense officials for consideration. Ideas that have been proposed include creating a technical information-sharing system with policy and operational resources; continuing military-to-military coordination; and improving civil–military relations by building on the civil–military coordination efforts to improve HADR operations in the region.[43]

Working with UN Agencies

Since 2004 ASEAN has been working closely with various UN agen-cies, including OCHA, WFP, UNDP, the UN Office for Disaster Risk Reduction, and the Office of the United Nations High Commissioner for Refugees, as articulated in the ASEAN–UN Joint Strategic Plan of Action on Disaster Management. This cooperation framework drives capacity-building initiatives in Southeast Asia in areas such as training for the UN Disaster Assessment and Coordination team, recovery planning, and logistics stockpiling.[44]

The collaboration between the United Nations and ASEAN was put to the test during the responses to Cyclone Nargis and Typhoon Haiyan. The two organizations jointly identified lessons learned from these events and integrated them into the ASEAN–UN Joint Strategic Plan of Action on Disaster Management 2016–2020.[45] In the areas of prevention and mitiga-tion as well as early warning and risk assessment, the collaborative work on disaster risk reduction reinforces the commitment of member states to achieving the Sendai Framework for Disaster Risk Reduction (2015–2030), which focuses on "preventing new and reducing existing disaster risks" through a holistic HADR framework that involves both disaster prevention and response.[46] ASEAN regards the United Nations as an important actor and partner as it continues to improve its collaboration with other partners in disaster risk reduction, and disaster management and response.

Non-State Actors: Partners and Security Governors in HADR

The devastation caused by large-scale disasters could easily turn into complex humanitarian emergencies absent the critical intervention of different actors at various stages of disaster operations. The world has seen a number of these humanitarian emergencies, mostly in less-developed and poorer countries. For states and communities with little adaptive capacity, human casualties are much higher, destruction to property more severe, and recovering and bouncing back takes much longer. It is in these types of disaster settings that the role of non-state actors becomes critical.

NGO Networks

Non-state actors are usually the first responders on the ground, leading states in the region to recognize that partnering with them in disaster operations is a must. Partnerships between state and non-state actors ensure that relief assistance reaches affected populations, especially those in remote areas, and helps reduce loss and damage. Such partnerships also help in building resilience and preparing communities to effectively respond to disasters through further stakeholder coordination.

As argued persuasively by former ASEAN secretary-general Ong Keng Yong at the Post-2015 AADMER Strategic Policy Dialogue in Singapore in November 2015, "partnerships on the ground will make ASEAN more confident to respond to disasters."[47] Ong stressed the importance of multistakeholder engagement at multiple levels. This was echoed by the current ASEAN secretary-general, H. E. Le Luong Minh, who remarked that the "participation of the people is key in the next ten years, as ASEAN forges together towards a more people-oriented, people-centred and resilient ASEAN Community" while advocating for a multisectoral and multipillar approach.[48] Such sentiments capture the many processes and HADR activities that have been initiated by a wide range of non-state actors in the region that not only boost partnerships with state actors but, more importantly, also promote the critical agenda of providing protection for vulnerable populations. After the 2004 Indian Ocean tsunami, ASEAN had made a concerted effort to build partnerships with civil society organizations throughout the region. It engaged with the ICRC and the International Federation of Red Cross and Red Crescent Societies on disaster response exercises and is currently working with several NGOs on issues related to disaster preparedness.[49]

In 2009 the AADMER Partnership Group was formed by several international civil society organizations to support ASEAN mechanisms on HADR (such as AADMER, the ASEAN Committee on Disaster Management, and the AHA Centre). It collaborates with ASEAN through a consortium of seven NGOs: ChildFund International, HelpAge International, Mercy Malaysia, Oxfam, Plan International, Save the Children International, and World Vision International.[50] The AADMER Partnership Group acts as a facilitator between ASEAN, the governments of ASEAN member states, and civil society; in so doing, it empowers homegrown NGOs within the region to realize the vision of a people-oriented and people-centered ASEAN.

The AADMER Partnership Group has made contributions to the development of the strategies of the AADMER Work Programme on partnership, resource mobilization, training, and knowledge management. It has also supported the implementation of AADMER across ASEAN member states through conducting country-level orientations, information dissemination, and policy analysis.[51] Through the collaboration between the AADMER Partnership Group and ASEAN, and because of ASEAN's recognition that civil society has a role in crafting and executing HADR policy, the ability of civil society organizations to inform or influence policies at the regional and national levels has increased.[52] A direct outcome of the group's involvement in HADR governance is seen in the enhancement of draft national disaster management laws in Cambodia, Laos, and Myanmar. In Cambodia, a review of the national emergency management policy to accommodate AADMER was also partially influenced by the research results of the AADMER Partnership Group.

Also among the NGO networks involved in HADR in the region is the Asian Disaster Reduction and Response Network, founded in 2003. This network has thirty-four members across Asia and a secretariat in Malaysia. Its main aim is to promote coordination, information sharing, and collaboration among NGOs and other stakeholders for effective and efficient disaster reduction and response in the Asia-Pacific region. Among its activities are promoting best practices and standards in disaster reduction and response, providing a mechanism for sharing reliable information, and facilitating capacity building among network members and other stakeholders.

The Asia Pacific Alliance for Disaster Management, meanwhile, is a transnational disaster aid alliance that works to facilitate cooperation and understanding between governments, private companies, and NGOs in the Asia-Pacific region. Founded in 2009 with members from Bangladesh, Indonesia, Japan, South Korea, the Philippines, and Sri Lanka, the alliance wants to change the way relief efforts are being delivered. It promotes ideas such as a pre-agreement among governments, private companies, and NGOs that could allow aid to be delivered faster and to more people.[53]

Local NGOs

In her study of NGOs in East Asia, Yukie Osa argues that local NGOs are highly effective as service providers.[54] They can leverage their existing experience, expertise, facilities, and community networks to distribute relief items quickly, deliver medical and psychosocial services, and provide shelter and protection to vulnerable communities, thus saving lives and livelihoods as well as limiting the physical and psychological damage of a catastrophic event. In many cases, because of their proximity to the ground, they are also more trusted than government actors, particularly by minorities and marginalized communities. This puts them in a better position than the government to assess the needs of these communities, which promotes human security and prevents societal grievances. NGOs may also bring greater transparency to HADR initiatives and offer useful alternative policies to governments to improve their national disaster management system. In the ASEAN region, faith-based NGOs such as Muhammadiyah in Indonesia and the National Secretariat for Social Action in the Philippines exemplify this kind of engagement (see boxes 6.4 and 6.5).

MUHAMMADIYAH AND HADR

Muhammadiyah, founded in 1912, is one of the biggest and oldest social welfare organizations in Indonesia. The faith-based group operates thousands of
schools, clinics, hospitals, and universities across the archipelago.

Muhammadiyah brings to HADR efforts the advantage of a large network of
volunteers as well as experience in delivering health, educational, and social services. Importantly, as a Muslim organization, it has religious and political legitimacy not just among its members but across many communities in Indonesia. In
the wake of the 2004 tsunami, it was Muhammadiyah that many international
organizations chose to partner with, especially if they wanted access to the con-
servative province of Aceh, which was among the hardest hit by the disaster.

The 2004 tsunami saw Muhammadiyah collaborate with organizations such
as IOM and Save the Children on gathering food, water, and other supplies for
survivors. And it continued such collaborations during the Yogyakarta earthquake of 2006, the Sumatra earthquake of 2009, and the Mount Merapi eruption in 2010. During the 2006 earthquake, Muhammadiyah worked with World
Vision International to provide educational services, emergency kits, and sustainable livelihoods to the people. It also worked with Won Buddhism of Korea,
which provided temporary shelters, wheelchairs, and crutches. In all three disasters, Muhammadiyah worked with the Australian government through AusAID
in the areas of emergency response and education, and with Direct Relief International in providing health support such as medicine, medical equipment, and
ambulances.

In addition to collaborations with other organizations, Muhammadiyah also
undertakes its own disaster response activities. Following the 2004 tsunami, for
instance, Muhammadiyah mobilized its activists and students to organize donations of basic necessities while its doctors were deployed to Aceh for emergency
response. As part of disaster recovery, Muhammadiyah teachers and activists
were tasked with providing educational and psychosocial guidance to children
and young adult survivors. Temporary shelters were given to internally displaced
people.

The Private Sector

One of the newest actors in HADR in the region is the private sector. As
with their engagement with other security challenges like migration,
human trafficking, and environmental security, private-sector actors have
demonstrated their ability to provide technical and logistical support as well
as much-needed resources for effective disaster management and response.

NATIONAL SECRETARIAT FOR SOCIAL ACTION AND HADR

The National Secretariat for Social Action, launched in 2015, is the development, advocacy, and humanitarian arm of the Catholic Bishops Conference of the Philippines. One of its main activities is a three-year program called #REACHPhilippines (Recovery Assistance to Vulnerable Communities Affected by Typhoon Haiyan in the Philippines). The program serves nine provinces: Leyte, Western Samar, Eastern Samar, Palawan, Aklan, Antique, Capiz, Iloilo, and Cebu.

#REACHPhilippines targets the poorest of the poor and those worst-hit by Typhoon Haiyan. It is involved in providing disaster-resilient shelters, water and sanitation facilities, sustainable livelihoods, and disaster risk-reduction and capacity-building training to the communities. Aside from rehabilitation activities aimed at the people, #REACHPhilippines also aims to rehabilitate the ecosystem. Its community-based programs include mangrove and reforestation projects. It is also involved in formulating environmental protection policies and resiliency plans, installing material recovery facilities, and establishing watersheds.

The National Secretariat for Social Action is implementing its programs in partnership with Caritas Internationalis member organizations from different parts of the world. Almost 2 million people have already benefited from its programs.

ASEAN has in fact called on the private sector to play a bigger role to enhance disaster management in the region. At the ASEAN Strategic Policy Dialogue on Disaster Management held in 2016 in Singapore, ASEAN Secretary-General Minh described the private sector as a "key stakeholder" that "plays a vital role in realising the vision of a disaster-resilient ASEAN Community."[55] He notes that "as disasters have a direct impact on businesses and their customers, it is important that the private sector becomes more involved in disaster management, especially through their business continuity plans as well as innovation to respond to disasters and reduce disaster losses."[56] According to Minh, the private sector has a key role "in facilitating innovation and forging change in disaster management and humanitarian assistance," and ASEAN has "buttressed that role with regional efforts through policies and frameworks that support the strong involvement of the private sector and their active and meaningful participation in disaster management and humanitarian assistance."[57] The ASEAN Vision 2025 on Disaster Management also suggests that private-sector contributions could complement national contributions, the traditional source of funding, and that this could be encouraged through tax incentives.[58] The Philippine Disaster Resilience Foundation and the Singapore-based Corporate Citizen Foundation are key examples of private-sector collaborations in preparing and responding to disasters.

The Philippine Disaster Resilience Foundation, backed by the country's largest conglomerates and industries and top corporate leaders, is the most prominent private-sector vehicle for HADR efforts in the Philippines (see box 6.6). Right after Typhoon Haiyan, there was no efficient way of providing relief goods and responding to the needs of the victims. The foundation thus saw a need for more robust solutions for managing disasters—and saw that this would involve coordinating and collaborating among HADR stakeholders not just those within the business sector but also with the government and local and international organizations. Also, while most of its members are large companies, the Philippine Disaster Resilience Foundation takes the view that large companies are only as effective as the strength of the supply chain and small- and medium-sized enterprises. As such, it conducts business continuity workshops for small- and medium-sized enterprises to enable them to quickly recover and revive the supply chain for its member companies.

Due to the failure in risk governance on the part of the government, especially local governments, the private sector is also stepping into the humanitarian space. The member companies of the Philippine Disaster Resilience Foundation have donated disaster-resilient school buildings that can also be used as evacuation centers and mobile high-tech health clinics that can be deployed to disaster areas. The foundation has also established an emergency operations center that can monitor and assess disasters and their impact as well as facilitate coordination among its member companies and the government.

In Singapore a group of companies under the umbrella of the Corporate Citizen Foundation has become the first from the private sector to make a contribution to the AHA Centre. The Corporate Citizen Foundation, launched in 2014, is a platform for corporate partnerships to help improve lives and safety in Asia. Along with a cash donation, ten water purification systems were presented to the center. Speaking at the presentation ceremony, the center's executive director said that "the private sector does not only bring relief items and donations, but also introduces innovation and change for the humanitarian landscape."[59]

BOX 6.6
PHILIPPINE DISASTER RESILIENCE FOUNDATION
AND HADR

The Philippine Disaster Resilience Foundation, founded in 2009, is a major private-sector actor in the HADR space in the Philippines. The foundation's work includes coordinating between government agencies, civil society groups, and local government units. Its activities can be summarized into three program areas: emergency preparedness, disaster rehabilitation, and disaster recovery.

In 2016 it launched a national emergency operations center in Makati City, the first such center in the world led by the private sector. Established with the cooperation of seventy-nine local companies from diverse sectors, the center aims to be an operations hub for disaster preparedness and HADR. Nationally, the center works with the National Disaster Risk Reduction and Management Council and the Department of Science and Technology. Internationally, it is linked to the Pacific Disaster Center in Hawaii, which gives it the ability to track any storm, volcanic eruption, or earthquake.

The foundation has also been active in helping the communities affected by Typhoon Haiyan to rebuild and strengthen resilience, with many of its projects incorporating state-of-the-art technology:

• In 2015 it installed four Eco-Loos in a community in Tacloban, Leyte. By collecting human waste and urine and turning it into liquid compost, the Eco-Loos make it unnecessary to use valuable potable water for sewage treatment.

• In 2015 and 2016 emergency-ready evacuation centers were opened in Tanauan and Tacloban, respectively. The centers were built in cooperation with the United Methodist Committee on Relief.

• In 2016 the foundation launched mobile e-health clinics in Tacloban, Leyte and Biliran Province. These clinics use telemedicine and video conferencing to provide free medical services. This project marries the strengths of several private-sector actors: a cloud-based information system from Hewlett Packard Enterprise; connectivity services from Smart Communications, Inc.; and top-tier physicians and medical specialists from the Makati Medical Center Foundation.

From these examples the potential value of collaborations between state actors and private-sector actors is evident not just in terms of providing resources or funds but also in bringing in innovative perspectives and products that could help improve HADR operations. It is also important to acknowledge that HADR does not simply end with relief delivery. There are also long-term socioeconomic issues that must be addressed to reduce the vulnerabilities of the poor and increase their resilience. This is another potential area of contribution for the private sector, which could work with the government as well as other non-state actors to address such issues and restore sources of livelihood in affected communities. Governments could facilitate the process by establishing a platform where all humanitarian actors could come together to coordinate their HADR efforts.[60]

Epistemic Communities

The contributions of academic institutions, think tanks, and advisory boards have been recognized by ASEAN, which has made these actors key stakeholders in HADR. The ASEAN Vision statements underscore the need to build partnerships with regional knowledge networks, such as the APEC Business Advisory Council, the ASEAN University Network, the NTS-Asia Consortium, NADI, the Council for Security Cooperation in the Asia Pacific, the Network of East Asian Think-Tanks, and the Digital Humanitarian Network as well as other sectoral leaders like business schools and professional associations.

A good example of a knowledge partnership is in the development of the AADMER Post-2016 agenda. In 2015 the ASEAN Secretariat sought the help of the Centre for Non-Traditional Security Studies (NTS Centre) of the S. Rajaratnam School of International Studies in Singapore in developing the AADMER Work Programme 2016–2020. To lay the groundwork for the document, researchers from the center were also asked to design and facilitate a strategic policy dialogue that would bring together representatives from the ASEAN Committee on Disaster Management, OCHA, and other international and national humanitarian organizations such as the ICRC, Médecins Sans Frontières, and Mercy Relief. The dialogue, which was held in August 2015, was to be the first of many organized by the ASEAN Secretariat and the AHA Centre and supported by the Singapore Civil Defence Force in collaboration with the United Nations and other humanitarian agencies.

Following the dialogue, the NTS Centre developed its Post-2015 AADMER Strategic Policy Document, which outlined key themes and recommended policy areas for ASEAN to consider in its new AADMER agenda.[61] The document was submitted to the ASEAN Secretariat in November 2015, and it became the basis for the ASEAN Vision 2025 on Disaster

Management, which was adopted by the ASEAN Committee on Disaster Management and endorsed by the AMMDM in December 2015 in Cambodia; it subsequently became the framework for the new AADMER Work Programme.

The experience of the NTS Centre in being directly involved in crafting the ASEAN HADR agenda underscores the potential for non-state actors to provide valuable contributions to regional governance processes. In this regard, the role of educational institutions, foundations, think tanks, and policy research organizations in offering thought leadership and strategic policy inputs therefore becomes extremely significant in addressing different types of regional security challenges. With the rich experience of the region in HADR and the help of its knowledge communities, ASEAN's role is also enhanced. In the humanitarian world, ASEAN will be able to establish itself as a research and development hub for HADR research and innovation.

HADR Issues and Challenges

The preceding discussion on regional frameworks shows that the region is definitely not short of institutions and actors that are, in one way or another, engaged in the complex and multifaceted task of HADR. But even with the proliferation of mechanisms and actors that constitute the vast network of institutions that are shaping the regional humanitarian landscape, significant challenges remain.

Coordination remains a major challenge. Although Southeast Asia and the wider East Asia has been recognized as having the most advanced forms of regional disaster management cooperation, the emergence of multiple sites of HADR cooperation has raised serious issues about coordination and duplication of effort. So far there is no overarching structure that can organize all these mechanisms and activities into one coherent and integrated system. While the AHA Centre is the designated coordinator of all regional HADR-related activities, it faces serious challenges, given its nascent status, in its ability to manage and integrate the multiple regional efforts that are continuing to evolve. At the moment the center simply does not have enough capacity both in terms of financial and human resources to play a more decisive leadership role in coordinating HADR operations. With the multiplicity of humanitarian actors involved in large-scale HADR operations, coordinating assistance from UN agencies and foreign governments and partners can be daunting.

Moreover, while AADMER is the cornerstone of regional disaster management, its 2016–2025 work program extends beyond disaster assistance to building resilience and sustainable development, which makes it very challenging to implement. There will be a need for more resources and sufficient institutional support including establishing the necessary legal frameworks. The latter is crucial if mechanisms such as the ASEAN Militaries Ready Group on HADR and the Changi Regional HADR Coordination Center are deployed to carry out rapid response operations. For these mechanisms to be operational, issues of state consent, internal interference, and legitimacy should have already been considered and addressed.

Closely related to the issue of legal frameworks that address HADR-related issues is the need to deal with some of the normative practices that have constrained regional collective action on HADR. The Haiyan experience is a case in point. As observed by one analyst, the requirement that ASEAN consensus be solicited before the AHA Centre and ASEAN-ERAT teams could be deployed to the affected area led to a delay in their coordination of regional relief assistance to the affected communities, despite their having arrived in Tacloban before the typhoon.[62] That it also took two weeks for the ASEAN secretary-general to call for an inspection of the damaged area reflected constraints on the ability of ASEAN's processes to respond in a timely manner to a disaster. The delay was roundly criticized given that just a few months before Haiyan struck the Philippines, the ASEAN Regional Forum disaster relief exercise and the ADMM-Plus HADR and military medicine exercise had just been held in the region. The delay, it was noted, led to an unintended consequence: loss of credibility for ASEAN.[63]

Affected states also lacked confidence in the capability of the AHA Centre. Quite understandably, during Typhoon Haiyan, the Philippines relied more on its trusted sources of support like the United States. In fact, within Southeast Asia, states still send their aid and support bilaterally instead of channeling their contributions through an ASEAN-led mechanism. The assistance provided by the ASEAN HADR mechanisms during Typhoon Haiyan paled in comparison with that provided by the United States, Japan, and the United Kingdom. Hence, unless ASEAN member states themselves make concerted efforts to strengthen their own regional capacity, HADR operations will continue to rely on external assistance.

Another difficult issue is the role of the military in humanitarian operations within the context of managing civil–military relations. In East Asia, the military is often the primary responder during disasters, given that their organizational capacity and operational abilities are better compared with civilian authorities. In some countries in the region, military participation in HADR must first be authorized by the civilian government, and in most, if not all cases, HADR operations are under civilian control. However, in large-scale and complex humanitarian emergencies, the military often takes on a much bigger role, and this often leads to maintaining the difficult balance between military and civilian control, especially when foreign military assets are deployed. Even when civilian control is maintained and the rules of engagement are observed, there are also uncertainties about the military's relationship with local NGOs and whether they have the skills and sensitivity to understand the needs of vulnerable groups.

In complex humanitarian crises resulting from armed conflict and violence, questions arise as to whether humanitarian principles are being applied. International guidelines on civil–military coordination, such as the Oslo Guidelines, are not yet fully implemented in many of the national legislation in the region. One of the reasons for this is that these guidelines are seen to be not applicable to the national context of these countries.[64] While regional guidelines, such as the Standard Operating Procedure for Regional Standby Arrangements and Coordination of Joint Disaster Relief and Emergency Response Operations stipulated in AADMER, are more likely to gain ground, countries in the region still prefer to develop context-specific civil–military coordination guidelines. An example of a context-specific initiative is the Regional Consultative Group on Humanitarian Civil–Military Coordination for Asia and the Pacific. The problem arises when national actors follow a certain set of guidelines that international actors are not familiar with. Thus, without a common framework, some actors would respond in an ad hoc manner, leading to misunderstanding and unintended consequences.[65]

Another issue is how best to localize humanitarian assistance and response, an issue that has been voiced by many national and international NGOs. They argue that more locally led responses should be enabled, given the concerns about increasing local ownership of HADR operations, thereby ensuring sensitivity to local context and situations and building and empowering local actors while promoting a more bottom-up approach to disaster relief operations. An initiative called the Charter4Change gathered about fifty signatures from NGOs and was brought to the World Humanitarian Summit in May 2016.[66] The charter outlines practical measures to implement changes to the way the humanitarian system operates. One of the measures proposed is to increase the transparency of resource transfers from the international community to southern-based national and local NGOs.[67] The charter also highlights the need to reaffirm the principles of partnership, to stop undermining local capacity, and to emphasize the importance of national actors.

As part of the international effort to promote localization, a national civil society forum called Balik-Bayan: Localizing Humanitarian Response was held in Quezon City in the Philippines in 2016. The forum saw the participation of sixty local civil society organizations.[68] The organizers noted that such efforts are driven by the desire to correct the perceived imbalances within the current humanitarian collaboration environment between, on the one hand, national and local civil society organizations, and, on the other, international NGOs and UN agencies. They argue that, rather than working under a subcontract with international humanitarian organizations, as often happens, local civil society organizations should be provided with the support to design and implement HADR responses themselves. They are more familiar with the local context and are better able to facilitate dialogue with local communities; they are thus better placed to ensure that resources and help go to where they are needed most.

Conclusion

With the high likelihood of more extreme weather patterns and large-scale natural disasters, HADR work in the region in the short- to medium-term will continue to focus on disaster management and response. As we have seen, the region has developed a range of mechanisms for HADR response. But with catastrophic natural disasters also come massive displacement of people. The issue of providing protection to internally displaced populations is something that has yet to be discussed seriously in the region's humanitarian agenda. Resettling those who are displaced often takes a much longer time and entails a longer commitment, while the region has mostly engaged in disaster management and response of a limited time span. But addressing this will not be easy.

The displacement of people due to natural disasters is one that is under-addressed even at the international level. There is a global framework, the UN Guiding Principles on Internal Displacement, but that deals with protection of internally displaced populations due to armed conflict and violence. There has yet to be one for the protection of people forced out their national borders due to natural disasters. International refugee law provides strong protection for people fleeing abroad and provides refugees with legal status with attributed status rights. However, international refugee law was not conceived to protect persons displaced across borders by the effects of climate change, even though they may find themselves in a refugee-like situation. There are platforms that discuss the plight of climate-induced "refugees" such as the Nansen Conference, but in the main, this is an issue that East Asia needs to lead the way on. As a disaster-prone region, the probability of more people displaced by natural disasters is high, which makes it imperative that the region confront the issue—and soon.

Finally, as AADMER progresses to deal with all types of disasters, natural and human-induced, the question as to whether the region is ready to deal with humanitarian crises caused by armed conflicts and political violence cannot be ignored. Thus far, AADMER's use of the term "human-induced" has been left ambiguous by omission: it is silent on situations of humanitarian crises in conflict settings. In an integrated community like ASEAN and East Asia, the consequences of humanitarian crises from armed conflict (such as displacements, violence, and human rights issues) have transboundary effects. There is therefore the expectation that ASEAN, through its established HADR frameworks, should be able to cooperate in providing assistance to vulnerable communities. In this regard, ASEAN and its East Asian neighbors cannot continue to avoid dealing with hard and difficult issues, nor can they remain constrained by regional norms of consensus building.

To be sure, humanitarian crises from armed conflict and political violence increase the complexity of humanitarian assistance. Pushing ahead, there are developments that could serve as entry points for more proactive response by ASEAN's HADR mechanisms. For example, the prolonged armed conflict that broke out in Marawi in the Philippines between government troops and Muslim extremists has galvanized regional support to help the four hundred thousand internally displaced persons there. Aside from humanitarian aid provided by the United States, Australia, and the

European Union, ASEAN countries such as Malaysia and Singapore, together with China, South Korea, and Japan, have joined to provide relief and assistance. The AHA Centre also sent relief goods at the request of the Philippine government. Together with NGOs and civil society organizations, actors from the private sector have been providing communication facilities and medical missions to attend to the needs of the internally displaced persons. Civil society organizations have also been alerting authorities to possible human rights abuses in the camps for those persons.

Meanwhile, in Myanmar, with the latest humanitarian crisis that emerged from the forced displacement of more than six hundred thousand Rohingyas to the Bangladesh border as a result of violent military operations against the Arakan Rohingya Salvation Army (discussed in chapter 5), the ASEAN region is once again under pressure to act decisively to avert an escalation of the crisis. ASEAN officials have asked the AHA Centre to work with a Myanmar-led disaster relief mechanism to provide humanitarian assistance to the displaced Rohingya communities. At the time of writing, the AHA Centre's humanitarian efforts have extended beyond providing relief assistance to affected communities in Rakhine state to also include those in the refugee camps in Bangladesh. This development—the use of ASEAN's AHA Centre as a mechanism to provide humanitarian assistance in a conflict setting—is significant and is worth monitoring.

Thus, while it may indeed take time for governments to make the mandate of AADMER more explicit on humanitarian crises arising from conflict and violence, the vibrant presence of multiple non-state actors working with governments and international NGOs can help advance the culture of protection for the vulnerable communities and address the complexities of issues that come with these human insecurities.

CHAPTER VII

Governance of Nuclear Energy

C hapter 6 raises the agenda of preparedness and protection in dealing with disasters, both natural and human-induced. Among the key governance issues that are critical in preventing risks and mitigating the human security threats from disasters are disaster preparedness and response; the active engagement and participation of all stakeholders, state and non-state; and effective coordination among multiple actors at different levels from the local to the international. Equally important is the need to have the legal and normative frameworks that underpin the standards of safety and inform the nature of humanitarian assistance and disaster relief (HADR) operations in Southeast Asia and the wider East Asian region.

These governance issues are relevant in our discussion of nuclear energy governance in the region. The increasing interest in building nuclear power plants in Southeast Asia has raised two major concerns: first is the policy choice of having nuclear energy as a suitable and viable alternative energy source and second are the safety and security concerns of operating nuclear power plants in the region. The latter concerns have been amplified by the Fukushima Daiichi Nuclear Power Plant accident in Japan in 2011. Paradoxically, in spite of the anxieties and worries post-Fukushima, nuclear power plants are still being constructed in East Asia. China, South Korea, India, and Russia are aggressively constructing nuclear power plants and are also vendors of such plants to their neighbors in Southeast Asia. In fact, it has been projected that the nuclear power industry will shift more from the developed world to developing states in Asia, raising not only geopolitical issues but, more importantly, bringing closer to the region the issues of nuclear safety and security. Against this background, we ask whether the construction of more nuclear power plants will bring with it higher risks of more nuclear accidents, whether countries in the region are prepared, and, if so, how they are prepared.

In the traditional perspective on security, nuclear energy is usually seen through the prism of geopolitics and within the context of energy security, a notion born out the 1973 oil crisis. The main issues are the balance between energy supply and demand and which countries wield more power due to the vastness of their energy resources. According to Daniel Yergin, energy security is all about ensuring the undisrupted access of oil supplies from producing countries.[1] In fact, energy security is often viewed as a key national security agenda, with a strong military defense being critical to protect energy assets and infrastructure against external aggression. This has been the prevailing view of energy security until emergent environmental and socioeconomic issues came to the fore.

First is the global agenda of mitigating the impact of climate change as a result of greenhouse gas emissions from the burning of fossil fuels. The need to address greenhouse gas emissions and their environmental impact expanded the notion of energy security to include environmental concerns. Second, starting from the early 2000s, there was increasing concern about the volatility of oil supply and prices. This concern about skyrocketing prices was compounded by the 2008 global financial crisis. The supply and price instability has had serious implications for the accessibility and affordability of energy to the populace, resulting in the notion of "energy-poor" communities despite availability of oil supply. Such concerns have generated significant discourse among non-state actors and the academic and policy community who lent their voice to the critique that the concept of energy security should not be too narrow and should include environmental and socioeconomic concerns. By adopting the concept of human security as an alternative lens, non-state actors such as civil society organizations, scholars, and practitioners have advocated for a more comprehensive view of energy security that includes the various dimensions of the subject and examines non-traditional energy security concerns.[2] The human security paradigm therefore formed the basis for a more holistic approach to examine the contemporary nuclear energy issues in East Asia.

Against that background this chapter examines key developments in the governance of nuclear energy in Southeast Asia and the wider East Asian region. It begins by looking at the factors driving countries in the region to turn to nuclear energy and by examining the current state of nuclear energy use and plans in the region. This is followed by a sober look at the governance challenges facing countries in the region and the frameworks that have been developed thus far to address them. Overarching the discussion in this chapter is the reality that nuclear disasters could have transboundary impacts and as such should concern the entire region, not just those countries currently operating nuclear power plants or those contemplating their adoption.

Why Nuclear Energy?

The interest in nuclear energy in East Asia is driven by many factors: the need for alternative sources of energy due to concerns over future volatility in oil prices and supply; increasing demand spurred by rapid economic growth; a slow transition to alternative energy sources; and the urgency of addressing greenhouse gas emissions. The climate change dimension has been gaining traction. For example, the 2016 Report on Climate Change and Nuclear Energy released by the International Atomic Energy Agency (IAEA) noted that 75 percent of greenhouse gas emissions are energy related.[3] In the global effort to address climate change, countries have agreed to reduce emissions and limit the global increase in temperature to below 2 degrees Celsius. The Paris Agreement of 2015 went even further, aspiring to a 1.5-degree target. The push to decarbonize the energy sector represents one of the more persuasive reasons for choosing nuclear energy since nuclear reactors do not emit greenhouse gases. And nuclear reactors do not emit pollutants such as nitrous oxides and sulfur dioxide, a major consideration for an urbanizing Asia struggling with issues of air pollution.

Apart from climate change concerns, stability of energy supply remains salient. Note that the International Energy Agency defines energy security as "the uninterrupted availability of energy sources at an affordable price."[4] Although the price of oil started to drop in 2014, states remain wary of future price increases and disruptions in supply, especially from politically volatile areas. Nuclear power is also considered more stable compared to other alternatives to fossil fuels. Unlike wind and solar power plants, nuclear power plants have a constant baseload with high capacity factors.

Uranium, which is required for making nuclear fuel, is available from reliable sources.[5] It also is easier to build up strategic uranium fuel reserves than fossil fuel reserves because uranium has greater energy density, which allows even small volumes of uranium fuel to provide reserve fuel for a longer time.[6]

In terms of the cost of generating electricity, nuclear energy also compares favorably with fossil fuels. Any increase in the cost of uranium for nuclear-generated electricity is far less than the price of generating electricity from fossil fuels and natural gas. Moreover, unlike power plants that use fossil fuels, nuclear power plants are not affected by greenhouse gas restrictions, carbon taxes, permit fees, or emission penalties.[7] From this perspective, electricity generated from nuclear energy is not only stable but also affordable. For the countries of Southeast Asia, which currently depend on fossil fuels for a major part of their electricity needs, that makes nuclear an attractive option as they seek to diversify their energy mix to ensure that their economies and people continue to have access to a sufficient supply of energy to meet increase in projected demand. Table 7.1 illustrates the reliance of ASEAN countries on fossil fuels.

TABLE 7.1

Electricity Generation by Fuel in Southeast Asia

Source	Share	
	2013 (%)	2040 (%)
Fossil Fuels	82	77
Coal	32	50
Gas	44	26
Oil	6	1
Nuclear		1
Renewables	18	22
Hydro	14	12
Geothermal	2	3
Bioenergy	1	3
Other*	0	4
Total	100	100

*Includes wind and solar PV
Source: International Energy Agency, *World Energy Outlook 2015 Special Report: Southeast Asia Energy Outlook* (Paris: IEA, 2015), 39.

TABLE 7.2

Number of Nuclear Reactors Planned for Newcomer Countries in East Asia, as of October 2016

Country	Number of nuclear reactors (planned)
Indonesia	4
Malaysia	4
Thailand	2
Vietnam	4*

*Vietnam has since suspended its plans. Newcomer countries are countries introducing nuclear power for the first time.

Source: World Nuclear Association, *World Nuclear Performance Report 2016, Asia Edition* (Singapore: WNA, 2016), 27.

There is another reason, not often stated, as to why states in the region would pursue nuclear energy: prestige. That a country could build and run a nuclear power plant signals development and progress. This, when combined with the other reasons outlined earlier, explains why developing countries plan to build nuclear power plants—despite the prohibitive cost involved. Thus, even after Fukushima, the nuclear energy development plans of Indonesia, Malaysia, Thailand, and Vietnam remained in place (see table 7.2, although Vietnam has since suspended its plans, as discussed in the next section).

Nuclear Energy in Southeast Asia

In terms of adoption of nuclear power, China, Japan, and South Korea are far ahead compared to the countries of Southeast Asia. Nuclear energy is already a credible energy resource in the three countries. As of 2017 China has thirty-six nuclear power reactors, with twenty-one under construction and plans for more.[8] Japan has over fifty reactors, although seven have been decommissioned after Fukushima, while South Korea has twenty-five.

Southeast Asia may soon have its own nuclear power plants, with several countries already showing strong interest in developing them. Vietnam had been the furthest along, having incorporated nuclear energy into its long-term development plans since 1976. It had approved the construction of two nuclear power plants in 2009, financed by Russia and Japan, respectively. In November 2016, however, the Vietnamese government decided to suspend its plans, citing soaring costs.[9] Despite this unexpected announcement, the government has nonetheless said that it will continue "promoting" nuclear power.[10]

Malaysia has been conducting feasibility studies with a view to having a nuclear power plant in the country by 2030. An assessment by an IAEA mission in October 2016 concluded that "Malaysia has developed a considerable base of knowledge and is well prepared to make an informed decision about introducing nuclear power."[11]

Indonesia has explored the idea of constructing a nuclear power plant but does not yet have any. However, it does have three research reactors used mainly for agricultural and medical purposes as well as safety laboratories, a waste treatment center, and a nuclear fuel center.[12] There are strong proponents of nuclear energy in the country who argue that renewable sources of energy are simply not enough to meet the country's needs. As the deputy chairman of the National Nuclear Energy Agency of Indonesia (BATAN) said, "like or dislike, nuclear must be included for the demand of electricity by 2025."[13] The country's state-run electricity company, PT PLN, is also open to the idea of going nuclear, especially if other sources of energy are insufficient to meet the country's energy targets.[14]

However, Indonesia's vulnerability to earthquakes, tsunamis, and volcanic eruptions has raised issues of safety, and public opposition over such concerns has meant that no specific target dates have been set for the construction of a nuclear power plant. Public officials have argued against such worries, saying that they are overstated. The chairman of BATAN, for example, said that "the fact is that some parts of Indonesia are not on the Ring of Fire. In Kalimantan, in Bangka and even near Singapore on Batam island. That side is a good and appropriate site for the nuclear power plant."[15] It is also of note that BATAN released the results of a public survey in 2016 that found most people supported plans to build nuclear power plants in the country due to the prospect of cheaper electricity prices, solving blackout problems, and opening up job opportunities.[16]

Two other ASEAN countries have shown interest in nuclear power: the Philippines and Cambodia. In 2016 the Philippine government announced that it was assessing the feasibility of recommissioning the Bataan Nuclear Power Plant.[17] Bataan, built between 1976 and 1984, would have been the first nuclear power plant to operate in Southeast Asia. But the plant was mothballed after being hit by charges of corruption and due to concerns over safety, given that the plant is located near an active volcano and a fault line. As another indication of the country's interest in nuclear energy, a memorandum of cooperation was signed between the country's Department of Science and Technology and Russia's State Atomic Energy Corporation ROSATOM in May 2017 with the goal of developing nuclear infrastructure, training personnel, and promoting public acceptance of nuclear technologies.[18]

Cambodia has not officially announced any plans for a nuclear power plant but has signed two deals with Russia to set up a nuclear energy information center, which could lay the foundation for a nuclear power project in the future.[19]

These developments reveal a regionalization of nuclear energy, which has significant implications for regional nuclear energy governance. This raises several critical issues that are starting to shape the regional security agenda on nuclear safety: ensuring nuclear energy safety and security; enhancing nuclear emergency preparedness and response capabilities; strengthening regional regulatory frameworks; and advancing the norms of nonproliferation of nuclear weapons in the region.

Securitizing Nuclear Energy

Many of the arguments against having nuclear power plants center on the impact on health, the environment, and population displacements in cases of nuclear accidents. Radiation poses a severe health risk, with acute radiation poisoning being mostly fatal (see box 7.1). In the case of nuclear accidents or nuclear test sites, the impact is long term and may come not just from immediate exposure but also from environmental contamination. The Chernobyl accident in 1986 led to some five thousand cases of thyroid cancer among children aged up to eighteen at the time of accident, which has been traced to drinking milk contaminated with radioactive iodine.[20] It is estimated that 120,000 people—emergency workers, evacuees, and residents of the strictly controlled zones in Ukraine, Belarus, and the Russian Federation—may eventually die of cancer.

Another direct impact of nuclear explosions, whether from nuclear accidents or nuclear testing, is the displacement of people from affected areas.

THE HEALTH EFFECTS OF RADIATION EXPOSURE

The following lists the major radiation-associated long-term health effects among the survivors of the Hiroshima and Nagasaki bombings:[1]

1. Excess leukemia deaths
2. Solid-cancer deaths
   • Cancers of the bladder, female breast, and lung cancer
   • Cancers of the brain/central nervous system, ovary, thyroid, colon, and esophagus
3. Non-cancer (chronic) disease deaths
   • Lens opacities (cataracts, ocular lesions)
   • Thyroid diseases and hyperparathyroidism
   • Cardiovascular and other late-onset diseases (diseases of the circulatory, digestive, and respiratory systems)
   • Psychological effects (higher frequencies of anxiety and somatization symptoms, posttraumatic stress disorder)
   • Life-span shortening
   • Cytogenetic changes and somatic mutations (chromosomal aberrations)
   • Immune responses
4. In utero exposure
   • Neurological effects (frank mental retardation)
5. Genetic effects in second generation
   • Congenital malformations
   • Still births
   • Perinatal deaths

1. Evan B. Douple et al., "Long-Term Radiation-Related Health Effects in a Unique Human Population: Lessons Learned from the Atomic Bomb Survivors of Hiroshima and Nagasaki," *Disaster Medicine Public Health Preparedness* 5, no. 1 (2011): S122–33.

Mass population displacement is one of the most significant humanitarian consequences of a nuclear explosion. Displaced populations will have immediate humanitarian needs such as shelter, uncontaminated food and water, and health care. This will require relocating them to sites beyond the contaminated areas, a challenge when nuclear explosions happen along international borders, spreading displaced populations to neighboring states. For example, in 1986, 116,000 residents were evacuated from the areas surrounding the Chernobyl reactor, with 230,000 more evacuated in later years.[21] Relocation had an impact on the displaced population's mental health: high levels of stress and anxiety are still being reported among those affected.

A more recent example is the Fukushima Daiichi nuclear disaster (see box 7.2). The accident led to 83,000 "nuclear refugees" from eleven towns contaminated by the radiation. Two years later, those eleven towns remained uninhabitable, despite efforts by the government to decontaminate them.[22] As noted by Silva Meybatyan, "in the context of both crises [Chernobyl and Fukushima], tens of thousands were permanently displaced from the immediate vicinities; thousands made the decision to move because of health concerns, environmental degradation and collapsed infrastructure; and millions remained in contaminated areas due to an absence of resources and/or opportunities, financial constraints and special attachment to their home."[23]

Securitizing actors in the region have warned that nuclear power plants pose an existential threat to human life. They highlight the safety issues related to nuclear power plants, including such risks as a nuclear accident and contamination of food sources by radioactive materials. Such concerns have gained resonance since Fukushima. One civil society organization that has consistently securitized nuclear power plants is the Malaysian Physicians for Peace and Social Responsibility. In response to rising interest in nuclear energy in the region, the group released its "Ten Reasons Against Nuclear Power." The group argued that nuclear power produces radioactive waste and limits spending on clean energy since resources would go toward developing nuclear power plants. Also, nuclear power is not completely safe; nuclear power plants are potential targets for terrorists; nuclear power is a cause of nuclear arms proliferation; and nuclear power plants are expensive.[24] The group's former president captures these concerns, saying: "Look at Fukushima. They have good technology, but when there was an earthquake and then came the tsunami, it caused the Japanese a lot of problems. The situation at the affected areas still remain uncertain until now."[25]

Greenpeace is another organization involved in securitizing nuclear power plants. A representative from Greenpeace Philippines called the planned revival of the Bataan Nuclear Power Plant an "expensive distraction," citing issues such as the disposal of nuclear waste and the location of the plant near a fault line.[26] Over in Indonesia, another Greenpeace representative argued that "science tells us that nuclear is inherently dangerous, especially in a country like Indonesia," adding that "nuclear is not safe, nuclear is not clean, nuclear is a false solution for climate change."[27] Despite

BOX 7.2
FUKUSHIMA DAIICHI NUCLEAR ACCIDENT, 2011

On March 11, 2011, a 9.1-magnitude earthquake struck the eastern coast of Japan's Tohoku region, causing a tsunami with waves measuring up to almost forty meters. The catastrophe triggered a major nuclear accident at the Fukushima Daiichi Nuclear Power Plant. Electricity was cut off and the backup generators did not work, disrupting the operation of the cooling system. This resulted in the overheating and meltdown of three of the power plant's reactors. Radioactive materials were released into the air, and radioactive water leaked into the ocean. The accident forced the evacuation of more than 150,000 people. While there were no reported deaths by radiation, more than thirty people died as a result of the physical and mental stress of having to evacuate. A few workers also died at the plant due to the accident while others have been diagnosed with leukemia because of radiation exposure.

Why Did the Accident Happen?
A 2012 report by the Fukushima Nuclear Accident Independent Investigation Commission labeled the event as a "manmade disaster—that could and should have been foreseen and prevented."[1] The report cited lack of governance and collusion between the government, regulators, and the Tokyo Electric Power Company (TEPCO), the owner of the plant.

The power plant was not sturdy enough to withstand the March 11 earthquake and tsunami. TEPCO and the regulators had known since 2006 that a tsunami that reached the level of the site could lead to a power loss, but they had failed to do anything about it.[2] There was also a lack of tsunami countermeasures. And although there were countermeasures for severe accidents, they were not up to international standards. The report also cited organization-related problems within TEPCO, including shortcomings in the areas of knowledge and training given to the workers.

Emergency Response
According to the report by the commission, emergency response was also affected by ambiguity in the roles and responsibilities of the government, the regulators, and TEPCO. The report also pointed to inadequacies in the way the regulators managed the crisis. Not only was the delivery of information regarding the nuclear accident slow, the severity was not conveyed properly, creating confusion among the evacuating public.

1. National Diet of Japan, "The Official Report of The Fukushima Nuclear Accident Independent Investigation Commission: Executive Summary" (Tokyo: National Diet of Japan, 2012), 9.
2. National Diet of Japan, 16.

the lack of information on when national plans to build nuclear power plants in Southeast Asia might be finalized, civil society groups continue to advocate against such plants.

In this regard, there is an interesting case further afield that serves as a good reference for successful advocacy by non-state actors in phasing out nuclear power plants. In Taiwan, a plan in the 1980s to build a fourth nuclear power plant, the Lungmen Nuclear Power Plant, drew the attention of several environmental groups and antinuclear organizations. Construction began in 1999, but the protests continued, with the groups using various means to make their case, including concerts, movie screenings, and events in local farmer markets.[28] These antinuclear movements in Taiwan escalated following the Fukushima disaster in 2011. Between 2011 and 2014, NGOs and nonpartisan activists led by the Taiwan Environmental Protection Union and the Green Citizens' Action Alliance pressed on to rally massive popular support, presenting themselves as citizens' groups while avoiding affiliation with the two opposing political parties in the country. The sustained engagement of these groups, and particularly the Green Citizens' Action Alliance, earned them the authority, expert knowledge, and legitimacy to build an antinuclear constituency by strengthening networks with local groups, urban artists, and university clubs. The sustained engagement eventually yielded results when, in April 2014, the Ma Ying-jeou government sealed off the first reactor of the controversial Lungmen plant and halted construction of the second one, which was 90 percent complete. In January 2017 the Taiwan legislature passed an amendment to the country's Electricity Act that will shut down all the island's nuclear power plants by 2015.[29]

Issues and Challenges of Nuclear Security Governance

While non-state actors have voiced fears about nuclear safety and human security, governments in the region have similarly raised concerns. The Fukushima accident was a reality check to governments eager to pursue nuclear energy. More importantly, Fukushima served as an important reminder that the security of the states and the people in the region is closely intertwined. And it is in their mutual interest to work together to address their shared concerns over nuclear energy plans in the region, the presence of nuclear power plants near the region's borders, and the use of radioactive sources.

The thinking in ASEAN is, if at least one member state starts to operate a nuclear power plant, all member states would have a vested interest in collectively institutionalizing nuclear safety standards and joint nuclear emergency preparedness and response. The transboundary radioactive plumes from a nuclear meltdown may have severe regional consequences, including risks to public health and contamination of food and water sources. And while Southeast Asia does not currently have any operational nuclear power plants, a nuclear disaster in China may still affect the region. China has nuclear power plants near Vietnam and may in future deploy offshore reactors in the South China Sea. Already, in 2015, one of the three nuclear power plants near the Vietnamese border, the Yangjiang Nuclear Power Plant in Guangdong Province, has experienced an operational mistake, which was compounded by the operators attempting to cover up the problem.[30] Thus, the need for vigilance and nuclear disaster preparedness cannot be overstated, particularly since nuclear power plant accidents could have severe transboundary security implications. These events have given impetus to ASEAN, China, Japan, and South Korea to examine their national and regional regulatory frameworks, identify the challenges and gaps in regional nuclear security governance, and strengthen existing regional and international cooperation on nuclear safety and security.

A recent study on nuclear safety by the Centre for Non-Traditional Security Studies at the S. Rajaratnam School of International Studies in Singapore highlights three key challenges for nations pursuing the development of nuclear power plants in Southeast Asia.[31] The first relates to national legislative and regulatory frameworks. There is a need for stronger regulatory and legislative frameworks that institutionalize the norms of nuclear safety and security as well as adherence to global nonproliferation obligations. In this regard it is vital for nuclear regulatory agencies at the national level to be independent. The director-general of the IAEA, Yukiya Amano, has stressed that regulatory independence lends itself to greater transparency and ensures that the agencies will not have to face pressures and conflicts of interest that may endanger safety and security.[32] As demonstrated in the Fukushima accident, the lack of independence of the regulatory body from proponents of nuclear energy such as ministries and the nuclear industry greatly compromised safety and was identified as one of the causes of the accident (see box 7.2). Nuclear-aspiring states in the region have yet to introduce the laws that would empower their nuclear regulatory bodies to independently perform their mandated functions, particularly inspection and licensing, to ensure nuclear safety.

A second challenge relates to the lack of knowledge and expertise in nuclear technology and nuclear engineering. Operating a nuclear power plant requires a pool of local nuclear professionals with actual relevant experience in the nuclear industry. Well-trained and experienced nuclear professionals are also critical in institutionalizing competent and independent regulatory bodies. The region currently does not have enough personnel with the expertise to safely operate its future nuclear power plants. Indonesia, for example, has an aging pool of nuclear experts at its nuclear energy agency and its other nuclear facilities. It needs to train young professionals as well as enhance the skills of its older professionals, particularly in nuclear safety and security. Malaysia has a similar problem. It also does not have enough experienced personnel to teach its nuclear engineering courses. Moreover, the focus of nuclear knowledge and expertise in the country has previously been on nonnuclear power applications such as in medicine, agriculture, industry, and manufacturing. In the case of Vietnam, it still needs to train enough nuclear engineers, reactor operators, and emergency personnel, given that it takes years to decades for a country to master nuclear power technology.[33]

The third challenge relates to developing the capacity to dispose of high-level nuclear waste (i.e., spent or used reactor fuel). Presently, there is no final repository site for the high-level waste accumulated globally over the past six decades, although progress has been made in France, Sweden, and Finland in developing deep geological disposal sites that are tentatively to be made available after 2020.[34] The IAEA has strongly advised newcomers in Asia to first address the waste issue by developing a national policy for radioactive waste management and the required infrastructure, even before commissioning a nuclear power plant.[35] In Vietnam's case, as part of its nuclear deal with Moscow, its future spent fuel would have been reprocessed in Russia, but the treated waste would still have been returned to Vietnam, where a disposal facility would have been required.[36] Indonesia has ratified the Joint Convention on the Safety of Spent Fuel Management and on the Safety of Radioactive Waste Management. While its nuclear research facilities are capable of managing and disposing low- and intermediate-level radioactive waste produced from educational, medical, and industrial activities, there is yet to be a comprehensive plan on the final disposal of high-level waste, should Indonesia decide to commission nuclear power plants. In Malaysia, questions of capacity in waste disposal have been raised because of the controversy over the case of Lynas, an Australian company with a rare-earth processing plant in Kuantan, Malaysia. An IAEA team assessed the Lynas project in 2011 and found it lacking a comprehensive, long-term waste management program.[37] Moreover, unlike Indonesia, Malaysia has yet to ratify the Joint Convention on the Safety of Spent Fuel Management and on the Safety of Radioactive Waste Management.

Closely related to these three issues is the weak nuclear security culture in the region. Nuclear security culture is defined by the IAEA as "the assembly of characteristics, attitudes and behavior of individuals, organizations and institutions which serves as a means to support and enhance nuclear security."[38] Developing a strong nuclear security culture needs to be not only an agenda of the United States or the West but a common agenda for all states. The risks associated with nuclear energy is not only from poor or substandard technology but also from the mindsets, attitudes, and behaviors of those involved in the operation and regulation of nuclear facilities. A critical component of the nuclear security culture is a strong safety culture. The IAEA defines a strong safety culture as "the assembly of characteristics and attitudes in organizations and individuals which establishes that, as an overriding priority, protection and safety issues receive the attention warranted by their significance."[39] A safety culture is a high priority for regulators and operators, particularly when, aside from preventing radiation exposure of workers and the public, there is also the risk of radioactive materials falling into the hands of terrorists. Ensuring a strong nuclear security culture with a sustained focus on protection and safety is one of the more challenging areas of nuclear security governance. The culture has to be developed locally, but domestic institutions can also learn from the best practices of other countries.

Another significant concern is the transport of nuclear materials through important regional sea lanes in Southeast Asia, which requires improvements in controls. Relevant government bodies have been urged to include in their assessments thorough background checks, physical barriers and personnel access controls, security plans or procedures, coordination and response planning, coordination and tracking of shipments, and security barriers to discourage theft of illicit material.

Against the many challenges faced by ASEAN countries, there is perhaps nothing that preoccupies the wider East Asia more than being able to uphold nuclear safety and security and avert any possibility of mishaps. Nuclear safety and security is indeed a regional issue since nuclear incidents may range from accidents with localized radiological impact to large-scale nuclear terrorist attacks or even nuclear disasters that can cause transnational spillovers.[40] As one Japanese practitioner in nuclear security puts it, an important lesson learned from Fukushima is the need to have broad perspectives on (and preparedness for) "unthinkable" events and unforeseen circumstances.[41] In this regard, nuclear emergency preparedness is extremely important, the goal of which is to ensure that an adequate capability is in place within the operating organization as well as at the local, national, and international levels. This is necessary to respond effectively in a nuclear emergency. Response should also consider crises related to the transportation of nuclear and radioactive materials through (or near) various territories and possible terrorist acts. It is crucial to be adequately prepared to prevent and quickly respond to new types of events, for instance, cyberattacks.[42]

Another important lesson from the Fukushima accident is the need to establish clear lines of responsibility in crisis management. As observed by a former IAEA expert, vague or overlapping responsibilities among stakeholders (operators, local governments, national government, regulators) make for ineffective crisis management. Regular nuclear emergency drills would help improve cooperation and coordination during an emergency response. Drills should involve the nuclear industry, regulatory bodies, local and national emergency teams, police, military, customs, coast guard, local governments, communities, NGOs, and media, among others. Emergency drills should be designed to test existing response procedures and capabilities of all sectors for various unforeseen scenarios.[43]

Regional Frameworks and Actors in Nuclear Energy Governance

Given the many issues and challenges identified in the previous section, it has become even more important for states and communities to come together and collectively address nuclear safety and security. There are obvious constraints to instituting many of the ideas on nuclear security at the national level. In Southeast Asia, aside from the structural impediments and lack of capacity, there is also the issue of having to work around the norm of noninterference in the internal affairs of states, a challenge that is constant in many of the regional efforts related to transboundary security issues. That said, there are regional frameworks that allow states to manage their differences and work toward realistic areas where collective efforts can be had. From the perspective of regional governance in nuclear energy, ASEAN remains among the most relevant platforms for developing policies and frameworks that help advance nuclear energy governance in East Asia.

ASEAN had established its first regional governance framework on nuclear safety and nonproliferation in its 1995 Treaty on the Southeast Asia Nuclear Weapon-Free Zone (Bangkok Treaty). The treaty obliges parties "not to develop, manufacture or otherwise acquire, possess or have control over nuclear weapons; station nuclear weapons; or test or use nuclear weapons anywhere inside or outside the treaty zone." While the treaty is primarily on nuclear weapons, it contains several provisions that recognize each state's right to use nuclear energy for peaceful purposes, particularly for economic development and social progress. The treaty therefore serves as the regional normative framework that guides member states should they decide to pursue nuclear energy. It promotes the norms of peaceful use of nuclear material and facilities; encourages adherence to the safety assessments, guidelines, and standards recommended by the IAEA; informs fellow members, if requested, of the outcome of safety assessments; upholds the international nonproliferation system through strict adherence to the Treaty on the Non-Proliferation of Nuclear Weapons and the IAEA safeguard system; and disposes of radioactive wastes and other radioactive material in accordance with IAEA standards and procedures.

State Actors

ASEAN leaders and officials are often heard calling on the regional community to adhere to these norms. This is often seen at the annual summit meetings of ASEAN leaders and at other political and security forums like the ASEAN Regional Forum and the East Asia Summit. In particular, at the regular meetings of the energy ministers and officials of ASEAN and the East Asia Summit, the agendas of enhancing capacity-building activities on civilian nuclear energy and pursuing regional nuclear safety cooperation are often discussed.

ASEAN NETWORK OF REGULATORY BODIES ON ATOMIC ENERGY

In response to the 2011 Fukushima incident and given the likely increase in nuclear and radiation use in ASEAN and the potential transboundary impacts of any nuclear incident, the idea of creating the ASEAN Network of Regulatory Bodies on Atomic Energy (ASEANTOM) was proposed by Thailand's Office of Atoms for Peace. Established in 2013, ASEAN-TOM is one of building blocks of the regional frameworks to institutionalize the culture of nuclear safety and security. It serves as a platform for nuclear regulatory bodies and relevant authorities in Southeast Asia to exchange information, experiences, and best practices as well as to enhance cooperation and jointly develop capacities on nuclear safety, security, and safeguards.

ASEANTOM plays a key role in agenda setting in the region. Four key governance agenda areas were identified following a series of consultation meetings with its members: emergency preparedness and response; environmental radiation monitoring; nuclear security; and nuclear safety.[44] In 2015 ASEANTOM's efforts in enhancing nuclear governance earned it political recognition when it was designated a sectoral body under the ASEAN Political-Security Community.[45] The designation increases its profile, with top leadership involvement and oversight of its activities, which may provide it with greater influence over nuclear energy governance in the region.[46]

Even though ASEANTOM is a relatively new body, it is already advancing practical cooperation with various stakeholders on the four agenda areas. It advances the agenda areas by building human-resource capacity through technical workshops and intensive training. Apart from regional workshops, ASEANTOM organizes tabletop and field exercises. For instance, under the ASEANTOM framework, Malaysia and Thailand have been cohosting annual nuclear security border exercises since 2015 that bring together nuclear regulatory bodies, customs, police, and emergency response teams. ASEANTOM has also coordinated meetings on creating an ASEAN-wide environmental monitoring network.[47] Thailand, Malaysia, the Philippines, and Vietnam have their respective environmental radiological monitoring systems or radiation monitoring portals that could alert authorities if there is an unusual increase in radiation that may indicate a leakage or an accident. Vietnam, in particular, has an ongoing project called Radiation Monitoring and Emergency Response that aims to monitor nuclear accidents in the country and its borders, which is important given that China has begun operating three nuclear power plants near Vietnam's northern border.[48] ASEANTOM is expected to consolidate all these state radiation monitoring initiatives, leading to the strengthening of nuclear energy governance in the region. ASEANTOM has also forged cooperation with international organizations and institutions such as the IAEA and the European Union, which is important in terms of transfer of knowledge and in terms of financial resources to implement various activities aimed at enhancing nuclear energy governance in the region.

Going forward, important challenges for ASEANTOM include lack of funding, the need to address the varying degrees of knowledge and expertise among ASEAN member states, the absence of a binding regional framework, and weak commitment from policymakers down to the technical staff.

Cooperation among nuclear regulatory bodies is extremely important in verifying the capability of the region to uphold nuclear safety, security, and safeguards and in addressing the gaps at the national and regional levels. ASEANTOM is a relatively young regional body, but its annual activities have been crafted in such a way that its members can jointly develop a coordinated ASEAN approach to improve nuclear governance with the assistance of the IAEA. But ASEANTOM's activities remain limited to state actors, when the whole business of nuclear governance also involves non-state actors. This suggests that ASEANTOM should also facilitate multisectoral information sharing and communication among state and non-state actors.

Non-State Actors

Track 2 regional networks in nuclear energy governance play an extremely crucial role in allowing non-state knowledge actors to contribute to nuclear governance policies and to filling the gap in expertise in Southeast Asia.

Most of the participants in these networks come from universities, research think tanks (such as the Singapore-based S. Rajaratnam School of International Studies), NGOs, and state agencies (foreign ministry, national security) that are not part of the traditional slate of nuclear governance actors. Regional networks can facilitate regional cooperation on nuclear safety in Asia; pooling and sharing of information, knowledge and practical experience; and development of a regional capacity-building system; among others. The Asia-Pacific region has a wealth of experience (including best practices, know-how, and resources) that can be shared with the region's "newcomers." There are also regional networks that can be tapped to widely disseminate this wealth of experience.[49]

COUNCIL FOR SECURITY COOPERATION IN THE ASIA PACIFIC NUCLEAR ENERGY EXPERTS GROUP

One of the relevant Track 2 networks is the Nuclear Energy Experts Group of the Council for Security Cooperation in the Asia Pacific (CSCAP). CSCAP includes members from all the major countries in the Asia-Pacific and has been consolidating its links and continuing to add value to the ASEAN Regional Forum. The goal of its Nuclear Energy Experts Group is to serve as a multilateral forum to discuss methods and processes to develop and manage nuclear energy programs in a safe, secure, and proliferation-resistant manner. It is neither pro- nor antinuclear energy per se. The annual CSCAP Nuclear Energy Experts Group meetings provide a constituency of around forty experts from Asia and beyond, all attending in their private capacities. These experts come from universities, think tanks, nuclear companies, and government agencies, and they develop policy recommendations to strengthen regional nuclear governance for consideration by Track 1 regional officials. This indeed highlights the important role of the epistemic community of experts and scholars in contributing to nuclear governance.

Another important aspect of nuclear energy governance in the region is the convergence of agenda setting between Track 1 security governance actors and Track 2 knowledge actors. In the case of the CSCAP Nuclear Energy Experts Group, its agenda intersects with the four governance agendas of ASEANTOM for Southeast Asia. Recent CSCAP discussions on nuclear energy have focused on nuclear security governance, nuclear safety, radioactive source management, nuclear waste management, and nuclear accident/incident response.[50] These generate policy inputs that can enrich the four governance agendas of ASEANTOM. In addition, the issues of cyber nuclear security threats and physical protection of nuclear facilities have been discussed at recent meetings and can also be considered under the broader nuclear security governance agenda.

Recognizing that they share similar agendas, the CSCAP Nuclear Energy Experts Group invites ASEANTOM representatives to its annual meetings. This gives experts from ASEANTOM, a Track 1 network, the opportunity to update the experts group on the network's activities and agenda and to field policy questions from them. CSCAP discussions are often candid and frank. This type of exchange allows for CSCAP experts to contribute to the Track 1 process through sharing and discussing with their ASEANTOM counterparts their recommendations on how to improve nuclear energy cooperation in Southeast Asia. Apart from nuclear governance issues, the experts group has also provided ideas on how to enhance the role of ASEANTOM. For example, it suggested that ASEANTOM should have a dedicated, permanent secretariat (currently the ASEANTOM chair rotates each year to coincide with that of the ASEAN chair), arguing that that would provide continuity and enhance regulatory cooperation. The experts group has also encouraged stronger collaboration between ASEANTOM and the ASEAN Coordinating Centre for Humanitarian Assistance on Disaster Management (AHA Centre) to better incorporate nuclear emergency preparedness and response within ASEAN's HADR framework.[51] As indication of the value of such interactions, ASEANTOM has told CSCAP that they do in fact take the ideas, recommendations, and outcomes from the experts group meetings back to ASEANTOM for discussion.

ASIA-PACIFIC LEADERSHIP NETWORK FOR NUCLEAR NON-PROLIFERATION AND DISARMAMENT

The Asia-Pacific Leadership Network for Nuclear Non-Proliferation and Disarmament (APLN) is a Track 2 network that works on strengthening nuclear governance in the wider Asia-Pacific region. It aims to inform policymakers, especially high-level policymakers, to take seriously the threats posed by nuclear weapons. The APLN has more than eighty members from fifteen countries across Asia and the Pacific, consisting of former political, official, diplomatic, and military leaders in senior executive positions as well as opinion leaders and shapers from other sectors of society.[52] While the APLN is meant to be a Track 2 forum, the participation of some officials from the foreign ministries of certain countries, although acting in their personal capacity, sometimes makes it a Track 1.5 body.

APLN members contribute to the debate on nuclear safety and security governance in the Asia-Pacific by making public statements, engaging in direct advocacy with governments in the region, commissioning research, and hosting regional seminars and conferences. It is deeply committed to encouraging the development and adoption of regional nuclear arms control measures, together with related nuclear safety and security measures, among regional nuclear actors. As noted earlier, APLN meetings, particularly its subregional ones, are attended by officials acting in their private capacity and have become important avenues for candid deliberations on policies related to nuclear safety and security, sidestepping the sensitivities in discussing matters of national concern in official meetings.

In the context of Southeast Asia, the APLN has been able to feed into the four governance agendas of ASEANTOM for Southeast Asia. For instance, the APLN Southeast Asia Meeting in 2016 saw strong arguments that ASEAN member states should strengthen normative frameworks related to nuclear safety, security, and safeguards—even those not intending to pursue nuclear energy development. States should sign all safety and security conventions (such as the Convention on Nuclear Safety, the Joint Convention on Spent Fuel and Radioactive Waste, and the Convention on Physical Protection of Nuclear Materials and its amendment) and IAEA regulations.[53] The meeting also urged ASEAN member states to extend their regular field and tabletop exercises under the purview of ADMM-Plus to include all types of disasters, including nuclear accidents.[54] Much like the CSCAP Nuclear Energy Experts Group, the deliberations among APLN members provide for more thoughtful analysis of and candid exchange on difficult issues such as the development of North Korea as a nuclear power state and the perceived militarization of Japan.

CENTERS OF EXCELLENCE IN EAST ASIA

Successful cooperation also requires engaging local stakeholders, such as universities and research centers. There is a need for training courses to develop a group of experts to maintain nuclear facilities. Given Southeast Asia's interest in nuclear energy, the lack of expertise, both in nuclear safety and nuclear security, is problematic.

According to members of the CSCAP Nuclear Energy Experts Group, the United States and the Northeast Asian states could play a major role by sharing best practices and providing know-how. The centers of excellence in China, Japan, and South Korea were mentioned as excellent venues for training officials from Asia.[55] For instance, Japan's Center of Excellence, together with the Japan Atomic Energy Agency and the Japan Atomic Energy Commission, has been providing robust technical training assistance to the Philippines, Malaysia, Vietnam, Indonesia, and Thailand in improving their capacity in nuclear safety and security.

The role of companies is also critical in this process. The China General Nuclear Power Group, for instance, has been organizing, together with the ASEAN Centre for Energy, the ASEAN–China Capacity Building on Nuclear Energy Workshop since 2015. The Korea Nuclear Association for International Cooperation also organized courses and site visits to nuclear facilities for ASEAN senior policymakers and working-level personnel between 2010 and 2015.

ASEAN NETWORK ON NUCLEAR POWER SAFETY RESEARCH

The ASEAN Network on Nuclear Power Safety Research is a Track 1.5/2 network based in Southeast Asia that could potentially complement the nuclear safety agenda of ASEANTOM. It was initiated by the Vietnam Atomic Energy Institute and the Thailand Institute of Nuclear Technology in 2017.[56] The network sees itself potentially playing a role in advancing the region's nuclear safety agenda and norm-building efforts through providing a regional platform for research collaboration and for sharing of knowledge and experience among the academic and research institutions of Southeast Asia. The member institutes of this network have been working closely with their respective national nuclear regulatory agencies (which are also members of ASEANTOM).

Given the shared interest of advancing nuclear governance on security issues that have serious transboundary implications, it is useful to note that there is a web of non-state actor networks beyond Southeast Asia that promote knowledge and expertise, encourage multilateral cooperation at multiple levels, and foster trust and confidence among states and societies. A few of these are described here.

INTERNATIONAL NUCLEAR SECURITY EDUCATION NETWORK

Established in 2010, the International Nuclear Security Education Network is an international web of universities and institutions focused on developing educational programs under the auspices of the IAEA's Nuclear Security Program. It is a global platform for drawing expertise, networks, and materials on nuclear security. Four research institutions and universities from Singapore, Malaysia, Thailand, and Indonesia are members of the network. Activities include joint research and development efforts, professional development courses, student–faculty exchange, workshops, and the development of teaching and training materials. These help to strengthen nuclear security education and governance in Southeast Asia.

ASIA-PACIFIC SAFEGUARDS NETWORK

Established in 2009 as an initiative of the Australian government, the Asia-Pacific Safeguards Network facilitates the exchange of information, knowledge, and practical experience on nuclear safeguards among members in order to strengthen capacity in this area. It also ensures that the safeguards activities in the region are conducted to IAEA standards. Its membership includes nuclear regulatory bodies from Australia, Bangladesh, Cambodia, Canada, Indonesia, Japan, Laos, Malaysia, Mongolia, Myanmar, New Zealand, the Philippines, Singapore, South Korea, Thailand, the United States, and Vietnam as well as representatives from the European Commission and the IAEA.

This network helps influence national and regional governance on nuclear safeguards in the Asia Pacific by assisting its members to improve safeguards implementation, and its annual meetings afford members the opportunity to come together to exchange best practices in the implementation of safeguards, to reflect on the outcomes of cooperative efforts, and to explore new collaborations.[57]

ASIAN NETWORK FOR EDUCATION IN NUCLEAR TECHNOLOGY

The Asian Network for Education in Nuclear Technology is a regional partnership supported by the IAEA that brings state and non-state actors together to improve capacity building, human-resource development, and knowledge management in nuclear science and technology. The network focuses on sharing nuclear information and knowledge relevant to nuclear education and training; providing expert assistance and review services to members; and helping to facilitate communication between members and other regional and global networks.[58] One of its important contributions in advancing nuclear energy governance is its e-learning platform. The platform helps disseminate relevant information and facilitates knowledge exchange between experienced nuclear professionals and younger staff. It also helps attract talented youth to the nuclear profession.

Conclusion

The concern about meeting future energy needs for a rapidly developing region while addressing climate change presents multiple considerations in ensuring that policy choices do not sacrifice human and state security. To be sure, there are no easy answers when it comes to the best policy option for achieving a stable and secure source of energy that is available, accessible, and affordable. Although nuclear energy has been in the mix of energy sources for some countries in East Asia, challenges related to nuclear energy governance still abound—nuclear safety being paramount.

While states in the ASEAN region have witnessed the impact of the Fukushima nuclear disaster, it has not dampened plans to consider nuclear power as a potential energy source. But set against the frequency of catastrophic natural disasters hitting the region, the prospect of more humanitarian crises can no longer be ignored. Nuclear energy governance is clearly now an agenda that must be taken seriously on board as governments and communities grapple with the many other transboundary security challenges affecting the region. In this regard, the interlocking governance processes that help advance the agendas of nuclear safety, emergency preparedness response, and nuclear security along with protection of civilians and the most vulnerable in times of humanitarian crises cannot be left to states alone. As with other transboundary non-traditional security threats, the participation and active involvement of non-state actors is a must.

Getting both public and private actors together in Track 1.5 and Track 2 forums has contributed significantly to the often difficult task of governing nuclear energy security. The challenge of having to manage the interest of states in protecting their sovereignty against that of promoting norms and practices that will enhance nuclear safety and security is dealt with in an informal setting where, in an atmosphere of camaraderie and trust, participants who are either recently retired or still officially active are able to present their national perspectives and explain their respective issues and constraints. Such frank exchanges go a long way in fostering better understanding of the kinds of issues and challenges facing states in meeting the demands of energy security. More importantly, these dialogues provide avenues to build capacity in areas and places where they are most needed.

CHAPTER VIII

Governance of Food Security

F ood security is one of the critical global challenges today. It is also a security challenge that connects with and brings together all other security threats confronting the world, from climate change to poverty, water and energy security, health, disasters, migration, wars, and conflict. At the height of the 2008 global food crisis, the executive director of the World Food Programme, Josette Sheeran, called for global action to deal with the "silent tsunami" that threatened to push over 100 million people into hunger.[1]

The Food and Agriculture Organization of the United Nations (FAO) defines food security as "a situation that exists when all people, at all times, have physical, social and economic access to sufficient, safe and nutritious food that meets their dietary needs and food preferences for an active and healthy life."[2] This definition suggests that food security is achieved only if four aspects of food security—availability of food, physical access, economic access, and the extent to which food is utilized to create better nutrition outcomes—are simultaneously met. The FAO often adds a fifth dimension, "stability," to emphasize the importance of the stability of the four dimensions over time.

Amid changes in the global security and economic environment, the quest for food security for all has become extremely challenging. Food prices remain high and volatile, making it difficult for millions across the world to gain access to food. With climate change and degradation of the environment, scarcity of resources, population growth, rising urbanization, and rising incomes, the urgency for the global and regional community to respond collectively has become more compelling. Failure to do so could gravely affect the security and well-being of individuals, communities, and states.

What can be a shared concern for collective action can also be a divisive one. Policies on food security and agriculture are highly contentious as protectionism, subsidies, and import and export controls continue to dominate policy thinking in almost all countries around the world. As the global community is forced to address contemporary food security challenges, finding pathways for solving food-related issues becomes more critical than ever. This is particularly relevant for Asia, where undernourishment and poverty continue to plague a large number of communities, despite the region enjoying steady economic growth. And while the region is home to the world's largest rice exporters, it is also the largest importer and consumer of rice per capita globally. Against rising incomes and changing diet patterns, on the one hand, and rising urbanization and declining agricultural production, on the other, the state of food security in East Asia presents several paradoxes that need the collective will of state and non-state actors to work together in addressing the new realities of food insecurity in the region and beyond.

This chapter begins by laying out why and how food was securitized in East Asia. It then looks at the food security governance arrangements and actors in the region, both state and non-state, observing that there are now efforts at the regional level to address food security (and insecurity) as a multidimensional challenge that requires multipronged approaches. The case of urban farming is highlighted as an example of an innovative solution that is seeing traction because of increasing urbanization, the need for sustainable development, and, importantly, the engagement of a multiplicity of actors in agenda setting and advocacy right through to implementation.

Why Securitize?

Food security is fundamental to human security and sustainable development. It featured in the 2005 UN Millennium Development Goals, and again in the Sustainable Development Goals adopted in 2015. While food security had been regarded largely as a development issue, there has been a clear move to elevate the issue into the realm of national and human security, as shown by the statements of leaders across East Asia in box 8.1.

Why securitize the issue? Securitization allows us to examine the different layers of insecurities faced by various groups of people who are affected differently. It also helps us identify the disparate perspectives of individuals and communities who suffer disproportionately from the multidimensional facets of food security. Starting with the first aspect of food security—availability—we note that, from a macro perspective, an estimated 795 million people globally still suffer from hunger or chronic undernourishment.[3] This is more than 10 percent of the world population.[4] Behind this number is the "hidden hunger" faced by 2 billion people, roughly a fourth of the world's population, who are undernourished.[5]

Asia has its own story to tell about food insecurity (figure 8.1). More than 512 million people, or over half the global total, who do not have enough food are found in the region.[6] The prospect of food insecurity becomes more acute when stacked against global population growth, which is projected to reach 9.1 billion by 2050, 34 percent higher than today. More than 30 percent of that increase is expected to be in Asia.[7]

The accelerating pace of urbanization will also have an influence on the food security status in Asia. An estimated 51 percent of the increase in global urban populations will be in Asia.[8] This will have a significant bearing on food availability since the issue of whether there is sufficient food to meet the increasing demand is affected by the state of the region's food production base. In this regard, the significant fall in the rural population is a concern as that has also meant that the number of people working in agriculture has declined.[9] The amount of arable land has been decreasing by approximately 710,000 hectares per year since 1991.[10] Investments in agriculture have also contracted. These trends have had a negative impact on food production. The rate of annual yield growth in wheat, rice, and maize has slowed from close to 3.3 percent in 1960 to about 1.3 percent in 2010.[11] The Intergovernmental Panel on Climate Change has cited a finding that world yields for rice and maize may decline by up to 12 percent by 2050, while wheat yields may decline by up to 13 percent.[12]

Access to food is also constrained by factors such as the poor infrastructure and inadequate facilities for food transport and distribution in

BOX 8.1

SECURITIZATION OF FOOD SECURITY IN THE POLICY DISCOURSE IN EAST ASIA

Food affords the very basis for human survival and development. And food security bears on national stability and world peace.[1]
—WEN JIABAO, VICE-PREMIER OF THE STATE COUNCIL OF THE PEOPLE'S REPUBLIC OF CHINA, WORLD FOOD SUMMIT, 2002

The developing world is at a tipping point. In the Philippines, we feel the pain of high prices of food, fuel and rice. . . . To address these global challenges, we must go on building bridges among allies around the world. To bring rice to where it is needed to feed the people, investments to create jobs and keep the peace and stability in the world.[2]
—GLORIA MACAPAGAL-ARROYO, PRESIDENT OF THE PHILIPPINES, UNITED NATIONS GENERAL ASSEMBLY, 2008

Do hereby pledge to embrace food security as a matter of permanent and high priority policy, review our commitment to achieving objectives of the World Food Summit, the Millennium Development Goals . . .[3]
—ASEAN LEADERS, ASEAN SUMMIT, 2009

Food security remains a major challenge for ASEAN and the world as a whole, at a time of high commodity prices and economic uncertainty."[4]
—ASEAN LEADERS, ASEAN SUMMIT, 2012

Food security is "one of the most acute problems of our time . . ."[5]
—VLADIMIR PUTIN, PRESIDENT OF RUSSIA, ASIA-PACIFIC ECONOMIC COOPERATION (APEC) SUMMIT, 2012

1. Jiabao Wen, "Speech by HE Mr Wen Jiabao Vice-Premier of the State Council of the People's Republic of China at World Food Summit, June 10, 2002," Ministry of Foreign Affairs of the People's Republic of China, June 13, 2002, http://www.fmprc.gov.cn/mfa_eng/wjb_663304/zzjg_663340/gjs_665170/gjzzyhy_665174/2616_665220/2618_665224/t15367.shtml.

2. Gloria Macapagal-Arroyo, "National Statement of President Gloria Macapagal-Arroyo at the 63rd UN General Assembly General Debate, New York City, USA, September 23, 2008," *Official Gazette* (Philippines), September 23, 2002, http://www.officialgazette.gov.ph/2008/09/23/statement-president-arroyo-at-the-63rd-un-general-assembly-general-debate/.

3. Association of Southeast Asian Nations (ASEAN), "Statement on Food Security in the ASEAN Region" (14th ASEAN Summit, Cha-am, Thailand, March 1, 2009).

4. ASEAN, "2012 Phnom Penh Agenda for ASEAN Community Building" (20th ASEAN Summit, Phnom Penh, Cambodia, April 3, 2012).

5. Elaine Kurtenbach, "Pacific Rim Leaders Seek to Fortify Food Security," *San Diego Union-Tribune*, September 8, 2012, http://www.sandiegouniontribune.com/sdut-pacific-rim-leaders-seek-to-fortify-food-security-2012sep08-story.html.

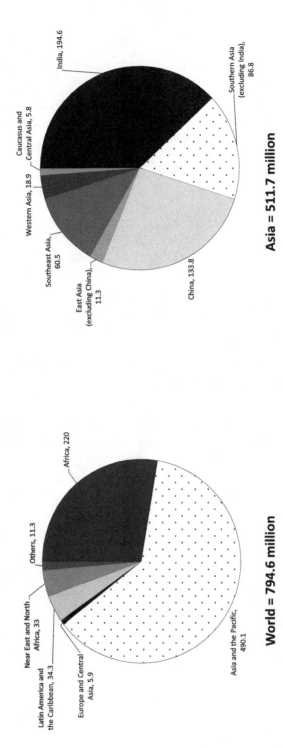

Figure 8.1 Where do the hungry live?

Source: Food and Agriculture Organization of the United Nations (FAO), International Fund for Agricultural Development (IFAD), and World Food Program (WFP), *The State of Food Insecurity in the World 2015* (Rome: FAO, 2015).

developing countries. The situation becomes worse in times of natural disasters and conflicts, when supply chains are suddenly disrupted. Economic access or ability to buy food is determined mainly by job and income security, with unstable food prices also an important factor.[13] The poor, who spend about 75 percent of their incomes on food alone, are among the most vulnerable in periods of rapid price increases, such as during the food crisis in 2007 to 2008, when the price of rice increased by up to three times the normal price.[14]

One of the reasons for the spike in food prices in 2008 was the rising cost of oil, which directly affected the price of fertilizers. Higher oil prices also affected the cost of transporting food from source to consumer. Another factor was the significant expansion of biofuel production due to pro-biofuel policies in countries such as India, Thailand, and China, which led to competition with food crops for available land and other resources.[15]

Since the food crisis happened at around the same time as the global financial crisis (2008–2009), the number of people who went hungry also reached a historic high of 1.2 billion, out of which 642 million were in Asia. Lack of physical and economic access to food can become a catalyst for civil unrest, as witnessed during the 2008 food crisis, which triggered riots across the globe (see box 8.2).

The increasing burden of getting access to food is most prevalent in urban areas where there is a high concentration of the urban poor. In tandem with rapid urbanization, the number of urban poor has increased by 25 percent from 1990 to 2008. This affects food utilization, typically reflected in the nutritional status of an individual. The urban poor is not only at risk of not having enough food but also faces issues with quality of food. Many live under suboptimal conditions in urban slums, for example, where food safety as well as nutritional value of food could be compromised.[16]

A paradox in the problem of hunger and malnutrition in East Asia is the challenge of obesity. Obesity in six ASEAN countries—Indonesia, Malaysia, Philippines, Singapore, Thailand, Vietnam—has grown faster than in the United States or the United Kingdom from 2010 to 2014. This brings with it its own challenges as diseases such as diabetes and hypertension accompany obesity. When all these factors are put together, food insecurity in East Asia presents a number of difficult challenges, illustrated in figure 8.2.

BOX 8.2
FOOD INSECURITY AND THE ARAB SPRING

In December 2010 Tunisian street vendor Mohamed Bouazizi set himself on fire, sparking off the Arab Spring, a series of antigovernment protests that swept across countries in the Middle East and North Africa. The people who took to the streets of Tunisia were not just protesting the death of Bouazizi; they were decrying the lack of freedom of speech, the rise in unemployment, and the pervasive corruption in their government. The riots were also symptomatic of a similarly burdensome issue: rising food prices.

Food Insecurity in the Middle East and North Africa
The world had experienced a dramatic increase in food prices over the course of 2007 and 2008. After plummeting in 2009, prices surged again from June 2010 to February 2011, going even higher than the peak in 2008.[1] Countries in the Middle East and North Africa like Tunisia were particularly vulnerable to the price increases and volatility since they were major food importers. In fact, the Middle East and North Africa region accounted for one-third of the global consumption of wheat. More than half of the sugar and cereal they consumed was also imported. Adding to their vulnerability, many of these countries, including Tunisia, Yemen, Jordan, Djibouti, Lebanon, and Iraq, had low grain reserve stocks and lacked the fiscal capacity to spend on subsidies and import costs. And the poor in these countries bore the brunt of the increase. Aside from the fact that more than half of their income went to food, their governments also happened to give a greater subsidy to fuel than to food.[2]

Impact on State Legitimacy and Credibility
A study released in 2011 concluded that high food prices can be a contributing factor in social disruptions like the ones witnessed during the Arab Spring. According to the study, riots are more likely to happen when the value of the FAO Food Price Index is more than 210. Whether it is the fault of the political system or of the global food supply system, the increase in food prices and eventually the food security failure can lead to loss of public support for their government. Given these circumstances, any random incident can trigger widespread violence.[3]

In the case of Tunisia, from June 2010 to February 2011 the FAO Food Price Index had risen to over 210 points, and amid the rising prices, its political system had failed to make its people feel secure. Ultimately, Bouazizi's self-immolation served as the random trigger event that would incite massive demonstrations in the country.[4] The Tunisian Revolution, which lasted until January 2011, led to the ouster of Zine al-Abidine Ben Ali, Tunisia's president for twenty-three years.

1. Aïcha L. Coulibaly, "The Food Price Increase of 2010–2011: Causes and Impacts" (background paper, 2013-02-E, Ottawa: Library of Parliament, 2013), 2.

2. Atif Kubursi, ed., *Food and Water Security in the Arab World—Proceedings of the First Arab Development Symposium* (Washington, D.C.: International Bank for Reconstruction and Development, World Bank, and Arab Fund for Economic and Social Development, 2012), 6–7.

3. Marco Lagi, Karla Z. Bertrand, and Yaneer Bar-Yam, "The Food Crises and Political Instability in North Africa and the Middle East" (Cambridge, Mass.: New England Computer Systems Institute, 2011).

4. Lagi, Bertrand, and Bar-Yam, "The Food Crises."

Food Security Governance:
Regional Frameworks and Actors

The task of ensuring that there is available, accessible, and safe and nutritious food is the responsibility of all states. The ability of a state to guarantee food security for its people is also a measure of its legitimacy. Food security policies are therefore the domain of national governments and reflect the national interest. But in a highly interconnected world, national food security is also contingent on regional and international food security. Moreover, the agenda of achieving food security is no longer just about having enough supply of food to meet demand. It is also about ensuring food safety and adequate nutrition, which requires investment and trade policies conducive to enhancing supply chains, infrastructure, research and development, and technology. More importantly, it is about promoting social protection, sustainable food production, and environmental security. Thus, to advance a more comprehensive agenda on food security, governments need the support and engagement of all stakeholders—state and non-state—to engender a multisectoral and multilevel approach to the governance of food security.

In discussing the response of Southeast Asia and the wider East Asian region to the complex challenges of food security, it bears reiterating here our notion of security governance, which is one that covers multilevel activities, structures, and processes undertaken by a range of actors working and coordinating their interdependent needs and interests through policymaking and implementation to address security challenges. In this regard, the region's experience with food security problems is instructive.

As with many regional efforts to respond to security challenges, ASEAN became the focal point and the platform for initiating regional policies to

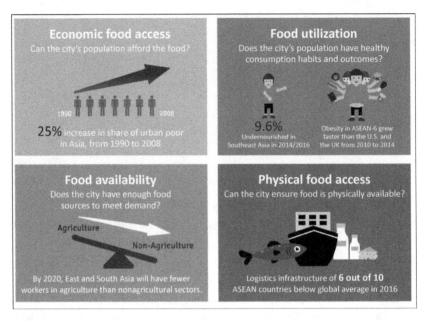

Figure 8.2 Key facets of urban food security
Source: Jose Ma Luis Montesclaros, "NTS Fast Facts: Food Security," factsheet (Singapore: RSIS, October 2016), accessed August 5, 2017, http://www.rsis.edu.sg/wp-content/uploads/2017/01/FastFacts-FoodSecurity-final.pdf.

help member states deal with food security issues. It was only after the 2008 global food crisis that regional efforts became more visible, with greater intraregional cooperation seen. Regional efforts have focused mainly on the first aspect of food security, which is ensuring food availability through boosting production and supply of food and through promoting regional trade and building food reserves.

The ASEAN platform has brought in actors such as the ASEAN Chambers of Commerce and Industry, the ASEAN Business Forum, and a number of national research institutions that work on agriculture and trade. It has also brought in China, Japan, and South Korea through the ASEAN Plus Three framework and, through this body, initiated a very important regional mechanism for building food reserves. The regional food security policies and frameworks are described briefly here.

ASEAN Integrated Food Security Framework

Learning from the impact of the 2007–2008 food crisis, ASEAN states have taken on a multipronged approach to deal with the complex challenges of food security. In 2009 ASEAN adopted the ASEAN Integrated Food Security Framework. This framework aims to, first, ensure long-term food security in ASEAN and, second, improve the livelihoods of farmers in the region. The framework was later translated into the Strategic Plan of Action on Food Security in the ASEAN Region 2015–2020. The framework outlines an ambitious and comprehensive plan aimed at achieving its two interrelated two goals. The plan has five key components with at least one target or strategic thrust to be achieved (figure 8.3). It is useful to go through each of the components briefly to understand which sectors are involved as well as to identify the key participating institutions and actors.[17]

FOOD SECURITY AND EMERGENCY/SHORTAGE RELIEF

The first component is food security and emergency/shortage relief, which includes the strategic thrust of strengthening food security, including through emergency or shortage relief arrangements. Under this component, a regional food security reserve is envisioned. This is to be done under the ASEAN Plus Three Emergency Rice Reserve (APTERR) framework, wherein the ASEAN Plus Three countries stock certain quantities of rice to draw from in the case of emergencies or to prevent crises similar to the 2007–2008 price increases (see box 8.3). The APTERR Council helps countries implement the APTERR mechanisms as well as conducts monitoring and evaluation. This is also to be coordinated with the ASEAN Plus Three Food Security Information System (AFSIS), which seeks to provide timely information on food security in the region.[18]

This component also seeks to ensure the sustainability of supply chains through providing support to the seed industry in consultation with the ASEAN Seed Council hosted in Malaysia.[19] Measures include promoting exchange of information on seeds in the region, making sure that farmers have access to quality seeds, and harmonizing the rules and regulations within the region's seed industry.

BOX 8.3
APTERR: A REGIONAL MECHANISM FOR ENHANCING
FOOD SECURITY

The conception of the APTERR mechanism has a long history in ASEAN. In the midst of a food crisis in 1979, ASEAN agriculture ministers met in Manila and agreed to develop the ASEAN Food Security Reserve Agreement to address the region's vulnerability to volatility in food production and hence food supply.[1] The agreement called for the creation of the ASEAN Emergency Rice Reserve (AERR), with pledges from Indonesia, Malaysia, the Philippines, Singapore, and Thailand.[2] However, these reserves were neither utilized nor prioritized.

It took the 2008 crisis for ASEAN—together with its Plus Three partners, China, Japan, and South Korea—to revisit the reserves mechanism and modify it to respond to new developments. In 2011 the APTERR framework was adopted. The provision for emergency food aid, as specified in the 1979 agreement, was enhanced to allow for sale of rice when a crisis is triggered by price hikes. The mechanism has since been used several times, albeit only during emergencies brought on by disasters. It is yet to be used in response to price volatility that could potentially lead to a crisis.

While the two food reserve mechanisms were both created after crises, the institutional context behind the establishment of APTERR is different. The agreement on APTERR was reached faster, a consequence of the growing relationship that had been built from years of interaction and cooperation among the ASEAN Plus Three countries. By that point, from its first summit in 1997, ASEAN Plus Three had had eighteen years of discussions. More importantly, food security had already been in the agenda of ASEAN, as reflected in the ASEAN Integrated Food Security Framework.

The Institutionalization of the Mechanism
The activation of the emergency rice reserves follows a specific process. The release of rice stocks is subject to approval by the APTERR Council, which is made up of representatives of countries party to the mechanism and which receives its mandate from the ASEAN Ministers of Forestry and Agriculture and their Plus Three counterparts.[3] One of the tools used by the council is the food emergency monitoring and information system, which helps evaluate the need to release stocks, and the impacts of doing so.

Assessment of APTERR
APTERR has several important advantages over its predecessor, AERR. For one, it has a more streamlined process for releasing stocks in times of emergency. It uses automatic triggers to indicate when rice needs to be released, a process that has already facilitated the transfer of 7,200 tonnes of rice to the Philippines,

which has faced multiple typhoons since 2012.[4] Second, while the AERR included rice stockpiles earmarked from national rice reserves, APTERR has physical pledges of rice allocated exclusively to it from national reserves. The amount pledged to APTERR is also higher. The Plus Three countries (China, Japan, and South Korea) came in with 700,000 tonnes, adding to the 87,000 tonnes previously pledged to the AERR.[5] Finally, APTERR has a stronger institutional structure, having established a council and a secretariat, along with rules and procedures governing how rice stocks are to be released.[6]

While APTERR seems to be complete with the needed information for its operation, there remain challenges. There is still opacity regarding the amount of stocks held by member countries, which could hamper risk assessments on the impacts of disruptions in the rice supply chain. And while there are provisions for three tiers, or ways of releasing stocks, only Tier 3—which applies to emergencies—has been used.[7] Tier 1, which is based on forward contracts, and Tier 2, which provides for purchases using cash, a loan, or a grant, have yet to be used. This may be due to the size of the reserves. The pledge of 787,000 tonnes of rice is still small compared to the total rice demand in larger member countries, such as Indonesia and China; thus, it would be more efficient to simply source from foreign markets. Yet, that we have not seen any increase in pledges could also partly be because of lack of utilization of the reserves.[8]

The Role of the Epistemic Community

As the first East Asian mechanism on food security, APTERR has attracted much attention from scholars and policy analysts, and several studies have been conducted to assess its impact and effectiveness. These studies and analyses have also suggested ways to improve the mechanism. For instance, an analysis by Jose Ma Luis P. Montesclaros offers the observation that the effectiveness of the reserves must be measured by more than size, suggesting that how the reserves are used could be more important.[9] Another analysis from the Centre for Non-Traditional Security Studies (NTS Centre) at the S. Rajaratnam School of International Studies in Singapore called for, among others, greater transparency in how national reserves are managed and more private-sector involvement in the procurement, storage, and distribution of stocks.[10] The Second Murdoch Commission recommended in a 2015 report that ASEAN Plus Three expand APTERR to cover wheat (not just rice), given the experience of countries outside the region such as India, which have seen dietary patterns change as incomes increase.[11] Other recommendations include increasing the size of the reserves (current contributions are only sufficient to meet one to two days of consumption in ASEAN); expanding what the reserves could be used for (from emergency uses during natural disasters, to the sale of grains to prevent price crises); and promoting private–public partnerships in managing aspects of the reserves.

(continued)

1. ASEAN, "Agreement on the ASEAN Food Security Reserve" (New York City, October 4, 1979).

2. ASEAN, "Agreement on the ASEAN Food Security Reserve," Art. 4, pt. 1.

3. ASEAN Plus Three Emergency Rice Reserve, "Rules and Procedures of the APTERR Council," undated, accessed August 12, 2017, accessed at http://apterr.org/images/download/document_operation_of_APTERR/Rules_and_Procedures_of_the_APTERR_Council.pdf; no longer available.

4. "ASEAN Rice Reserve Available During Emergencies," *Philippine News Agency*, April 3, 2017, http://www.canadianinquirer.net/2017/04/03/asean-rice-reserve-available-during-emergencies/.

5. See Sally Trethewie, "The ASEAN Plus Three Emergency Rice Reserve (APTERR): Cooperation, Commitment and Contradictions" (working paper, Singapore: S. Rajaratnam School of International Studies, 2013).

6. Trethewie, "The ASEAN Plus Three Emergency Rice Reserve."

7. Leonard Leung, "Food Security and Resilience of the Association of Southeast Asian Nations Member States to Food Price Volatility" (completion report for project 47208-001, Manila: Asian Development Bank, 2017).

8. Trethewie, "The ASEAN Plus Three Emergency Rice Reserve."

9. Jose Ma Luis P. Montesclaros, "It's Not the Size, But How It's Used: Lesson for ASEAN Rice Reserves," *RSIS Commentary* (Singapore), March 2015.

10. Mely Caballero-Anthony et al., "Public Stockpiling and Food Security" (Singapore: S. Rajaratnam School of International Studies, 2015).

11. Murdoch Commission, *Food Security, Trade and Partnerships: Towards Resilient Regional Food Systems in Asia, Full Report* (Perth, Australia: Murdoch University, 2015).

SUSTAINABLE FOOD TRADE DEVELOPMENT

The second component of the ASEAN Integrated Food Security Network is sustainable food trade development, which includes the thrust of promoting a conducive food market and trade. This component seeks to reconfigure the regional food trade to allow for "more diverse and affordable food at more stable prices."[20] As part of this component, a rice trade forum has been organized where restrictions in food trade are discussed along with ways to strengthen the food value chain. The deliberations feed into decisions by the ASEAN Food Security Reserve Board, which provides policy advice to the Senior Officials Meeting of the ASEAN Ministers on Agriculture and Forestry.

INTEGRATED FOOD SECURITY
INFORMATION SYSTEM

The third component relates to the region's integrated food security information system. The goal is to strengthen the system to effectively forecast, plan, and monitor supply and utilization for basic food commodities. AFSIS is the key body for this, providing "real time market intelligence, use of existing data and quantitative analysis."[21] It develops quality standards for information systems within the region.

AGRICULTURAL INNOVATION

The fourth component is agricultural innovation, and under this fall three strategic thrusts. The first is to promote sustainable food production through institutions under the country-specific National Agricultural Research Systems and the International Agricultural Research Centers, which are encouraged to help with and disseminate technologies and practices across agri-based and food value chains that will be of benefit to the seed sector, fish feeds, and agribusiness. The ASEAN Technical Working Group on Agricultural Research and Development takes the lead in technologies that can reduce or prevent postharvest losses.

The second thrust looks to encourage greater investments in the food and agri-based industry to enhance food security. To expand investments in the sector requires working closely with the ASEAN Chambers of Commerce and Industry, the ASEAN Business Forum, the ASEAN Sectoral Working Group on Crops, the ASEAN Sectoral Working Group on Fisheries, and the ASEAN Sectoral Working Group on Livestock in preparing roadmaps for agri- and food-based value chains within the region.

The third thrust is to identify and address emerging issues related to food security. Separate bodies have yet to be determined for this future-oriented task, apart from the ASEAN Secretariat and the FAO, but the goals are to investigate the implications of bioenergy development on food production, to pilot climate-smart agricultural technologies, and to look at the long-term implications of demographic structural changes in the region.

NUTRITION-ENHANCING AGRICULTURE DEVELOPMENT

The fifth component is nutrition-enhancing agriculture development. This involves three strategic thrusts. The first is to use nutrition information to support evidence-based food security and agriculture policies. AFSIS, the Senior Officials Meeting of the ASEAN Ministers on Agriculture and Forestry, and the Senior Officials Meeting of the ASEAN Ministers on Health Development are all involved. The nutrition information will be integrated

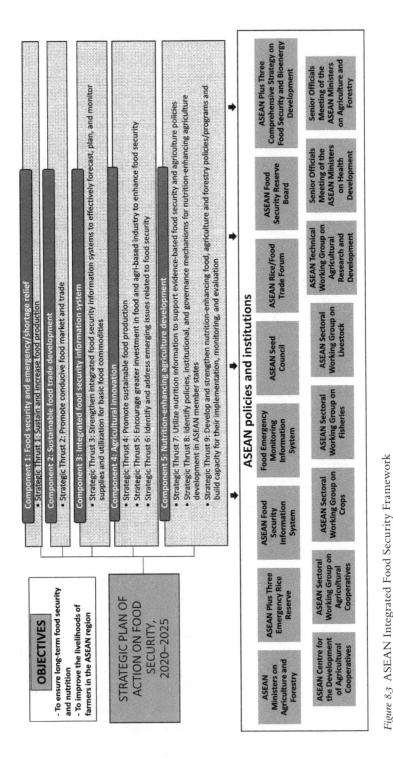

Figure 8.3 ASEAN Integrated Food Security Framework

Source: Based on Association of Southeast Asian Nations (ASEAN), "ASEAN Integrated Food Security (AIFS) Framework and Strategic Plan of Action on Food Security in the ASEAN Region (SPA-FS) 2015–2020" (Jakarta: ASEAN Secretariat, 2014).

into AFSIS activities, with implications for capacity-building efforts within the region.

The second thrust of the fifth component involves identifying policies and institutional and governance mechanisms for nutrition-enhancing agriculture development in ASEAN member states. The goal is to build awareness of the importance of nutrition among key stakeholders in food, agriculture, and forestry. In this area, the role and participation of academic and research institutions, the FAO, and other development partners are critical in order to develop strategic partnerships and alliances within countries and across the region in addressing nutrition and health issues.

The third thrust under the fifth component is to develop and strengthen nutrition-enhancing food, agriculture, and forestry policies and programs and to build capacity for their implementation, monitoring, and evaluation. The parties responsible for this include the FAO and other development partners as well as the ASEAN Seed Council, given the need to "mainstream nutrition in sectoral and cross-sectoral policies and programs" related to the food, agriculture, and forestry sector, and develop national and regional policy guidelines and tools to this end.[22]

Figure 8.3 summarizes the key thrusts, policies, and institutions in relation to the ASEAN Integrated Food Security Framework. As can be seen, the framework presents a wide array of policies, measures, and institutions that are envisioned to work together in addressing the multifaceted dimensions and challenges on food security. For all intents and purposes, the framework reflects a regional governance system that draws on a proliferation of actors who are expected to work collaboratively in each of the areas and targets identified that could help deal with food security problems.

Non-State Actors and the ASEAN Food Security Agenda

The complexities of regional and global food security challenges have driven a number of non-state actors in the region to be part of the agenda-setting process and to support the development of regional food security policies. Among the more active are members of the region's epistemic community, some of which are described here.

Centre for Non-Traditional Security Studies (NTS Centre)

A major contribution of the NTS Centre at the S. Rajaratnam School of International Studies in Singapore is its program on food security, which aims to provide a platform to engage the different stakeholders in the region to generate more exchange of views and innovative ideas on how to meet the challenges posed by emerging food security issues. In line with this, it has convened expert meetings and high-level consultations.

One of its most significant events is the International Conference on Asian Food Security, which first took place in August 2011, "Feeding Asia in the 21st Century: Building Urban–Rural Alliances." The conference attracted more than two hundred public, private, and civil society players in Asia's food security space.[23] The success of the first conference led to another, held in 2013. This second iteration was distinguished by the participation of private companies in the agricultural sector like Syngenta and Bayer, which felt the need to be part of the conversation on the region's food security challenges.

In addition, the NTS Centre's food security team has collaborated with public and private partners to deliver innovative food security tools that have transformed knowledge on food security. One of these is the Rice Bowl Index, a measure of the robustness of a country's food security policy, which was developed through a partnership with private-sector actors Syngenta and the Frontier Strategy Group.[24] The NTS Centre was also involved in Singapore's Inter-Ministry Committee on Food Security, one of the first intersectoral bodies to look at food security in the region.

The NTS Centre has produced dozens of well-received publications on many aspects of food security and has highlighted food security concerns through media interviews and commentaries. Through its program of research, events, and outreach that brings in multiple stakeholders at different levels, the center has been an effective actor in elevating and shaping the food security agenda of the region.

Southeast Asian Regional Center for Graduate Study and Research in Agriculture

The Southeast Asian Regional Center for Graduate Study and Research in Agriculture (SEARCA) was established by the Southeast Asian Ministers of Education Organization in 1966 and was a co-organizer of the International Conference on Asian Food Security in 2011 and 2013, mentioned earlier. Through its research activities in the region, it provides the knowledge base for highlighting areas of action for the region. For example, SEARCA published a report in 2010 that had implications for the notion of a regional rice reserve. In its analysis of the impact of the 2007–2008 food crisis in the Greater Mekong Subregion (Cambodia, Laos, Thailand, and Vietnam), it found that export restrictions and export taxes imposed by governments in the subregion had led to more panic, driving world rice prices to increase even faster and aggravating the food crisis. In its recommendations, it resurfaced the AERR of 1979 and the East Asia Emergency Rice Reserve under ASEAN Plus Three.[25]

Economic Research Institute for ASEAN and East Asia

The Economic Research Institute for ASEAN and East Asia, an international organization formally established at the Third East Asia Summit in 2007, is based in Jakarta. The institute has contributed to the internalization of food security within ASEAN and in the larger East Asian context.[26] As early as 2008, the institute was already organizing meetings. At the Energy Ministers' Meeting during the Second East Asia Summit in Bangkok, Thailand, in August 2008, a joint ministerial statement was released affirming the need to balance food production with biofuel production. A later meeting in August 2008 resulted in a joint media statement from the ASEAN Economic Ministers Plus Six Working Lunch, wherein the foreign ministers of the Plus Six countries (Australia, China, India, Japan, New Zealand, South Korea) sought to respond to the global food crisis. These efforts eventually translated into the Declaration of the 8th East Asia Summit on Food Security in 2013.[27]

Second Murdoch Commission

There are also actors beyond the Asian region who form part of the epistemic community influencing the food security agenda in the region. The Second Murdoch Commission is an example of this. Launched in 2014, it included experts in food security from Australia, China, India, Japan, and a number of ASEAN countries and was jointly chaired by the head of the NTS Centre (who is also a former director of the ASEAN Secretariat) and an official from the FAO.[28] These experts were brought together to examine the issue of how to ensure greater food security in Asia. The commission's final report in 2015 includes suggestions on areas of improvement for APTERR (see box 8.3).

There are many more members of the region's epistemic communities and other non-state actors who have been keenly interested in shaping the agenda of food security in the region and have in one way or another contributed to efforts to identify policies to deal with the multifaceted challenges to food security. While the discussion here is not able to cover them, suffice it to say that these knowledge networks form part of the thick web of governance processes undertaken by multiple actors, wedded together by the shared goal of developing knowledge, building capacity, and strengthening transnational networks to advance policy agendas that address the problems of food insecurity to states and societies in the region.

The Case of the Urban Farming Agenda

Another significant issue that is being advanced by the policy and knowledge networks in the region is urban farming as a response to growing urbanization. The number and size of cities and the share of the world living in cities are only expected to swell (figure 8.4). Most of the increase in the urban population will be in low- and middle-income countries (figure 8.5).

These numbers can be troubling for Asia, given that alongside Asia's rapid urbanization, it also experienced a 25 percent increase in the share of urban poor from 1990 to 2008.[29] With the urban–rural migration that has occurred over the past decades, combined with impacts of climate change on food production, the challenge of meeting urban food needs may worsen in the long term. Policy advocacies that advance urban farming examine how cities can contribute to urban food security.[30] While 15 to 20 percent of food is already produced within cities, the ever greater concentration of people in cities will give impetus to mechanisms that will allow urbanites to participate in farming and food production.[31] Already we have seen heightened interest in urban and peri-urban agriculture, which, proponents argue, shows benefits beyond providing food. Jobs are created, which in

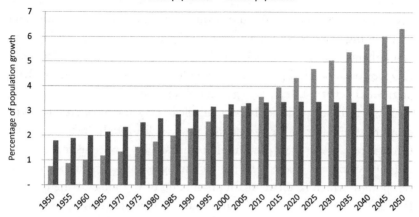

Figure 8.4 Growth in global urban and rural populations, to 2050
Source: Based on United Nations, Department of Economic and Social Affairs,
Population Division, *World Urbanization Prospects: The 2014 Revision*, CD-ROM ed.
(New York: United Nations, 2014); and Food and Agriculture Organization of the
United Nations (FAO), *The Future of Food and Agriculture—Trends and Challenges*
(Rome: FAO, 2017).

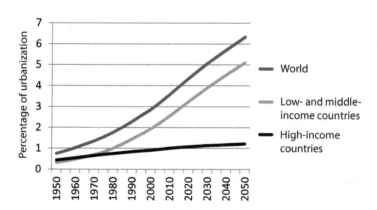

Figure 8.5 Urbanization trends by region
Source: Based on United Nations, Department of Economic and Social Affairs,
Population Division, *World Urbanization Prospects: The 2014 Revision*, CD-ROM ed.
(New York: United Nations, 2014); and Food and Agriculture Organization of the
United Nations (FAO), *The Future of Food and Agriculture—Trends and Challenges*
(Rome: FAO, 2017).

turn contributes to poverty alleviation. Urban and peri-urban agriculture also allows for greater inclusion of women and migrant communities and for greening in cities, which feeds into the goal of sustainable development that enhances human well-being and security. A few examples of successful cases of urban and peri-urban agriculture are Hanoi; Shanghai; Beijing; Mexico City; Dakar, Senegal; and Accra, Ghana.[32]

The private sector has an important role to play. It contributes inputs to growers at the start of the production process. It may also help add value through processing the agricultural products. The private sector can lead in prototyping and mainstreaming technologies such as hydroponics and aeroponics, which facilitate urban production of vegetables. An emerging field is data-enabled or "smart" agriculture, which makes use of sensors to track environmental conditions, complemented with crop analytics that use this data to provide recommendations on the ideal quantities of nutrients to give the plants. Further technologies allow for varying the rate of release of nutrients.[33]

The private sector could also link urban farms and urban agricultural technologies with investors looking for new opportunities. AgFunder is an example of such a platform. Its cofounder, Michael Dean, shared at the World Agricultural Forum 2017 that it raised US$34 million for sixteen companies.[34] Apart from supply-side technologies, there are also e-commerce technologies that allow for the delivery of fresh produce straight to the doorsteps of consumers.[35] Globally, US$3.23 billion was raised in 2016, with over 670 different investors, to support the growth of companies in the field of agricultural technology.

Think tanks also have an important role to play in mainstreaming new technologies. One way is by helping contextualize challenges. The International Food Policy Research Institute, for instance, projects the long-term impacts of climate change on food production and further links this to potential reductions in daily per capita consumption and potential increases in the millions of children facing malnutrition. The institute then shows the extent to which these impacts can be prevented with the use of different combinations of agricultural technologies and infrastructure.[36]

Other actors involved are the organizations that help build farmers' organizations and cooperatives. The Asian Farmers' Association for Sustainable Rural Development, for example, enables farmers to collectively gain access to new technologies, and it lobbies for secure tenurial rights to land for agricultural production.[37] In Singapore, the Kranji Countryside

Association pushes for policies that will enable more agricultural innovation, such as the need for farmers to be given longer land tenure, which will give them enough time to reap the benefits of investments in new agricultural technologies.[38]

Conclusion

With climate change upon us, the challenges to making the world community food secure have become more daunting. Food security is no longer just ensuring availability of food commodities, and the governance approach to food security can no longer be confined to agricultural and trade policies alone. As discussed in this chapter, a sustainable food security approach is one that goes beyond food availability to include physical and economic access to food as well as nutrition and food safety. The global agenda of food security is expanding and underscores the fact that the food security ecosystem is complex and multidimensional and requires the engagement of multiple actors to ensure its sustainability.

Given the politically sensitive and restricted nature of food policies in the region and globally, there are indeed no easy pathways to meet these challenges. These impediments notwithstanding, regional cooperation matters. There are ongoing efforts at different levels by different actors in East Asia to encourage more regional cooperation in addressing the different issues of food security.

Within the existing regional frameworks of ASEAN and ASEAN Plus Three, regional mechanisms have been established to address issues of ensuring food reserves in times of sudden shortfalls in supply and during emergencies. Meanwhile, knowledge networks are actively engaged in generating new ideas and setting policy agendas like urban farming to fill in the gaps in food policies and build networks with other stakeholders of food security in the region. Similarly, we are seeing partnerships being established with the private sector in tapping investments, research and development, and state-of-the-art technology to respond to the higher risks associated with food production under a changing global environment and climatic conditions. All these and more illustrate the multiple processes that are present in the region, advancing new ideas and innovative approaches to make governments and other stakeholders more prepared to respond to the emerging global threats and challenges to food security.

Conclusion

Building Security Governance in Times of
Turbulence and Uncertainty

We live in a dangerous world . . .

If one looks at the interconnection of the global megatrends—population growth and movements of people, climate change, food insecurity, water scarcity—we see how they are more and more inter-combined, enhancing each other and creating situations in which more people are displaced or tension, conflicts can emerge.

[Thus] absolutely crucial is the enhancement of a new generation of partnerships, partnerships not only with governments, not only with civil society and academia but equally partnerships with the business community . . . , creating the conditions for an inclusive and sustainable development—the best way to prevent crises and conflicts in today's world."
—ANTÓNIO GUTERRES, UN SECRETARY-GENERAL, JANUARY 2017

S can the news today and dive into the latest bestsellers on global futures, and we see a world in turbulence. With daily headlines of natural disasters, migrants in distress and lost at sea, images of hunger and deprivation, looming threats of the next global pandemic influenza along with horrific news of war, terrorism, and violence in certain regions in the world—it is easy to be despondent about the future. Richard Haass, in his 2017 book *A World in Disarray*, speaks of a global order in decline. He points to a future that is unstable, writing that "the 21st century will prove extremely difficult to manage, representing as it does a departure from almost four centuries of history—what is normally thought of as the modern era—that came before it."[1]

Haass suggests that there is a need for World Order 2.0, a new operating system for a globalized world, where sovereign states take on the responsibility of regulating developments within their borders that could adversely affect others outside those borders. The notion of World Order 2.0 speaks also to the need for an updated system of global governance that requires states to provide leadership on, and assume responsibility for, domestic issues that have transboundary implications. Within this new system of governance, states are no longer the sole provider of security; other actors will be compelled to become involved and be part of the governance processes as they step in to help manage and resolve the challenges of the future. This reality would apply not just to the major powers but also to the rest of the world, the ASEAN states plus China, Japan, and South Korea included.

This book begins by observing that, in Southeast Asia and wider East Asia, a region known for placing a premium on sovereignty and noninterference in the affairs of other states, security governance not only exists but is developing in dynamic ways. Notwithstanding the bilateral tensions and territorial disputes in the region, we see a pattern of security governance where state and non-state actors work together to address a host of non-traditional security (NTS) threats. There are numerous regional frameworks focused on such threats, including regional agreements to regulate transboundary air pollution, institutionalize disease surveillance and reporting to prevent the spread of pandemics, speed up operations in disaster relief and emergency response, promote peaceful use of nuclear energy, and manage the movements of people through strengthening norms and practices on preventing trafficking in persons.

The abundance of governance frameworks found in the region goes beyond state-led institutions, agencies, and bodies. There are also institutions and multiple networks led by non-state actors that focus on specific security issues and aim to promote and protect the security of groups and communities while contributing to the overarching goal of governing security challenges. The plethora of emerging frameworks presents an interesting mosaic of governance architecture geared toward preventing instability and promoting peace and security in East Asia. (Some of these frameworks have been beset by problems, but this should not diminish the efforts by a range of actors emerging from different sites to collectively work at addressing regional security challenges.)

In showing the multiple sites of security governance present in the region, I move beyond the conventional security lenses to the premise that NTS challenges pose grave threats to both the peoples and the states in the region. The extent of the human suffering from such challenges as pandemics, transboundary air pollution, and natural disasters means that we can no longer ignore their impact on human and state security, nor can we just relegate them to the development agenda. What is needed is a broader perspective of what security is. There is a need to understand how security is defined by multiple actors and how these actors regard certain issues as affecting and threatening their well-being and security. Failure to do so would be a huge injustice to humanity. The framing of these transboundary challenges as a security imperative is not accidental. That the NTS concept has now become part of the security lexicon not only of academics but, more importantly, among government officials in East Asia and that it has, over the past two decades, been included in national and regional agendas, indicate that these kinds of security issues are as critical as traditional security threats. This is reflected in several official pronouncements and documents on political and security cooperation in the ASEAN, ASEAN Plus Three, and East Asia Summit frameworks. It is useful to note, for example, that in the agenda of the East Asia Summit (the framework that includes major powers in the Asia-Pacific including the United States and Russia), food and energy security as well as pandemics loom large, together with issues of maritime security and nuclear proliferation. Within ASEAN's Political–Security Community, NTS threats dominate the security agenda.

In recognizing that NTS issues are no less grave than conventional security threats, I have argued for the need to move beyond a strictly state-centric analysis to identify and examine the other actors that are able to contribute to security discourses and practices. As I argued earlier, in a changed and rapidly changing security environment, the notion that the state is *the* sole security provider is no longer valid. The international system is much more dynamic today, with different security actors actively engaging and negotiating with state actors and international organizations in crafting strategies, building mechanisms, and promoting norms that help protect against the threats posed by transboundary security challenges. As defined in this book, these security actors include, but are not limited to, non-state actors that have been able to exercise influence across borders as well as those providing security at the local level. With a certain degree of legitimacy and continuity, these actors—or "security governors," as described in chapter 1 of this book—affect policies, set agendas, establish and implement rules, and assess or adjudicate their outcomes. I have therefore described and analyzed these governance processes as "state-plus" processes that bring states within the frameworks of regional organizations like ASEAN and ASEAN Plus Three together with a range of non-state actors—civil society organizations, NGOs, international foundations, the private sector—that are interacting and engaging in the multilevel processes of addressing security challenges. The different modalities of governance processes are indeed significant since these configurations of actors, in more ways than one, negotiate and accommodate interests while constantly recalibrating security governance in the region.

The security-governance dynamics unfolding in Southeast Asia and beyond in no small measure represent what ought to be the new type of governance in the twenty-first century, one that is no longer state-centric but rather based on multiple layers of actors working in partnership to prevent crises and promote peace, security, and development. I do not disregard or diminish the role of the state. In the case studies discussed in this book, I have noted the importance of getting governments to take ownership of the implementation of regional agreements. Failure to get their cooperation and buy-in makes these regional processes and interventions less effective and does little to improve the human security of affected communities, as illustrated by the case of the ASEAN Agreement on Transboundary Haze Pollution (see chapter 4), and the difficulties in getting states experiencing the aftermath of natural disasters or forced displacements to agree to allow regional actors operating under the framework of the ASEAN Agreement on Disaster Management and Emergency Response (AADMER) into the affected country to render humanitarian relief to the victims (see chapter 6). Also, to be sure, these governance processes have had their share of problems, including tensions and conflicts among actors. Nevertheless, it is in these dynamic processes that we are able to capture and analyze how multiple interests are managed and negotiated, and it is where we are able to appreciate the multiple sites of governance that exist in the region that would otherwise have been left understudied or ignored.

This book therefore has sought to provide a better understanding of the nature of the security governance taking place in Southeast Asia and, by extension, the rest of East Asia by providing examples of cases where we see different actors at play and by investigating how the different actors participate in governance processes from different sites of authority. This allows us to broaden and deepen our conceptual understanding of what security is for states and societies and what and how security governance is unfolding in this new century.

Another aim is to bring more awareness to the complexities of each of the NTS issues presented as well as the challenges of governing the issues across multiple scales in the region. The cases in this book highlight the risks and vulnerabilities faced by different communities and observe that states face capacity deficits when it comes to dealing with the complexities of NTS threats. Given the region's incredible diversity in population size, political systems, levels of economic growth, and societal composition, different states and communities vary in how they are affected by different NTS challenges. Less developed states with poorer communities have less adaptive capacity and tend to be disproportionately affected by natural disasters, health crises, and other NTS challenges. For instance, as we have seen with Cyclone Nargis and Typhoon Haiyan, vulnerable communities experience greater population displacement and higher exposure to related threats such as infectious diseases. They are also often without access to basic needs such as food, water, shelter, and proper sanitation following a disaster, and they usually take a much longer time to rebuild their lives and livelihoods. The inability to respond quickly and prevent the escalation of any NTS threat would compound preexisting vulnerabilities and exacerbate societal fault lines, which in turn could lead to instability and conflict.

What is unique about the story of governance of NTS threats in Southeast Asia and the wider region is their shared vulnerabilities to transnational threats and the common challenges in capacity and response. Even more interesting is how they have channeled these common interests to develop frameworks of cooperation, building on a history of cooperation and working around competing interests and normative constraints while providing space for non-state actors to get involved. As a consequence, what we are seeing as security-governance responses are a combination of (1) state-led action (for example, the introduction of emergency measures like border control and quarantine during health crises) supported by education and awareness-raising programs undertaken by NGOs and faith-based organizations; and (2) regional policies strengthening cooperation in humanitarian assistance and disaster relief (HADR), which bring together the militaries in the region and relief agencies, civil society organizations, and international foundations. We also see the establishment of regional frameworks like the ASEAN Plus Three Emergency Rice Reserve agreement to ameliorate food shortages in times of crisis caused by factors like a sudden economic downturn and natural disasters. These measures are complemented by efforts and ideas advanced by academic and policy communities as well as NGOs to improve food policies across the region, mindful that these kinds of crises disproportionately impact on the more vulnerable communities in the region.

As to whether the region has become less insecure in the face of NTS challenges and whether we have changed the outcomes of human security in the region, my aim in this book is not to claim that the engagement of non-state actors with state actors has successfully resolved the complex problems and challenges related to ensuring health security, food security, or the human security of trafficked victims and refugees. What I have endeavored to do is to shed light and examine how the proliferation of "security actors" has advanced efforts to address and govern these issues and to argue that the mosaic of formal and informal governance processes are themselves works in progress that incrementally serve to advance human security without having to immediately yield definitive results. The book therefore recognizes the limitations of measuring the level of success while acknowledging this to be an important area for further research.

Trends in NTS Governance in East Asia

In this conclusion, I present a few brief observations on the trends, challenges, and practices of NTS governance in East Asia based on the case studies in this book.

Securitization Remains an Essential but Not Sufficient Means to Govern NTS Challenges

The process of securitization—framing an NTS issue as an existential threat to state and human security—remains an efficient means to convey the urgency of addressing a security threat and bring it to the attention of the national, regional, and international community. Securitization provides the logic as to why an NTS issue should be part of the agenda of security cooperation among states and the basis to rally support and participation from other actors within and outside the region.

Securitization helps governments work together through regional mechanisms. For example, ASEAN, ASEAN Plus Three, and the ASEAN Regional Forum could institute emergency measures to respond to a threat, including immediately allocating resources for disaster relief, or releasing vaccines from regional stockpiles in a health emergency, or rice during a food crisis. Securitization also justifies strong responses by states, such as compulsory temperature screening and quarantine to contain spread of diseases, border controls to stave off irregular migrants, and legal actions against those responsible for haze-causing forest fires.

While securitization helps to define the security agenda, it is neither a sustainable nor an optimal way to comprehensively address an NTS threat that cuts across other NTS issues. For instance, food insecurities and health emergencies are linked to climate change, but they are also associated with political decisions such as policies that favor export controls for food commodities at the expense of open trade and the failure of governments to strengthen public health systems. And, as noted earlier, structural factors such as poverty also define the kinds of risks and vulnerabilities facing different communities as well as their resilience capacity.

Thus, while securitization draws immediate attention to the seriousness of a food crisis or a pandemic outbreak and brings about the necessary mechanisms to organize and coordinate regional responses to the problem, this is only one part of the security-governance process. The immediate measures following securitization are often reactive and intense, for example, the imposition of travel restrictions during an infectious disease outbreak or the road-space rationing in times of heavy air pollution to curb car emissions. It is not realistic or necessary to sustain such measures for long.

To effectively address the impacts of NTS threats, it is equally important to consider the structural impediments that can aggravate the kinds of risks and challenges people face. Removing the impediments requires structural reforms that by nature involve incremental processes—for example, building the capacity of communities at risk, particularly vulnerable groups, to cope with NTS threats. This is where inputs from other actors to fill in policy gaps and address capacity deficits are critical.

The Nature of an NTS Issue Influences Governance

Regional security-governance frameworks serve as constitutive processes in shaping regional norms and security practices. However, these dynamic, interactive processes do not necessarily produce positive results in all cases. Successful governance of NTS issues would depend on how the material and the ideational variables are configured and whether there is a convergence of these factors in each of the NTS issues being dealt with. For instance, in the case study on migration, analyses show that, while there are regional frameworks for managing regular and irregular (forced) migration, the governance processes in place led to more contestation and even conflict among actors and affected communities. Many international and regional NGOs have criticized the approach often taken of criminalizing trafficking victims, who they argue need protection instead. There has also been discord within ASEAN on how Rohingya refugees and "boat people" have been dealt with. Similarly, despite states signing on to the ASEAN agreement on transboundary pollution, there has yet to be a year when the contiguous neighbors in the region are not affected by forest fires from Indonesia's Kalimantan and Sumatra provinces.

While one can expect that the norms of protection, prevention, and disaster preparedness would be promoted and institutionalized in the security practices of states through these regional frameworks, shared risks do not automatically translate to common interests and collective action. Certain domestic interests may trump regional interests, and balancing the two is often easier said than done. Moreover, in responding to transboundary NTS challenges, the countries concerned cooperate and coordinate based on respect for each other's sovereignty, which means there is a limit to the extent of one government's involvement in the NTS governance of another country unless consent is granted by the host government. Singapore passed a law in 2014 that allows the government to punish companies that, through indiscriminate burning in Indonesia, cause the forest fires that lead to serious haze in Singapore, but sovereignty impedes enforcement of that law. Singapore foreign minister Vivian Balakrishnan explicitly stated that the law is to complement rather than replace the laws and activities of other countries.[2]

Success in advancing human security norms is therefore uneven, despite member states adopting the ASEAN Political–Security Community framework, which specifies as one of its aims the goal of strengthening regional cooperation on NTS challenges. There is more cooperation on less contentious and more urgent issues like pandemics and large-scale disasters than in managing human trafficking and refugees. Similarly, the implementation of the haze agreement is complicated by the lack of capacity and the conflicting national interests. Complexity, capacity, and interest all play a role in the progress and success of NTS governance. However, acknowledging the variations in progress does not mean that the governance processes are not in place. I would argue that despite challenges in achieving the desired results, it is nonetheless important to capture these dynamic processes of security governance to be able to understand the future of the region's security landscape.

States Take the Lead in Setting Agendas and Policy Responses

That NTS governance involves multiple actors from a variety of sectors indicates the necessity of leadership to ensure the activities of different actors are coordinated and synergies in governance achieved. In East Asia, states take the lead in setting out the security agenda, crafting domestic policies and frameworks, allocating resources, and issuing declarations to respond to a security threat. While NTS challenges have transboundary reach, the principle of state sovereignty still largely defines national policy responses and regional and international efforts in this area. Sovereignty constitutes the primary source of the authority of national governments as security actors and legitimizes their status as the lead security governor. For instance, the Responsibility to Protect norm emphasizes that the state has primary responsibility for protecting its population from four types of mass atrocities. The Hyogo Framework for Action 2005–2015 also recognizes that the state holds primary responsibility in disaster response and relief. In addition, national governments set the laws and regulations that govern the activities of other actors such as intergovernmental organizations and NGOs in their territories. When an NTS threat unfolds, a national framework guides the response and outlines the roles and responsibilities as well as the procedures for different actors to get involved.

This is not to say that security governance that is participatory and inclusive does not exist in East Asia. Regional and international organizations play a major role at the regional and national levels, but their involvement is shaped by the principle of sovereignty. ASEAN and its related regional frameworks facilitate the mobilization of financial and human resources in times of need, but the focus is on providing support and complementing the efforts at the national level rather than replacing them. An official request by the affected state for assistance is required before regional and international actors can go in and help. Recognition and appreciation of the necessity of this procedure facilitate provision and acceptance of external assistance and support. For instance, it is clearly stated in the Emergency Response Framework of the World Health Organization that the organization should "negotiate access and clearances with the government . . . on behalf of health sector partners" in the event of an outbreak of a health emergency.[3] For challenges with transboundary implications, regional organizations provide the framework for interstate and multistakeholder cooperation and coordination. This general trend has translated into tangible results in specific issue areas. For instance, the ASEAN Coordinating Centre for Humanitarian Assistance on Disaster Management (AHA Centre) was established in 2011 to facilitate information exchange and updates among member states and partners as well as to coordinate the region's humanitarian efforts.

Spaces have opened up for other non-state actors to provide support, contribute ideas, and offer assistance to affected communities. During the SARS and H5N1 health crises in Indonesia, for instance, while the government set out the policies to contain disease spread, it was the civil society organizations and faith-based groups in the country that translated those policies into community-level activities. The groups helped raise awareness of the disease, disseminated critical information on disease prevention and treatment, and taught local communities how to handle infected poultry.

While non-state actors make important contributions to dealing with NTS challenges, they need to coordinate their activities with the national policies and frameworks of the host country. For instance, in disaster response, foreign NGOs need to align their provision of assistance with the government-led response, to avoid gaps and duplication.

Regional Institutions Matter

Despite the existence of bilateral tensions and many serious problems that affect cooperation among states in the region, it has become even more important for governments to work together and collectively respond to the many transnational NTS challenges facing the region. There has been significant progress. Several regional frameworks for regional cooperation on NTS issues have been established: ASEAN, the ASEAN Regional Forum, ASEAN Plus Three, the ASEAN Defence Ministers' Meeting (ADMM) and ADMM-Plus, among others. This reflects the value that states place on regional institutions.

As demonstrated across the case studies in this book, ASEAN has taken the lead in creating many of the regional frameworks to respond to specific

NTS challenges. ASEAN health officials are spearheading efforts to fight infectious diseases; the environment and forestry officials deal with managing forest fires; committees on migrant workers and the protection of women and children deal with issues of labor migration and human trafficking; the committee on disaster management and climate change as well as energy officials deal with nuclear security issues; and agriculture and forestry officials deal with food security. The work of these ASEAN sectoral bodies is reflected, as discussed in the preceding chapters, in a range of agreements and frameworks, including an emerging infectious diseases framework and an emergency rice reserve as well as agreements on tackling transboundary air pollution, trafficking in persons, and disaster management and emergency relief.

The emergence of these regional frameworks offers a number of benefits to the member states of ASEAN and its Plus Three partners, China, Japan, and South Korea. First, these regional frameworks facilitate assistance to members in addressing NTS problems. The assistance comes in many forms: direct financial support, human resources training, technical support, and use of military assets in times of natural disasters like typhoons and forest fires. Second, these frameworks provide a common platform for knowledge sharing and information exchange. During the SARS and the H5N1 outbreaks, joint efforts on information exchange, sharing of expertise and good practices, laboratory and diagnostic support, and outbreak investigation proved extremely useful in preventing the spread and tackling future outbreaks. Third, these frameworks allow for joint and coordinated regional responses and cooperation in times of humanitarian crises. After the Indian Ocean tsunami experience, there are now more efforts to provide coordinated and immediate assistance and disaster relief to states hit by natural disasters. Aside from establishing the AHA Centre as the regional coordinator for HADR operations, ASEAN holds disaster emergency response simulation exercises annually, and the ASEAN Regional Forum holds them biannually. These exercises are not limited to representatives from member states' national disaster management offices but also bring in participants from international humanitarian bodies like the UN Office for the Coordination of Humanitarian Affairs, the UN Development Programme, the Office of the United Nations High Commissioner for Refugees (UNHCR), the International Committee of the Red Cross, local and regional civil society organizations, and local NGOs. Militaries in the region are also involved in these exercises. Aside from the important objective of improving coordination among the many actors in large-scale humanitarian response, these exercises also help develop capacity, raise standards, set common standards in operating procedures, and strengthen regional disaster management capacity and interoperability.

Finally, these regional frameworks, by promoting inclusivity and habits of dialogue, have helped build confidence and trust among East Asian states. While Northeast Asia lacks any formal institutions similar to ASEAN, China, Japan, and South Korea engage in ad hoc cooperative activities in times of NTS emergencies. During China's Sichuan earthquake in 2008, the Japanese government sent a search-and-rescue team and a medical team. China was among the first countries to send a rescue team after the Great East Japan earthquake in 2011. To a certain extent, the centrality of ASEAN facilitates communication with the Northeast Asian countries as the ASEAN Plus mechanisms open channels for ASEAN countries and their dialogue partners to work together on a range of NTS issues. Put together, these regional efforts foster and deepen regional cooperation and advance security governance.

The engagement between and among states within regional frameworks and between state and non-state actors points to an important feature of the security governance of NTS in the region: in an increasingly interconnected and integrated region, states have been compelled to reach out to one another, cognizant of the fact that unilateral policies and responses are not sufficient to address the crosscutting impact of any one of the NTS challenges that threaten their states and societies. The motivations driving states to work together—by sharing information and through compulsory reporting in addressing pandemics, by committing to enforce national laws to prevent transboundary pollution, and by consenting to outside "intervention" or help in times of humanitarian disasters despite the implications for the principles of sovereignty and noninterference—are salient features of security governance and regionalism that are often missed in the narrow approaches of security through power and competition.

Indeed, what makes the story of "ASEAN in East Asia" and "East Asia through ASEAN" worth telling is that while many security analysts still talk about the underinstitutionalization of Asia compared to Europe, there in fact exists a myriad of frameworks and processes that are not limited to state-led institutions but also include non-state actors. What is therefore instructive in the experiences of ASEAN and wider East Asia is that while Westphalian norms are sacrosanct, flexibility is possible when there are shared vulnerabilities and recognition of collective responsibility. These are illustrated when regional measures that are inherently intrusive, such as sharing information on hotspots of forest fires, implementing compulsory reporting of disease outbreaks, promoting transparency by sharing nuclear policies, and allowing access for humanitarian assistance, have been adopted.

Non-State Actors as Security Governors

Non-state actors include a swathe of different groups ranging from local community groups, NGOs, civil society organizations, and international NGOs to private companies, business chambers, and private foundations as well as think tanks. As discussed in the NTS cases in this book, non-state actors play a highly significant role, engaging with state and other actors and participating in the multiple governance processes that are taking place at different levels. How they carry out their security-governance roles is often defined by their respective attributes, capacities, and the bases of their legitimacy. The variety of the non-state actors presents a large pool of different resources and capabilities for NTS governance. Three particular strengths enable non-state actors to complement NTS governance by state actors: capabilities in terms of resources, skills, technologies, and knowledge; access to the people and communities in need; and public trust.

Agenda Setting

With their expert knowledge and linkages with governments, epistemic communities (represented by think tanks and research institutions) have made important contributions in helping shape the agenda of regional cooperation on a number of NTS issues. For example, in the drive to improve disaster preparedness and HADR operations, the Track 2 Network of ASEAN Defense and Security Institutions (NADI) has provided a forum for security and defense analysts, and practitioners to discuss issues of military-to-military cooperation, interoperability, and military–civilian relations. These important deliberations in a non-official environment help generate policy recommendations for ADMM, ADMM-Plus, and the ASEAN Regional Forum, which are the regional platforms for HADR operations. Meanwhile, the Centre for Non-Traditional Security

Studies (NTS Centre) at the S. Rajaratnam School of International Studies in Singapore has been actively engaged in helping the ASEAN Secretariat and the AHA Centre craft the post-2015 agenda for AADMER, the cornerstone of the HADR framework in ASEAN. Among the issues and policy agenda identified in the new AADMER workplan are how best to institutionalize AADMER and the AHA Centre as the core frameworks of regional HADR cooperation and measures to improve coordination among the many humanitarian actors involved in HADR operations. The recommendations include ideas to improve finance and resource mobilization, build partnerships with a range of stakeholders, find innovative ways to draw on local knowledge, and strengthen the capacity of civil society organizations who work directly with affected communities.

Promoting Norms and Best Practices

Civil society organizations and NGOs have been important actors in pushing governments to observe the norm of protection. As discussed in chapter 5, civil society groups like the Asia Pacific Refugee Rights Network have worked with international organizations like the International Organization for Migration and UNHCR to pressure states to observe and implement the norm of protection for all people on the move, including refugees and displaced populations. Equally important is their advocacy for a more human-centric approach to migration by focusing on providing protection, particularly for vulnerable groups and communities. Local NGOs also help educate workers about their rights and responsibilities as well as increase their awareness of the risks involved in being a foreign migrant worker.

While Greenpeace and the World Wide Fund for Nature work with local NGOs in Indonesia on efforts to monitor forest fires, the Roundtable on Sustainable Palm Oil sets standards and criteria for palm oil companies to minimize the environmental and social costs of palm oil production. Environmental NGOs in China are also working to get big companies to release information on pollution in order to reduce emission of wastes. As part of this push, one NGO publishes annual evaluations of the environmental performance of big foreign and domestic companies. Such certification and evaluation processes by NGOs essentially promote sustainable production and consumption.

Civil society is also a driving force for improvements in the governing performance of states. Environmental NGOs in the region have called for greater transparency, such as better access to information related to environmental insecurities. There has been some progress made. For example, the Beijing municipal government began releasing data on toxic air pollutants in 2012.[4] Representatives of different NTS governors in the region also adopted the Jakarta Declaration for Strengthening the Right to Environmental Information for People and the Environment in May 2013.[5] The various activities by non-state actors serve to encourage and even compel governments, corporate actors, and other stakeholders to adopt good practices.

Building Capacity

Lack of knowledge on local conditions, poor understanding of people's interests and concerns, and low cultural sensitivity result in a mismatch between the assistance and support provided and a community's needs, leading to ineffective governance. This was seen in the disaster response to the 2015 Nepal earthquake, where some food items that were distributed to victims contained beef, which is against the religious practices of the Nepali communities.[6] Civil society groups that are familiar with local context and maintain good access to people at the local level are in a better position to assess local risks and gaps in capacity. Muhammadiyah, a faith-based organization with extensive presence across Indonesia and strong ability to mobilize people, serves as a good example. Local NGOs and civil society groups may also be more effective as they have gained public trust through their activities that contribute to public good, and that trust enhances people's reception of NGO assistance and support.

Local communities should be empowered to play a role in disaster management and response. They are usually the immediate source of early-warning signs and the first to be on the scene helping those affected by a disaster; they are also more committed to long-term reconstruction and preparedness. Their role is particularly important in emergencies and small disasters that do not catch headlines but leave people affected, and when, due to limitations in its resources and capabilities, the government may not be able to act as swiftly and effectively as in large disasters.

Working closely with local communities, civil society groups and NGOs come in and provide the critical intervention in areas that are either missed or overlooked by government or intergovernmental mechanisms. For instance, people residing in slums are more vulnerable in the face of extreme weather and natural disasters due to the packed living conditions. It is critical that evacuation routes are planned in advance and residents are informed about evacuation procedures as well as self-rescue skills. However, the governments of many developing countries are too stretched by the many challenges to place sufficient emphasis on the needs of all communities. NGOs like Mercy Relief have stepped into this gap and have implemented activities to build the capacity of vulnerable communities in disaster preparedness. In Indonesia, Muhammadiyah responded to the threat of infectious diseases by providing training to communities and strengthening surveillance at the local level.

As we have seen from the case studies in this book, philanthropic foundations, multinational corporations, and international NGOs are a significant source of support. They help fund responses to natural disasters and climate change, control and treatment of infectious diseases, and environmental protection. In times of natural disasters, the private sector provides the much-needed financial, logistical, and technical support for HADR. For instance, power companies and communications providers play a critical role in the early stage of disaster response as they help restore and maintain electricity supply and communication systems for rescue and relief efforts. Multinational pharmaceutical companies like GlaxoSmithKline and Tekmira Pharmaceuticals have been involved in developing vaccines for Ebola, while companies like AgFunder and Syngenta have helped prototype and mainstream technologies to help farmers address problems of food production caused by climate change.

The visible engagement of non-state actors as de facto security actors and part of the patterns of security-governance processes that are defining the broader East Asia's regional security architecture constitutes, for all intents and purposes, the normative impulses that change state behavior and recalibrate norms toward achieving human security.

The Expanding Role of Military Actors

The involvement of the military in NTS governance is important but delicate. The traditional role of military forces is to defend sovereignty and territorial integrity from external military threats. But with the emergence of NTS threats, there has been a push to expand their mission, and the importance of noncombat missions have increased. The unique characteristics of disaster response makes this the NTS issue area that sees a bigger role for the military than other areas. The military is often the primary responder in the immediate aftermath of disasters. It commands certain resources and capabilities not available to other security governors, including the civilian government. In the immediate aftermath of the Sichuan earthquake in 2008, for example, many parts of the disaster zone were inaccessible as roads and bridges were blocked or destroyed, seriously hampering HADR operations. Soldiers were deployed and parachuted into certain areas to open access.[7]

Noncombat operations like disaster rescue and relief have become a regular mission of the military in many countries. China's 2009 defense white paper lists it as a component of the People's Liberation Army missions. In the Philippines, in the post-Haiyan period, each of the three forces of the Armed Forces of the Philippines has dedicated a battalion for HADR. Military cycles in the Philippines are also planned according to weather threats.

Despite the growing recognition of the importance of noncombat operations, there remain serious reservations and sensitivity among humanitarian actors regarding the involvement of the military beyond their primary mission of national defense. For example, the Nepali authorities were disconcerted when, in the midst of HADR operations after the 2015 Nepal earthquake, the local government lost contact with some foreign military teams for a period of time.[8] Preestablished procedures and rules for the involvement of the military in NTS governance are therefore necessary as a guard against unintended complications. There is also the concern that military involvement leads to the militarization of the NTS issue and brings it into the more sensitive domain of traditional security. It is therefore essential to clarify key issues concerning the role of the military in NTS governance, such as the exit procedures and the relationship with the civilian government and the coordination mechanism.

Preparing for Future Disruptors

One other critical message of this book is to underscore the need for the international community to be prepared for future disruptors. The world is now dealing with many unknowns, and states and communities have had to grapple with the phenomena of new normals. News about hurricanes, typhoons, floods, and prolonged drought show how much more devastation and immense suffering are in the offing as the global climate changes and brings more catastrophic impact. After the region's experience with the SARS pandemic, the global health community has also been vigilant about the next big shoe to drop. These are not standalone security challenges.

Against the prospects of an increasingly complex security environment, the need to ensure sustainable development has become more compelling than ever. This also means that we need to bring back the imperatives of human security to strengthen preparedness and societal resilience and promote anticipatory adaptation to manage climate change; deepen regional and international multilateral cooperation and build more partnerships; and foster more global compacts to advance security governance at all levels.

Technological innovation has had a significant impact on NTS governance. The application of technologies in HADR operations and the use of social media have made it easier to provide updated information and data in such areas as disaster early warning and response, disease control, and pollution regulation as well as easier to share them widely. Meanwhile, the increasing pace of automation continues to affect the job market, and this has raised new anxieties about widening inequality, marginalization, and alienation. It is therefore important for NTS governance to keep pace with advancements in technology and the accompanying challenges.

Two decades ago, R. A. W. Rhodes introduced the idea of "governance without government."[9] He argued that *governance* brings state and non-state actors together through shared goals, in contrast to *government*, which is backed by formal authority. The case studies in this book suggest the increasing salience of the notion of governance through shared goals in East Asia, given the proliferation of actors involved in NTS governance. These security governors contribute their respective strengths—including material and ideational resources, unique capabilities, and expert knowledge—to the region's multigovernance processes. East Asian security actors have shown that their collective efforts provide the critical building blocks for moving security governance to meet future global challenges ahead.

Notes

1. Security Governance in Southeast Asia and Beyond

1. ASEAN was established in August 1967. Regarded as one of the most successful regional organizations in the world, it is a significant actor in managing regional security in East Asia.

2. United Nations General Assembly, "In Larger Freedom: Towards Development, Security and Human Rights for All" (A/59/2005, March 21, 2005).

3. Deborah D. Avant, Martha Finnemore, and Susan K. Sell, eds., *Who Governs the Globe?* (New York: Cambridge University Press, 2010), 2.

4. Robert Keohane, *International Institutions and State Power: Essays in International Relations Theory* (Boulder, Colo.: Westview Press, 1989).

5. See Michael J. Green and Bates Gill, eds., *Asia's New Multilateralism: Cooperation, Competition, and the Search for Community* (New York: Columbia University Press, 2009), 12.

6. Cited in See Seng Tan, introduction to *Do Institutions Matter? Regional Institutions and Regionalism in East Asia*, ed. See Seng Tan (Singapore: S. Rajaratnam School of International Studies, 2008), 1.

7. Barry Buzan, Ole Waever, and Jaap de Wilde, *Security: A New Framework for Analysis* (Boulder, Colo.: Lynne Rienner, 1998), 2.

8. Barry Buzan, *People, States and Fear: An Agenda for International Security Studies in the Post-Cold War Era*, 2nd ed. (Hemel Hempstead, U.K.: Harvester Wheatsheaf, 1991), 131.

9. Graeme Cheeseman, "Asia-Pacific Security Discourse in the Wake of the Asian Economic Crisis," *Pacific Review* 12, no. 3 (1999): 336.

10. Alexis McGinnes, "The Human Face of the Asian Financial Crisis in Malaysia and Indonesia," *Swords and Ploughshares: A Journal of International Affairs* (Spring 2003): 45–58.

11. Ralf Emmers and John Ravenhill, "The Asian and Global Financial Crises: Consequences for East Asian Regionalism" (working paper, Singapore: S. Rajaratnam School of International Studies, 2010), 3; and Joseph Y. S. Cheng, "Broadening the Concept of Security in East and Southeast Asia: The Impact of the Asian Financial Crisis and the September 11 Incident," *Journal of Contemporary China* 15, no. 46 (2006): 92. See also Mely Caballero-Anthony, "Revisioning Human Security in Southeast Asia," *Asian Perspective* 28, no. 3 (2006): 155–89.

12. See also Denis Hew, "Economic Integration in East Asia: An ASEAN Perspective" (Madrid: Research Unit on International Security and Cooperation, University of Madrid, 2006), 55–56.

13. Mely Caballero-Anthony, "SARS in Asia: Crisis, Vulnerabilities, and Regional Responses," *Asian Survey* 45, no. 3 (2005): 475–95.

14. Elke Krahmann, "Conceptualizing Security Governance," *Cooperation and Conflict: Journal of the Nordic International Studies Association* 38, no. 1 (2003): 16.

15. Buzan, Waever, and de Wilde, *Security*; and Avant, Finnemore, and Sell, *Who Governs the Globe?*

16. Arnold Wolfers, " 'National Security' as an Ambiguous Symbol," *Political Science Quarterly* 67, no. 4 (1952): 485, cited in David A. Baldwin, "The Concept of Security," *Review of International Studies* 23, no. 1 (1997): 13.

17. Buzan, Waever, and de Wilde, *Security*, 2. For a detailed discussion on different understandings of security, see Steve Smith, "The Contested Concept of Security," in *Critical Security Studies and World Politics*, ed. Ken Booth (Boulder, Colo.: Lynne Rienner, 2005). See also Mely Caballero-Anthony, ed., *An Introduction to Non-Traditional Security Studies: A Transnational Approach* (London: Sage, 2016).

18. Buzan, *People, States and Fear*. The 1983 edition is titled *People, States and Fear: The National Security Problem in International Relations*, published by the Copenhagen School of Security Studies.

19. United Nations Development Programme (UNDP), *Human Development Report 1994* (New York: Oxford University Press, 1994).

20. See Mely Caballero-Anthony and Alistair Cook, eds., *Non-Traditional Security in Asia: Issues, Challenges and Frameworks for Action* (Singapore: Institute of Southeast Asian Studies, 2013).

21. Tsuneo Akaha, "Non-Traditional Security Cooperation for Regionalism in Northeast Asia," in *Broadening Asia's Security Discourse and Agenda: Political and Environmental Perspectives*, ed. Ramesh Thakur and Edward Newman (Tokyo: United Nations University, 2004), 306–39.

22. See Caballero-Anthony and Cook, *Non-Traditional Security in Asia*.

23. Andrew Jacobs, "Typhoon Response Highlights Weaknesses in Philippine Military," *New York Times*, November 19, 2013, http://www.nytimes.com/2013/11/20/world/asia/typhoon-response-highlights-weaknesses-in-philippine-military.html?page wanted=all.

24. Melissa Leach, "The Ebola Crisis and Post-2015 Development," *Journal of International Development* 27, no. 6 (2015): 816–34.

25. Elke Krahmann, "National, Regional and Global Governance: One Phenomenon or Many?," *Global Governance* 9, no. 3 (2003): 325.

26. S. E. Finer, *Comparative Government* (London: Allen Lane / Penguin, 1970), cited in R. A. W. Rhodes, "The New Governance: Governing Without Government," *Political Studies* 44, no. 4 (1996): 652.

27. Jan Kooiman, "Social-Political Governance: Introduction," in *Modern Governance*, ed. Jan Kooiman (London: Sage, 1993), cited in Rhodes, "The New Governance," 657.

28. James N. Rosenau, "Governance in the Twenty-First Century," *Global Governance* 1, no. 1 (1995): 14.

29. Krahmann, "National, Regional and Global Governance," 329.

30. Avant, Finnemore, and Sell, *Who Governs the Globe?*; Ramesh Thakur and Thomas G. Weiss, "United Nations 'Policy': An Argument with Three Illustrations," *International Studies Perspectives* 10, no. 1 (2009): 18–35; and Rosenau, "Governance in the Twenty-First Century," 14.

31. See Krahmann, "Conceptualizing Security Governance," 11.

32. Heiner Hänggi, "Making Sense of Security Sector Governance," in *Challenges of Security Sector Governance*, ed. Heiner Hänggi and Theodor Winkler (Munster: LIT Verlag, 2004), 8.

33. Daniel Flemes and Michael Radseck, "Creating Multilevel Security Governance in South America" (working paper, Hamburg: German Institute of Global and Area Studies, December 2009), 7.

34. Deborah D. Avant, Martha Finnemore, and Susan K. Sell, "Who Governs the Globe?," in *Who Governs the Globe?*, ed. Deborah D. Avant, Martha Finnemore, and Susan K. Sell (New York: Cambridge University Press, 2010), 1–32.

35. For a detailed discussion on securitization, see Buzan, Waever, and de Wilde, *Security*. See also Mely Caballero-Anthony and Ralf Emmers, "The Dynamics of Securitization in Asia," in *Studying Non-Traditional Security in Asia: Trends and Issues*, ed. Ralf Emmers, Mely Caballero-Anthony, and Amitav Acharya (Singapore: Marshall Cavendish, 2006), 21–35.

36. Anne Roemer-Mahler and Stefan Elbe, "The Race for Ebola Drugs: Pharmaceuticals, Security, and Global Health Governance," *Third World Quarterly* 37, no. 3 (2016): 494–95.

37. See International Commission on Intervention and State Sovereignty, *The Responsibility to Protect: Report of the International Commission on Intervention and State Sovereignty* (Ottawa: International Development Research Centre, 2001).

38. In normal cases, it would be unethical to use experimental drugs or treatments on patients without prior human tests. See Roemer-Mahler and Elbe, "The Race for Ebola Drugs," 489.

39. James Sperling, "Governance and Security in the Twenty-First Century," in *Handbook of Governance and Security*, ed. James Sperling (Cheltenham, U.K.: Edward Elgar, 2014), 9; and Marie-Claude Smouts, "The Proper Use of Governance in International Relations," *International Social Science Journal* 50, no. 155 (1998): 87, cited in Mark

Webber, "Security Governance," in *Handbook of Governance and Security*, ed. James Sperling (Cheltenham, U.K.: Edward Elgar, 2014), 20.

40. Buzan, Waever, and de Wilde, *Security*, 28.

41. Yanzhong Huang, "China's Response to the 2014 Ebola Outbreak in West Africa," *Global Challenges* 1, no. 2 (2017): 1.

42. "Typhoon Haiyan: Philippines Declares State of Calamity," *BBC News*, November 12, 2013, http://www.bbc.com/news/world-asia-24901993.

43. For Asian debates on human security, see, for example, Caballero-Anthony, "Revisioning Human Security in Southeast Asia"; William Tow, Ramesh Thakur, and In-Taek Hyun, eds., *Asia's Emerging Regional Order* (Tokyo: United Nations University Press, 2000); Japan Institute of International Affairs, *In Quest of Human Security* (Tokyo: JIIA, 2001); and Pranee Thiparat, ed., *The Quest for Human Security: The Next Phase of ASEAN?* (Bangkok: Institute of Security and International Studies, 2001). For works on the general topic on human security, see Fen Osler Hampson, Jean Daudelin, John B. Hay, Todd Martin, and Holly Reid, *Madness in the Multitude: Human Security and World Disorder* (Oxford: Oxford University Press, 2002); and Jennifer Leaning and Sam Arie, "Human Security: A Framework for Assessment in Conflict and Transition" (working paper, Cambridge, Mass.: Harvard Center for Population and Development Studies, September 2001).

44. United Nations, "Goal 2: End Hunger, Achieve Food Security and Improved Nutrition and Promote Sustainable Agriculture," *Sustainable Development Goals*, undated, accessed June 25, 2017, http://www.un.org/sustainabledevelopment/hunger/.

45. Security essentially refers to "safety from the constant threats of hunger, disease, crime and repression." It also means "protection from sudden and hurtful disruptions in the pattern of our daily lives—whether in our homes, in our jobs,in our communities or in our environment." UNDP, *Human Development Report 1994*, 3.

46. Buzan, Waever, and de Wilde, *Security*, 36.

47. Roland Paris, "Human Security: Paradigm Shift or Hot Air?," *International Security* 26, no. 2 (2001): 102.

48. Smith, "The Contested Concept of Security," 32.

49. United Nations General Assembly, "Securing Peace and Development: The Role of the United Nations in Supporting Security Sector Reform" (A/62/659–S/2008/39, January 23, 2008).

50. Mark Beeson and Alex J. Bellamy, *Securing Southeast Asia: The Politics of Security Sector Reform* (Oxon, U.K.: Routledge, 2008).

51. Tine Hanrieder and Christian Kreuder-Sonnen, "WHO Decides on the Exception? Securitization and Emergency Governance in Global Health," *Security Dialogue* 45, no. 4 (2014): 337.

52. Alistair D. B. Cook, Maxim Shreshta and Zin Bo Htet, "The 2015 Nepal Earthquake: Implications for Future International Relief Efforts" (Singapore: S. Rajaratnam School of International Studies, 2016).

53. World Health Organization (WHO), "Barriers to Rapid Containment of the Ebola Outbreak," August 11, 2014, http://www.who.int/csr/disease/ebola/overview-august -2014/en/.

54. Julius Cesar I. Trajano, "Building Resilience from Within: Enhancing Humanitarian Civil–Military Coordination in Post-Haiyan Philippines" (Singapore: S. Rajaratnam School of International Studies, December 2016), 12–16.

55. Peter M. Haas, "Introduction: Epistemic Communities and International Policy Coordination," *International Organization* 46, no. 1 (1992): 1–35.

56. Diane Stone, "The 'Policy Research' Knowledge Elite and Global Policy Processes," in *Non-State Actors in World Politics*, ed. Daphne Josselin and William Wallace (Hampshire, U.K.: Palgrave, 2001), 124.

2. State and Non-State Actors and NTS Governance in Southeast Asia and Beyond

1. Different dichotomies have been used to describe actors of governance: state versus non-state; governmental versus nongovernmental; public versus private. The former part of the dichotomies generally represents the category that is official and formal, and the latter refers to the informal. While there are differences between non-state, nongovernmental, and private actors, the three concepts largely converge at the point that their authorities for governance are based outside the traditional domain created by the Westphalian sovereignty.

2. Rodney Bruce Hall and Thomas J. Biersteker, "The Emergence of Private Authority in the International System," in *The Emergence of Private Authority in Global Governance*, ed. Rodney Bruce Hall and Thomas J. Biersteker (Cambridge: Cambridge University Press, 2002), 4; and Elke Krahmann, "Conceptualizing Security Governance," *Cooperation and Conflict: Journal of the Nordic International Studies Association* 38, no. 1 (2003): 5–26.

3. Deborah D. Avant, Martha Finnemore, and Susan K. Sell, "Who Governs the Globe?," in *Who Governs the Globe?*, ed. Deborah D. Avant, Martha Finnemore, and Susan K. Sell (New York: Cambridge University Press, 2010), 8.

4. Hall and Biersteker, "The Emergence of Private Authority in the International System," 3; and Richard A. Higgott, Geoffrey R. D. Underhill, and Andreas Bieler, "Introduction: Globalisation and Non-State Actors," in *Non-State Actors and Authority in the Global System*, ed. Richard A. Higgott, Geoffrey R. D. Underhill, and Andreas Bieler (London: Routledge, 2000), 1.

5. James Sperling, "Regional Security Governance," in *Handbook of Governance and Security*, ed. James Sperling (Cheltenham: Edward Elgar, 2014), 98. The United Nations emphasizes the importance of regional efforts: The Security Council has held annual meetings to discuss cooperation between the United Nations and regional and subregional organizations in the maintenance of international peace and security since 2003. Former UN secretary-general Ban Ki-moon devoted the annual report on implementing the Responsibility to Protect in 2011 to affirming the role of regional and subregional arrangements, in United Nations General Assembly, "The Role of Regional and Sub-Regional Arrangements in Implementing the Responsibility to Protect" (A/65/877–S/2011/393, June 27, 2011).

6. James Sperling, "State Attributes and System Properties: Security Multilateralism in Central Asia, Southeast Asia, the Atlantic and Europe," in *Multilateralism and Security Institutions in an Era of Globalization*, ed. Dimitris Bourantonis, Kostas Ifantis, and Panayotis Tsakonas (London: Routledge, 2008), 102–3.

7. See Krahmann, "Conceptualizing Security Governance"; Avant, Finnemore, and Sell, "Who Governs the Globe?"; David Held, "The Diffusion of Authority," in *International Organization and Global Governance*, ed. Thomas G. Weiss and Rorden Wilkinson (Abingdon: Routledge, 2014), 60–72; Higgott, Underhill, and Bieler, "Introduction: Globalisation and Non-State Actors"; and Emil J. Kirchner, "Regional and Global Security: Changing Threats and Institutional Responses," in *Global Security Governance: Competing Perceptions of Security in the 21st Century*, ed. Emil J. Kirchner and James Sperling (London: Routledge, 2007).

8. See, for example, Baogang He, *Contested Ideas of Regionalism in Asia* (London: Routledge, 2016); Hiro Katsumata, "East Asian Regional Security Governance: Bilateral Balancing and ASEAN's Informal Cooperative Security," in *Comparative Regional Security Governance*, ed. Shaun Breslin and Stuart Croft (London: Routledge, 2012); and Anja Jetschke, "Is ASEAN a Provider of Regional Security Governance?" (Hamburg: German Institute of Global and Area Studies, 2011).

9. Erin Zimmerman, *Think Tanks and Non-Traditional Security: Governance Entrepreneurs in Asia* (Hampshire, U.K.: Palgrave Macmillan, 2016); and Shahar Hameiri and Lee Jones, *Governing Borderless Threats: Non-Traditional Security and the Politics of State Transformation* (Cambridge: Cambridge University Press, 2015).

10. Nicolas Carrillo Santarelli, "Nonstate Actors," *Oxford Bibliographies*, modified July 24, 2013, http://www.oxfordbibliographies.com/view/document/obo-9780199796953/obo-9780199796953-0085.xml.

11. Thomas G. Weiss, D. Conor Seyle, and Kelsey Coolidge, "The Rise of Non-State Actors in Global Governance: Opportunities and Limitations" (Broomfield, Colo.: One Earth Future Foundation, 2013), 7.

12. Daphne Josselin and William Wallace, "Non-State Actors in World Politics: A Framework," in *Non-State Actors in World Politics*, ed. Daphne Josselin and William Wallace (New York: Palgrave, 2001), 3–4.

13. Avant, Finnemore, and Sell, "Who Governs the Globe?," 1.

14. Johanna Hanefeld, "Global Fund to Fight AIDS, Tuberculosis, and Malaria," in *Handbook of Transnational Governance: Institutions and Innovations*, ed. Thomas Hale and David Held (Oxford: Polity, 2011), 161–2.

15. Catia Gregoratti, "UN–Business Partnerships," in *Handbook of Transnational Governance: Institutions and Innovations*, ed. Thomas Hale and David Held (Oxford: Polity, 2011), 309.

16. Higgott, Underhill, and Bieler, "Introduction: Globalisation and Non-State Actors," 1–2.

17. Chris Buckley, "Uncertainty over New Chinese Law Rattles Foreign Nonprofits," *New York Times*, December 29, 2016, https://www.nytimes.com/2016/12/29/world/asia/china-foreign-ngo.html.

18. Cambodia adopted a law in 2015 that requires NGOs to register with and report annually to the authorities. Laos issued a series of decrees in 2014 to supervise the activities of overseas NGOs in the country. In 2017, Indonesia adopted a regulation that expedites the banning or disbanding of organizations, such as radical Islamic groups, that promote ideals that are contrary to the state ideology Pancasila. Prominent Muslim organizations like Muhammadiyah and the Nahdlatul Ulama gave their support to the regulation, while some NGOs expressed concern. Amnesty International said that the regulation will only "impose restrictions on freedom of association, expression, thought, conscience and religion." See, respectively, Harriet Sherwood, "Human Rights Groups Face Global Crackdown 'Not Seen in a Generation,'" *Guardian*, August 26, 2015, https://www.theguardian.com/law/2015/aug/26/ngos-face-restrictions-laws-human-rights-generation; Erin Hale and Aleksander Solum, "Laos NGO Restrictions Threaten Development, Say Non-Profit Groups," *South China Morning Post*, September 17, 2014, http://www.scmp.com/news/asia/article/1594490/laos-ngo-restrictions-threaten-development-say-non-profit-groups; Alin Almanar et al., "Gov't Issues Perppu to Expedite Disbanding of Anti-Pancasila Organizations, Including HTI," *Jakarta Globe* (Indonesia), July 12, 2017, http://jakartaglobe.id/news/govt-issues-perppu-expedite-disbanding-anti-pancasila-organizations-including-hti/; and Amnesty International, "Indonesia: Amendment of the Mass Organizations Law Expands Threats to the Freedom of Association" (public statement, ASA 21/6722/2017, July 12, 2017).

19. Save the Children, *Save the Children in China: 2013 Annual Review* (Beijing: Save the Children in China, 2013).

20. Josselin and Wallace, "Non-State Actors in World Politics," 3–4.

21. Kendall Stiles, "Grassroots Empowerment: States, Non-State Actors and Global Policy Formulation," in *Non-State Actors and Authority in the Global System*, ed. Richard A. Higgott, Geoffrey R. D. Underhill, and Andreas Bieler (London: Routledge, 2000).

22. Muhammad Yunus, "Economic Security for a World in Crisis," *World Policy Institute* 26, no. 2 (2009): 9.

23. Held, "The Diffusion of Authority," 64.

24. Julius Cesar I. Trajano, "Building Resilience from Within: Enhancing Humanitarian Civil-Military Coordination in Post-Haiyan Philippines" (Singapore: S. Rajaratnam School of International Studies, 2016), 12–16.

25. Kenneth W. Abbott and Duncan Snidal, "The Governance Triangle: Regulatory Standards Institutions and the Shadow of the State," in *The Politics of Global Regulation*, ed. Walter Mattli and Ngaire Woods (Princeton, N.J.: Princeton University Press, 2009), 44–88.

26. Mely Caballero-Anthony, "Non-State Regional Governance Mechanism for Economic Security: The Case of the ASEAN People's Assembly," *Pacific Review* 17, no. 4 (2004): 567–85.

27. Avant, Finnemore, and Sell, "Who Governs the Globe?," 1.

28. Diane Coleman, "Policy Networks, Non-State Actors, and Internationalized Policy-Making: A Case Study of Agricultural Trade," in *Non-State Actors in World Politics*, ed. Daphne Josselin and William Wallace (Hampshire, U.K.: Palgrave, 2001), 94.

29. Hall and Biersteker, "The Emergence of Private Authority in the International System," 6.

30. A. Claire Cutler, "Private International Regimes and Interfirm Cooperation," in *The Emergence of Private Authority in Global Governance*, ed. Rodney Bruce Hall and Thomas J. Biersteker (Cambridge: Cambridge University Press, 2002), 23.

31. Nigel Haworth and Steve Hughes, "Labor," in *International Organization and Global Governance*, ed. Thomas G. Weiss and Rorden Wilkinson (Abingdon, U.K.: Routledge, 2014), 340.

32. Peter J. Hoffman, "Private Military and Security Companies," in *International Organization and Global Governance*, ed. Thomas G. Weiss and Rorden Wilkinson (Abingdon, U.K.: Routledge, 2014), 388; Krahmann, "Conceptualizing Security Governance," 15.

33. Ase Gilje Ostensen, "In the Business of Peace: The Political Influence of Private Military and Security Companies on UN Peacekeeping," *International Peacekeeping* 20, no. 1 (2013): 38.

34. Caballero-Anthony, "Non-State Regional Governance," 570.

35. Jan Aart Scholte, "Civil Society and NGOs," in *International Organization and Global Governance*, ed. Thomas G. Weiss and Rorden Wilkinson (Abingdon, U.K.: Routledge, 2014), 323–24.

36. Nathan Grills, "The Paradox of Multilateral Organizations Engaging with Faith-Based Organizations," *Global Governance* 15, no. 4 (2009): 505.

37. Grills, "The Paradox of Multilateral Organizations," 505.

38. Michael Moran, "Global Philanthropy," in *International Organization and Global Governance*, ed. Thomas G. Weiss and Rorden Wilkinson (Abingdon, U.K.: Routledge, 2014), 372.

39. Peter M. Haas, "Introduction: Epistemic Communities and International Policy Coordination," *International Organization* 46, no. 1 (1992): 3.

40. James G. McGann, "Think Tanks and Global Policy Networks," in *International Organization and Global Governance*, ed. Thomas G. Weiss and Rorden Wilkinson (Abingdon, U.K.: Routledge, 2014), 361; and Diane Stone, *Knowledge Actors and Transnational Governance* (Hampshire: Palgrave Macmillan, 2013), 64.

41. Alex J. Bellamy, *Responsibility to Protect: The Global Effort to End Mass Atrocities* (Cambridge, U.K.: Polity, 2009), 37.

42. Deepa Seetharaman, "Zuckerberg Family Fund to Invest $3 Billion in Research Technology," *Wall Street Journal*, September 22, 2016, https://www.wsj.com/articles/zuckerberg-family-fund-to-invest-3-billion-in-research-technology-1474489559.

43. Yanzhong Huang, "Global Health, Civil Society, and Regional Security," in *A Growing Force: Civil Society Role in Asian Regional Security*, ed. Rizal Sukma and James Gannon (Tokyo: Japan Center for International Exchange, 2013), 27.

44. Heiner Hänggi, "Making Sense of Security Sector Governance," in *Challenges of Security Sector Governance*, ed. Heiner Hänggi and Theodor H. Winkler (Munster: LIT Verlag, 2004), 8.

45. United Nations Peacekeeping, "Security Sector Reform," undated, accessed July 5, 2017, http://www.un.org/en/peacekeeping/issues/security.shtml.

46. United Nations Peacekeeping, "Security Sector Reform."

47. Hänggi, "Making Sense of Security Sector Governance," 9.

48. Barry Buzan, Ole Waever, and Jaap de Wilde, *Security: A New Framework for Analysis* (Boulder, Colo.: Lynne Rienner,1998); and United Nations Development Programme (UNDP), *Human Development Report 1994* (New York: Oxford University Press, 1994).

49. Buzan, Waever, and de Wilde, *Security*, 21. See also pp. 36–40.

50. International Campaign to Ban Landmines, "Timeline of the International Campaign to Ban Landmines," (campaigning tool, Geneva: ICBL, undated), accessed February 15, 2017, http://www.icbl.org/media/342067/icb009_chronology_a5_v4-pages.pdf.

51. Margaret Chan, "WHO Director-General Addresses UN Security Council on Ebola" (address to the Emergency Session of the UN Security Council on Peace and Security in Africa (Ebola), New York, September 18, 2014), http://www.who.int/dg/speeches /2014/security-council-ebola/en/.

52. Colin McInnes, "Crisis! What Crisis? Global Health and the 2014–15 West African Ebola Outbreak," *Third World Quarterly* 37, no. 3 (2016): 389.

53. See High-Level Advisory Panel on the Responsibility to Protect in Southeast Asia, "Mainstreaming the Responsibility to Protect in Southeast Asia: Pathway Towards a Caring ASEAN Community" (report presented at the United Nations, New York, September 9, 2014).

54. Buzan, Waever, and de Wilde, *Security*, 36.

55. Nike, Inc., *FY 14/15 Nike, Inc. Sustainable Business Report* (Beaverton, Ore.: Nike, 2016), 14. Nike came up with its 2020 targets, which are outlined in the report, as a means to minimize their environmental footprint. The company seeks to double their business while halving their environmental impact.

56. Temasek Foundation Ecosperity, "Who We Are," undated, accessed September 5, 2017, http://www.temasekfoundation-ecosperity.org.sg/.

57. Joe Cochrane, "Blazes in Southeast Asia May Have Led to Deaths of over 100,000, Study Says," *New York Times*, September 19, 2016, https://www.nytimes.com/2016 /09/20/world/asia/indonesia-haze-smog-health.html.

58. Friends of Nature, Institute of Public and Environmental Affairs, and Green Beagle, "2010 Study of Heavy Metal Pollution by IT Brand Supply Chain: The IT Industry Has a Critical Duty to Prevent Heavy Metal Pollution," April 24, 2010, http://chinawater risk.org/wp-content/uploads/2011/04/Initial-Study-of-Heavy-Metal-Pollution-by-IT -Brand-Supply-Chain-English-Final.pdf; and Friends of Nature, et al., "Green Choice Apparel Supply Chain Investigation—Draft Report: Cleaning up the Fashion Industry," April 9, 2012, http://wwwoa.ipe.org.cn//Upload/Report-Textiles-One-EN.pdf.

59. Consent refers to the agreement among actors that a problem is of common concern to allow resource mobilization and coordination among actors. Legitimacy means governance is accepted and desirable by the referent. Mark Webber, "Security Governance," in *Handbook of Governance and Security*, ed. James Sperling (Cheltenham, U.K.: Edward Elgar, 2014), 21–22.

60. See Michael Barnett and Martha Finnemore, *Rules for the World: International Organizations in Global Politics* (Ithaca, N.Y.: Cornell University Press, 2004), 21; and Avant, Finnemore, and Sell, "Who Governs the Globe?"

61. Barnett and Finnemore, *Rules for the World*.

62. Avant, Finnemore, and Sell, "Who Governs the Globe?," 11.

63. The securitizing audience varies according to the context and issue concerned. At the national level, the audience can be the general public; at the regional and international level, the audience can include states, regional and international organizations, and non-state actors. For more on "audience," see Thierry Balzacq, "The Three Faces of Securitization: Political Agency, Audience and Context," *European Journal of International Relations* 11, no. 2 (2005): 171–201; Paul Roe, "Actor, Audience(s) and Emergency Measures: Securitization and the UK's Decision to Invade Iraq," *Security Dialogue* 39, no. 6 (2008): 615–35; Nicole J. Jackson, "International Organizations, Security Dichotomies and the Trafficking of Persons and Narcotics in Post-Soviet Central Asia: A Critique of the Securitization Framework," *Security Dialogue* 37, no. 3 (2006): 299–317; and Claire Wilkinson, "The Copenhagen School on Tour in Kyrgyzstan: Is Securitization Theory Useable Outside Europe?," *Security Dialogue* 38, no. 1 (2007): 5–25.

64. Buzan, Waever, and de Wilde, *Security*, 77.

65. Buzan, Waever, and de Wilde, *Security*, 72.

66. Haas, "Introduction," 5.

67. See Adam Kamradt-Scott, "Evidence-Based Medicine and the Governance of Pandemic Influenza," *Global Public Health* 7, no. 2 (2012): S112–17.

68. Council for Security Cooperation in the Asia Pacific (CSCAP), "The Security Implications of Climate Change" (memorandum, Kuala Lumpur: CSCAP, June 2010). CSCAP was founded in 1995, a year after the ASEAN Regional Forum. Its role is to provide expert advice on security issues to the ASEAN Regional Forum and other political and security institutions in the Asia-Pacific like ASEAN.

69. Task Force on ASEAN Migrant Workers, "Making Advocacy Work," *Justice and Peace Commission of the H.K. Catholic Diocese*, undated, accessed February 20, 2017, http://www.hkjp.org/files/files/focus/humanright/task%20force%20on%20ASEAN%20Migrant.pdf.

70. Task Force on ASEAN Migrant Workers, "Making Advocacy Work," 3.

71. Task Force on ASEAN Migrant Workers, "Making Advocacy Work," 4.

72. Task Force on ASEAN Migrant Workers, "ASEAN Civil Society Organizations (CSOs)-Trade Unions Consultation on Protection and Promotion of the Rights of Migrant Workers 12 May 2007, Jakarta, Indonesia" (Jakarta: ASEAN, 2007), http://asean.org/storage/2016/05/I2_ASEAN-Civil-Soc-Org-Trade-Unions-Consul-on-Protection-n-Promotion-of-the-Rights-of-MW-2007.pdf; and Kelly Gerard, "From the ASEAN People's Assembly to the ASEAN Civil Society Conference: The Boundaries of Civil Society Advocacy," *Contemporary Politics* 19, no. 4 (2013): 414.

73. See section titled "Recommendations to the Government of Indonesia," in Task Force for ASEAN Migrant Workers, "ASEAN Civil Society Organizations," 4–6.

74. Jorge V. Tigno, "Walk the Talk: CSOs, Migrant Workers, and Overseas Employment from the Philippines," in *Asia on the Move: Regional Migration and the Role of Civil Society*, ed. Mely Caballero-Antony and Toshihiro Menju (Tokyo: Japan Center for International Exchange, 2015), 143.

75. Tigno, "Walk the Talk," 155.

76. Dicky Pelupessy and Diane Bretherton, "Disaster, Mental Health, and Community Resilience: Lessons from the Field in Aceh Province, Indonesia," in *Natural Disaster Management in the Asia-Pacific: Policy and Governance*, ed. Caroline Brassard, David W. Giles, and Arnold M. Howitt (London: Springer, 2015), 150.

77. Pelupessy and Bretherton, "Disaster, Mental Health, and Community Resilience," 152–53.

78. National Bureau of Asian Research, *Strategic Assistance: Disaster Relief and Asia-Pacific Stability* (Seattle: NBR, 2014), 12–13.

79. As mentioned in chapter 1, while the discussion on security governance processes in the book are largely about Southeast Asia, the repeated reference to East Asia reflects Southeast Asia/ASEAN's deep engagement and integration with its three Northeast Asian neighbors, China, Japan, and South Korea.

80. Charles E. Morrison, "Track 1 / Track 2 Symbiosis in Asia Pacific Regionalism," *Pacific Review* 17, no. 4 (2004): 548–9.

81. See United States Institute of Peace, "Glossary: Tracks of Diplomacy," undated, accessed February 15, 2018, https://www.usip.org/glossary/tracks-diplomacy.

82. Caballero-Anthony, "Non-State Regional Governance," 577.

83. Examples include Mely Caballero-Anthony et al., "Health Governance and Dengue in Southeast Asia" (Singapore: S. Rajaratnam School of International Studies, 2015); Mely Caballero-Anthony, "Non-Traditional Security and Infectious Diseases in ASEAN: Going Beyond the Rhetoric of Securitisation to Deeper Institutionalisation," *Pacific Review* 12, no. 4 (2008): 507–25; Mely Caballero-Anthony, "Combating Infectious Diseases in East Asia: Securitisation and Global Public Goods for Health and Human Security," *Journal of International Affairs* 59. no. 2 (2006): 105–27; Mely Caballero-Anthony, "Securitising Infectious Diseases in Asia," *Indonesian Quarterly* 34, no. 1 (2006): 45–52; Mely Caballero-Anthony, "SARS in Asia: Crisis, Vulnerabilities and Regional Responses," *Asian Survey* 45, no. 3 (2005): 475–95; and Huang, "Global Health, Civil Society, and Regional Security," 35.

84. Huang, "Global Health, Civil Society, and Regional Security," 30.

85. Jun Honna, "The Role of Civil Society Organizations in Combating Human Trafficking in Southeast Asia," in *A Growing Force: Civil Society Role in Asian Regional Security*, ed. Rizal Sukma and James Gannon (Tokyo: Japan Center for International Exchange, 2013), 56.

86. Sheldon W. Simon, "Evaluating Track II Approaches to Security Diplomacy in the Asia-Pacific: The CSCAP Experience," *Pacific Review* 15, no. 2 (2002): 176–77.

87. Desmond Ball, "CSCAP and the ARF," in *Assessing Track 2 Diplomacy in the Asia-Pacific Region: A CSCAP Reader*, ed. Desmond Ball and Kwa Chong Guan (Singapore: S. Rajaratnam School of International Studies, 2010), 65.

88. Sheldon W. Simon, "Evaluating Track 2 Approaches to Security Dialogue in the Asia-Pacific Region: The CSCAP Experience (2002)," in *Assessing Track 2 Diplomacy in the Asia-Pacific Region: A CSCAP Reader*, ed. Desmond Ball and Kwa Chong Guan (Singapore: S. Rajaratnam School of International Studies, 2010), 105.

89. Seng Chye Tan, "NADI: Supporting ADMM and Promoting Defence Diplomacy," in *Forward Engagement: RSIS as a Think Tank of International Studies and Security in the Asia-Pacific*, ed. Alan Chong (Singapore: World Scientific, 2016), 89–96.

90. Simon, "Evaluating Track II Approaches," 172.

91. Tan, "NADI," 94.

92. Caballero-Anthony, "Non-State Regional Governance," 579–80.

93. Helen E. S. Nesadurai, "The ASEAN People's Forum (APF) as Authentic Social Forum: Regional Civil Society Networking for an Alternative Regionalism," in *Routledge Handbook of Asian Regionalism*, ed. Mark Beeson and Richard Stubbs (Abingdon, U.K.: Routledge, 2012), 169.

94. Gerard, "From the ASEAN People's Assembly," 416–17; and Nesadurai, "The ASEAN People's Forum," 170.

95. Gerard, "From the ASEAN People's Assembly," 418.

96. Gerard, "From the ASEAN People's Assembly," 418.

97. Gerard, "From the ASEAN People's Assembly," 417.

98. Robin Bush, "Muhammadiyah and Disaster Response: Innovation and Change in Humanitarian Assistance," in *Natural Disaster Management in the Asia-Pacific: Policy and Governance*, ed. Caroline Brassard, David W. Giles, and Arnold M. Howitt (Tokyo: Springer, 2015), 39.

99. Bush, "Muhammadiyah and Disaster Response: Innovation and Change in Humanitarian Assistance," 33.

100. Robin Bush, "Muhammadiyah and Disaster Response: Innovation and Change in Social Welfare" (working paper, Hong Kong: Southeast Asia Research Centre, City University of Hong Kong, 2014), 17–18.

101. Bush, "Muhammadiyah and Disaster Response: Innovation and Change in Humanitarian Assistance," 34.

102. Buddhist Tzu Chi Foundation, "Tzu Chi Foundation Exceeds 1 Billion Pesos in Material Aid to Typhoon Haiyan Survivors," *Reliefweb*, January 30, 2014, http://reliefweb .int/report/philippines/tzu-chi-foundation-exceeds-1-billion-pesos-material-aid-ty phoon-haiyan-survivors.

3. Governance of Health Security

1. The 1978 Alma-Ata Declaration stated that health must be considered a worldwide social goal requiring the collaborative efforts of many other social and economic sectors in addition to the health sector.

2. Commission on Human Security, *Human Security Now: Protecting and Empowering People* (New York: Commission on Human Security, 2003), 96. The Commission on Human Security defines human security as "[the protection of] the vital core of all human lives in ways that enhance human freedoms and human fulfilment" (4).

3. See United Nations, "Home Page," *Millennium Development Goals and Beyond 2015*, undated, accessed June 15, 2017, http://www.un.org/millenniumgoals/.

4. See United Nations, "Sustainable Development Goals," *Sustainable Development Knowledge Platform*, undated, accessed June 15, 2017, https://sustainabledevelopment.un.org/?menu=1300.

5. See Mely Caballero-Anthony, "Non-Traditional Security and Infectious Diseases in ASEAN: Going Beyond the Rhetoric of Securitization to Deeper Institutionalisation," *Pacific Review* 21, no. 4 (2008): 507–25.

6. See Mely Caballero-Anthony, "SARS in Asia: Crisis, Vulnerabilities, and Regional Responses," *Asian Survey* 45, no. 3 (2005): 475–95.

7. World Health Organization (WHO), "WHO Strategic Action Plan for Pandemic Influenza 2006–2007" (WHO/CDS/EPR/GIP/2006.2, 3, Geneva: WHO, 2006).

8. Lorna Weir and Eric Mykhalovskiy, *Global Public Health Vigilance: Creating a World on Alert* (London: Routledge, 2010), 150–51.

9. WHO, *The World Health Report: A Safer Future: Global Public Health Security in the 21st Century* (Geneva: WHO, 2007), 17–33.

10. See Simon Rushton, "Global Health Security: Security for Whom? Security from What?," *Political Studies* 59, no. 4 (2011): 779–96; Steven J. Hoffman, "The Evolution, Etiology and Eventualities of the Global Health Security Regime," *Health Policy and Planning* 25, no. 6 (2010): 510–22; Catherine Yuk-ping Lo and Nicholas Thomas, "How Is Health a Security Issue? Politics, Responses and Issues," *Health Policy and Planning* 25, no. 6 (2010): 447–53; and Colleen O'Manique and Pieter Fourie, "Security and Health in the Twenty-First Century," in *The Routledge Handbook of Security Studies*, ed. Myriam Dunn Cavelty and Victor Mauer (London: Routledge, 2010).

11. Jai P. Narain and R. Bhatia, "The Challenge of Communicable Diseases in the WHO South-East Asia Region," *Bulletin of the World Health Organization* 88, no. 3 (2010): 162.

12. WHO Regional Office for South-East Asia, "South-East Asia Countries Adopt Call for Action to Accelerate Efforts to End TB," media release, SEAR/PR/1644, March 16, 2017, http://www.searo.who.int/mediacentre/releases/2017/1644/en/. Note that WHO regions are different from the geographic regions commonly referred to in international politics. The WHO South-East Region and WHO Western Pacific Region essentially cover South Asia, East Asia, Southeast Asia, and the Pacific region in the traditional sense.

13. WHO Regional Office for South-East Asia, *Progress Report on HIV in the WHO South-East Asia Region 2016* (New Delhi: WHO, 2016), 10.

14. WHO, "Summary of Probable SARS Cases with Onset of Illness from 1 November 2002 to 31 July 2003," 2004, http://www.who.int/csr/sars/country/table2004_04_21/en/.

15. WHO, "Middle East Respiratory Syndrome Coronavirus (MERS-CoV)—Republic of Korea," July 7, 2015, http://www.who.int/csr/don/07-july-2015-mers-korea/en/.

16. Caballero-Anthony, "SARS in Asia," 482.

17. Caballero-Anthony, "SARS in Asia," 482; and Melissa Curley and Nicholas Thomas, "Human Security and Public Health in Southeast Asia: The SARS Outbreak," *Australian Journal of International Affairs* 58, no. 1 (2004): 23.

18. Caballero-Anthony, "SARS in Asia," 482–83.

19. Yanzhong Huang, "Pursuing Health as Foreign Policy: The Case of China," *Indiana Journal of Global Legal Studies* 17, no. 1 (2010): 140–44.

20. See the discussion in chapter 2 on securitizing actors, their role, and their sources of authority.

21. L. O. Kallings, "The First Postmodern Pandemic: 25 Years of HIV/AIDS (Review)," *Journal of Internal Medicine* 263, no. 3 (2008): 239.

22. There is sufficient existing research showing the negative impacts of the disease on many aspects of the states and societies affected, such as Kallings, "The First Post-modern Pandemic"; Gwyn Prins, "AIDS and Global Security," *International Affairs* 80, no. 5 (2004): 931–52; Simon Rushton, "AIDS and International Security in the United Nations System;" *Health Policy and Planning* 25, no. 6 (2010): 495–504; Colin McInnes, "HIV/AIDS and Security," *International Affairs* 82, no. 2 (2006): 315–26; and Tony Barnett and Gwyn Prins, "HIV/AIDS and Security: Fact, Fiction and Evidence," *International Affairs* 82, no. 2 (2006): 359–68.

23. Sara E. Davies, "Securitizing Infectious Diseases," *International Affairs* 84, no. 2 (2008): 298.

24. Rushton, "AIDS and International Security," 497.

25. See Prins, "Aids and Global Security," 940–41.

26. Jonathan Herington, "Securitization of Infectious Diseases in Vietnam: The Cases of HIV and Avian Influenza," *Health Policy and Planning* 25, no. 6 (2010): 471.

27. Herington, "Securitization of Infectious Diseases," 471.

28. Catherine Yuk-ping Lo, *HIV/AIDS in China and India: Governing Health Security* (New York: Palgrave Macmillan, 2015), 86.

29. Huang, "Pursuing Health as Foreign Policy," 117.

30. Gao Qiang, "Speech at the HIV/AIDS High-Level Meeting of the UN General Assembly," Permanent Mission of the People's Republic of China to the United Nations Office at Geneva and Other International Organizations in Switzerland, September 22, 2003, http://www.china-un.ch/eng/dbtyw/zmjg_1/jgthsm/t85551.htm.

31. ASEAN Secretariat, "ASEAN Regional Security: The Threats Facing It and the Way Forward," ASEAN, April 10, 2006, http://asean.org/?static_post=asean-regional-security-the-threats-facing-it-and-the-way-forward-by-asean-secretariat.

32. Tine Hanrieder and Christian Kreuder-Sonnen, "WHO Decides on the Exception? Securitization and Emergency Governance in Global Health," *Security Dialogue* 45, no. 4 (2014): 337.

33. WHO, "World Health Organization Issues Emergency Travel Advisory," media release, March 15, 2003, http://www.who.int/mediacentre/news/releases/2003/pr23/en/.

34. "Reaching a Common Understanding, Strengthening Leadership, Carrying Out Responsibilities, Feasibly Completing SARS Prevention and Treatment Work (in Chinese)," *People's Daily* (China), April 14, 2003, cited in Huang, "Pursuing Health as Foreign Policy."

35. Ministry of Foreign Affairs Policy Lab, "Diplomacy: Towards Openness, Transparency and Cooperation," *World Affairs*, no. 12 (2003): 12, cited in Huang, "Pursuing Health as Foreign Policy."

36. For more on regional efforts to address SARS, see Caballero-Anthony, "SARS in Asia."

37. See Heads of States of ASEAN and China, "Joint Statement" (Special ASEAN–China Leaders' Meeting on the Severe Acute Respiratory Syndrome [SARS], Bangkok, Thailand, April 29, 2003).

38. See Asia-Pacific Economic Cooperation (APEC), "APEC Health Ministers' Statement" (APEC Health Ministerial Meeting, Bangkok, Thailand, June 28, 2003).

39. Zhongyi He, "Feichuantong Anquan yu Zhongguo: Xueshu Yantaohui Zongshu [Non-Traditional Security in China: Conference Report]," *Shijie Jingji yu Zhengzhi* [World Economics and Politics], no. 3 (2004): 55.

40. Caballero-Anthony, "SARS in Asia," 476. On the discussion in the late 1980s, see Muthiah Alagappa, "Comprehensive Security: Interpretations in ASEAN Countries," in *Asian Security Issues: Regional and Global*, ed. Robert Scalapino et al. (Berkeley: Institute of East Asian Studies, University of California, 1989).

41. Institute of Defence and Strategic Studies, "Non-Traditional Security in Asia: The Dynamics of Securitization" (workshop report, Singapore: IDSS, 2004). This workshop was part of a bigger project on NTS sponsored by the Ford Foundation. It shows that the interest in reconceptualizing security and understanding NTS in Southeast Asia started in the early 2000s.

42. Center for Non-Traditional Security Studies, *Pandemic Preparedness in Asia* (Singapore: S. Rajaratnam School of International Studies, 2009).

43. WHO Regional Office for the Western Pacific, "Meeting on Laboratory Strengthening for Emerging Infectious Diseases in the Asia Pacific Region, Kuala Lumpur, Malaysia, 19–21 October 2011" (report, Manila: WHO, 2012), 6.

44. WHO Regional Office for the Western Pacific, "Meeting on Laboratory Strengthening," 16–17.

45. WHO Regional Office for the Western Pacific, "Meeting on Laboratory Strengthening," 13, 20.

46. WHO Regional Office for the Western Pacific, "Meeting on Laboratory Strengthening," 20.

47. WHO, "Human Infection with Avian Influenza A(H7N9) Virus—China," March 15, 2017, http://www.who.int/csr/don/15-march-2017-ah7n9-china/en/.

48. Bill Rau, "The Politics of Civil Society in Confronting HIV/AIDS," *International Affairs* 82, no. 2 (2006): 288.

49. WHO, *World Health Statistics 2016: Monitoring Health for the SDGs* (Geneva: WHO, 2016), 50.

50. WHO Regional Office for South-East Asia, *Progress Report on HIV*, 10.

51. WHO Regional Office for the Western Pacific, "Meeting on Laboratory Strengthening," 9.

52. "Singapore a Role Model in Its Handling of Zika: WHO," *Straits Times* (Singapore), September 3, 2016, http://www.straitstimes.com/singapore/environment/singapore -a-role-model-in-its-handling-of-zika-who.

53. Ministry of Health and National Environment Agency of Singapore, "Additional Measures against Zika Virus," media release, February 3, 2016, https://www.moh.gov.sg /content/moh_web/home/pressRoom/pressRoomItemRelease/2016/additional -measures-against-zika-virus.html; and Ministry of Health and National Environment

Agency of Singapore, "Precautionary Measures against Zika Virus Infection," media release, January 27, 2016, https://www.moh.gov.sg/content/moh_web/home/press Room/pressRoomItemRelease/2016/precautionary-measures-against-zika-virus -infection-.html.

54. Purnawan Junadi, "Pandemic Preparedness Operations, Systems and Networks: The Indonesian Case," in *Pandemic Preparedness in Asia*, ed. Mely Caballero-Anthony (Singapore: S. Rajaratnam School of International Studies, 2009), 27.

55. Percy W. Hawkes et al., "USAID/Indonesia Avian and Pandemic Influenza (API) Program Evaluation: 2009–2014" (Washington, D.C.: GH Tech Project Bridge IV, 2014),14.

56. Herington, "Securitization of Infectious Diseases in Vietnam," 471.

57. This has also been noted by Fidler when he identified infectious diseases, HIV/AIDS, SARS, avian influenza, and H1N1 as examples of health cooperation issues in APEC and ASEAN. See David Fidler, "Asia and Global Health Governance: Power, Principles and Practice," in *Asia's Role in Governing Global Health*, ed. Kelley Lee, Tikki Pang, and Yeling Tan (London: Routledge, 2013), 208.

58. WHO, "WHO Collaborating Centres," undated, accessed June 27, 2017, http://www .who.int/collaboratingcentres/database/en/.

59. For comprehensive discussions on China's and Japan's development assistance for health, see Christine Pilcavage, "Japan's Overseas Development Assistance in the Health Sector and Global Health Governance," in *Asia's Role in Governing Global Health*, ed. Kelley Lee, Tikki Pang, and Yeling Tan (London: Routledge, 2013), 19–38; and Jenny Qu Wang et al., "Global Health Governance in China: The Case of China's Health Aid to Foreign Countries," in *Asia's Role in Governing Global Health*, ed. Kelley Lee, Tikki Pang, and Yeling Tan (London: Routledge, 2013), 39–65.

60. Heads of States of China, Japan, and Republic of Korea, "Joint Statement" (Tenth Anniversary of Trilateral Cooperation Among the People's Republic of China, Japan, and the Republic of Korea, Beijing, China, October 10, 2009).

61. Heads of States of China, Japan, and Republic of Korea, "Joint Declaration on the Enhancement of Trilateral Comprehensive Cooperative Partnership" (Fifth Trilateral Summit Meeting among the People's Republic of China, the Republic of Korea and Japan, Beijing, China, May 13, 2012).

62. Heads of States of ASEAN and Japan, "The ASEAN–Japan Plan of Action (2011–2015)" (14th ASEAN–Japan Summit, Bali, Indonesia, November 18, 2011).

63. Heads of States of ASEAN and Republic of Korea, "Plan of Action to Implement the Joint Declaration on ASEAN–ROK Strategic Partnership for Peace and Prosperity (2011–2015)" (13th ASEAN–Republic of Korea Summit, Hanoi, Vietnam, October 29, 2010).

64. ASEAN Secretariat, "ASEAN Response to Combat Avian Influenza" (5th JICA–ASEAN Regional Cooperation Meeting, Yangon, Myanmar, April 19–21, 2006).

65. ASEAN Secretariat, "ASEAN Response to Combat Avian Influenza."

66. East Asia Summit, "Declaration on Avian Influenza Prevention, Control and Response" (1st East Asia Summit, Kuala Lumpur, Malaysia, December 14, 2005).

67. See East Asia Summit, "Declaration on Regional Responses to Malaria Control and Addressing Resistance to Antimalarial Medicines" (7th East Asia Summit, Phnom Penh, Cambodia, November 20, 2012).

68. Mekong Basin Disease Surveillance Foundation Secretariat, "MBDS Background," Mekong Basin Disease Surveillance, undated, accessed May 15, 2017, http://www .mbdsnet.org/about-mbds/mbds-background/.

69. Nancy MacPherson et al., "Key Findings and Lessons from an Evaluation of the Rockefeller Foundation's Disease Surveillance Networks Initiative," *Emerging Health Threats Journal* 6 (2013): 3.

70. Asia–Europe Foundation, *Regional Mechanisms of Communicable Disease Control in Asia and Europe* (Singapore: ASEF, 2013), 22.

71. Asia–Europe Foundation, *Regional Mechanisms of Communicable Disease Control*, 21.

72. Asia–Europe Foundation, *Regional Mechanisms of Communicable Disease Control*, 21; and Bounlay Phommasack et al., "Mekong Basin Disease Surveillance (MBDS): A Trust-based Network," *Emerging Health Threats Journal* 6 (2013): 4.

73. The amount for Gavi is derived from disbursements as of March 2013 to the following countries: Cambodia, China, Laos, Papua New Guinea, Vietnam, Indonesia, Korea, Myanmar, and Timor Leste. Gavi, "Disbursements and Commitments (by country)," Gavi: The Vaccine Alliance, undated, accessed June 27, 2013, http://www.gavialliance .org/results/disbursements/. The amount for the Global Fund to Fight AIDS, Tuberculosis and Malaria is derived from the Global Fund portfolio as of June 2013, to the following countries: China, Indonesia, Myanmar, the Philippines, Cambodia, Korea, Laos, Malaysia, Papua New Guinea, Thailand, Timor Leste, and Vietnam, in Global Fund, "Global Fund Portfolio Downloads," undated, accessed June 27, 2013, http://portfolio .theglobalfund.org/en/Downloads/DisbursementsInDetail.

74. World Bank, "Projects and Operations: By Theme," undated, accessed June 27, 2013, http://www.worldbank.org/projects/theme?lang=en; and World Trade Organization, "Specific TRIPS Issues," undated, accessed June 12, 2017, http://www.wto.org/eng lish/tratop_e/trips_e/trips_e.htm#issues. Within the United Nations system, there are three main bodies that explicitly recognize the linkages between health and development and focus on the social determinants of health: the United Nations Children's Fund, the United Nations Population Fund, and the United Nations Development Programme. For more on their roles, see Sophie Harman, *Global Health Governance* (London: Routledge, 2012), 40–46.

75. Generated from the World Bank database, using the following search criteria: East Asia and Pacific (region), Health (sector). See World Bank, "Projects and Operations," accessed June 27, 2013, http://www.worldbank.org/projects/search?lang=en&search Term=&mjthemecode_exact=8.

76. See Asian Development Bank, "Operational Plan for Health, 2015–2020," undated, accessed June 5, 2017, https://www.adb.org/sectors/health/operational-plan-for -health-2015-2020.

77. See Sara Bennett et al., "Global Health Research Governance: An Asian Perspective on the Need for Reform," in *Asia's Role in Governing Global Health*, ed. Kelley Lee, Tikki Pang, and Yeling Tan (London: Routledge, 2013),172–73.

78. Asia Partnership on Emerging Infectious Diseases Research, "APEIR Milestone," undated, accessed June 15, 2017, http://apeir.net/.
79. Asia Pacific Observatory on Health Systems and Policies, "Informing Policies, Building Partnerships" (flyer, New Delhi: Asia Pacific Observatory on Health Systems and Policies, 2016).
80. Philips News Center, "ASEAN Non-Communicable Diseases (NCD) Network Launched," *Philips*, April 8, 2013, https://www.philips.com/a-w/about/news/archive/standard/news/press/2013/20130408-asean-ncd-network.html.
81. For more, see Yanzhong Huang, "Global Health, Civil Society and Regional Security," in *A Growing Force: Civil Society's Role in Asian Regional Security*, ed. Rizal Sukma and James Gannon (Tokyo: Japan Center for International Exchange, 2013), 40.
82. Huang, "Global Health, Civil Society and Regional Security," 36–37.
83. Hawkes et al., "USAID/Indonesia Avian and Pandemic Influenza," 9–10; and Huang, "Pursuing Health as Foreign Policy," 29.
84. Huang, "Global Health, Civil Society and Regional Security," 28–29.

4. Governance of Environmental Security

1. David A. Baldwin, "The Concept of Security," *Review of International Studies* 23, no. 1 (1997): 5–26; and Barry Buzan, Ole Waever, and Jaap de Wilde, *Security: A New Framework for Analysis* (Boulder, Colo.: Lynne Rienner, 1998).
2. United Nations Development Programme (UNDP), *Human Development Report 2016* (New York: UNDP, 2016), 38; and United Nations Educational, Scientific and Cultural Organization (UNESCO), "Facts and Figures on Marine Biodiversity," undated, accessed June 8, 2017, http://www.unesco.org/new/en/natural-sciences/ioc-oceans/focus-areas/rio-20-ocean/blueprint-for-the-future-we-want/marine-biodiversity/facts-and-figures-on-marine-biodiversity/.
3. UNDP, *Human Development Report 2016*, 38.
4. According to World Bank data as of 2015, the population of China is 1.37 billion; Indonesia, 257 million; the Philippines, 100.6 million; Vietnam, 91.7 million; and Thailand, 67.9 million.
5. A survey by the International Monetary Fund in 2016 observed that Asia would remain the world's economic engine, despite some moderation. International Monetary Fund, "IMF Survey: Asia: Growth Remains Strong, Expected to Ease Only Modestly," May 3, 2016, http://www.imf.org/en/News/Articles/2015/09/28/04/53/socar050316b.
6. United Nations, Department of Economic and Social Affairs, Population Division, "World Population Prospects: The 2015 Revision, Key Findings and Advance Tables" (working paper, ESA/P/WP.241, New York: United Nations, 2015).
7. World Bank, "World Development Indicators—Rural Population," n.d., http://data.worldbank.org/indicator/SP.RUR.TOTL.ZS.
8. Organisation for Economic Co-operation and Development (OECD), *OECD Environmental Outlook to 2050: The Consequences of Inaction* (Paris: OECD, 2012).

9. Lester R. Brown, "Redefining National Security," *Challenge* 29, no. 3 (1986): 25.

10. Brown, "Redefining National Security," 25.

11. Millennium Project, "Environmental Security Study: Section 2—Definitions of Environmental Security," undated, accessed June 21, 2017, http://www.millennium -project.org/millennium/es-2def.html. Other possible definitions of environmental security are also found at this site.

12. Millennium Project, "Environmental Security Study."

13. Millennium Project, "Environmental Security Study."

14. Buzan, Waever, and de Wilde, *Security*, 71.

15. World Commission on Environment and Development, *Our Common Future* (Oxford: Oxford University Press, 1987), 9.

16. World Commission on Environment and Development, *Our Common Future*, 290.

17. White House, *National Security Strategy of the United States* (Washington, D.C.: White House, 1991), 22.

18. Shahar Hameiri and Lee Jones, *Governing Borderless Threats: Non-Traditional Security and the Politics of State Transformation* (Cambridge: Cambridge University Press, 2015), 77.

19. United Nations Secretary-General, "An Agenda for Peace" (A/47/277, June 17, 1992).

20. United Nations Security Council, "6587th Meeting" (S/PV.6587, July 20, 2011).

21. According to the 1994 Human Development Report, human security has seven dimensions: economic security, food security, health security, environmental security, personal security, community security, and political security. UNDP, *Human Development Report 1994* (New York: Oxford University Press, 1994).

22. Lorraine Elliott, "Human Security/Environmental Security," *Contemporary Politics* 21, no. 1 (2015): 11–24.

23. United Nations Security Council, "5663rd Meeting" (S/PV.5663, April 17, 2007).

24. United Nations Security Council, "6587th Meeting."

25. United Nations Security Council, "6587th Meeting."

26. Association of Southeast Asian Nations (ASEAN), *ASEAN Political-Security Community Blueprint* (Jakarta: ASEAN Secretariat, 2009), para. 9.

27. Kheng-Lian Koh, Nicholas A. Robinson, and Lin-Heng Lye, *ASEAN Environmental Legal Integration: Sustainable Goals?* (Cambridge: Cambridge University Press, 2016), 37–81.

28. ASEAN Secretariat, "ASEAN Regional Security: The Threats Facing It and the Way Forward," *ASEAN*, April 10, 2006, http://asean.org/?static_post=asean-regional -security-the-threats-facing-it-and-the-way-forward-by-asean-secretariat.

29. ASEAN Secretariat, "ASEAN Regional Security."

30. Tom Phillips, "Beijing Smog: Pollution Red Alert Declared in China Capital and 21 Other Cities," *Guardian*, December 17, 2016, https://www.theguardian.com/world /2016/dec/17/beijing-smog-pollution-red-alert-declared-in-china-capital-and-21 -other-cities.

31. Donald Mosteller, "Air Pollution's Hazy Future in South Korea," *Data-Driven Yale*, June 30, 2016, http://datadriven.yale.edu/air-quality-2/air-pollutions-hazy-future-in -south-korea-2/.

32. He-rim Jo, "South Korea Has OECD's Second-Worst Air Quality," *Korea Herald*, February 16, 2017, http://www.koreaherald.com/view.php?ud=20170216000831; and Health Effects Institute, *State of Global Air* 2017 (Boston, MA: HEI, 2017).

33. Woosuk Jung, "South Korea's Air Pollution: Gasping for Solutions" (policy brief, Stockholm: ISDP, 2017).

34. Jung, "South Korea's Air Pollution," 1.

35. Health Effects Institute, *State of Global Air 2017*.

36. Korea Meteorological Administration, "Asian Dust," undated, accessed June 3, 2017, https://web.kma.go.kr/eng/weather/asiandust/intro.jsp.

37. Eric Johnston, "Yellow Dust Storms Getting Worse," *Japan Times*, April 22, 2008, http://www.japantimes.co.jp/news/2008/04/22/reference/yellow-dust-storms -getting-worse/#.WXtiStJ97IU. See also Souleymane Coulibaly et al., "Seasonal Fluctuations in Air Pollution in Dazaifu, Japan, and Effect of Long-Range Transport from Mainland East Asia," *Biological and Pharmaceutical Bulletin* 38, no. 9 (2015): 1395– 403; and Souleymane Coulibaly et al., "Long-Range Transport of Mutagens and Other Air Pollutants from Mainland East Asia to Western Japan," *Genes and Environment* 37, no. 25 (2015): 1–10.

38. This section is largely taken from Mely Caballero-Anthony and Tian Goh, "ASE- AN's Haze Shroud: Grave Threat to Human Security," *RSIS Commentary* (Singapore), October 2015.

39. Health Effects Institute, *State of Global Air 2017*, 1.

40. Health Effects Institute, *State of Global Air 2017*, 7.

41. "Hazardous Air Quality Detected in Kalimantan and Riau," *Jakarta Post*, September 28, 2015, http://www.thejakartapost.com/news/2015/09/28/hazardous-air-quality-detected -kalimantan-and-riau.html.

42. John O'Callaghan, "Singapore, Malaysia Face Economic Hit from Prolonged Smog," *Reuters*, June 24, 2013, http://www.reuters.com/article/us-southeastasia-haze-impact /singapore-malaysia-face-economic-hit-from-prolonged-smog-idUSBRE95N0BS 20130624.

43. "Haze Fires Cost Indonesia $22b, Twice Tsunami Bill: World Bank," *Straits Times* (Singapore), December 16, 2015, http://www.straitstimes.com/asia/se-asia/haze-fires -cost-indonesia-22b-twice-tsunami-bill-world-bank.

44. "Singapore GDP Will Take Hit from Haze as Countries Issue Travel Warnings," *Business Times* (Singapore), October 7, 2015, http://www.businesstimes.com.sg/govern ment-economy/singapore-gdp-will-take-hit-from-haze-as-countries-issue-travel -warnings.

45. World Bank and Institute for Health Metrics and Evaluation, *The Cost of Air Pollution: Strengthening the Economic Case for Action* (Washington, D.C.: World Bank, 2016), 93.

46. "Indonesia's Vice-President Jusuf Kalla Criticises Neighbours for Grumbling about Haze," *Straits Times* (Singapore), March 5, 2015, http://www.straitstimes.com/asia /se-asia/indonesias-vice-president-jusuf-kalla-criticises-neighbours-for-grumbling -about-haze.

47. Jennifer Duggan, "Kunming Pollution Protest Is Tip of Rising Chinese Environmental Activism," *Guardian*, May 16, 2013, https://www.theguardian.com/environment

/chinas-choice/2013/may/16/kunming-pollution-protest-chinese-environmental
-activism.

48. Buzan, Waever, and de Wilde, *Security*, 76.

49. Buzan, Waever, and de Wilde, *Security*.

50. The United Nations Environment Programme adopted a decision to promote China's "ecological civilization," which was introduced by China in 2007. According to China, the industrial civilization has been based on the development model of polluting first, treatment and protection later. The ecological civilization represents a more advanced form of civilization characterized by green development. To build such a civilization, it is important that human beings follow rules of nature and protect the environment.

51. Buzan, Waever, and de Wilde, *Security*, 77.

52. World Bank, *Cost of Pollution in China: Economic Estimates of Physical Damage* (Washington, D.C.: World Bank, 2007).

53. Alejandro Litovsky, "Antibiotic Waste Is Polluting India and China's Rivers; Big Pharma Must Act," *Guardian*, October 25, 2016, https://www.theguardian.com/sustainable-business/2016/oct/25/antibiotic-waste-pollution-india-china-rivers-big-pharma-superbugs-resistance.

54. Hameiri and Jones, *Governing Borderless Threats*, 93.

55. Margareth Sembiring, "Here Comes the Haze, Yet Again: Are New Measures Working?," *RSIS Commentary* (Singapore), September 2015.

56. Raman Letchumanan, "Southeast Asia's Recurring Smoke Haze Crisis: What Can Be Done?," *RSIS Commentary* (Singapore), October 2015.

57. Letchumanan, "Southeast Asia's Recurring Smoke Haze Crisis."

58. Inkyoung Kim, "Environmental Cooperation of Northeast Asia: Transboundary Air Pollution," *International Relations of the Asia-Pacific* 7, no. 3 (2007): 446.

59. See North-East Asian Subregional Program for Environmental Cooperation, "Home Page," undated, accessed September 3, 2017, http://www.neaspec.org/.

60. Nazia Nazeer and Fumitaka Furuoka, "Overview of ASEAN Environment, Transboundary Haze Pollution Agreement and Public Health," *International Journal of Asia Pacific Studies* 13, no. 1 (2017): 77–84.

61. Nazeer and Furuoka, "Overview of ASEAN Environment."

62. Sembiring, "Here Comes the Haze, Yet Again"; and Tama Salim, "One-Map Policy Helps Resolve Land Disputes, Overlapping Permits," *Jakarta Post*, December 26, 2014, http://www.thejakartapost.com/news/2014/12/26/one-map-policy-helps-resolve
-land-disputes-overlapping-permits.html.

63. Margareth Sembiring, "Combating Haze—Holding One's Breath a Year On," *RSIS Commentary* (Singapore), August 2016.

64. The 11th Meeting of the Conference of the Parties to the ASEAN Agreement on Transboundary Haze Pollution in October 2015 in Hanoi supported Indonesia's plan to host the ASEAN Coordinating Centre for Transboundary Haze Pollution Control.

65. The companies include Asia Pulp and Paper, Rimba Hutani Mas, Sebangun Bumi Andalas Wood Industries, Bumi Sriwijaya Sentosa, and Wachyuni Mandira. "Singapore Moves Against Indonesian Firms Over Haze," *Jakarta Post*, September 26,

2015, http://www.thejakartapost.com/news/2015/09/26/singapore-moves-against
-indonesian-firms-over-haze.html.

66. Zakir Hussain, "Singapore Taking Action Against Companies Responsible for Haze, Says Masagos Zulkifli," *Straits Times* (Singapore), April 21, 2016, http://www.straitstimes .com/singapore/environment/singapore-taking-action-against-companies-responsible -for-haze-says-masagos.

67. Greenpeace, *Indonesia's Forests: Under Fire* (Amsterdam: Greenpeace, 2015).

68. Sujadi Siswo, "Greenpeace Indonesia Launches Map to Track Haze-Causing Fires," *Channel NewsAsia*, March 16, 2016, http://www.channelnewsasia.com/news/asiapa-cific/greenpeace-indonesia-launches-map-to-track-haze-causing-fires-8160040.

69. Greenpeace, *Dirty Bankers: How HSBC Is Financing Forest Destruction for Palm Oil* (Amsterdam: Greenpeace, 2017).

70. HSBC, "HSBC Statement on Revised Agricultural Commodities Policy: Palm Oil," media release, February 20, 2017, http://www.hsbc.com/news-and-insight/media -resources/media-releases/2017/hsbc-statement-on-revised-agricultural-commodities -policy.

71. Greenpeace, *Dirty Bankers.*

72. HSBC, "HSBC Statement."

73. Aidenvironment, "Aidenvironment Asia Takes Up a Lead Role in Halting Deforestation in SE Asia," undated, accessed June 23, 2017, http://www.aidenvironment.org/project /aidenvironment-asia-takes-up-a-lead-role-in-halting-deforestation-in-se-asia/.

74. Hameiri and Jones, *Governing Borderless Threats*, 102.

75. World Wide Fund for Nature (WWF), "Singapore Companies—Causing the Haze?," September 27, 2016, http://www.wwf.sg/?279350/Singapore-companies-causing-or -preventing-the-haze.

76. "Haze & Us: We Breathe What We Buy," *We Breathe What We Buy*, undated, accessed June 22, 2017, https://webreathewhatwebuy.com/_2015/haze/.

77. Nurul Firmansyah, Romes Hirawan, and Isnandi, "Indonesia Declares Haze Emergency" (Utrecht, Neth.: ICCO Cooperation, 2015), 10.

78. Firmansyah, Hirawan, and Isnandi, "Indonesia Declares Haze Emergency."

79. Hameiri and Jones, *Governing Borderless Threats*, 103.

80. Institute of Public and Environmental Affairs, "CITI Evaluation Guideline 3.1," undated, accessed June 27, 2017, http://www.ipe.org.cn/greensupplychain/userguide /CITI%20Evaluation%20Guideline%20V3.1.pdf.

81. Asia-Pacific Economic Cooperation (APEC), "2014 Leaders' Declaration" (22nd APEC Economic Leaders' Meeting, Beijing, China, November 11, 2014).

82. "Tianjin to Build APEC Green Supply Chain Cooperation Network Demonstration Center," *China Daily*, updated October 13, 2016, http://www.chinadaily.com.cn/m /tianjin2012/2016-10/13/content_27049434.htm.

83. Ruge Gao, "Rise of Environmental NGOs in China: Official Ambivalence and Contested Messages," *Journal of Political Risk* 1, no. 8 (2013).

84. Gao, "Rise of Environmental NGOs in China."

85. "Liang Congjie," *Economist*, November 18, 2010, http://www.economist.com/node /17519870.

86. Gao, "Rise of Environmental NGOs in China."
87. Alan Khee-Jin Tan, "The 'Haze' Crisis in Southeast Asia: Assessing Singapore's Transboundary Haze Pollution Act" (NUS Law working paper no. 2015/002, Singapore: National University of Singapore, 2015).

5. Governance of Migration

1. United Nations, Department of Economic and Social Affairs, Population Division, *International Migration Report 2015: Highlights* (New York: UN, 2016), 1.
2. International Organization for Migration (IOM), "Key Migration Terms," undated, accessed August 13, 2017, https://www.iom.int/key-migration-terms.
3. IOM, "Key Migration Terms."
4. See, for example, United Nations Educational, Scientific and Cultural Organization (UNESCO), "Migrant/Migration," undated, accessed February 12, 2015, http://www.unesco.org/new/en/social-and-human-sciences/themes/international-migration/glossary/migrant.
5. IOM, "Key Migration Terms."
6. IOM Regional Office for Asia and the Pacific, *Regional Strategy for Asia and the Pacific 2012–2015* (Bangkok: IOM, 2012), 3.
7. IOM Regional Office for Asia and the Pacific, *Regional Strategy for Asia.*
8. Asian Development Bank, *Asian Economic Integration Report 2015: How Can Special Economic Zones Catalyze Economic Development?* (Manila: ADB, 2015), ix.
9. Asia accounted for nearly 50 percent of global remittances (US$583.4 billion) in 2014, with India, China, and the Philippines receiving the most, amounting to US$163 billion, or 61 percent of the Asian total. See Asian Development Bank, 37.
10. IOM, "International Dialogue on Migration 2008, Challenges of Irregular Migration: Addressing Mixed Migration Flows, Discussion Note" (MC/INF/294, IOM, 2008), para. 6; and United Nations High Commissioner for Refugees (UNHCR), *Refugee Protection and Mixed Migration: The 10-Point Plan in Action* (Geneva: UNHCR, 2011), 8.
11. UNHCR, *Global Trends: Forced Displacement in 2015* (Geneva: UNHCR, 2016), 5.
12. UNHCR, *Global Trends,* 5.
13. IOM Regional Office for Asia and the Pacific, *Regional Strategy,* 4.
14. United Nations Office on Drugs and Crime (UNODC), *United Nations Convention Against Transnational Organized Crime and the Protocols Thereto* (Vienna: UNODC, 2004), 42.
15. UNODC, *United Nations Convention Against Transnational Organized Crime.*
16. International Labour Office, *Profits and Poverty: The Economics of Forced Labour* (Geneva: ILO, 2014), 13.
17. UNODC, *Global Report on Trafficking in Persons 2016* (New York: United Nations Publication, 2016).
18. UNODC, *Global Report on Trafficking in Persons 2016,* 7.
19. UNODC, *Global Report on Trafficking in Persons 2016,* 1.

20. UNODC, *Global Report on Trafficking in Persons 2016*, 6.

21. UNHCR, *Global Trends*, 2.

22. Catherine Putz, "Thailand Deports 100 Uyghurs to China," *Diplomat*, July 11, 2015, http://thediplomat.com/2015/07/thailand-deports-100-uyghurs-to-china/.

23. Andy Hall, *Migrant Workers' Rights to Social Protection in ASEAN: Case Studies of Indonesia, Philippines, Singapore and Thailand* (Singapore: Friedrich Ebert Stiftung, 2011), 101–2.

24. See Joseph Wah, "Is ASEAN Closer to Legal Protection of the Rights of Migrant Workers?," *ASEAN People's Forum*, March 22, 2014; and Paul Vandenberg, "Ensuring the Triple Win of Labour Migration in Asia" (policy brief, Tokyo: Asian Development Bank Institute, 2015).

25. ASEAN Secretariat, "ASEAN Welcomes Entry into Force of ACTIP," ASEAN, media release, March 8, 2017, http://asean.org/asean-welcomes-entry-into-force-of-actip/.

26. See Rebecca Surtees, *After Trafficking: Experiences and Challenges in the (Re)integration of Trafficked Persons in the Greater Mekong Sub-Region* (Bangkok: United Nations Inter-Agency Project on Human Trafficking in the Greater Mekong Sub-Region, 2013).

27. Matthew Friedman, "Coordinated Mekong Ministerial Initiative" (presentation at the Dakar Consultation on the Role of Regional and Sub-Regional Mechanisms in International Efforts to Counter Trafficking in Persons, Especially Women and Children, Dakar, Senegal, October 4–5, 2010).

28. Ruji Auethavornpipat, "Tackling Human Trafficking in ASEAN," *New Mandala*, March 2, 2017, http://www.newmandala.org/tackling-human-trafficking-asean/.

29. Mely Caballero-Anthony, "Movement of People in Asia and Civil Society: Managing Complex Challenges," in *Asia on the Move: Regional Migration and the Role of Civil Society*, ed. Mely Caballero-Anthony and Toshihiro Menju (Tokyo: Japan Center for International Exchange, 2015).

30. Jorge V. Tigno, "Walk the Talk: CSOs, Migrant Workers, and Overseas Employment from the Philippines," in *Asia on the Move: Regional Migration and the Role of Civil Society*, ed. Mely Caballero-Antony and Toshihiro Menju (Tokyo: Japan Center for International Exchange, 2015), 140–62.

31. Tigno, "Walk the Talk."

32. Nicola Piper, "Bridging Gender, Migration and Governance: Theoretical Possibilities in the Asian Context," *Asian and Pacific Migration Journal* 12, no. 1–2 (2003): 21–48, cited in Tigno, "Walk the Talk," 157.

33. Avyanthi Azis, "Indonesia and Labor Outmigration: The Role of Civil Society," in *Asia on the Move: Regional Migration and the Role of Civil Society*, ed. Mely Caballero-Anthony and Toshihiro Menju (Tokyo: Japan Center for International Exchange, 2015).

34. Atsuko Y. Geiger, "Regional Frameworks for Managing Migration and the Role of Civil Society Organizations," in *Asia on the Move: Regional Migration and the Role of Civil Society*, ed. Mely Caballero-Antony and Toshihiro Menju (Tokyo: Japan Center for International Exchange, 2015).

35. For more on the ASEAN Civil Society Conference, see Stefan Rother and Nicola Piper, "Alternative Regionalism from Below: Democratizing ASEAN's Migration Governance," *International Migration* 53, no. 3 (2015): 36–49.

36. Bali Process on People Smuggling, Trafficking in Persons and Related Transnational Crime, "Bali Declaration on People Smuggling, Trafficking in Persons and Related Transnational Crime" (Sixth Ministerial Conference, Bali, Indonesia, March 23, 2016), para. 12.

37. Catriona Martin, "Pro Bono Support of the Bali Process on People Smuggling, Trafficking in Persons and Related Transnational Crime," *Australian Pro Bono News*, October 2016, http://www.probonocentre.org.au/apbn/oct-2016/pro-bono-support-bali -process/.

38. Julie Bishop, "Bali Process Government and Business Forum on Human Trafficking," *Minister for Foreign Affairs*, media release, March 16, 2017, http://foreignminister.gov .au/releases/Pages/2017/jb_mr_170316.aspx.

39. Bishop, "Bali Process Government."

40. U.S. Department of State, *Trafficking in Persons Report June 2005* (Washington, D.C.: U.S. Department of State, 2005), 7.

41. UNHCR, *Mixed Movements in South-East Asia 2016* (Geneva: UNHCR, 2017), 2.

42. See Penny Green, Thomas MacManus, and Alicia de la Cour Venning, *Countdown to Annihilation: Genocide in Myanmar* (London: International State Crime Initiative, 2015).

43. Emanuel Stoakes, Chris Kelly, and Annie Kelly, "Revealed: How the Thai Fishing Industry Trafficks, Imprisons and Enslaves," *Guardian*, July 20, 2015, https://www .theguardian.com/global-development/2015/jul/20/thai-fishing-industry-impli cated-enslavement-deaths-rohingya.

44. Syed Jaymal Zahiid, "Rightless, Rohingya Children at Risk to Vice and Slave Labor," *Malay Mail Online*, December 20, 2016, http://www.themalaymailonline.com/malay- sia/article/rightless-rohingya-children-at-risk-to-vice-and-slave-labour#sthash .qpFXdsm3.dpuf.

45. UNHCR, *South-East Asia Mixed Maritime Movements April–June 2015* (Geneva: UNHCR, 2015), 1.

46. UNHCR, "UNHCR Alarmed at Reports of Boat Pushbacks in South-East Asia," media release, May 13, 2015, http://www.unhcr.org/555345959.html; Praveen Menon, "Malaysia, Indonesia to Let 'Boat People' Come Ashore Temporarily," *Reuters*, May 20, 2015, https://www.reuters.com/article/us-asia-migrants/malaysia-indonesia -to-let-boat-people-come-ashore-temporarily-idUSKBN0O50MV20150520; and "Govt Starts to Repatriate Bangladeshi Refugees," *Jakarta Post*, July 24, 2015, http:// www.thejakartapost.com/news/2015/07/24/govt-starts-repatriate-bangladeshi -refugees.html.

47. UNHCR, *South-East Asia Mixed Maritime Movements*, 1.

48. Surin Pitsuwan and Prashanth Parameswaran, "Why Southeast Asia's Refugee Crisis Matters," *Diplomat*, July 23, 2015, http://thediplomat.com/2015/07/southeast-asia -refugees-in-crisis/.

49. Panu Wongcha-um, "Refugees Vulnerable in Southeast Asia as Global Displaced Hits Record High," *Channel NewsAsia* (Singapore), June 19, 2015, http://www .channelnewsasia.com/news/asiapacific/refugees-vulnerable-in-southeast-asia-as -global-displaced-hits-r-8275722.

50. Amnesty International, "Open Letter: Southeast Asia Refugee Crisis" (ASA 03/1717/2015, May 22, 2015).
51. Amnesty International, "Open Letter."
52. Human Rights Watch, "Southeast Asia: End Rohingya Boat Pushbacks," May 14, 2015, https://www.hrw.org/news/2015/05/14/southeast-asia-end-rohingya-boat-pushbacks.
53. "Don't Treat Rohingyas as Criminals, Gov't Told," *Malaysiakini*, May 14, 2015, http://www.malaysiakini.com/news/298343.
54. Office of the United Nations High Commissioner on Human Rights, "High Commissioner Zeid: Pushbacks Endanger Thousands in Bay of Bengal," May 15, 2015, http://www.ohchr.org/EN/NewsEvents/Pages/DisplayNews.aspx?NewsID=15960&LangID=E#sthash.uADsVG7K.dpuf.
55. See Peter Sutherland et al., "Search and Rescue at Sea, Disembarkation, and Protection of the Human Rights of Refugees and Migrants Now Imperative to Save Lives in the Bay of Bengal and Andaman Sea" (Joint Statement, May 19, 2015), http://www.un.org/en/development/desa/population/migration/partners/docs/Joint_Statement_on_Andaman_Sea.pdf.
56. Ministry of Foreign Affairs of Thailand, "Summary: Special Meeting on Irregular Migration in the Indian Ocean, 29 May 2015, Bangkok, Thailand," media release, May 29, 2015, http://www.mfa.go.th/main/en/media-center/14/56880-Summary-Special-Meeting-on-Irregular-Migration-in.html.
57. Peter Sutherland et al., "A Comprehensive People-Oriented Approach to the Irregular Movement of Migrants and Refugees in South East Asia" (Joint Statement, July 1, 2015), http://www.un.org/en/development/desa/population/migration/partners/docs/Joint_Statement_South_East_Asia.pdf.
58. Ministry of Foreign Affairs of Thailand, "Result of the 2nd Special Meeting on Irregular Migration in the Indian Ocean," December 4, 2015, http://www.mfa.go.th/main/en/media-center/28/62757-Result-of-the-2nd-Special-Meeting-on-Irregular-Mig.html.
59. William Lacy Swing, "Speech at the Special Meeting on Irregular Migration in the Indian Ocean, Bangkok, Thailand, 29 May 2015," International Organization for Migration, June 3, 2015, https://www.iom.int/speeches-and-talks/special-meeting-irregular-migration-indian-ocean. See also IOM, "Better Policies Needed to Help Migrants, IOM Tells Special Meeting in Bangkok," media release, December 4, 2015, https://www.iom.int/news/better-policies-needed-help-migrants-iom-tells-special-meeting-bangkok.
60. Evan Jones, "The Special Meeting on Irregular Migration in the Indian Ocean: Falling Short of Expectations," *Asia Pacific Refugee Rights Network*, media release, June 1, 2015, http://aprrn.info/press-release-the-special-meeting-on-irregular-migration-in-the-indian-ocean-falling-short-of-expectations/.
61. Antje Missbach, "Rohingya Refugees in Aceh, Indonesia: Hostile Hospitality," Middle East Institute, June 2, 2016, http://www.mei.edu/content/map/rohingya-refugees-aceh-indonesia-hostile-hospitality.
62. Missbach, "Rohingya Refugees in Aceh, Indonesia."

63. Sriprapha Petcharamesree, "ASEAN and Its Approach to Forced Migration Issues," *International Journal of Human Rights* 20, no. 2 (2016): 173–90.
64. Susan Kneebone, "The Labeling Problem in Southeast Asia's Refugee Crisis," *Diplomat*, August 12, 2015, http://thediplomat.com/2015/08/the-labeling-problem-in-southeast-asias-refugee-crisis/.
65. Kneebone, "The Labeling Problem."
66. Asia Pacific Refugee Rights Network, "APRRN Joint Statement on the Australia–Malaysia Refugee Swap Agreement," May 17, 2011, http://aprrn.info/aprrn-joint-statement-on-the-australia-malaysia-refugee-swap-agreement/.
67. Asia Pacific Refugee Rights Network, "APRRN Joint Statement."
68. Brian Kelly and Anita J. Wadud, "Asian Labour Migrants and Humanitarian Crises: Lessons from Libya" (policy brief, Bangkok: International Organization for Migration, 2012).
69. Imelda Nicolas and Dovelyn Rannveig Agunias, "The Global Forum on Migration and Development: Perspectives from Asia and the Pacific" (policy brief, Bangkok: International Organization for Migration, 2014).
70. See, for example, Graeme Hugo, "Migration in the Asia-Pacific" (Grand-Saconnex, Switz.: GCIM, 2005); and Nicolas and Agunias, "The Global Forum on Migration and Development."
71. Asian Development Bank, *Impact of Global Crisis on Migrant Workers and Families: Gender Perspective* (Manila: ADB, 2013).
72. United Nations, "UN Human Rights Chief Points to 'Textbook Example of Ethnic Cleansing' in Myanmar," *UN News*, September 11, 2017, https://news.un.org/en/story/2017/09/564622-un-human-rights-chief-points-textbook-example-ethnic-cleansing-myanmar.

6. Governance of Humanitarian Assistance and Disaster Relief Operations

1. Center for Research on the Epidemiology of Disasters (CRED), *The Human Cost of Natural Disasters—2015: A Global Perspective* (Brussels: CRED, 2015), 10.
2. United Nations Office for the Coordination of Humanitarian Affairs (UN OCHA) Regional Office for Asia and the Pacific, *2016 Year in Review*, January 17, 2017, https://ocharoap.exposure.co/2016-year-in-review.
3. The total affected is the sum of injured, homeless, and affected. Those affected are the people requiring immediate assistance during a period of emergency, including displaced or evacuated people. See CRED, *The Human Cost*, 10.
4. CRED, *The Human Cost*.
5. Abhishek Bhati, Aditya Upadhayaya, and Amit Sharma, "National Disaster Management in the ASEAN-5: An Analysis of Tourism Resilience," *Tourism Review* 71, no. 2 (2016): 148–64.

6. UN OCHA, "Asia-Pacific Region: Overview of El Niño Responses—July 2016" (information update, July 15, 2016).

7. M. Assar, *Guide to Sanitation in Natural Disasters* (Geneva: WHO, 1971), 14.

8. See Bantaro Bandoro, "In Indonesia, Natural Disasters Are a Security Concern," *Jakarta Post*, December 18, 2014, http://jakartaglobe.id/opinion/in-indonesia-natural-disasters-are-a-security-concern/.

9. John T. Watson, Michelle Gayer, and Maire A. Connolly, "Epidemics After Natural Disasters," *Emerging Infectious Diseases Journal* 13, no. 1 (2007): 1–5.

10. Internal Displacement Monitoring Centre, *Global Report on Internal Displacement 2017* (Geneva: IDMC, 2017).

11. The eleven countries affected were Mongolia, Vietnam, Indonesia, the Philippines, Timor Leste, Papua New Guinea, Palau, Micronesia, the Marshall Islands, Vanuatu, and Fiji. UN OCHA, "El Niño in Asia," undated, www.UNOCHA.org/legacy/el-nino-asia-pacific; and UN OCHA, "Asia-Pacific Region."

12. CRED, *The Human Cost*, 28.

13. CRED, *The Human Cost*, 30.

14. See, for example, Hannah Brock, "Climate Change: Drivers of Insecurity and the Global South" (London: Oxford Research Group, 2012).

15. The Hyogo Framework for Action 2005–2015 is a ten-year plan adopted by 168 countries that seeks to make the world a safer place for natural hazards by building resilience among nations and communities. It was adopted during the 2005 Second World Conference on Disaster Risk Reduction in Kobe, Japan.

16. ASEAN Coordinating Centre for Humanitarian Assistance (AHA Centre). "About AHA Center," undated, accessed June 28, 2017. https://ahacentre.org/about-us/.

17. See ASEAN, "Strategy and Priorities for AADMER Work Programme Phase 2 2013–2015" (Jakarta: ASEAN Secretariat, 2013).

18. Center for Excellence in Disaster Management and Humanitarian Assistance (CFE-DMHA), *ASEAN Disaster Management Reference Handbook* (Hickam, Hawaii: CFE-DMHA, 2015), 30.

19. CFE-DMHA, *ASEAN Disaster Management Reference Handbook*, 32.

20. ASEAN, "Chairman's Statement" (30th ASEAN Summit, Manila, Philippines, April 29, 2017), http://asean.org/chairmans-statement-30th-asean-summit/.

21. ASEAN, "Terms of Reference of the ASEAN Committee on Disaster Management" (December 2003).

22. ASEAN Coordinating Centre for Humanitarian Assistance (AHA Centre), "ASEAN Committee on Disaster Management (ACDM)," undated, accessed June 28, 2017, accessed from https://ahacentre.org/acdm/; no longer available.

23. Daniel Petz, *Strengthening Regional and National Capacity for Disaster Risk Management: The Case of ASEAN* (Washington, D.C.: Brookings, 2014).

24. ASEAN, "Strategy and Priorities for AADMER."

25. CFE-DMHA, *ASEAN Disaster Management Reference Handbook*.

26. Petz, *Strengthening Regional and National Capacity*.

27. ASEAN Secretariat, "ASEAN to Deepen and Broaden Cooperation in Disaster Management and Emergency Response," ASEAN, media release, April 6, 2017,

http://asean.org/asean-deepen-broaden-cooperation-disaster-management
-emergency-response/.

28. Singapore Civil Defense Force, "4th ASEAN Ministerial Meeting on Disaster Management 2016," media release, October 13, 2016, accessed from https://www.scdf.gov
.sg/general/news/news-releases/2016/4th-asean-ministerial-meeting-disaster
-management-2016; no longer available.

29. See ASEAN, "ASEAN Declaration on One ASEAN One Response: ASEAN Responding to Disasters as One in the Region and Outside the Region" (28th ASEAN Summit, Vientiane, Laos, September 6, 2016).

30. ASEAN, "Joint Declaration of the ASEAN Defence Ministers on Promoting Defence Cooperation for a Dynamic ASEAN Community" (ASEAN Defence Ministers' Meeting, Vientiane, Laos, May 25, 2016).

31. ASEAN, "ASEAN Militaries Ready Group on Humanitarian Assistance and Disaster Relief (AMRG on HADR): Concept Paper" (adopted at the 9th ASEAN Defence Meeting, Langkawi, Malaysia, March 16, 2015).

32. ASEAN, "ASEAN Militaries Ready Group."

33. ASEAN, "Joint Declaration of the ASEAN Defence Ministers."

34. In May 2017, a meeting on the ASEAN Militaries Ready Group on HADR was held in Kuala Lumpur. The participants sought to develop standard operating procedures for the group, which would be necessary in determining the minimum national military personnel, assets, capacities, and capabilities that will be deployed in disaster affected areas. ASEAN Coordinating Centre for Humanitarian Assistance on Disaster Management (AHA Centre), "ASEAN Militaries Ready Group on Humanitarian Assistance and Disaster Relief (AMRG on HADR)," *The Column: AHA Centre News Bulletin* 29 (May 2017): 11.

35. Ministry of Defense of Singapore, "Changi Regional HADR Coordination Centre (RHCC)," media release, January 25, 2017, https://www.mindef.gov.sg/web/portal
/mindef/news-and-events/latest-releases/article-detail/2017/january/25jan17_fact
sheet.

36. CFE-DMHA, *ASEAN Disaster Management Reference Handbook.*

37. ASEAN Defence Ministers' Meeting, "About the ASEAN Defence Ministers' Meeting (ADMM-Plus)," February 6, 2017, https://admm.asean.org/index.php/about-admm
/about-admm-plus.html.

38. CFE-DMHA, *ASEAN Disaster Management Reference Handbook.*

39. Michito Tsuruoka, "An Era of the ADMM-Plus? Unique Achievements and Challenges," *PacNet*, no. 69 (newsletter, Washington, D.C.: Center for Strategic and International Studies, September 2013).

40. ASEAN Defence Ministers' Meeting, "About the ASEAN Defence Ministers' Meeting."

41. ASEAN Regional Forum, "ARF Strategic Guidance for Humanitarian Assistance and Disaster Relief (Draft Version 8)" (ASEAN Regional Forum, March 2010).

42. Mohamed Thajudeen bin Abdul Wahab, "Speech on the Occasion of the ASEAN Regional Forum (ARF) Disaster Relief Exercise (DiREx) 2015 Closing Ceremony" (Kedah, Malaysia, May 28, 2015), https://www.mkn.gov.my/page/speech

-by-ybhg-datuk-mohamed-thajudeen-bin-abdul-wahab-secretary-of-the-national
-security-council-prime-minister-s-department-on-the-occasion-of-the-asean
-regional-forum-arf-disaster-relief-exercise-direx-2015-closing-ceremony-28-may
-2015-kedah.

43. Track 2 Network of ASEAN Defense and Security Institutions, "Chairman's Report" (8th Annual Meeting of the Track 2 Network of ASEAN Defense and Security Institutions [NADI], Kuala Lumpur, Malaysia, February 9–11, 2015).

44. ASEAN and United Nations, "ASEAN–UN Joint Strategic Plan of Action on Disaster Management 2016–2020" (Meeting of the ASEAN Committee on Disaster Management, Semarang, Indonesia, April 26, 2016).

45. ASEAN and United Nations, "ASEAN–UN Joint Strategic Plan of Action."

46. ASEAN and United Nations, "ASEAN–UN Joint Strategic Plan of Action."

47. ASEAN Secretariat, "ASEAN–UN Joint Strategic Plan of Action and Building Disaster- Resilient ASEAN Community," ASEAN, media release, November 3, 2015, http://asean.org/asean-secretaries-general-talk-on-humanitarian-action-and-building-disaster-resilient-asean-community/.

48. ASEAN Secretariat, "ASEAN–UN Joint Strategic Plan of Action."

49. Yukie Osa, "The Growing Role of NGOs in Disaster Relief and Humanitarian Assistance in East Asia," in *A Growing Force: Civil Society's Role in Asian Regional Security*, ed. Rizal Sukma and James Gannon (Tokyo: Japan Center for International Exchange, 2013).

50. CFE-DMHA, *ASEAN Disaster Management Reference Handbook*.

51. G. Tanyang, "Summing-up APG Phase 2: Facilitating Partnerships Between ASEAN and CSOs for AADMER" (AADMER Partnership Group, January 28, 2014).

52. See Laura Allison and Monique Taylor, "ASEAN's 'People-Oriented' Aspirations: Civil Society Influences on Non-Traditional Security Governance," *Australian Journal of International Affairs* 71, no. 1 (2017): 24–41.

53. Allison and Taylor, "ASEAN's 'People-Oriented' Aspirations."

54. Osa, "The Growing Role of NGOs."

55. ASEAN Secretariat, "Private Sector Invited to Play a Bigger Role to Enhance Disaster Management in ASEAN," ASEAN, media release, August 22, 2016, http://asean.org/private-sector-invited-to-play-a-bigger-role-to-enhance-disaster-management-in-asean/.

56. ASEAN Secretariat, "Private Sector Invited to Play a Bigger Role."

57. Corporate Citizen Foundation, "CCF @ Strategic Policy Dialogue in Disaster Management," August 19, 2016, http://corporatecitizen.org/2016/09/ccf-asean-strategic-policy-dialogue-on-disaster-management-2016/.

58. ASEAN, "ASEAN Vision 2025 on Disaster Management" (Jakarta: ASEAN Secretariat, 2015), 13.

59. Keng Gene Ng, "Private Sector Strengthens Commitment Towards Regional Emergency Relief," *Straits Times* (Singapore), March 11, 2016, http://www.straitstimes.com/singapore/private-sector-strengthens-commitment-towards-regional-emergency-relief.

60. Julius Cesar I. Trajano, "Building Resilience from Within: Enhancing Humanitarian Civil–Military Coordination in Post-Haiyan Philippines" (Singapore: S. Rajaratnam School of International Studies, 2016), 12–16.

61. The Post-2015 AADMER Strategic Policy Document suggests that AADMER expand its efforts in the areas of institutionalization, finance and resource mobilization, and partnerships and innovation. The document also proposes to position ASEAN as the focal point for disaster management and emergency response in Southeast Asia, and as a vehicle for wider coordination beyond its immediate neighborhood.

62. Dylan Ming Hui Loh, "ASEAN's Norm Adherence and Its Unintended Consequences in HADR and SAR Operations," *Pacific Review* 29, no. 4 (2016): 556–9.

63. Loh, "ASEAN's Norm Adherence," 558.

64. Josephine Flint, Gloria Martinez, and Kate Sutton, "Asian Perspectives on Civil–Military–Police Relations and Coordination in Disaster Management" (Australian Civil-Military Centre, 2015).

65. Flint, Martinez, and Sutton, "Asian Perspectives on Civil–Military–Police Relations," 12–14.

66. Charter4Change, "Charter for Change: Localization of Humanitarian Aid" (London: Chater4Change, 2015).

67. Global Humanitarian Assistance, *Global Humanitarian Assistance Report 2015* (Bristol, U.K.: Development Initiatives, 2015), cited in Charter4Change, "Charter for Change."

68. Rowel Garcia, "CSOs Call for Localization of Humanitarian Response," *Veritas*, April 26, 2016, http://www.veritas846.ph/csos-call-localization-humanitarian-response/.

7. Governance of Nuclear Energy

1. Daniel Yergin, "Ensuring Energy Security," *Foreign Affairs* 85, no. 2 (2006): 69–82.

2. See, for example, Mely Caballero-Anthony and Collin Koh, "Energy and Non-Traditional Security" (policy brief, Singapore: RSIS, 2008); and Rajesh Basrur and Collin Koh, *Nuclear Energy and Energy in Asia* (Oxford: Routledge, 2012). The policy brief on energy and non-traditional security reflects the discussion points raised at the Regional Workshop on Energy and Non-Traditional Security, held on August 28, 2008, and organized by Centre for Non-Traditional Security Studies of Singapore's S. Rajaratnam School of International Studies.

3. International Atomic Energy Agency (IAEA), *Climate Change and Nuclear Power* (Vienna: IAEA, 2016), 9.

4. International Energy Agency, "Energy Supply Security, Emergency Response of IEA Countries" (Paris: OECD Publishing, 2014), cited in IAEA, 59.

5. Reliable sources of uranium include Australia, Canada, Kazakhstan, and Russia. IAEA, "Energy Supply Security," 60.

6. IAEA, "Energy Supply Security," 61.

7. IAEA, "Energy Supply Security,"62.

8. World Nuclear Association, "Nuclear Power in China," updated June 2017, http://www.world-nuclear.org/information-library/country-profiles/countries-a-f/china-nuclear-power.aspx.

9. "NA Adopts Halt to Ninh Thuan Nuclear Power Plant Project," *Voice of Vietnam*, November 22, 2016, http://english.vov.vn/domestic/na-adopts-halt-to-ninh-thuan-nuclear-power-plant-project-337386.vov.

10. "Vietnam to Scrap Nuclear Plant Construction Plans," *Bangkok Post*, November 9, 2016.

11. IAEA, "IAEA Reviews Malaysia's Nuclear Power Infrastructure Development," media release, October 18, 2016, https://www.iaea.org/newscenter/pressreleases/iaea-reviews-malaysias-nuclear-power-infrastructure-development.

12. Samantha Yap, "Inside Indonesia's Nuclear Dream," *Channel NewsAsia* (Singapore), February 16, 2016, http://www.channelnewsasia.com/news/asiapacific/inside-indonesia-s-nuclear-dream-8166246.

13. Yap, "Inside Indonesia's Nuclear Dream."

14. Fedina S. Sundaryani, "PLN to Go Nuclear if Renewable Energy Goal Flops," *Jakarta Post*, April 25, 2017, http://www.thejakartapost.com/news/2017/04/25/pln-to-go-nuclear-if-renewable-energy-goal-flops.html.

15. Yap, "Inside Indonesia's Nuclear Dream."

16. Haeril Halim, "Most People Approve of Nuclear Power Plant: Batan," *Jakarta Post*, January 16, 2017, http://www.thejakartapost.com/news/2017/01/16/most-people-approve-nuclear-power-plant-batan.html.

17. Victor V. Saulon, "DoE Considering Sulu as Site for Nuclear Plant," *Business World Online,* March 20, 2017, http://www.bworldonline.com/content.php?section=Economy&title=doe-considering-sulu-as-site-for-nuclear-plant&id=142413.

18. "Russia, Philippines' New Partner, Showcases Nuclear Energy," *ABS-CBN News*, June 19, 2017, http://news.abs-cbn.com/business/06/19/17/russia-philippines-new-partner-showcases-nuclear-energy.

19. Hui Yee Tan, "Cambodia and Thailand Edging Closer to Nuclear Power," *Straits Times* (Singapore), May 30, 2016, http://www.straitstimes.com/asia/cambodia-and-thailand-edging-closer-to-nuclear-power.

20. World Health Organization (WHO), "Health Effects of the Chernobyl Accident: An Overview," April 2006, http://www.who.int/ionizing_radiation/chernobyl/backgrounder/en/.

21. WHO, "Health Effects of the Chernobyl Accident."

22. Martin Fackler, "Japan's Nuclear Refugees, Still Stuck in Limbo," *New York Times*, October 1, 2013, http://www.nytimes.com/2013/10/02/world/asia/japans-nuclear-refugees-still-stuck-in-limbo.html.

23. Silva Meybatyan, "Nuclear Disasters and Displacement," *Forced Migration Review*, February 2014, http://www.fmreview.org/crisis/meybatyan.html.

24. "Ten Reasons Against Nuclear Power," *Malaysian Physicians for Peace and Social Responsibility*, updated March 7, 2017, http://mpsr.org/wp/2017/03/07/ten-reasons-against-nuclear-power-updated/.

25. "Nuke Plans on Power Plant, Doctors at Global Meet Tell Putrajaya," *Malay Mail Online*, August 28, 2014, http://www.themalaymailonline.com/malaysia/article/nuke-plans-on-power-plant-doctors-at-global-meet-tell-putrajaya.

26. Anna Estanislao, "Nuclear Power: A Go or No?," *CNN Philippines*, September 1, 2016, http://cnnphilippines.com/news/2016/09/01/nuclear-power-bataan-powerplant-alternative-source-energy-senate-power-crisis.html.

27. Yap, "Inside Indonesia's Nuclear Dream."

28. Hsui Wen Liu, "Taiwan Joins Global Anti-Nuclear Trend," *Asia Times*, January 18, 2017, http://www.atimes.com/article/taiwan-finally-joins-anti-nuclear-movement/.

29. Ming-sho Ho, "The Fukushima Effect: Explaining the Resurgence of the Anti-nuclear Movement in Taiwan," *Environmental Politics* 23, no. 6 (2014): 965–83.

30. Eric Ng, "China's Nuclear Error and Cover-up Unlikely to Hurt Reactor Exports, Industry Competitiveness," *South China Morning Post*, August 14, 2016, http://www.scmp.com/business/companies/article/2002990/chinas-nuclear-error-and-cover-unlikely-hurt-reactor-exports.

31. Mely Caballero-Anthony et al., "The Sustainability of Nuclear Energy in Southeast Asia: Opportunities and Challenges" (Singapore: S. Rajaratnam School of International Studies, 2014).

32. Yukiya Amano, "Atoms for Peace in the 21st Century" (speech at the Energy Market Authority's Distinguished Speaker Program, Singapore, January 26, 2015), International Atomic Energy Agency, www.iaea.org/newscenter/statements/atoms-peace-21st-century-1.

33. T. N. T. Ninh, "Human Resources and Capacity-building: Issues and Challenges for Vietnam" (presentation at the ESI-RSIS International Conference on Nuclear Governance Post-Fukushima, Singapore, October 31, 2013).

34. Yukiya, "Atoms for Peace in the 21st Century."

35. Yukiya, "Atoms for Peace in the 21st Century."

36. Nguyen Nu Hoai Vi, "Viet Nam's Experience in the Area of Nuclear Security" (presentation at the International Cooperation to Enhance a Worldwide Nuclear Security Culture, Amsterdam, March 20, 2014).

37. See IAEA, "Report of the International Review Mission of the Radiation Safety Aspects of a Proposed Rare Earths Processing Facility (the Lynas Project), May 29–June 3, 2011, Malaysia" (IAEA: 2011).

38. See IAEA, *Nuclear Security Culture: Implementing Guide* (Vienna: IAEA, 2008), 3.

39. See IAEA, *Nuclear Security Culture*.

40. Olli Heinonen, "Regional Norms for Cooperation on Nuclear Safety and Emergency Preparedness in Southeast Asia" (RSIS Distinguished Public Lecture, Singapore, November 2, 2016).

41. Tatsujiro Suzuki, "Nuclear Safety and Cooperation in ASEAN" (presentation at the RSIS Roundtable at the Singapore International Energy Week 2016, Singapore, October 28, 2016).

42. Heinonen, "Regional Norms for Cooperation."

43. Heinonen, "Regional Norms for Cooperation."

44. Siriritana Biramontri, "The ASEANTOM and Regional Cooperation on Nuclear Safety in Southeast Asia" (presentation at the Singapore International Energy Week RSIS Roundtable on Nuclear Safety and Cooperation in ASEAN, Singapore, October 28, 2016).

45. See Association of Southeast Asian Nations (ASEAN), "Joint Communique: Turning Vision into Reality for a Dynamic ASEAN Community" (49th ASEAN Foreign Ministers' Meeting, Vientiane, Laos, July 24, 2016).

46. See ASEAN, "Chairman's Statement: Turning Vision into Reality for a Dynamic ASEAN Community" (28th and 29th ASEAN Summits, Vientiane, Laos, September 28, 2016).

47. ASEAN, "Chairman's Statement."

48. Hoang Sy Than, "Vietnam Nuclear Power Program and the New Research Reactor Project" (presentation at the Singapore International Energy Week RSIS Roundtable on Nuclear Safety and Cooperation in ASEAN, Singapore, October 28, 2016).

49. Heinonen, "Regional Norms for Cooperation."

50. See Carl Baker and David Santoro, "Key Findings: Nuclear Energy Experts Group Singapore, Singapore, Feb. 27–28, 2017" (Honolulu: Pacific Forum CSIS, 2017).

51. Carl Baker and Federica Dall'Arche, "Nuclear Governance in Asia after the Nuclear Security Summit Process: A Conference Report of the CSCAP Nuclear Energy Experts Group Meeting, Singapore, September 2016," *Issues & Insights* 16, no. 19 (Honolulu: Pacific Forum CSIS, 2016).

52. Asia-Pacific Leadership Network for Nuclear Non-Proliferation and Disarmament (APLN), "About APLN," undated, accessed July 22, 2017, http://www.a-pln.org/about/about/.

53. APLN, "Southeast Asia Regional Meeting 2016," December 23, 2016, http://www.a-pln.org/meetings/meetings_view/Southeast_Asia_Regional_Meeting_2016.

54. APLN, "Southeast Asia Regional Meeting 2016."

55. Baker and Dall'Arche, "Nuclear Governance in Asia."

56. See ASEAN Network on Nuclear Power Safety Research, "Kick-off Meeting for ASEAN Network on Nuclear Power Safety Research and the 2nd ASEAN Workshop on Nuclear Power Safety Research," 2017, https://docs.google.com/viewer?a=v&pid=sites&srcid=ZGVmYXVsdGRvbWFpbnxhc2Vhbm5ldHdvcmtmb3JucHNyMXxneDooYThhZDUiNGZjMDgwMDhm.

57. Kazuko Hikawa, "Asia-Pacific Safeguards Network—Regional Cooperation in the Field of Safeguards" (presentation at the 23rd WiN Global Annual Conference, Vienna, Austria, August 26, 2015); see also Asia-Pacific Safeguards Network, "Fundamentals and Good Practices of Safeguards Regulatory Authorities," (October 30, 2012), in "Communication dated 14 December 2012 Received from the Australian Government" (INFCIRC/845, IAEA, 2013).

58. As of 2015 the Asian Network for Education in Nuclear Technology comprises members from nineteen states: Australia, Bangladesh, China, India, Indonesia, Japan, Jordan, Republic of Korea, Lebanon, Malaysia, Mongolia, Pakistan, Philippines, Sri Lanka, Syria, Thailand, United Arab Emirates, Vietnam, and Yemen. See IAEA,

"ANENT: Asian Network for Education in Nuclear Technology," November 11, 2015, https://www.iaea.org/nuclearenergy/nuclearknowledge/networking/ANENT/.

8. Governance of Food Security

1. United Nations, "Global Food Crisis 'Silent Tsunami' Threatening over 100 million People, Warns UN," *UN News Centre*, April 22, 2008, http://www.un.org/apps/news /story.asp?NewsID=26412#.Waa8qtJ97IU.

2. Food and Agriculture Organization of the United Nations (FAO), International Fund for Agricultural Development (IFAD), and World Food Program (WFP), *The State of Food Insecurity in the World 2015* (Rome: FAO, 2015), 53.

3. World Food Program (WFP), "Working for Zero Hunger" (factsheet, Rome: WFP, 2017), https://docs.wfp.org/api/documents/WFP-0000016221/download/?_ga=2.6295 9465.770084067.1503629024-295218535.1489636463.

4. United Nations, Department of Economic and Social Affairs, Population Division, "World Population Prospects: The 2017 Revision, Key Findings and Advance Tables" (working paper, ESA/P/WP/248, New York: United Nations, 2017).

5. United Nations, Department of Economic and Social Affairs, Population Division, "World Population Prospects."

6. FAO, IFAD, and WFP, *The State of Food Insecurity in the World 2014* (Rome: FAO, 2014); and FAO, IFAD and WFP, *The State of Food Insecurity in the World 2015*.

7. United Nations, Department of Economic and Social Affairs, Population Division, "World Population Prospects."

8. United Nations, Department of Economic and Social Affairs, Population Division, "World Urbanization Prospects: The 2014 Revision, Highlights" (ST/ESA/ SER.A/352, New York: United Nations, 2014).

9. World Bank, "World Development Indicators—Rural Population," undated, accessed August 25, 2017, http://data.worldbank.org/indicator/SP.RUR.TOTL.ZS.

10. World Bank, "World Development Indicators."

11. Tony Fischer, Derek Byerlee, and Greg Edmeades, *Crop Yields and Global Food Security: Will Yield Increase Continue to Feed the World?* (Canberra, Australia: ACIAR, 2014).

12. John R. Porter et al., "Food Security and Food Production Systems," in *Climate Change 2014: Impacts, Adaptation, and Vulnerability—Summaries, Frequently Asked Questions, and Cross-Chapter Boxes*, ed. Christopher B. Field et al. (Cambridge: Cambridge University Press, 2014).

13. See Barry Desker, Mely Caballero-Anthony, and Paul Teng, "ASEAN Food Security: Towards a More Comprehensive Framework" (paper presented at the Jakarta Framework Project, July 2013).

14. C. Peter Timmer, "Reflections on Food Crises Past," *Food Policy* 35, no.1 (2010): 1–11.

15. Desker, Caballero-Anthony, and Teng, "ASEAN Food Security."

16. See Paul Teng and Margarita Escaler, "The Case for Urban Food Security: A Singapore Perspective" (Singapore: S. Rajaratnam School of International Studies, 2010).

17. ASEAN, "ASEAN Integrated Food Security (AIFS) Framework and Strategic Plan of Action on Food Security in the ASEAN Region (SPA-FS) 2015–2020" (Jakarta: ASEAN Secretariat, 2014).

18. See the AFSIS website, http://www.aptfsis.org/index.php.

19. "ASEAN Seed Council for Strengthening Food Security," *India-ASEAN News on Agriculture and Forestry* (March 2013): 11–12.

20. ASEAN, "ASEAN Integrated Food Security (AIFS) Framework."

21. ASEAN, "ASEAN Integrated Food Security (AIFS) Framework."

22. ASEAN, "ASEAN Integrated Food Security (AIFS) Framework."

23. "Feeding Asia in the 21st Century: Building Urban-Rural Alliances at International Conference on Asian Food Security (ICAFS) 2011 in Singapore," *Asia Pacific Biotech News* 15, no. 8 (2011): 40.

24. See Syngenta and Frontier Strategy Group, *Rice Bowl Index: Translating Complexity into an Opportunity for Action* (Singapore: Syngenta, 2012).

25. Mercedita A. Sombilla et al., "Policy Responses to the Food Price Crisis and Their Implications: The Case of Four Greater Mekong Subregion Countries" (Rome: International Fund for Agriculture Development, 2011).

26. ASEAN Secretariat, *East Asia Summit Documents Series 2005–2014* (Jakarta: ASEAN Secretariat, 2015).

27. ASEAN, "Declaration of the 8th East Asia Summit on Food Security" (8th East Asia Summit, Bandar Seri Begawan, Brunei, October 10, 2013).

28. Murdoch University, "The Murdoch Commission: Commission Members," undated, accessed August 9, 2017, http://www.murdoch.edu.au/Murdoch-Commission/Com missions/Second-Murdoch-Commission/Commission-Members/

29. Jose Ma Luis Montesclaros, "NTS Fast Facts: Food Security" (factsheet, Singapore: S. Rajaratnam School of International Studies, October 2016), http://www.rsis.edu .sg/wp-content/uploads/2017/01/FastFacts-FoodSecurity-final.pdf.

30. Paul Teng, "Food Security: Cities as Part of the Solution and Not the Problem," *RSIS Commentary* (Singapore), August 2012.

31. Teng, "Food Security."

32. Teng, "Food Security."

33. Paul Teng, "Knowledge Intensive Agriculture: The New Disruptor in World Food?," *RSIS Commentary* (Singapore), June 2017.

34. Michael Dean, "Investing in Agriculture Technology" (presentation at the World Agricultural Forum, Singapore, July 7, 2017).

35. AgFunder, *AgTech Investing Report: Year in Review 2016* (San Francisco: AgFunder, 2017).

36. Gerald C. Nelson et al., *Climate Change: Impact on Agriculture and Costs of Adaptation* (Washington, D.C.: IFPRI, 2009).

37. Asian Farmers' Association for Sustainable Rural Development, "About AFA," undated, accessed August 21, 2017, http://asianfarmers.org/?page_id=53.

38. Justin Ong, "Unanswered Questions, Uncertain Future for Kranji Farmers," *Channel NewsAsia* (Singapore), May 28, 2016, http://www.channelnewsasia.com/news/sin gapore/unanswered-questions-uncertain-future-for-kranji-farmers-8030608.

Conclusion: Building Security Governance in Times of Turbulence and Uncertainty

1. Richard Haass, *A World in Disarray: American Foreign Policy and the Crisis of the Old Order* (New York: Penguin Press, 2017).
2. S. Jayakumar and Tommy Koh, "Sovereignty, Jurisdiction and International Law," *Straits Times* (Singapore), June 25, 2016, http://www.straitstimes.com/opinion/sovereignty -jurisdiction-and-international-law; see also Rene L. Pattiradjawane, "Weighing Environmental Diplomacy against Sovereignty Diplomacy," *Straits Times* (Singapore), May 24, 2016, http://www.straitstimes.com/opinion/weighing-environmental-diplo macy-against-sovereignty-diplomacy.
3. World Health Organization (WHO), *Emergency Response Framework* (Geneva: WHO, 2013), 23.
4. Jonathan Watts, "NGOs Upbeat over China's Environmental Transparency Progress," *Guardian*, January 16, 2012, https://www.theguardian.com/environment/2012/jan/16 /green-transparency-china.
5. Carole Excell, "New Jakarta Declaration Aims to Strengthen Rights to Environmental Information in Asia," *World Resources Institute*, May 9, 2013, http://www.wri.org /blog/2013/05/new-jakarta-declaration-aims-strengthen-rights-environmental -information-asia.
6. Alistair D. B. Cook, Maxim Shrestha, and Zin Bo Htet, *International Response to 2015 Nepal Earthquake: Lessons and Observations* (Singapore: S. Rajaratnam School of International Studies, 2016), 22.
7. Jake Hooker, "Quake Revealed Deficiencies of China's Military," *New York Times*, July 2, 2008, http://www.nytimes.com/2008/07/02/world/asia/02china.html.
8. Cook, Shrestha, and Zin, *International Response to 2015 Nepal Earthquake*, 22.
9. R. A. W. Rhodes, "The New Governance: Governance Without Government," *Political Studies* 44 (1996): 652–67.

Bibliography

Abbott, Kenneth W., and Duncan Snidal. "The Governance Triangle: Regulatory Standards Institutions and the Shadow of the State." In *The Politics of Global Regulation*, ed. Walter Mattli and Ngaire Woods, 44–88. Princeton, N.J.: Princeton University Press, 2009.

Abdul Wahab, Mohamed Thajudeen bin. "Speech on the Occasion of the ASEAN Regional Forum (ARF) Disaster Relief Exercise (DiREx) 2015 Closing Ceremony." Kedah, Malaysia, May 28, 2015. https://www.mkn.gov.my/page/speech-by-ybhg-datuk-mohamed -thajudeen-bin-abdul-wahab-secretary-of-the-national-security-council-prime -minister-s-department-on-the-occasion-of-the-asean-regional-forum-arf-disaster -relief-exercise-direx-2015-closing-ceremony-28-may-2015-kedah.

AgFunder. *AgTech Investing Report: Year in Review 2016*. San Francisco: AgFunder, 2017.

Aidenvironment. "Aidenvironment Asia Takes Up a Lead Role in Halting Deforestation in SE Asia." Undated. Accessed June 23, 2017. http://www.aidenvironment.org/project /aidenvironment-asia-takes-up-a-lead-role-in-halting-deforestation-in-se-asia/.

Akaha, Tsuneo. "Non-Traditional Security Cooperation for Regionalism in Northeast Asia." In *Broadening Asia's Security Discourse and Agenda: Political and Environmental Perspectives*, ed. Ramesh Thakur and Edward Newman, 306–39. Tokyo: United Nations University, 2004.

Alagappa, Muthiah. "Comprehensive Security: Interpretations in ASEAN Countries." In *Asian Security Issues: Regional and Global*, ed. Robert Scalapino, Seizaburo Sata, Jusuf Wanandi, and Sung Joo-Han, 50–78. Berkeley: Institute of East Asian Studies, University of California, 1989.

Allison, Laura, and Monique Taylor. "ASEAN's 'People-Oriented' Aspirations: Civil Society Influences on Non-Traditional Security Governance." *Australian Journal of International Affairs* 71, no. 1 (2017): 24–41.

Almanar, Alin, Dames Alexander Sinaga, Anselmus Bata, and Robert Isidorus. "Gov't Issues Perppu to Expedite Disbanding of Anti-Pancasila Organizations, Including HTI." *Jakarta Globe.* July 12, 2017. http://jakartaglobe.id/news/govt-issues-perppu-expedite -disbanding-anti-pancasila-organizations-including-hti/.

Amnesty International. "Indonesia: Amendment of the Mass Organizations Law Expands Threats to the Freedom of Association." Public statement, ASA 21/6722/2017, July 12, 2017.

——. "Open Letter: Southeast Asia Refugee Crisis." ASA 03/1717/2015, May 22, 2015.

ASEAN and United Nations. "ASEAN–UN Joint Strategic Plan of Action on Disaster Management 2016–2020." *Meeting of the ASEAN Committee on Disaster Management,* Semarang, Indonesia, April 26, 2016.

ASEAN Coordinating Center for Humanitarian Affairs (AHA Centre). "About AHA Centre." Undated. Accessed June 28, 2017. https://ahacentre.org/about-us/.

——. "ASEAN Committee on Disaster Management (ACDM)." Undated. Accessed June 27, 2017, from https://ahacentre.org/acdm/; no longer available.

——. "ASEAN Militaries Ready Group on Humanitarian Assistance and Disaster Relief (AMRG on HADR)." *AHA Centre News Bulletin* 29 (May 2017): 11.

ASEAN Defence Ministers' Meeting. "About the ASEAN Defence Ministers' Meeting (ADMM-Plus)." February 6, 2017. https://admm.asean.org/index.php/about-admm /about-admm-plus.html.

ASEAN Network on Nuclear Power Safety Research. "Kick-off Meeting for ASEAN Network on Nuclear Power Safety Research and the 2nd ASEAN Workshop on Nuclear Power Safety Research." 2017. https://docs.google.com/viewer?a=v&pid=sites&srcid =ZGVmYXVsdGRvbWFpbnxhc2Vhbm5ldHdvcmttb3JucHNyMXxneneDoo YThhZDUiNGZjMDgwMDhm.

ASEAN Plus Three Emergency Rice Reserve. "Rule and Procedures of the APTERR Council." Undated. Accessed August 12, 2017, from http://apterr.org/images/down load/document_operation_of_APTERR/Rules_and_Procedures_of_the_APTERR _Council.pdf; no longer available.

ASEAN Regional Forum. "ARF Strategic Guidance for Humanitarian Assistance and Disaster Relief (Draft Version 8)." ASEAN Regional Forum, March 2010.

"ASEAN Rice Reserve Available During Emergencies." *Philippine News Agency*, April 3, 2017. http://www.canadianinquirer.net/2017/04/03/asean-rice-reserve-available-during -emergencies/.

ASEAN Secretariat. "ASEAN to Deepen and Broaden Cooperation in Disaster Management and Emergency Response." ASEAN, media release, April 6, 2017. http:// asean.org/asean-deepen-broaden-cooperation-disaster-management-emergency -response/.

——. "ASEAN Forges Stronger Multi-Stakeholder Partnership for Disaster Management Makati City, Philippines." ASEAN, media release, May 20, 2016. http://asean.org/asean -forges-stronger-multi-stakeholder-partnership-for-disaster-management-makati -city-philippines-20-may-2010/.

——. "ASEAN Secretaries-General Talk on Humanitarian Action and Building Disaster-Resilient ASEAN Community." ASEAN, media release, November 3, 2015. http://

asean.org/asean-secretaries-general-talk-on-humanitarian-action-and-building
-disaster-resilient-asean-community/.

——. "ASEAN Regional Security: The Threats Facing It and the Way Forward." ASEAN,
April 10, 2006. http://asean.org/?static_post=asean-regional-security-the-threats-faci
ng-it-and-the-way-forward-by-asean-secretariat.

——. "ASEAN Response to Combat Avian Influenza." 5th JICA–ASEAN Regional
Cooperation Meeting, Yangon, Myanmar, April 19–21, 2006.

——. "ASEAN Welcomes Entry into Force of ACTIP." ASEAN, media release, March 8,
2017. http://asean.org/asean-welcomes-entry-into-force-of-actip/.

——. East Asia Summit Documents Series 2005–2014. Jakarta: ASEAN Secretariat, 2015.

——. "Private Sector Invited to Play a Bigger Role to Enhance Disaster Management in
ASEAN." ASEAN, media release, August 22, 2016. http://asean.org/private-sector
-invited-to-play-a-bigger-role-to-enhance-disaster-management-in-asean/.

"ASEAN Seed Council for Strengthening Food Security." India-ASEAN News on Agriculture and Forestry, March 2013, 11–12.

Asia–Europe Foundation. Regional Mechanisms of Communicable Disease Control in Asia and
Europe. Singapore: ASEF, 2013.

Asia-Pacific Economic Cooperation (APEC). "2014 Leaders' Declaration." 22nd APEC
Economic Leaders' Meeting, Beijing, China, November 11, 2014.

——. "APEC Health Ministers' Statement." APEC Health Ministerial Meeting, Bangkok, Thailand, June 28, 2003.

Asia-Pacific Leadership Network for Nuclear Non-Proliferation and Disarmament
(APLN). "About APLN." Undated. Accessed July 22, 2017. http://www.a-pln.org
/about/about/.

——. "Southeast Asia Regional Meeting 2016." December 23, 2016. http://www.a-pln
.org/meetings/meetings_view/Southeast_Asia_Regional_Meeting_2016.

Asia Pacific Observatory on Health Systems and Policies. "Informing Policies, Building
Partnerships." Flyer, New Delhi: APO, 2016.

Asia Pacific Refugee Rights Network. "APRRN Joint Statement on the Australia–Malaysia
Refugee Swap Agreement." May 17, 2011. http://aprrn.info/aprrn-joint-statement-on
-the-australia-malaysia-refugee-swap-agreement/.

——. "Who We Are." Undated. Accessed September 21, 2017. http://aprrn.info/about
-us/who-we-are/.

Asia-Pacific Safeguards Network. "Fundamentals and Good Practices of Safeguards Regulatory Authorities." October 30, 2012. In "Communication dated 14 December 2012
Received from the Australian Government." INFCIRC/845, IAEA, January 8, 2013.

Asia Partnership on Emerging Infectious Diseases Research. "APEIR Milestone." Undated.
Accessed June 15, 2017. http://apeir.net/.

Asian Development Bank. Asian Economic Integration Report 2015: How Can Special Economic
Zones Catalyze Economic Development? Manila: ADB, 2015.

——. Impact of Global Crisis on Migrant Workers and Families: Gender Perspective. Manila:
ADB, 2013.

——. "Operational Plan for Health, 2015–2020." Undated. Accessed June 5, 2017. https://
www.adb.org/sectors/health/operational-plan-for-health-2015-2020.

Asian Farmers' Association for Sustainable Rural Development. "About AFA." Undated. Accessed August 21, 2017. http://asianfarmers.org/?page_id=53.

Assar, M. *Guide to Sanitation in Natural Disasters*. Geneva: WHO, 1971.

Association of Southeast Asian Nations (ASEAN). "Agreement on the ASEAN Food Security Reserve" (New York City, October 4, 1979).

——. "ASEAN Declaration on One ASEAN One Response: ASEAN Responding to Disasters as One in the Region and Outside the Region." 28th ASEAN Summit, Vientiane, Lao, September 6, 2016.

——. "ASEAN Integrated Food Security (AIFS) Framework and Strategic Plan of Action on Food Security in the ASEAN Region (SPA-FS) 2015–2020." Jakarta: ASEAN Secretariat, 2014.

——. "ASEAN Militaries Ready Group on Humanitarian Assistance and Disaster Relief (AMRG on HADR: Concept Paper)." Adopted at the 9th ASEAN Defence Meeting, Langkawi, Malaysia, March 16, 2015.

——. *ASEAN Political-Security Community Blueprint*. Jakarta: ASEAN Secretariat, 2009.

——. "ASEAN Vision 2025 on Disaster Management." Jakarta: ASEAN Secretariat, 2015.

——. "Chairman's Statement." *30th ASEAN Summit*, Manila, Philippines, April 29, 2017. http://asean.org/chairmans-statement-30th-asean-summit/.

——. "Chairman's Statement: Turning Vision into Reality for a Dynamic ASEAN Community." 28th and 29th ASEAN Summits, Vientiane, Laos, September 28, 2016.

——. "Declaration of the 8th East Asia Summit on Food Security." 8th East Asia Summit, Bandar Seri Begawan, Brunei Darussalam, October 10, 2013.

——. "Joint Communique: Turning Vision into Reality for a Dynamic ASEAN Community." 49th ASEAN Foreign Ministers' Meeting, Vientiane, Laos, July 24, 2016.

——. "Joint Declaration of the ASEAN Defence Ministers on Promoting Defence Cooperation for a Dynamic ASEAN Community." ASEAN Defence Ministers' Meeting, Vientiane, Laos, May 25, 2016.

——. "Statement on Food Security in the ASEAN Region." *14th ASEAN Summit*, Cha-am, Thailand, March 1, 2009.

——. "Strategy and Priorities for AADMER Work Programme Phase 2 2013–2015." Jakarta: ASEAN Secretariat, 2013.

——. "Terms of Reference of the ASEAN Committee on Disaster Management." December 2003.

——. "2012 Phnom Penh Agenda for ASEAN Community Building." 20th ASEAN Summit, Phnom Penh, Cambodia, April 3, 2012.

Auethavornpipat, Ruji. "Tackling Human Trafficking in ASEAN." *New Mandala*, March 2, 2017. http://www.newmandala.org/tackling-human-trafficking-asean/.

Avant, Deborah D., Martha Finnemore, and Susan K. Sell, eds. *Who Governs the Globe?* New York: Cambridge University Press, 2010.

——. "Who Governs the Globe?" In *Who Governs the Globe?*, ed. Deborah D. Avant, Martha Finnemore, and Susan K. Sell, 1–32. New York: Cambridge University Press, 2010.

Azis, Avyanthi. "Indonesia and Labor Outmigration: The Role of Civil Society." In *Asia on the Move: Regional Migration and the Role of Civil Society*, ed. Mely Caballero-Anthony and Toshihiro Menju, 103–19. Tokyo: Japan Center for International Exchange, 2015.

Baker, Carl, and Federica Dall'Arche. "Nuclear Governance in Asia after the Nuclear Security Summit Process: A Conference Report of the CSCAP Nuclear Energy Experts Group Meeting." *Issues & Insights* 16, no. 19. Honolulu: Pacific Forum CSIS, 2016.

Baker, Carl, and David Santoro. "Key Findings: Nuclear Energy Experts Group Singapore, Feb. 27–28, 2017." Honolulu: Pacific Forum CSIS, 2017.

Baldwin, David A. "The Concept of Security." *Review of International Studies* 23, no. 1 (1997): 5–26.

Bali Process on People Smuggling, Trafficking in Persons and Related Transnational Crime. "Bali Declaration on People Smuggling, Trafficking in Persons and Related Transnational Crime." Sixth Ministerial Conference, Bali, Indonesia, March 23, 2016.

Ball, Desmond. "CSCAP and the ARF." In *Assessing Track 2 Diplomacy in the Asia-Pacific Region: A CSCAP Reader*, ed. Desmond Ball and Kwa Chong Guan, 62–76. Singapore: S. Rajaratnam School of International Studies, 2010.

Balzacq, Thierry. "The Three Faces of Securitization: Political Agency, Audience and Context." *European Journal of International Relations* 11, no. 2 (2005): 171–201.

Bandoro, Bantaro. "In Indonesia, Natural Disasters Are a Security Concern." *Jakarta Post*, December 18, 2014. http://jakartaglobe.id/opinion/in-indonesia-natural-disasters-are-a-security-concern/.

Barnett, Michael, and Martha Finnemore. *Rules for the World: International Organizations in Global Politics*. Ithaca, N.Y.: Cornell University Press, 2004.

Barnett, Tony, and Gwyn Prins. "HIV/AIDS and Security: Fact, Fiction and Evidence." *International Affairs* 82, no. 2 (2006): 359–68.

Basrur, Rajesh, and Collin Koh. *Nuclear Energy and Energy in Asia*. Oxford: Routledge, 2012.

Beeson, Mark, and Alex J. Bellamy. *Securing Southeast Asia: The Politics of Security Sector Reform*. Oxon, U.K.: Routledge, 2008.

Bellamy, Alex J. *Responsibility to Protect: The Global Effort to End Mass Atrocities*. Cambridge: Polity, 2009.

Bennett, Sara, Tikki Pang, Somsak Chunharas, and Thaworn Sakhunpanit. "Global Health Research Governance: An Asian Perspective on the Need for Reform." In *Asia's Role in Governing Global Health*, ed. Kelley Lee, Tikki Pang, and Yeling Tan, 158–76. London: Routledge, 2013.

Bhati, Abhishek, Aditya Upadhayaya, and Amit Sharma. "National Disaster Management in the ASEAN-5: An Analysis of Tourism Resilience." *Tourism Review* 71, no. 2 (2016): 148–64.

Biramontri, Siriritana. "The ASEANTOM and Regional Cooperation on Nuclear Safety in Southeast Asia." Presentation at the Singapore International Energy Week RSIS Roundtable on Nuclear Safety and Cooperation in ASEAN, Singapore, October 28, 2016.

Bishop, Julie. "Bali Process Government and Business Forum on Human Trafficking." Minister for Foreign Affairs, media release, March 16, 2017. http://foreignminister.gov.au/releases/Pages/2017/jb_mr_170316.aspx.

Boykoff, Pamela, and Alexandra Field. "Vietnamese Girls Smuggled into China and Sold as Child Brides." *CNN*, updated April 19, 2016. http://edition.cnn.com/2016/04/17/asia/vietnamese-girls-child-brides-china/index.html.

Brock, Hannah. "Climate Change: Drivers of Insecurity and the Global South." London: Oxford Research Group, 2012.

Brown, Lester R. "Redefining National Security." *Challenge* 29, no. 3 (1986): 25.

Buckley, Chris. "Uncertainty over New Chinese Law Rattles Foreign Nonprofits." *New York Times*, December 29, 2016. https://www.nytimes.com/2016/12/29/world/asia /china-foreign-ngo.html.

Buddhist Tzu Chi Foundation. "Tzu Chi Foundation Exceeds 1 Billion Pesos in Material Aid to Typhoon Haiyan Survivors." *Reliefweb*, January 30, 2014. http://reliefweb.int /report/philippines/tzu-chi-foundation-exceeds-1-billion-pesos-material-aid -typhoon-haiyan-survivors.

Bush, Robin. "Muhammadiyah and Disaster Response: Innovation and Change in Humanitarian Assistance." In *Natural Disaster Management in the Asia-Pacific: Policy and Governance*, ed. Caroline Brassard, David W. Giles, and Arnold M. Howitt, 33–48. Tokyo: Springer, 2015.

——. "Muhammadiyah and Disaster Response: Innovation and Change in Social Welfare." Working paper, Hong Kong: Southeast Asia Research Centre, City University of Hong Kong, 2014.

Buzan, Barry. *People, States and Fear: An Agenda for International Security Studies in the Post– Cold War Era*, 2nd ed. Hemel Hempstead, U.K.: Harvester Wheatsheaf, 1991.

Buzan, Barry, Ole Waever, and Jaap de Wilde. *Security: A New Framework for Analysis*. Boulder, Colo.: Lynne Rienner, 1998.

Caballero-Anthony, Mely. "Combating Infectious Diseases in East Asia: Securitisation and Global Public Goods for Health and Human Security." *Journal of International Affairs* 59, no. 2 (2006): 105–27.

——, ed. *An Introduction to Non-Traditional Security Studies: A Transnational Approach*. London: Sage, 2016.

——. "Movement of People in Asia and Civil Society: Managing Complex Challenges." In *Asia on the Move: Regional Migration and the Role of Civil Society*, ed. Mely Caballero-Anthony and Toshihiro Menju, 7–23. Tokyo: Japan Center for International Exchange, 2015.

——. "Non-State Regional Governance Mechanism for Economic Security: The Case of the ASEAN People's Assembly." *Pacific Review* 17, no. 4 (2004): 567–85.

——. "Non-Traditional Security and Infectious Diseases in ASEAN: Going Beyond the Rhetoric of Securitization to Deeper Institutionalization." *Pacific Review* 12, no. 4 (2008): 507–25.

——. "Revisioning Human Security in Southeast Asia." *Asian Perspective* 28, no. 3 (2006): 155–89.

——. "SARS in Asia: Crisis, Vulnerabilities, and Regional Responses." *Asian Survey* 45, no. 3 (2005): 475–95.

——. "Securitizing Infectious Diseases in Asia." *Indonesian Quarterly* 34, no. 1 (2006): 45–52.

Caballero-Anthony, Mely, and Alistair Cook, eds. *Non-Traditional Security in Asia: Issues, Challenges and Frameworks for Action*. Singapore: Institute of Southeast Asian Studies, 2013.

Caballero-Anthony, Mely, Alistair D. B. Cook, Gianna Gayle Herrera Amul, and Akanksha Sharma. "Health Governance and Dengue in Southeast Asia." Singapore: S. Rajaratnam School of International Studies, 2015.

Caballero-Anthony, Mely, Alistair Cook, Julius Trajano, and Margareth Sembiring. "The Sustainability of Nuclear Energy in Southeast Asia: Opportunities and Challenges." Singapore: S. Rajaratnam School of International Studies, 2014.

Caballero-Anthony, Mely, and Ralf Emmers. "The Dynamics of Securitization in Asia." In *Studying Non-Traditional Security in Asia: Trends and Issues*, ed. Ralf Emmers, Mely Caballero-Anthony, and Amitav Acharya, 21–35. Singapore: Marshall Cavendish, 2006.

Caballero-Anthony, Mely, and Tian Goh. "ASEAN's Haze Shroud: Grave Threat to Human Security." *RSIS Commentary* (Singapore), October 2015.

Caballero-Anthony, Mely, and Collin Koh. "Energy and Non-Traditional Security." Policy brief, Singapore: S. Rajaratnam School of International Studies, 2008.

Caballero-Anthony, Mely, Paul P. S. Teng, Maxim Shrestha, Tamara Nair, and Jonatan A. Lassa. "Public Stockpiling and Food Security." Singapore: S. Rajaratnam School of International Studies, 2015.

Center for Excellence in Disaster Management and Humanitarian Assistance (CFE-DMHA). *ASEAN Disaster Management Reference Handbook*. Hickam, Hawaii: CFE-DMHA, 2015.

Center for Non-Traditional Security Studies. *Pandemic Preparedness in Asia*. Singapore: S. Rajaratnam School of International Studies, 2009.

Center for Research on the Epidemiology of Disasters (CRED). *The Human Cost of Natural Disasters—2015: A Global Perspective*. Brussels: CRED, 2015.

Chan, Margaret. "WHO Director-General Addresses UN Security Council on Ebola." Address to Emergency Session of the UN Security Council on Peace and Security in Africa (Ebola), New York, September 18, 2014. http://www.who.int/dg/speeches/2014/security-council-ebola/en/.

Charter4Change. "Charter for Change: Localization of Humanitarian Aid." London: Charter4Change, 2015.

Cheeseman, Graeme. "Asia-Pacific Security Discourse in the Wake of the Asian Economic Crisis." *Pacific Review* 12, no. 3 (1999): 333–56.

Cheng, Joseph Y. S. "Broadening the Concept of Security in East and Southeast Asia: The Impact of the Asian Financial Crisis and the September 11 Incident." *Journal of Contemporary China* 15, no. 46 (2006): 89–111.

Cochrane, Joe. "Blazes in Southeast Asia May Have Led to Deaths of over 100,000, Study Says." *New York Times*, September 19, 2016. https://www.nytimes.com/2016/09/20/world/asia/indonesia-haze-smog-health.html.

Coleman, Diane. "Policy Networks, Non-State Actors, and Internationalized Policy-Making: A Case Study of Agricultural Trade." In *Non-State Actors in World Politics*, ed. Daphne Josselin and William Wallace, 93–112. Hampshire, U.K.: Palgrave, 2001.

Commission on Human Security. *Human Security Now: Protecting and Empowering People*. New York: Commission on Human Security, 2003.

Cook, Alistair D. B., Maxim Shrestha, and Zin Bo Htet. *International Response to 2015 Nepal Earthquake: Lessons and Observations*. Singapore: S. Rajaratnam School of International Studies, 2016.

——. "The 2015 Nepal Earthquake: Implications for Future International Relief Efforts." Singapore: S. Rajaratnam School of International Studies, 2016.

Corporate Citizen Foundation. "CCF @ Strategic Policy Dialogue in Disaster Management." August 19, 2016. http://corporatecitizen.org/2016/09/ccf-asean-strategic-policy-dialogue-on-disaster-management-2016/.

Coulibaly, Aïcha L. "The Food Price Increase of 2010–2011: Causes and Impacts." Background paper, 2013-02-E, Ottawa: Library of Parliament, 2013.

Coulibaly, Souleymane, Hiroki Minami, Maho Abe, Tomohiro Hasei, Tadashi Oro, Kunihiro Funasaka, Daichi Asakawa, Masanari Watanabe, Naoko Honda, Keiji Wakabayashi, and Tetsushi Watanabe. "Long-Range Transport of Mutagens and Other Air Pollutants from Mainland East Asia to Western Japan." *Genes and Environment* 37, no. 25 (2015): 1–10.

Coulibaly, Souleymane, Hiroki Minami, Maho Abe, Tomohiro Hasei, Nobuyuki Sera, Shigekazu Yamamoto, Kunihiro Funasaka, Daichi Asakawa, Masanari Watanabe, Naoko Honda, Keiji Wakabayashi, and Tetsushi Watanabe, "Seasonal Fluctuations in Air Pollution in Dazaifu, Japan, and Effect of Long-Range Transport from Mainland East Asia." *Biological and Pharmaceutical Bulletin* 38, no. 9 (2015): 1395–403.

Council for Security Cooperation in the Asia Pacific (CSCAP). "The Security Implications of Climate Change." Memorandum, Kuala Lumpur: CSCAP, June 2010.

Curley, Melissa, and Nicholas Thomas. "Human Security and Public Health in Southeast Asia: The SARS Outbreak." *Australian Journal of International Affairs* 58, no. 1 (2004): 17–32.

Cutler, A. Claire. "Private International Regimes and Interfirm Cooperation." In *The Emergence of Private Authority in Global Governance*, ed. Rodney Bruce Hall and Thomas J. Biersteker, 23–40. Cambridge: Cambridge University Press, 2002.

Davies, Sara E. "Securitizing Infectious Diseases." *International Affairs* 84, no. 2 (2008): 295–313.

Dean, Michael. "Investing in Agriculture Technology." Presentation at the World Agricultural Forum, Singapore, July 7, 2017.

Desker, Barry, Mely Caballero-Anthony, and Paul Teng. "ASEAN Food Security: Towards a More Comprehensive Framework." Paper presented at the Jakarta Framework Project, July 2013.

"Don't Treat Rohingyas as Criminals, Gov't Told." *Malaysiakini*, May 14, 2015. http://www.malaysiakini.com/news/298343.

Douple, Evan B., Kiyohiko Mabuchi, Harry M. Cullins, Dale L. Preston, Kazunori Kodama, Yukiko Shimizu, Saeko Fujiwara, and Roy E. Shore. "Long-Term Radiation-Related Health Effects in a Unique Human Population: Lessons Learned from the Atomic Bomb Survivors of Hiroshima and Nagasaki." *Disaster Medicine Public Health Preparedness* 5, no. 1 (2011): S122–33.

Duggan, Jennifer. "Kunming Pollution Protest Is Tip of Rising Chinese Environmental Activism." *Guardian*, May 16, 2013. https://www.theguardian.com/environment/chinas-choice/2013/may/16/kunming-pollution-protest-chinese-environmental-activism.

East Asia Summit. "Declaration on Avian Influenza Prevention, Control and Response." 1st East Asia Summit, Kuala Lumpur, Malaysia, December 14, 2005.

——. "Declaration on Regional Responses to Malaria Control and Addressing Resistance to Antimalarial Medicines." 7th East Asia Summit, Phnom Penh, Cambodia, November 20, 2012.

Elliott, Lorraine. "Human Security/Environmental Security." *Contemporary Politics* 21, no. 1 (2015): 11–24.

Emmers, Ralf, and John Ravenhill. "The Asian and Global Financial Crises: Consequences for East Asian Regionalism." Working paper, Singapore: S. Rajaratnam School of International Studies, 2010.

Estanislao, Anna. "Nuclear Power: A Go or No?" *CNN Philippines*, September 1, 2016. http://cnnphilippines.com/news/2016/09/01/nuclear-power-bataan-powerplant-alternative-source-energy-senate-power-crisis.html.

Excell, Carole. "New Jakarta Declaration Aims to Strengthen Rights to Environmental Information in Asia." *World Resources Institute*, May 9, 2013. http://www.wri.org/blog/2013/05/new-jakarta-declaration-aims-strengthen-rights-environmental-information-asia.

Fackler, Martin. "Japan's Nuclear Refugees, Still Stuck in Limbo." *New York Times*, October 1, 2013. http://www.nytimes.com/2013/10/02/world/asia/japans-nuclear-refugees-still-stuck-in-limbo.html.

"Feeding Asia in the 21st Century: Building Urban-Rural Alliances at International Conference on Asian Food Security (ICAFS) 2011 in Singapore." *Asia Pacific Biotech News* 15, no. 8 (2011): 40.

Fidler, David. "Asia and Global Health Governance: Power, Principles and Practice." In *Asia's Role in Governing Global Health*, ed. Kelley Lee, Tikki Pang, and Yeling Tan, 198–214. London: Routledge, 2013.

Finer, S. E. *Comparative Government*. London: Allen Lane / Penguin, 1970.

Firmansyah, Nurul, Romes Hirawan, and Isnandi. "Indonesia Declares Haze—Emergency." Utrecht, Neth.: ICCO Cooperation, 2015.

Fischer, Tony, Derek Byerlee, and Greg Edmeades. *Crop Yields and Global Food Security: Will Yield Increase Continue to Feed the World?* Canberra, Australia: ACIAR, 2014.

Flemes, Daniel, and Michael Radseck. "Creating Multilevel Security Governance in South America." Working paper, Hamburg: German Institute of Global and Area Studies, 2009.

Flint, Joesphine, Gloria Martinez, and Kate Sutton. "Asian Perspectives on Civil–Military–Police Relations and Coordination in Disaster Management." Australian Civil-Military Centre, 2015.

Food and Agriculture Organization of the United Nations (FAO). *The Future of Food and Agriculture—Trends and Challenges*. Rome: FAO, 2017.

Food and Agriculture Organization of the United Nations (FAO), International Fund for Agricultural Development (IFAD), and World Food Program (WFP). *The State of Food Insecurity in the World 2014*. Rome: FAO, 2014.

——. *The State of Food Insecurity in the World 2015*. Rome: FAO, 2015.

Friedman, Matthew. "Coordinated Mekong Ministerial Initiative." Presentation at the Dakar Consultation on the Role of Regional and Sub-Regional Mechanisms in International

Efforts to Counter Trafficking in Persons, Especially Women and Children, Dakar, Senegal, October 4–5, 2010.

Friends of Nature, Institute of Public and Environmental Affairs, and Green Beagle. "2010 Study of Heavy Metal Pollution by IT Brand Supply Chain: The IT Industry Has a Critical Duty to Prevent Heavy Metal Pollution." April 24, 2010. http://chinawaterrisk .org/wp-content/uploads/2011/04/Initial-Study-of-Heavy-Metal-Pollution-by-IT -Brand-Supply-Chain-English-Final.pdf.

Friends of Nature, Institute of Public and Environmental Affairs, Green Beagle, Environmental Protection Commonwealth Association, and Nanjing Green Stone Environmental Action Network. "Green Choice Apparel Supply Chain Investigation, Draft Report: Cleaning up the Fashion Industry." April 9, 2012. http://wwwoa.ipe.org.cn //Upload/Report-Textiles-One-EN.pdf.

Gao, Ruge. "Rise of Environmental NGOs in China: Official Ambivalence and Contested Messages." *Journal of Political Risk* 1, no. 8 (2013).

Gao Qiang. "Speech at the HIV/AIDS High-Level Meeting of the UN General Assembly." Permanent Mission of the People's Republic of China to the United Nations Office at Geneva and Other International Organizations in Switzerland, September 22, 2003. http://www.china-un.ch/eng/dbtyw/zmjg_1/jgthsm/t85551.htm.

Garcia, Rowel. "CSOs Call for Localization of Humanitarian Response." *Veritas*, April 26, 2016. http://www.veritas846.ph/csos-call-localization-humanitarian-response/.

Gavi. "Disbursements and Commitments (by Country)." Gavi: The Vaccine Alliance. Undated. Accessed June 27, 2013. http://www.gavialliance.org/results/disbursements/.

Geiger, Atsuko Y. "Regional Frameworks for Managing Migration and the Role of Civil Society Organisations." In *Asia on the Move: Regional Migration and the Role of Civil Society*, ed. Mely Caballero-Antony and Toshihiro Menju, 183–202. Tokyo: Japan Center for International Exchange, 2015.

Gerard, Kelly. "From the ASEAN People's Assembly to the ASEAN Civil Society Conference: The Boundaries of Civil Society Advocacy." *Contemporary Politics* 19, no. 4 (2013): 411–26.

Global Fund. "Global Fund Portfolio Downloads." Undated. Accessed June 27, 2013. http:// portfolio.theglobalfund.org/en/Downloads/DisbursementsInDetail.

Global Humanitarian Assistance. *Global Humanitarian Assistance Report 2015*. Bristol, U.K.: Development Initiatives, 2015.

"Govt Starts to Repatriate Bangladeshi Refugees." *Jakarta Post*, July 24, 2015. http://www .thejakartapost.com/news/2015/07/24/govt-starts-repatriate-bangladeshi-refugees .html.

Green, Michael J., and Bates Gill, eds. *Asia's New Multilateralism: Cooperation, Competition, and the Search for Community*. New York: Columbia University Press, 2009.

Greenpeace. *Dirty Bankers: How HSBC Is Financing Forest Destruction for Palm Oil*. Amsterdam: Greenpeace, 2017.

——. *Indonesia's Forests: Under Fire*. Amsterdam: Greenpeace, 2015.

Green, Penny, Thomas MacManus, and Alicia de la Cour Venning. *Countdown to Annihilation: Genocide in Myanmar*. London: International State Crime Initiative, 2015.

Gregoratti, Catia. "UN–Business Partnerships." In *Handbook of Transnational Governance: Institutions and Innovations*, ed. Thomas Hale and David Held, 309–21. Oxford: Polity, 2011.

Grills, Nathan. "The Paradox of Multilateral Organizations Engaging with Faith-Based Organizations." *Global Governance* 15, no. 4 (2009): 505–20.

Haas, Peter M. "Introduction: Epistemic Communities and International Policy Coordination." *International Organization* 46, no. 1 (1992): 1–35.

Haass, Richard. *A World in Disarray: American Foreign Policy and the Crisis of the Old Order.* New York: Penguin Press, 2017.

Hale, Erin, and Aleksander Solum. "Laos NGO Restrictions Threaten Development, Say Non- Profit Groups." *South China Morning Post*, September 17, 2014. http://www.scmp .com/news/asia/article/1594490/laos-ngo-restrictions-threaten-development-say-non -profit-groups.

Halim, Haeril. "Most People Approve of Nuclear Power Plant: Batan." *Jakarta Post*, January 16, 2017. http://www.thejakartapost.com/news/2017/01/16/most-people-approve -nuclear-power-plant-batan.html.

Hall, Andy. *Migrant Workers' Rights to Social Protection in ASEAN: Case Studies of Indonesia, Philippines, Singapore and Thailand.* Singapore: Friedrich Ebert Stiftung, 2011.

Hall, Rodney Bruce, and Thomas J. Biersteker. "The Emergence of Private Authority in the International System." In *The Emergence of Private Authority in Global Governance*, ed. Rodney Bruce Hall and Thomas J. Biersteker, 3–22. Cambridge: Cambridge University Press, 2002.

Hameiri, Shahar, and Lee Jones. *Governing Borderless Threats: Non-Traditional Security and the Politics of State Transformation.* Cambridge: Cambridge University Press, 2015.

Hampson, Fen Osler, Jean Daudelin, John B. Hay, Todd Martin, and Holly Reid. *Madness in the Multitude: Human Security and World Disorder.* Oxford: Oxford University Press, 2002.

Hanefeld, Johanna. "Global Fund to Fight AIDS, Tuberculosis, and Malaria." In *Handbook of Transnational Governance: Institutions and Innovations*, ed. Thomas Hale and David Held, 161–66. Oxford: Polity, 2011.

Hänggi, Heiner. "Making Sense of Security Sector Governance." In *Challenges of Security Sector Governance*, ed. Heiner Hänggi and Theodor Winkler, 3–23. Munster: LIT Verlag, 2004.

Hanrieder, Tine, and Christian Kreuder-Sonnen. "WHO Decides on the Exception? Securitization and Emergency Governance in Global Health." *Security Dialogue* 45, no. 4 (2014): 331–48.

Harman, Sophie. *Global Health Governance.* London: Routledge, 2012.

Hawkes, Percy W., Ricardo Echalar, Setyawan Budiharta, and Susy Soenarjo. "USAID/ Indonesia Avian and Pandemic Influenza (API) Program Evaluation: 2009–2014." Washington, D.C.: GH Tech Project Bridge IV, 2014.

Haworth, Nigel, and Steve Hughes. "Labor." In *International Organization and Global Governance*, ed. Thomas G. Weiss and Rorden Wilkinson, 335–48. Abingdon, U.K.: Routledge, 2014.

"Hazardous Air Quality Detected in Kalimantan and Riau." *Jakarta Post*, September 28, 2015. http://www.thejakartapost.com/news/2015/09/28/hazardous-air-quality-detected -kalimantan-and-riau.html.

"Haze & Us: We Breathe What We Buy." *We Breathe What We Buy*. Undated. Accessed June 22, 2017. https://webreathewhatwebuy.com/_2015/haze/.

"Haze Fires Cost Indonesia $22b, Twice Tsunami Bill: World Bank." *Straits Times* (Singapore), December 16, 2015. http://www.straitstimes.com/asia/se-asia/haze-fires-cost -indonesia-22b-twice-tsunami-bill-world-bank.

He, Baogang. *Contested Ideas of Regionalism in Asia*. London: Routledge, 2016.

He, Zhongyi. "*Feichuantong Anquan yu Zhongguo: Xueshu Yantaohui Zongshu* [Non-Traditional Security in China: Conference Report], *Shijie Jingji yu Zhengzhi* [World Economics and Politics], no. 3 (2004): 48–55.

Heads of States of ASEAN and China. "Joint Statement." Special ASEAN-China Leaders Meeting on the Severe Acute Respiratory Syndrome (SARS), Bangkok, Thailand, April 29, 2003.

Heads of States of ASEAN and Japan. "The ASEAN–Japan Plan of Action (2011–2015)." 14th ASEAN–Japan Summit, Bali, Indonesia, November 18, 2011.

Heads of States of ASEAN and Republic of Korea. "Plan of Action to Implement the Joint Declaration on ASEAN–ROK Strategic Partnership for Peace and Prosperity (2011–2015." 13th ASEAN–Republic of Korea Summit, Hanoi, Vietnam, October 29, 2010.

Heads of States of China, Japan, and Republic of Korea. "Joint Declaration on the Enhancement of Trilateral Comprehensive Cooperative Partnership." Fifth Trilateral Summit Meeting among the People's Republic of China, the Republic of Korea and Japan, Beijing, China, May 13, 2012.

——. "Joint Statement." Tenth Anniversary of Trilateral Cooperation Among the People's Republic of China, Japan, and the Republic of Korea, Beijing, China, October 10, 2009.

Health Effects Institute. *State of Global Air 2017*. Boston: HEI, 2017.

Heinonen, Olli. "Regional Norms for Cooperation on Nuclear Safety and Emergency Preparedness in Southeast Asia." RSIS Distinguished Public Lecture, Singapore, November 2, 2016.

Held, David. "The Diffusion of Authority." In *International Organization and Global Governance*, ed. Thomas G. Weiss and Rorden Wilkinson, 60–72. Abingdon, U.K.: Routledge, 2014.

Herington, Jonathan. "Securitization of Infectious Diseases in Vietnam: The Cases of HIV and Avian Influenza." *Health Policy and Planning* 25, no. 6 (2010): 467–75.

Hew, Denis. "Economic Integration in East Asia: An ASEAN Perspective." Madrid: Research Unit on International Security and Cooperation, University of Madrid, 2006.

Higgott, Richard A., Geoffrey R. D. Underhill, and Andreas Bieler. "Introduction: Globalisation and Non-State Actors." In *Non-State Actors and Authority in the Global System*, ed. Richard A. Higgott, Geoffrey R. D. Underhill, and Andreas Bieler, 1–12. London: Routledge, 2000.

High-Level Advisory Panel on the Responsibility to Protect in Southeast Asia. "Mainstreaming the Responsibility to Protect in Southeast Asia: Pathway Towards a Caring

ASEAN Community." Report presented at the United Nations, New York, September 9, 2014. https://r2pasiapacific.org/high-level-advisory-panel-r2p-southeast-asia.

Hikawa, Kazuko. "Asia-Pacific Safeguards Network—Regional Cooperation in the Field of Safeguards." Presentation at the 23rd WiN Global Annual Conference, Vienna, Austria, August 26, 2015.

Hoffman, Peter J. "Private Military and Security Companies." In *International Organization and Global Governance*, ed. Thomas G. Weiss and Rorden Wilkinson, 385–96. Abingdon, U.K.: Routledge, 2014.

Hoffman, Steven J. "The Evolution, Etiology and Eventualities of the Global Health Security Regime." *Health Policy and Planning* 25, no. 6 (2010): 510–22.

Ho, Ming-sho. "The Fukushima Effect: Explaining the Resurgence of the Anti-Nuclear Movement in Taiwan." *Environmental Politics* 23, no. 6 (2014): 965–83.

Honna, Jun. "The Role of Civil Society Organizations in Combating Human Trafficking in Southeast Asia." In *A Growing Force: Civil Society Role in Asian Regional Security*, ed. Rizal Sukma and James Gannon, 43–65. Tokyo: Japan Center for International Exchange, 2013.

Hooker, Jake. "Quake Revealed Deficiencies of China's Military." *New York Times*, July 2, 2008. http://www.nytimes.com/2008/07/02/world/asia/02china.html.

HSBC. "HSBC Statement on Revised Agricultural Commodities Policy: Palm Oil." Media release, February 20, 2017. http://www.hsbc.com/news-and-insight/media -resources/media-releases/2017/hsbc-statement-on-revised-agricultural-commodities -policy.

Huang, Yanzhong. "China's Response to the 2014 Ebola Outbreak in West Africa." *Global Challenges* 1, no. 2 (2017): 1–7.

——. "Global Health, Civil Society, and Regional Security." In *A Growing Force: Civil Society Role in Asian Regional Security*, ed. Rizal Sukma and James Gannon, 25–42. Tokyo: Japan Center for International Exchange, 2013.

——. "Pursuing Health as Foreign Policy: The Case of China." *Indiana Journal of Global Legal Studies* 17, no. 1 (2010): 105–46.

Hugo, Graeme. "Migration in the Asia-Pacific." Grand-Saconnex, Switz.: GCIM, 2005.

Human Rights Watch. "Southeast Asia: End Rohingya Boat Pushbacks." May 14, 2015. https://www.hrw.org/news/2015/05/14/southeast-asia-end-rohingya-boat-pushbacks.

Hussain, Zakir. "Singapore Taking Action Against Companies Responsible for Haze, Says Masagos Zulkifli." *Straits Times* (Singapore), April 21, 2016. http://www.straitstimes.com /singapore/environment/singapore-taking-action-against-companies-responsible-for -haze-says-masagos.

"Indonesia's Vice-President Jusuf Kalla Criticizes Neighbors for Grumbling about Haze." *Straits Times* (Singapore), March 5, 2015. http://www.straitstimes.com/asia/se-asia/indo nesias-vice-president-jusuf-kalla-criticises-neighbours-for-grumbling-about-haze.

Institute of Defence and Strategic Studies. "Non-Traditional Security in Asia: The Dynamics of Securitization." Workshop report, Singapore: IDSS, 2004.

Institute of Public and Environmental Affairs. "CITI Evaluation Guideline 3.1." Undated. Accessed June 27, 2017. http://www.ipe.org.cn/greensupplychain/userguide/CITI%20 Evaluation%20Guideline%20V3.1.pdf.

Internal Displacement Monitoring Centre. *Global Report on Internal Displacement 2017*. Geneva: IDMC, 2017.

International Atomic Energy Agency (IAEA). "ANENT: Asian Network for Education in Nuclear Technology." November 11, 2015. https://www.iaea.org/nuclearenergy/nucle arknowledge/networking/ANENT/.

——. *Climate Change and Nuclear Power*. Vienna: IAEA, 2016.

——. "IAEA Reviews Malaysia's Nuclear Power Infrastructure Development." Media release, October 18, 2016. https://www.iaea.org/newscenter/pressreleases/iaea-reviews -malaysias-nuclear-power-infrastructure-development.

——. *Nuclear Security Culture: Implementing Guide*. Vienna: IAEA, 2008.

——. "Report of the International Review Mission of the Radiation Safety Aspects of a Proposed Rare Earths Processing Facility (the Lynas Project), May 29–June 3, 2011, Malaysia." IAEA: 2011.

International Campaign to Ban Landmines. "Timeline of the International Campaign to Ban Landmines." Campaigning tool, Geneva: ICBL. Undated. Accessed February 15, 2017. http://www.icbl.org/media/342067/icb009_chronology_a5_v4-pages.pdf.

International Commission on Intervention and State Sovereignty. *The Responsibility to Protect: Report of the International Commission on Intervention and State Sovereignty*. Ottawa: International Development Research Centre, 2001.

International Energy Agency. *World Energy Outlook 2015 Special Report: Southeast Asia Energy Outlook*. Paris: IEA, 2015.

International Labour Office. *Profits and Poverty: The Economics of Forced Labour*. Geneva: ILO, 2014.

International Monetary Fund. "IMF Survey: Asia: Growth Remains Strong, Expected to Ease Only Modestly." May 3, 2016. http://www.imf.org/en/News/Articles/2015/09/28 /04/53/socar050316b.

International Organization for Migration (IOM). "Better Policies Needed to Help Migrants, IOM Tells Special Meeting in Bangkok." Media release, December 4, 2015. https://www .iom.int/news/better-policies-needed-help-migrants-iom-tells-special-meeting -bangkok.

——. "International Dialogue on Migration 2008, Challenges of Irregular Migration: Addressing Mixed Migration Flows, Discussion Note." MC/INF/294, IOM, 2008.

——. "Key Migration Terms." Undated. Accessed August 13, 2017. https://www.iom.int /key-migration-terms.

IOM Regional Office for Asia and the Pacific. *Regional Strategy for Asia and the Pacific 2012–2015*. Bangkok: IOM, 2012.

Jackson, Nicole J. "International Organizations, Security Dichotomies and the Trafficking of Persons and Narcotics in Post-Soviet Central Asia: A Critique of the Securitization Framework." *Security Dialogue* 37, no. 3 (2006): 299–317.

Jacobs, Andrew. "Typhoon Response Highlights Weaknesses in Philippine Military." *New York Times*, November 19, 2013. http://www.nytimes.com/2013/11/20/world/asia/typhoon -response-highlights-weaknesses-in-philippine-military.html?pagewanted=all.

Japan Institute of International Affairs. *In Quest of Human Security*. Tokyo: JIIA, 2001.

Jayakumar, S., and Tommy Koh. "Sovereignty, Jurisdiction and International Law." *Straits Times* (Singapore), June 25, 2016. http://www.straitstimes.com/opinion/sovereignty -jurisdiction-and-international-law.

Jetschke, Anja. "Is ASEAN a Provider of Regional Security Governance?" Hamburg: German Institute of Global and Area Studies, 2011.

Jo, He-rim. "South Korea Has OECD's Second-Worst Air Quality." *Korea Herald*, February 16, 2017. http://www.koreaherald.com/view.php?ud=20170216000831.

Johnston, Eric. "Yellow Dust Storms Getting Worse." *Japan Times*, April 22, 2008. http:// www.japantimes.co.jp/news/2008/04/22/reference/yellow-dust-storms-getting-worse /#.WXtiStJ97IU.

Jones, Evan. "The Special Meeting on Irregular Migration in the Indian Ocean: Falling Short of Expectations." *Asia Pacific Refugee Rights Network*, media release, June 1, 2015. http://aprrn.info/press-release-the-special-meeting-on-irregular-migration-in-the-in dian-ocean-falling-short-of-expectations/.

Josselin, Daphne, and William Wallace. "Non-State Actors in World Politics: A Framework." In *Non-State Actors in World Politics*, ed. Daphne Josselin and William Wallace, 1–20. New York: Palgrave, 2001.

Junadi, Purnawan. "Pandemic Preparedness Operations, Systems and Networks: The Indonesian Case." In *Pandemic Preparedness in Asia*, ed. Mely Caballero-Anthony, 27–34. Singapore: S. Rajaratnam School of International Studies, 2009.

Jung, Woosuk. "South Korea's Air Pollution: Gasping for Solutions." Policy brief. Stockholm: Institute for Security and Development Policy, 2017.

Kallings, L. O. "The First Postmodern Pandemic: 25 Years of HIV/AIDS (Review)." *Journal of Internal Medicine* 263, no. 3 (2008): 218–43.

Kamradt-Scott, Adam. "Evidence-Based Medicine and the Governance of Pandemic Influenza." *Global Public Health* 7, no. 2 (2012): S111–26.

Kan, Naoto. "Message from the Prime Minister." *Prime Minister of Japan and His Cabinet*, March 13, 2011. http://japan.kantei.go.jp/kan/statement/201103/13message_e.html.

——. "Press Conference by Prime Minister." Prime Minister of Japan and His Cabinet, August 26, 2011. http://japan.kantei.go.jp/kan/statement/201108/26kaiken_e.html.

Katsumata, Hiro. "East Asian Regional Security Governance: Bilateral Balancing and ASEAN's Informal Cooperative Security." In *Comparative Regional Security Governance*, ed. Shaun Breslin and Stuart Croft, 72–93. London: Routledge, 2012.

Kelly, Brian, and Anita J. Wadud. "Asian Labour Migrants and Humanitarian Crises: Lessons from Libya." Policy brief, Bangkok: International Organization for Migration, 2012.

Keohane, Robert. *International Institutions and State Power: Essays in International Relations Theory*. Boulder, Colo.: Westview Press, 1989.

Kim, Inkyoung. "Environmental Cooperation of Northeast Asia: Transboundary Air Pollution." *International Relations of the Asia-Pacific* 7, no. 3 (2007): 439–62.

Kirchner, Emil J. "Regional and Global Security: Changing Threats and Institutional Responses." In *Global Security Governance: Competing Perceptions of Security in the 21st Century*, ed. Emil J. Kirchner and James Sperling, 3–22. London: Routledge, 2007.

Kneebone, Susan. "The Bali Process and Global Refugee Policy in the Asia-Pacific Region." *Journal of Refugee Studies* 27, no. 4 (2014): 596–618.

——. "The Labeling Problem in Southeast Asia's Refugee Crisis." *Diplomat*, August 12, 2015. http://thediplomat.com/2015/08/the-labeling-problem-in-southeast-asias-refugee-crisis/.

Koh, Kheng-Lian, Nicholas A. Robinson, and Lin-Heng Lye. *ASEAN Environmental Legal Integration: Sustainable Goals?* Cambridge: Cambridge University Press, 2016.

Kooiman, Jan. "Social-Political Governance: Introduction." In *Modern Governance*, ed. Jan Kooiman, 1–6. London: Sage, 1993.

Korea Meteorological Administration. "Asian Dust." Undated. Accessed June 3, 2017. https://web.kma.go.kr/eng/weather/asiandust/intro.jsp.

Krahmann, Elke. "Conceptualizing Security Governance." *Cooperation and Conflict: Journal of the Nordic International Studies Association* 38, no. 1 (2003): 5–26.

——. "National, Regional and Global Governance: One Phenomenon or Many?" *Global Governance* 9 (2003): 323–46.

Kubursi, Atif, ed. *Food and Water Security in the Arab World—Proceedings of the First Arab Development Symposium.* Washington, D.C.: International Bank for Reconstruction and Development, World Bank, and Arab Fund for Economic and Social Development, 2012.

Kurtenbach, Elaine. "Pacific Rim Leaders Seek to Fortify Food Security." *San Diego Union-Tribune*, September 8, 2012. http://www.sandiegouniontribune.com/sdut-pacific-rim-leaders-seek-to-fortify-food-security-2012sep08-story.html.

Lagi, Marco, Karla Z. Bertrand, and Yaneer Bar-Yam. "The Food Crises and Political Instability in North Africa and the Middle East." Cambridge, Mass.: New England Computer Systems Institute, 2011.

Leach, Melissa. "The Ebola Crisis and Post-2015 Development." *Journal of International Development* 27, no. 6 (2015): 816–34.

Leaning, Jennifer, and Sam Arie. "Human Security: A Framework for Assessment in Conflict and Transition." Working paper, Cambridge, Mass.: Harvard Center for Population and Development Studies, 2000.

Letchumanan, Raman. "Southeast Asia's Recurring Smoke Haze Crisis: What Can Be Done?" *RSIS Commentary* (Singapore), October 2015.

Leung, Leonard. "Food Security and Resilience of the Association of Southeast Asian Nations Member States to Food Price Volatility." Completion report for project 47208-001, Manila: Asian Development Bank, 2017.

"Liang Congjie." *Economist*, November 18, 2010. http://www.economist.com/node/17519870.

Litovsky, Alejandro. "Antibiotic Waste Is Polluting India and China's Rivers; Big Pharma Must Act." *Guardian*, October 25, 2016. https://www.theguardian.com/sustainable-business/2016/oct/25/antibiotic-waste-pollution-india-china-rivers-big-pharma-superbugs-resistance.

Liu, Hsui Wen. "Taiwan Joins Global Anti-Nuclear Trend." *Asia Times*, January 18, 2017. http://www.atimes.com/article/taiwan-finally-joins-anti-nuclear-movement/.

Lo, Catherine Yuk-ping. *HIV/AIDS in China and India: Governing Health Security.* New York: Palgrave Macmillan, 2015.

Lo, Catherine Yuk-ping, and Nicholas Thomas. "How Is Health a Security Issue? Politics, Responses and Issues." *Health Policy and Planning* 25, no. 6 (2010): 447–53.

Loh, Dylan Ming Hui. "ASEAN's Norm Adherence and Its Unintended Consequences in HADR and SAR Operations." *Pacific Review* 29, no. 4 (2016): 549–72.

Macapagal-Arroyo, Gloria. "Statement: President Arroyo at the 63rd UN General Assembly General Debate." *Official Gazette* (Philippines), September 23, 2002. http://www .officialgazette.gov.ph/2008/09/23/statement-president-arroyo-at-the-63rd-un -general-assembly-general-debate/.

MacPherson, Nancy, Ann Marie Kimball, Charlanne Burke, Neil Abernethy, Sandra Tempongko, and Jakob Zinsstag. "Key Findings and Lessons from an Evaluation of the Rockefeller Foundation's Disease Surveillance Networks Initiative." *Emerging Health Threats Journal* 6 (2013): 1–5.

Martin, Catriona. "Pro Bono Support of the Bali Process on People Smuggling, Trafficking in Persons and Related Transnational Crime." *Australian Pro Bono News*, October 2016. http://www.probonocentre.org.au/apbn/oct-2016/pro-bono-support-bali -process/.

McInnes, Colin. "Crisis! What Crisis? Global Health and the 2014–15 West African Ebola Outbreak." *Third World Quarterly* 37, no. 3 (2016): 380–400.

——. "HIV/AIDS and Security." *International Affairs* 82, no. 2 (2006): 315–26.

McGann, James G. "Think Tanks and Global Policy Networks." In *International Organization and Global Governance,* ed. Thomas G. Weiss and Rorden Wilkinson, 360–71. Abingdon, U.K.: Routledge, 2014.

McGinnes, Alexis. "The Human Face of the Asian Financial Crisis in Malaysia and Indonesia." *Swords and Ploughshares: A Journal of International Affairs* (Spring 2003): 45–58.

Mekong Basin Disease Surveillance Foundation Secretariat. "MBDS Background." Mekong Basin Disease Surveillance. Undated. http://www.mbdsnet.org/about-mbds/mbds -background/.

Menon, Praveen. "Malaysia, Indonesia to Let 'Boat People' Come Ashore Temporarily." Reuters, May 20, 2015. https://www.reuters.com/article/us-asia-migrants/malaysia -indonesia-to-let-boat-people-come-ashore-temporarily-idUSKBN0O50MV 20150520.

Meybatyan, Silva. "Nuclear Disasters and Displacement." *Forced Migration Review,* February 2014. http://www.fmreview.org/crisis/meybatyan.html.

Millennium Project. "Environmental Security Study: Section 2—Definitions of Environmental Security." Undated. Accessed June 21, 2017. http://www.millennium-project .org/millennium/es-2def.html.

Ministry of Defense of Singapore. "Changi Regional HADR Coordination Centre (RHCC)." Media release, January 25, 2017. https://www.mindef.gov.sg/web/portal /mindef/news-and-events/latest-releases/article-detail/2017/january/25jan17_fact sheet.

Ministry of Foreign Affairs of Thailand. "Result of the 2nd Special Meeting on Irregular Migration in the Indian Ocean." December 4, 2015. http://www.mfa.go.th/main/en /media-center/28/62757-Result-of-the-2nd-Special-Meeting-on-Irregular-Mig .html.

——. "Summary: Special Meeting on Irregular Migration in the Indian Ocean, 29 May 2015, Bangkok, Thailand." Media release, May 29, 2015. http://www.mfa.go.th/main /en/media-center/14/56880-Summary-Special-Meeting-on-Irregular-Migration-in .html.

Ministry of Foreign Affairs Policy Lab. "Diplomacy: Towards Openness, Transparency and Cooperation." *World Affairs*, no. 12 (2003): 12.

Ministry of Health and National Environment Agency of Singapore. "Additional Measures against Zika Virus." Media release, February 3, 2016. https://www.moh.gov.sg/con tent/moh_web/home/pressRoom/pressRoomItemRelease/2016/additional-measures -against-zika-virus.html.

——. "Precautionary Measures Against Zika Virus Infection." Media release, January 27, 2016. https://www.moh.gov.sg/content/moh_web/home/pressRoom/pressRoomItem-Release/2016/precautionary-measures-against-zika-virus-infection-.html.

Missbach, Antje. "Rohingya Refugees in Aceh, Indonesia: Hostile Hospitality." *Middle East Institute*, June 2, 2016. http://www.mei.edu/content/map/rohingya-refugees-aceh -indonesia-hostile-hospitality.

Montesclaros, Jose Ma Luis. "It's Not the Size, But How It's Used: Lesson for ASEAN Rice Reserves." *RSIS Commentary* (Singapore), March 2015.

——. "NTS Fast Facts: Food Security." Factsheet, Singapore: S. Rajaratnam School of International Studies, October 2016. http://www.rsis.edu.sg/wp-content/uploads/2017 /01/FastFacts-FoodSecurity-final.pdf.

Moran, Michael. "Global Philanthropy." In *International Organization and Global Governance*, ed. Thomas G. Weiss and Rorden Wilkinson, 372–84. Abingdon, U.K.: Routledge, 2014.

Morrison, Charles E. "Track 1 / Track 2 Symbiosis in Asia Pacific Regionalism." *Pacific Review* 17, no. 4 (2004): 547–65.

Mosteller, Donald. "Air Pollution's Hazy Future in South Korea." *Data-Driven Yale*, June 30, 2016. http://datadriven.yale.edu/air-quality-2/air-pollutions-hazy-future -in-south-korea-2/.

Murdoch Commission. *Food Security, Trade and Partnerships: Towards Resilient Regional Food Systems in Asia, Full Report.* Perth, Australia: Murdoch University, 2015.

Murdoch University. "The Murdoch Commission: Commission Members." Undated. Accessed August 9, 2017. http://www.murdoch.edu.au/Murdoch-Commission/Com missions/Second-Murdoch-Commission/Commission-Members/.

"NA Adopts Halt to Ninh Thuan Nuclear Power Plant Project." *Voice of Vietnam*, November 22, 2016. http://english.vov.vn/domestic/na-adopts-halt-to-ninh-thuan-nuclear -power-plant-project-337386.vov.

Narain, Jai P., and R. Bhatia. "The Challenge of Communicable Diseases in the WHO South-East Asia Region." *Bulletin of the World Health Organization* 88, no. 3 (2010): 162.

National Bureau of Asian Research. *Strategic Assistance: Disaster Relief and Asia-Pacific Stability.* Seattle: NBR, 2014.

National Diet of Japan. "The Official Report of The Fukushima Nuclear Accident Independent Investigation Commission: Executive Summary." Tokyo: National Diet of Japan, 2012.

Nazeer, Nazia, and Fumitaka Furuoka. "Overview of ASEAN Environment, Transboundary Haze Pollution Agreement and Public Health." *International Journal of Asia Pacific Studies* 13, no. 1 (2017): 73–94.

Nelson, Gerald C., Mark W. Rosegrant, Jawoo Koo, Richard Robertson, Timothy Sulser, Tingju Zhu, Claudia Ringler, et al. *Climate Change: Impact on Agriculture and Costs of Adaptation*. Washington, DC: IFPRI, 2009.

Nesadurai, Helen E. S. "The ASEAN People's Forum (APF) as Authentic Social Forum: Regional Civil Society Networking for an Alternative Regionalism." In *Routledge Handbook of Asian Regionalism*, ed. Mark Beeson and Richard Stubbs, 166–76. Abingdon, U.K.: Routledge, 2012.

——. "Food Security, the Palm Oil–Land Conflict Nexus, and Sustainability: A Governance Role for a Private Multi-Stakeholder Regime like the RSPO?" *Pacific Review* 26, no. 5 (2013): 505–29.

Ng, Eric. "China's Nuclear Error and Cover-up Unlikely to Hurt Reactor Exports, Industry Competitiveness." *South China Morning Post*, August 14, 2016. http://www.scmp.com/business/companies/article/2002990/chinas-nuclear-error-and-cover-unlikely-hurt-reactor-exports.

Ng, Keng Gene. "Private Sector Strengthens Commitment Towards Regional Emergency Relief." *Straits Times* (Singapore), March 11, 2016. http://www.straitstimes.com/singapore/private-sector-strengthens-commitment-towards-regional-emergency-relief.

Nguyen Nu Hoai Vi. "Viet Nam's Experience in the Area of Nuclear Security." Presentation at the International Cooperation to Enhance a Worldwide Nuclear Security Culture, Amsterdam, March 20, 2014.

Nicolas, Imelda, and Dovelyn Rannveig Agunias. "The Global Forum on Migration and Development: Perspectives from Asia and the Pacific." Policy brief, Bangkok: International Organization for Migration, 2014.

Nike, Inc. *FY 14/15 Nike, Inc. Sustainable Business Report*. Beaverton, Ore.: Nike, 2016.

Ninh, T. N. T. "Human Resources and Capacity-Building: Issues and Challenges for Vietnam." Presentation at the ESI-RSIS International Conference on Nuclear Governance Post-Fukushima, Singapore, October 31, 2013.

North-East Asian Subregional Program for Environmental Cooperation. "Home Page." Undated. Accessed September 3, 2017. http://www.neaspec.org/.

"Nuke Plans on Power Plant, Doctors at Global Meet Tell Putrajaya." *Malay Mail Online*, August 28, 2014. http://www.themalaymailonline.com/malaysia/article/nuke-plans-on-power-plant-doctors-at-global-meet-tell-putrajaya.

O'Callaghan, John. "Singapore, Malaysia Face Economic Hit from Prolonged Smog." Reuters, June 24, 2013. http://www.reuters.com/article/us-southeastasia-haze-impact/singapore-malaysia-face-economic-hit-from-prolonged-smog-idUSBRE95N0BS20130624.

Office of the United Nations High Commissioner on Human Rights. "High Commissioner Zeid: Pushbacks Endanger Thousands in Bay of Bengal." May 15, 2015. http://

www.ohchr.org/EN/NewsEvents/Pages/DisplayNews.aspx?NewsID=15960&Lan
gID=E#sthash.uADsVG7K.dpuf.

O'Manique, Colleen, and Pieter Fourie. "Security and Health in the Twenty-First Century." In *The Routledge Handbook of Security Studies*, ed. Myriam Dunn Cavelty and Victor Mauer, 243–53. London: Routledge, 2010.

Ong, Justin. "Unanswered Questions, Uncertain Future for Kranji Farmers." *Channel News-
Asia* (Singapore), May 28, 2016. http://www.channelnewsasia.com/news/singapore
/unanswered-questions-uncertain-future-for-kranji-farmers-8030608.

Ong Keng Yong. "Message from the Secretary-General of ASEAN on the Occasion of the
2005 ASEAN Day for Disaster Management." Speech, October 12, 2005.

Organisation for Economic Co-operation and Development (OECD). *OECD Environmental Outlook to 2050: The Consequences of Inaction*. Paris: OECD, 2012.

Osa, Yukie. "The Growing Role of NGOs in Disaster Relief and Humanitarian Assistance in
East Asia." In *A Growing Force: Civil Society's Role in Asian Regional Security*, ed. Rizal
Sukma and James Gannon, 66–89. Tokyo: Japan Center for International Exchange, 2013.

Ostensen, Ase Gilje. "In the Business of Peace: The Political Influence of Private Military
and Security Companies on UN Peacekeeping." *International Peacekeeping* 20, no. 1
(2013): 33–47.

Paris, Roland. "Human Security: Paradigm Shift or Hot Air?" *International Security* 26, no. 2
(2001): 87–102.

Pattiradjawane, Rene L. "Weighing Environmental Diplomacy against Sovereignty Diplomacy." *Straits Times* (Singapore), May 24, 2016. http://www.straitstimes.com/opinion
/weighing-environmental-diplomacy-against-sovereignty-diplomacy.

Pelupessy, Dicky, and Diane Bretherton. "Disaster, Mental Health, and Community Resilience: Lessons from the Field in Aceh Province, Indonesia." In *Natural Disaster Management in the Asia-Pacific: Policy and Governance*, ed. Caroline Brassard, David W. Giles,
and Arnold M. Howitt, 139–55. London: Springer, 2015.

Petcharamesree, Sriprapha. "ASEAN and Its Approach to Forced Migration Issues." *International Journal of Human Rights* 20, no. 2 (2016): 173–90.

Petz, Daniel. *Strengthening Regional and National Capacity for Disaster Risk Management: The
Case of ASEAN*. Washington, D.C.: Brookings, 2014.

Philips News Center. "ASEAN Non-Communicable Diseases (NCD) Network Launched."
Philips, April 8, 2013. https://www.philips.com/a-w/about/news/archive/standard/news
/press/2013/20130408-asean-ncd-network.html.

Phillips, Tom. "Beijing Smog: Pollution Red Alert Declared in China Capital and 21 Other
Cities." *Guardian*, December 17, 2016. https://www.theguardian.com/world/2016/dec
/17/beijing-smog-pollution-red-alert-declared-in-china-capital-and-21-other-cities.

Phommasack, Bounlay, Chuleeporn Jiraphongsa, Moe Ko Oo, Katherine C. Bond, Nata-
lie Phaholyothin, Rapeepong Suphanchaimat, Kumnuan Ungchusak, and Sarah B.
Macfarlane. "Mekong Basin Disease Surveillance (MBDS): A Trust-Based Network."
Emerging Health Threats Journal 6 (2013): 1–9.

Pilcavage, Christine. "Japan's Overseas Development Assistance in the Health Sector and
Global Health Governance." In *Asia's Role in Governing Global Health*, ed. Kelley Lee,
Tikki Pang, and Yeling Tan, 19–38. London: Routledge, 2013.

Piper, Nicola. "Bridging Gender, Migration and Governance: Theoretical Possibilities in the Asian Context." *Asian and Pacific Migration Journal* 12, no. 1–2 (2003): 21–48.

Pitsuwan, Surin. "Keynote Address by ASEAN Secretary General at the Launch of the RSIS Centre for Non-Traditional Security Studies." Speech, Singapore, May 6, 2008.

Pitsuwan, Surin, and Prashanth Parameswaran. "Why Southeast Asia's Refugee Crisis Matters." *Diplomat*, July 23, 2015. http://thediplomat.com/2015/07/southeast-asia-refugees-in-crisis/.

Porter, John R., Liyoung Xie, Andrew J. Challinor, Kevern Cochrane, S. Mark Howden, Muhammad Mohsin Iqbal, David B. Lobell et al. "Food Security and Food Production Systems." In *Climate Change 2014: Impacts, Adaptation, and Vulnerability—Summaries, Frequently Asked Questions, and Cross-Chapter Boxes*, ed. Christopher B. Field, Vicente R. Barros, David Jon Dokken, Katharine J. Mach, Michael D. Mastrandrea, T. Eren Bilir, Monalisa Chaterjee et al., 485–533. Cambridge: Cambridge University Press, 2014.

Prins, Gwyn. "AIDS and Global Security." *International Affairs* 80, no. 5 (2004): 931–52.

Putz, Catherine. "Thailand Deports 100 Uyghurs to China." *Diplomat*, July 11, 2015. http://thediplomat.com/2015/07/thailand-deports-100-uyghurs-to-china/.

Quah, Euston. "Transboundary Pollution in Southeast Asia—The Indonesian Fires." *World Development* 30, no. 3 (2002): 429–41.

Rama, Siti Masyitah. "The Role of NGOs in Combating Avian Influenza in Indonesia: A Muhammadiyah Case Study." Singapore: S. Rajaratnam School of International Studies, 2010.

Rau, Bill. "The Politics of Civil Society in Confronting HIV/AIDS." *International Affairs* 82, no. 2 (2006): 285–95.

"Reaching a Common Understanding, Strengthening Leadership, Carrying Out Responsibilities, Feasibly Completing SARS Prevention and Treatment Work (in Chinese)." *People's Daily* (China), April 14, 2003.

Rhodes, R. A. W. "The New Governance: Governing Without Government." *Political Studies* 44, no. 4 (1996): 652–67.

Roe, Paul. "Actor, Audience(s) and Emergency Measures: Securitization and the UK's Decision to Invade Iraq." *Security Dialogue* 39, no. 6 (2008): 615–35.

Roemer-Mahler, Anne, and Stefan Elbe. "The Race for Ebola Drugs: Pharmaceuticals, Security and Global Health Governance." *Third World Quarterly* 37, no. 3 (2016): 487–506.

Rosenau, James N. "Governance in the Twenty-First Century." *Global Governance* 1, no. 1 (1995):13–43.

Rother, Stefan, and Nicola Piper. "Alternative Regionalism from Below: Democratizing ASEAN's Migration Governance." *International Migration* 53, no. 3 (2015): 36–49.

Rushton, Simon. "AIDS and International Security in the United Nations System." *Health Policy and Planning* 25, no. 6 (2010): 495–504.

——. "Global Health Security: Security for Whom? Security from What?" *Political Studies* 59, no. 4 (2011): 779–96.

"Russia, Philippines' New Partner, Showcases Nuclear Energy." *ABS-CBN News*, June 19, 2017. http://news.abs-cbn.com/business/06/19/17/russia-philippines-new-partner-showcases-nuclear-energy.

Salim, Tama. "One-Map Policy Helps Resolve Land Disputes, Overlapping Permits." *Jakarta Post*, December 26, 2014. http://www.thejakartapost.com/news/2014/12/26/one-map-policy-helps-resolve-land-disputes-overlapping-permits.html.

Santarelli, Nicolas Carrillo. "Nonstate Actors." *Oxford Bibliographies*. Modified July 24, 2013. http://www.oxfordbibliographies.com/view/document/obo-9780199796953/obo-9780199796953-0085.xml.

Saulon, Victor V. "DoE Considering Sulu as Site for Nuclear Plant." *Business World Online*, March 20, 2017. http://www.bworldonline.com/content.php?section=Economy&title=doe-considering-sulu-as-site-for-nuclear-plant&id=142413.

Save the Children. *Save the Children in China: 2013 Annual Review*. Beijing: Save the Children in China, 2013.

Scholte, Jan Aart. "Civil Society and NGOs." In *International Organization and Global Governance*, ed. Thomas G. Weiss and Rorden Wilkinson, 322–34. Abingdon, U.K.: Routledge, 2014.

Seetharaman, Deepa. "Zuckerberg Family Fund to Invest $3 Billion in Research Technology." *Wall Street Journal*, September 22, 2016. https://www.wsj.com/articles/zuckerberg-family-fund-to-invest-3-billion-in-research-technology-1474489559.

Sembiring, Margareth. "Combating Haze—Holding One's Breath a Year On." *RSIS Commentary* (Singapore), August 2016.

——. "Here Comes the Haze, Yet Again: Are New Measures Working?" *RSIS Commentary* (Singapore), September 2015.

Sherwood, Harriet. "Human Rights Groups Face Global Crackdown 'Not Seen in a Generation.'" *Guardian*, August 26, 2015. https://www.theguardian.com/law/2015/aug/26/ngos-face-restrictions-laws-human-rights-generation.

Simon, Sheldon W. "Evaluating Track II Approaches to Security Diplomacy in the Asia-Pacific: The CSCAP Experience." *Pacific Review* 15, no. 2 (2002): 167–200.

——. "Evaluating Track 2 Approaches to Security Dialogue in the Asia-Pacific Region: The CSCAP Experience." In *Assessing Track 2 Diplomacy in the Asia-Pacific Region: A CSCAP Reader*, ed. Desmond Ball and Kwa Chong Guan, 77–121. Singapore: S. Rajaratnam School of International Studies, 2010.

"Singapore a Role Model in Its Handling of Zika: WHO." *Straits Times* (Singapore), September 3, 2016. http://www.straitstimes.com/singapore/environment/singapore-a-role-model-in-its-handling-of-zika-who.

Singapore Civil Defense Force. "4th ASEAN Ministerial Meeting on Disaster Management 2016." Media release, October 13, 2016. Accessed from https://www.scdf.gov.sg/general/news/news-releases/2016/4th-asean-ministerial-meeting-disaster-management-2016; no longer available.

"Singapore GDP Will Take Hit from Haze as Countries Issue Travel Warnings." *Business Times* (Singapore), October 7, 2015. http://www.businesstimes.com.sg/government-economy/singapore-gdp-will-take-hit-from-haze-as-countries-issue-travel-warnings.

"Singapore Moves Against Indonesian Firms over Haze." *Jakarta Post*, September 26, 2015. http://www.thejakartapost.com/news/2015/09/26/singapore-moves-against-indonesian-firms-over-haze.html.

Siswo, Sujadi. "Greenpeace Indonesia Launches Map to Track Haze-Causing Fires." *Channel NewsAsia*, March 16, 2016. http://www.channelnewsasia.com/news/asiapacific/green peace-indonesia-launches-map-to-track-haze-causing-fires-8160040.

Smith, Steve. "The Contested Concept of Security." In *Critical Security Studies and World Politics*, ed. Ken Booth, 27–62. Boulder, Colo.: Lynne Rienner, 2005.

Smouts, Marie-Claude. "The Proper Use of Governance in International Relations." *International Social Science Journal* 50, no. 155 (1998): 81–89.

Sombilla, Mercedita A., Arsenio M. Balisacan, Donato B. Antiporta, and Rowell C. Dikitanan. "Policy Responses to the Food Price Crisis and Their Implications: The Case of Four Greater Mekong Subregion Countries." Rome: International Fund for Agriculture Development, 2011.

Sperling, James. "Governance and Security in the Twenty-First Century." In *Handbook of Governance and Security*, ed. James Sperling, 3–13. Cheltenham, U.K.: Edward Elgar, 2014.

——, ed. *Handbook of Governance and Security*. Cheltenham, U.K.: Edward Elgar, 2014.

——. "Regional Security Governance." In *Handbook of Governance and Security*, ed. James Sperling, 98–120. Cheltenham, U.K.: Edward Elgar, 2014.

——. "State Attributes and System Properties: Security Multilateralism in Central Asia, Southeast Asia, the Atlantic and Europe." In *Multilateralism and Security Institutions in an Era of Globalization*, ed. Dimitris Bourantonis, Kostas Ifantis, and Panayotis Tsakonas, 101–35. London: Routledge, 2008.

Stiles, Kendall. "Grassroots Empowerment: States, Non-State Actors and Global Policy Formulation." In *Non-State Actors and Authority in the Global System*, ed. Richard A. Higgott, Geoffrey R. D. Underhill, and Andreas Bieler, 32–47. London: Routledge, 2000.

Stoakes, Emanuel, Chris Kelly, and Annie Kelly. "Revealed: How the Thai Fishing Industry Trafficks, Imprisons and Enslaves." *Guardian*, July 20, 2015. https://www.theguar dian.com/global-development/2015/jul/20/thai-fishing-industry-implicated-enslave ment-deaths-rohingya.

Stone, Diane. *Knowledge Actors and Transnational Governance*. Hampshire, U.K.: Palgrave Macmillan, 2013.

——. "The 'Policy Research' Knowledge Elite and Global Policy Processes." In *Non-State Actors in World Politics*, ed. Daphne Josselin and William Wallace, 113–32. Hampshire, U.K.: Palgrave, 2001.

Sundaryani, Fedina S. "PLN to Go Nuclear if Renewable Energy Goal Flops." *Jakarta Post*, April 25, 2017. http://www.thejakartapost.com/news/2017/04/25/pln-to-go-nuclear-if -renewable-energy-goal-flops.html.

Surtees, Rebecca. *After Trafficking: Experiences and Challenges in the (Re)integration of Trafficked Persons in the Greater Mekong Sub-Region*. Bangkok: United Nations Inter-Agency Project on Human Trafficking in the Greater Mekong Sub-Region, 2013.

Sutherland, Peter, António Guterres, Zeid Ra'ad Al Hussein, and William Lacy Swing. "A Comprehensive People-Oriented Approach to the Irregular Movement of Migrants and Refugees in South East Asia." Joint Statement, July 1, 2015. http://www.un.org/en /development/desa/population/migration/partners/docs/Joint_Statement_South_East _Asia.pdf.

———. "Search and Rescue at Sea, Disembarkation, and Protection of the Human Rights of Refugees and Migrants Now Imperative to Save Lives in the Bay of Bengal and Andaman Sea." Joint Statement, May 19, 2015. http://www.un.org/en/development/desa/population/migration/partners/docs/Joint_Statement_on_Andaman_Sea.pdf.

Suzuki, Tatsujiro. "Nuclear Safety and Cooperation in ASEAN." Presentation at the *RSIS* Roundtable at Singapore International Energy Week 2016, Singapore, October 28, 2016.

Swing, William Lacy. "Speech at the Special Meeting on Irregular Migration in the Indian Ocean, Bangkok, Thailand, 29 May 2015." International Organization for Migration, June 3, 2015. https://www.iom.int/speeches-and-talks/special-meeting-irregular-migra tion-indian-ocean.

Syngenta and Frontier Strategy Group. *Rice Bowl Index: Translating Complexity into an Opportunity for Action.* Singapore: Syngenta, 2012.

Tan, Alan Khee-Jin. "The 'Haze' Crisis in Southeast Asia: Assessing Singapore's Transboundary Haze Pollution Ac." NUS Law working paper no. 2015/002, Singapore: National University of Singapore, 2015.

Tan, Hui Yee. "Cambodia and Thailand Edging Closer to Nuclear Power." *Straits Times* (Singapore), May 30, 2016. http://www.straitstimes.com/asia/cambodia-and-thailand -edging-closer-to-nuclear-power.

Tan, See Seng. Introduction to *Do Institutions Matter? Regional Institutions and Regionalism in East Asia*, ed. See Seng Tan, 1–18. Singapore: S. Rajaratnam School of International Studies, 2008.

Tan, Seng Chye. "NADI: Supporting ADMM and Promoting Defence Diplomacy." In *Forward Engagement: RSIS as a Think Tank of International Studies and Security in the Asia-Pacific*, ed. Alan Chong, 89–96. Singapore: World Scientific, 2016.

Tanyang, G. "Summing-up APG Phase 2: Facilitating Partnerships Between ASEAN and CSOs for AADMER." AADMER Partnership Group, January 28, 2014.

Task Force on ASEAN Migrant Workers. "ASEAN Civil Society Organizations (CSOs)-Trade Unions Consultation on Protection and Promotion of the Rights of Migrant Workers 12 May 2007, Jakarta, Indonesia." Jakarta: ASEAN, 2007. http://asean.org /storage/2016/05/I2_ASEAN-Civil-Soc-Org-Trade-Unions-Consul-on-Protection -n-Promotion-of-the-Rights-of-MW-2007.pdf.

———. "Making Advocacy Work." *Justice and Peace Commission of the H.K. Catholic Diocese.* Undated. Accessed February 20, 2017. http://www.hkjp.org/files/files/focus/human right/task%20force%20on%20ASEAN%20Migrant.pdf.

Tay, Simon. "The Environment and Security in Southeast Asia." In *Beyond the Crisis: Challenges and Opportunities*, ed. Mely Caballero-Anthony and Jawhar Hassan, 149–60. Kuala Lumpur, Malaysia: Institute of Security and International Studies, 2000.

Temasek Foundation Ecosperity. "Who We Are." Undated. Accessed September 5, 2017, http://www.temasekfoundation-ecosperity.org.sg/.

Teng, Paul. "Food Security: Cities as Part of the Solution and Not the Problem." *RSIS Commentary* (Singapore), August 2012.

———. "Knowledge Intensive Agriculture: The New Disruptor in World Food?" *RSIS Commentary* (Singapore), June 2017.

Teng, Paul, and Margarita Escaler. "The Case for Urban Food Security: A Singapore Perspective." Singapore: S. Rajaratnam School of International Studies, 2010.

"Ten Reasons Against Nuclear Power." *Malaysian Physicians for Peace and Social Responsibility*, updated March 7, 2017. http://mpsr.org/wp/2017/03/07/ten-reasons-against-nuclear-power-updated/.

Thakur, Ramesh, and Thomas G. Weiss. "United Nations 'Policy': An Argument with Three Illustrations." *International Studies Perspectives* 10, no. 1 (2009): 18–35.

Than, Hoang Sy. "Vietnam Nuclear Power Program and the New Research Reactor Project." Presentation at the Singapore International Energy Week RSIS Roundtable on Nuclear Safety and Cooperation in ASEAN, Singapore, October 28, 2016.

Thiparat, Pranee, ed. *The Quest for Human Security: The Next Phase of ASEAN?* Bangkok: Institute of Security and International Studies, 2001.

"Tianjin to Build APEC Green Supply Chain Cooperation Network Demonstration Center." *China Daily*, updated October 13, 2016. http://www.chinadaily.com.cn/m/tianjin2012/2016-10/13/content_27049434.htm.

Tigno, Jorge V. "Walk the Talk: CSOs, Migrant Workers, and Overseas Employment from the Philippines." In *Asia on the Move: Regional Migration and the Role of Civil Society*, ed. Mely Caballero-Antony and Toshihiro Menju, 140–62. Tokyo: Japan Center for International Exchange, 2015.

Timmer, C. Peter. "Reflections on Food Crises Past." *Food Policy* 35, no.1 (2010): 1–11.

Tow, William, Ramesh Thakur, and In-Taek Hyun, eds. *Asia's Emerging Regional Order*. Tokyo: United Nations University Press, 2000.

Track II Network of ASEAN Defence and Security Institutions. "Chairman's Report." 8th Annual Meeting of the Track II Network of ASEAN Defence and Security Institutions (NADI), Kuala Lumpur, Malaysia, February 9–11, 2015.

Trajano, Julius Cesar I. "Building Resilience from Within: Enhancing Humanitarian Civil–Military Coordination in Post-Haiyan Philippines." Singapore: S. Rajaratnam School of International Studies, 2016.

Trethewie, Sally. "The ASEAN Plus Three Emergency Rice Reserve (APTERR): Cooperation, Commitment and Contradictions." Working paper, Singapore: S. Rajaratnam School of International Studies, 2013.

Tsuruoka, Michiko. "An Era of the ADMM-Plus? Unique Achievements and Challenges." *PacNet* no. 69. Washington, D.C.: Center for Strategic and International Studies, September 2013.

Tumonong, Malyn. "Five Years of AHA Centre: Experiences, Challenges and Future Outlook of Disaster Management in the ASEAN." Presentation at the United Nations/India Workshop on the Use of Earth Observation Data in Disaster Management and Risk Reduction: Sharing the Asian Experience, Hyderabad, India, March 8–10, 2016. http://www.unoosa.org/documents/pdf/spider/activities/2016/india/Day3/Plenary_session2/5_Years_of_AHA_Centre_mmltumonong.pdf.

"Typhoon Haiyan: Philippines Declares State of Calamity." *BBC News*, November 12, 2013. http://www.bbc.com/news/world-asia-24901993.

United Nations. "Global Food Crisis 'Silent Tsunami' Threatening over 100 million People, Warns UN." *UN News Centre*, April 22, 2008. http://www.un.org/apps/news/story .asp?NewsID=26412#.Waa8qtJ97IU.

——. "Goal 2: End Hunger, Achieve Food Security and Improved Nutrition and Promote Sustainable Agriculture." *Sustainable Development Goals*. Undated. Accessed June 25, 2017. http://www.un.org/sustainabledevelopment/hunger/.

——. "Home Page." *Millennium Development Goals and Beyond 2015*. Undated. Accessed June 15, 2017. http://www.un.org/millenniumgoals/.

——. "Sustainable Development Goals." *Sustainable Development Knowledge Platform*. Undated. Accessed June 15, 2017. https://sustainabledevelopment.un.org/?menu=1300.

——. "UN Human Rights Chief Points to 'Textbook Example of Ethnic Cleansing' in Myanmar." *UN News*, September 11, 2017. https://news.un.org/en/story/2017 /09/564622-un-human-rights-chief-points-textbook-example-ethnic-cleansing -myanmar.

United Nations, Department of Economic and Social Affairs, Population Division. *International Migration Report 2015: Highlights*. New York: United Nations, 2016.

——. "World Population Prospects: The 2015 Revision, Key Findings and Advance Tables." Working paper, ESA/P/WP.241. New York: United Nations, 2015.

——. "World Population Prospects: The 2017 Revision, Key Findings and Advance Tables." Working paper, ESA/P/WP/248. New York: United Nations, 2017.

——. *World Urbanization Prospects: The 2014 Revision*, CD-ROM ed. New York: United Nations, 2014.

——. "World Urbanization Prospects: The 2014 Revision, Highlights." ST/ESA/ SER.A/352. New York: United Nations, 2014.

United Nations Development Programme (UNDP). *Human Development Report 1994*. New York: Oxford University Press, 1994.

——. *Human Development Report 2016*. New York: UNDP, 2016.

United Nations Educational, Scientific and Cultural Organization (UNESCO). "Facts and Figures on Marine Biodiversity." Undated. Accessed June 8, 2017. http://www.unesco .org/new/en/natural-sciences/ioc-oceans/focus-areas/rio-20-ocean/blueprint-for -the-future-we-want/marine-biodiversity/facts-and-figures-on-marine-biodiversity/.

——. "Migrant/Migration." Undated. Accessed February 12, 2015. http://www.unesco .org/new/en/social-and-human-sciences/themes/international-migration/glossary /migrant.

United Nations General Assembly. "In Larger Freedom: Towards Development, Security and Human Rights for All." A/59/2005, March 21, 2005.

——. "Securing Peace and Development: The Role of the United Nations in Supporting Security Sector Reform." A/62/659–S/2008/39, January 23, 2008.

——. "The Role of Regional and Sub-Regional Arrangements in Implementing the Responsibility to Protect." A/65/877–S/2011/393, June 27, 2011.

United Nations High Commissioner for Refugees (UNHCR). *Global Trends: Forced Displacement in 2015*. Geneva: UNHCR, 2016.

——. *Mixed Movements in South-East Asia 2016*. Geneva: UNHCR, 2017.

———. *Refugee Protection and Mixed Migration: The 10-Point Plan in Action.* Geneva: UNHCR, 2011.

———. *South-East Asia Mixed Maritime Movements April–June 2015.* Geneva: UNHCR, 2015.

———. "UNHCR Alarmed at Reports of Boat Pushbacks in South-East Asia." Media release, May 13, 2015. http://www.unhcr.org/555345959.html.

United Nations Office for the Coordination of Humanitarian Affairs (UN OCHA). "Asia-Pacific Region: Overview of El Niño Responses—July 2016." Information update, July 15, 2016.

———. "El Niño in Asia." Undated. www.UNOCHA.org/legacy/el-nino-asia-pacific.

United Nations Office on Drugs and Crime (UNODC). *Global Report on Trafficking in Persons 2016.* New York: United Nations Publication, 2016.

———. *United Nations Convention Against Transnational Organized Crime and the Protocols Thereto.* Vienna: UNODC, 2004.

United Nations Peacekeeping. "Security Sector Reform." Undated. Accessed July 5, 2017. http://www.un.org/en/peacekeeping/issues/security.shtml.

United Nations Secretary-General. "An Agenda for Peace." A/47/277, June 17, 1992.

United Nations Security Council. "6587th Meeting." S/PV.6587, July 20, 2011.

———. "5663rd Meeting." S/PV.5663, April 17, 2007.

United States Institute of Peace. "Glossary: Tracks of Diplomacy." Undated. Accessed February 15, 2018. https://www.usip.org/glossary/tracks-diplomacy.

UN OCHA Regional Office for Asia and the Pacific. *2016 Year in Review.* January 17, 2017. https://ocharoap.exposure.co/2016-year-in-review.

U.S. Department of State. *Trafficking in Persons Report June 2005.* Washington, D.C.: U.S. Department of State, 2005.

———. *2016 Trafficking in Persons Report.* Washington, D.C.: U.S. Department of State, 2016.

Vandenberg, Paul. "Ensuring the Triple Win of Labor Migration in Asia." Policy Brief no. 2015-1. Tokyo: Asian Development Bank Institute, 2015.

"Vietnam to Scrap Nuclear Plant Construction Plans." *Bangkok Post*, November 9, 2016.

Wah, Joseph. "Is ASEAN Closer to Legal Protection of the Rights of Migrant Workers?" *ASEAN People's Forum*, March 22, 2014.

Wang, Jenny Qu, Minquan Liu, Aming Liu, Tao Wei, and Hang Li. "Global Health Governance in China: The Case of China's Health Aid to Foreign Countries." In *Asia's Role in Governing Global Health*, ed. Kelley Lee, Tikki Pang, and Yeling Tan, 39–65. London: Routledge, 2013.

Watson, John T., Michelle Gayer, and Maire A. Connolly. "Epidemics After Natural Disasters." *Emerging Infectious Diseases Journal* 13, no. 1 (2007): 1–5.

Watts, Jonathan. "NGOs Upbeat over China's Environmental Transparency Progress." *Guardian*, January 16, 2012. https://www.theguardian.com/environment/2012/jan/16/green-transparency-china.

Webber, Mark. "Security Governance." In *Handbook of Governance and Security*, ed. James Sperling, 17–40. Cheltenham, U.K.: Edward Elgar, 2014.

Weir, Lorna, and Eric Mykhalovskiy. *Global Public Health Vigilance: Creating a World on Alert.* London: Routledge, 2010.

Weiss, Thomas G., D. Conor Seyle, and Kelsey Coolidge. "The Rise of Non-State Actors in Global Governance: Opportunities and Limitations." Broomfield, Colo.: One Earth Future Foundation, 2013.

Wen, Jiabao. "Speech by HE Mr. Wen Jiabao Vice-Premier of the State Council of the People's Republic of China at World Food Summit, June 10, 2002." *Ministry of Foreign Affairs of the People's Republic of China*, June 13, 2002. http://www.fmprc.gov.cn/mfa _eng/wjb_663304/zzjg_663340/gjs_665170/gjzzyhy_665174/2616_665220/2618 _665224/t15367.shtml.

White House. *National Security Strategy of the United States.* Washington, D.C.: White House, 1991.

World Health Organization (WHO). "Barriers to Rapid Containment of the Ebola Outbreak." August 11, 2014. http://www.who.int/csr/disease/ebola/overview-august -2014/en/.

——. *Emergency Response Framework.* Geneva: WHO, 2013.

——. "Health Effects of the Chernobyl Accident: An Overview." April 2006. http://www .who.int/ionizing_radiation/chernobyl/backgrounder/en/.

——. "Human Infection with Avian Influenza A(H7N9) Virus—China." March 15, 2017. http://www.who.int/csr/don/15-march-2017-ah7n9-china/en/.

——. "Middle East Respiratory Syndrome Coronavirus (MERS-CoV)—Republic of Korea." July 7, 2015. http://www.who.int/csr/don/07-july-2015-mers-korea/en/.

——. "Summary of Probable SARS Cases with Onset of Illness from 1 November 2002 to 31 July 2003." April 21, 2004. http://www.who.int/csr/sars/country/table2004_04_21/en/.

——. *The World Health Report: A Safer Future: Global Public Health Security in the 21st Century.* Geneva: WHO, 2007.

——. "WHO Collaborating Centres." Undated. Accessed June 27, 2013. http://www2 .wpro.who.int/sites/whocc/home.htm.

——. "WHO Strategic Action Plan for Pandemic Influenza 2006–2007." WHO/CDS /EPR/GIP/2006.2, 3, Geneva: WHO, 2006.

——. "World Health Organization Issues Emergency Travel Advisory." Media release, March 15, 2003. http://www.who.int/mediacentre/news/releases/2003/pr23/en/.

——. *World Health Statistics 2016: Monitoring Health for the SDGs.* Geneva: WHO, 2016.

WHO Regional Office for South-East Asia. *Progress Report on HIV in the WHO South-East Asia Region 2016.* New Delhi: WHO, 2016.

——. "South-East Asia Countries Adopt Call for Action to Accelerate Efforts to End TB." Media release, SEAR/PR/1644, March 16, 2017. http://www.searo.who.int/mediacentre /releases/2017/1644/en/.

WHO Regional Office for the Western Pacific. "Meeting on Laboratory Strengthening for Emerging Infectious Diseases in the Asia Pacific Region, Kuala Lumpur, Malaysia, 19–21 October 2011." Report, Manila: WHO, 2012.

Wilkinson, Claire. "The Copenhagen School on Tour in Kyrgyzstan: Is Securitization Theory Useable Outside Europe?" *Security Dialogue* 38, no. 1 (2007): 5–25.

Wolfers, Arnold. "'National Security' as an Ambiguous Symbol." *Political Science Quarterly* 67, no. 4 (1952): 481–502.

Wongcha-um, Panu. "Refugees Vulnerable in Southeast Asia as Global Displaced Hits Record High." *Channel NewsAsia* (Singapore), June 19, 2015. http://www.channelnews asia.com/news/asiapacific/refugees-vulnerable-in-southeast-asia-as-global-displaced -hits-r-8275722.

World Bank. *Cost of Pollution in China: Economic Estimates of Physical Damage.* Washington, D.C.: World Bank, 2007.

——. "Projects and Operations: By Theme." Undated. Accessed June 27, 2013. http:// www.worldbank.org/projects/theme?lang=en.

——. "Projects and Operations." Undated. Accessed June 27, 2013. http://www.worldbank .org/projects/search?lang=en&searchTerm=&mjthemecode_exact=8.

——. "World Development Indicators—Rural Population." Undated. Accessed August 25, 2017. http://data.worldbank.org/indicator/SP.RUR.TOTL.ZS.

World Bank and Institute for Health Metrics and Evaluation. *The Cost of Air Pollution: Strengthening the Economic Case for Action.* Washington, D.C.: World Bank, 2016.

World Commission on Environment and Development. *Our Common Future.* Oxford: Oxford University Press, 1987.

World Food Program (WFP). "Working for Zero Hunger." Factsheet, Rome: WFP, 2017. https://docs.wfp.org/api/documents/WFP-0000016221/download/?_ga=2.62959465 .770084067.1503629024-295218535.1489636463.

World Nuclear Association. "Nuclear Power in China." Updated June 2017. http://www .world-nuclear.org/information-library/country-profiles/countries-a-f/china-nuclear -power.aspx.

——. *World Nuclear Performance Report 2016, Asia Edition.* Singapore: WNA, 2016.

World Trade Organization. "Specific TRIPS Issues." Undated. Accessed June 12, 2017. http://www.wto.org/english/tratop_e/trips_e/trips_e.htm#issues.

World Wide Fund for Nature (WWF). "Singapore Companies—Causing the Haze?" September 27, 2016. http://www.wwf.sg/?279350/Singapore-companies-causing-or-pre venting-the-haze.

Yao Wenlong. "Statement by Mr. Yao Wenlong, Minister Counsellor of the Permanent Mission of China to the United Nations, at the 60th Session of the UNGA under Agenda Item 73 Entitled 'Strengthening of the Coordination of Humanitarian and Disaster Relief Assistance of the United Nations, including Special Economic Assistance.'" Permanent Mission of the People's Republic of China to the UN, November 14, 2005. http://www.china-un.org/eng/xw/t221480.htm.

Yap, Samantha. "Inside Indonesia's Nuclear Dream." *Channel NewsAsia* (Singapore), February 16, 2016. http://www.channelnewsasia.com/news/asiapacific/inside-indonesia-s -nuclear-dream-8166246.

Yergin, Daniel. "Ensuring Energy Security." *Foreign Affairs* 85, no. 2 (2006): 69–82.

Yudhoyono, Susilo Bambang. "Disasters Are 'Greatest Threats to Our National Security.'" Speech, Asian Ministerial Conference for Disaster Risk Reduction, Yogyakarta, Indonesia, October 23, 2012.

Yukiya Amano. "Atoms for Peace in the 21st Century." Speech at the Energy Market Authority's Distinguished Speaker Program, Singapore, January 26, 2015. International Atomic
Energy Agency, www.iaea.org/newscenter/statements/atoms-peace-21st-century-1.

Yunus, Muhammad. "Economic Security for a World in Crisis." *World Policy Institute* 26,
no. 2 (2009): 5–12.

Zahiid, Syed Jaymal. "Rightless, Rohingya Children at Risk to Vice and Slave Labor."
Malay Mail Online, December 20, 2016. http://www.themalaymailonline.com/malaysia
/article/rightless-rohingya-children-at-risk-to-vice-and-slave-labour#sthash.qpFXdsm3
.dpuf.

Zimmerman, Erin. *Think Tanks and Non-Traditional Security: Governance Entrepreneurs in Asia.*
Hampshire, U.K.: Palgrave Macmillan, 2016.

Index

Abbott, Kenneth, 31
ACSC. *See* ASEAN Civil Society
    Conference
ADB. *See* Asian Development Bank
ADInet. *See* ASEAN Disaster
    Information Network
ADMM. *See* ASEAN Defence Ministers
    Meeting
ADMM-Plus, 154–55, 156, 227
advocacy, 126, 142, 181, 231; advocacy
    groups, 39
AERR. *See* ASEAN Emergency Rice
    Reserve
Afghanistan, 121, 137
AFSIS. *See* ASEAN Plus Three Food
    Security Information System
AgFunder, 216, 233
agriculture policy: agriculture
    development, 209–11;
    agricultural innovation, 209;
    and food security, 197; urban
    and peri-urban agriculture, 197,
    214–17

AHA Centre. *See* ASEAN Coordinating
    Centre for Humanitarian Assistance
    on Disaster Management
Aidenvironment Asia, 106
AIDS Care China, 44
AIDS Society of Asia and the Pacific, 81
air pollution, 85; in China, Japan, and
    Korea, 92–93; health risks, 93–95;
    social and politcal impact, 95. *See also*
    environmental concerns; haze
Alagappa, Muthiah, 6
Alma-Ata Declaration, 53, 248
Amano, Yukiya, 182
AMMDM. *See* ASEAN Ministerial
    Meeting on Disaster
Amnesty International, 133
animal health: and food security, 67;
    governance of, 75
Annan, Kofi, 3
APA. *See* ASEAN Peoples' Assembly
APEC. *See* Asia-Pacific Economic
    Cooperation
APEC Business Advisory Council, 164

APLN. *See* Asia-Pacific Leadership
Network for Nuclear Non-
Proliferation and Disarmament
Arab Spring, 14, 202
Arakan Rohingya Salvation Army, 139
armaments industry, 27, 39
armed conflict, 13, 59, 167, 169
ASEAN. *See* Association of Southeast
Asian Nations
ASEAN Agreement on Disaster
Management and Emergency
Response (AADMER), 147, 148–49,
149; AADMER Strategic Policy
Dialogue, 157, 161; AADMER Work
Program, 148, 151–52, 164
ASEAN Agreement on Transboundary
Haze Pollution, 99–100, 101,
221
ASEAN Animal Health Trust Fund, 76
ASEAN Business Forum, 204, 209
ASEAN Centre for Energy, 192
ASEAN Chambers of Commerce and
Industry, 204, 209
ASEAN Charter, 133
ASEAN Civil Society Conference
(ACSC), 33, 128
ASEAN Committee on Disaster
Management, 151–52
ASEAN Convention Against Trafficking
in Persons, Especially Women and
Children, 124
ASEAN Coordinating Centre for
Humanitarian Assistance on Disaster
Management (AHA Centre), 147,
149–50, 165–66, 170, 227; One
ASEAN, One Response, 150
ASEAN Coordinating Centre for
Transboundary Haze Pollution
Control, 104
ASEAN Declaration on Mutual
Assistance on Natural Disasters, 151

ASEAN Declaration on the Protection
and Promotion of the Rights of
Migrant Workers, 40, 123–24
ASEAN Defence Ministers Meeting
(ADMM), 43, 46, 47, 227
ASEAN Disaster Information Network
(ADinet), 147
ASEAN Emergency Rapid Assessment
Team (ASEAN-ERAT), 147–49,
150
ASEAN Emergency Rice Reserve
(AERR), 206, 207
ASEAN-ERAT. *See* ASEAN
Emergency Rapid Assessment Team
ASEAN Expert Group on International
Forest Policy Processes, 102
ASEAN Food Security Reserve
Agreement, 206
ASEAN Food Security Reserve Board,
208
ASEAN Forum on Migrant Labor, 40
ASEAN Highly Pathogenic Avian
Influenza Task Force, 76
ASEAN Human Rights Declaration,
136
ASEAN-Institutes of Strategic and
International Studies (ASEAN-ISIS),
47
ASEAN Integrated Food Security
Framework. *See* Strategic Plan of
Action on Food Security in the
ASEAN Region
ASEAN Knowledge Networks on
Forest Law Enforcement and
Governance and Climate Change,
102
ASEAN Militaries Ready Group on
HADR, 153–54, 265
ASEAN Ministerial Meeting on
Disaster Management (AMMDM),
152

ASEAN Network of Regulatory Bodies on Atomic Energy (ASEANTOM), 187–88, 189–90

ASEAN Network on Nuclear Power Safety Research, 192

ASEAN Non-Communicable Diseases Network, 80

ASEAN Peatland Management Strategy, 102, 104

ASEAN Peoples' Assembly (APA), 47–48

ASEAN plus China, Japan, and South Korea (ASEAN Plus Three), 2, 9, 10, 62, 76–77; bilateral swap arrangements, 9

ASEAN Plus Three Emergency Rice Reserve (APTERR), 205–7

ASEAN Plus Three Emerging Infectious Diseases Program, 77

ASEAN Plus Three Field Epidemiology Training Network, 77

ASEAN Plus Three Food Security Information System (AFSIS), 205, 208–9

ASEAN Plus Three Health Ministers Meeting, 42, 62

ASEAN Plus Three Partnership Laboratories, 77

ASEAN Political-Security Community, 187

ASEAN Regional Forum, 155–56, 230

ASEAN Sectoral Working Group on Crops, 209

ASEAN Sectoral Working Group on Fisheries, 209

ASEAN Sectoral Working Group on Livestock, 209

ASEAN Seed Council, 205

ASEAN Senior Labour Officials Meeting, 40, 41

ASEAN Social Forestry Network, 102

ASEAN Specialized Meteorological Centre, 101

ASEAN Strategic Policy Dialogue on Disaster Management, 161

ASEAN Surveillance Process, 42

ASEAN Technical Working Group on Agricultural Research and Development, 209

ASEANTOM. See ASEAN Network of Regulatory Bodies on Atomic Energy

ASEAN Treaty on the Southeast Asia Nuclear Weapon-Free Zone, 186

ASEAN Trust Fund, 134

ASEAN University Network, 164

ASEAN–UN Joint Strategic Plan of Action on Disaster Management, 156–57

ASEAN Vision 2025 on Disaster Management, 152, 161

"ASEAN way," 18. See also noninterference; sovereignty

Asia Migrants Network, 33

Asia Pacific Alliance for Disaster Management, 159

Asia Pacific Alliance for Sexual and Reproductive Health and Rights, 81

Asia Pacific Economic Cooperation (APEC), 110

Asia Pacific Emerging Infectious Diseases Research Network, 79

Asia-Pacific Leadership Network for Nuclear Non-Proliferation and Disarmament (APLN), 190–91

Asia Pacific Observatory on Health Systems and Policies, 80

Asia Pacific Refugee Rights Network, 128–29, 134, 136

Asia-Pacific Safeguards Network, 193–194

Asia Pacific Strategy for Emerging Diseases, 75

Asia Partnership on Emerging Infectious Diseases Research, 80

Asia Security Initiative, 34

Asian Development Bank (ADB), 77, 79

Asian Disaster Reduction and Response Network, 159

Asian Farmers' Association for Sustainable Rural Development, 216

Asian financial crisis, 9

Asian Network for Education in Nuclear Technology, 194, 270

Asian Partnership on Emerging Infectious Disease Research, 79

Asian Regional Initiative Against Trafficking in Women and Children, 129

Asian-Pacific Resource and Research Centre for Women, 81

Association of Southeast Asian Nations (ASEAN), 7, 237; and epistemic communities, 164–65; lack of action on migration crises, 133, 139–40; limits and challenges of, 103; members of, 2–3; and the private sector, 161–62; regional frameworks, 228–29

asylum seekers, 115, 119, 121

AusAID. *See* Australian Agency for International Development

Australia, 153, 155, 160, 169, 193, 213

Australian Agency for International Development (AusAID), 73, 160

authority, sources of: capacity-based authority, 64; delegated authority, 38, 64; expert authority, 24, 38; formal authority, 235; institutional authority, 38; principled authority, 38; regional authority, 10; sovereign authority, 38, 63

Avant, Deborah, 4, 12

Badawi, Abdullah, 48

Balakrishnan, Vivian, 225

balance-of-power politics, 6

Bali Process Government and Business Forum, 129, 130

Bali Process on People Smuggling, Trafficking in Persons and Related Transnational Crime, 129–30

the Balkans, 121

Bangkok Treaty. *See* ASEAN Treaty on the Southeast Asia Nuclear Weapon-Free Zone

Bangladesh, 30, 121, 133, 137, 139–41, 159, 170, 193

BATAN. *See* National Nuclear Energy Agency of Indonesia

Belarus, 177

BIG. *See* Geospatial Information Agency, Indonesia

Bill & Melinda Gates Foundation, 33, 34

border control, 64, 222, 224

Botswana, 59

Bouazizi, Mohamed, 202

Boutros-Ghali, Boutros, 90

Brown, Lester, 88

Brundtland, Gro Harlem, 61

Brundtland Report. See *Our Common Future*

Brunei, 1, 94, 99, 155

Busan, Barry, 9

Cambodia, 1, 65, 69, 95, 132, 158, 165, 177, 193

Canada, 2, 39, 57, 193

carbon emissions, 73: carbon emissions policy, 173; emissions standards, 109. *See also* greenhouse gases

the Caribbean, 57

CCF. *See* Corporate Citizen Foundation

Centre for Non-Traditional Security Studies (NTS Centre), 34, 164–65, 212, 231

CERD. *See* Center for Research on the Epidemiology of Disasters

Chan, Margaret, 37

Chan Zuckerberg Initiative, 33, 34

Changi Regional HADR Coordination Center, 154

Charter4Change, 167–68

Chiang Mai Initiative, 9, 42

China, 1, 2, 5, 20, 23, 34, 119, 86, 97, 137, 175; and air pollution, 92–93, 109; Beijing, 206; Guangdong, 61, 182; and H1N1, 57; and H7N9, 67–68; Hebei, 109; and human trafficking, 120; and SARS, 62; securitizing SARS, 61–62; Shanghai, 216; Shanxi, 109; trilateral cooperation with Japan and South Korea, 75–76, 103; and the Uyghurs, 135

China Environmental Protection Foundation, 110

chronic diseases, 55, 58, 178

civil emergencies, 36

civil–military relations, 156, 167

civil society organizations, 11, 15, *32*, 33, 40–41, 81–82; and energy governance, 172; and environmental governance, 107–8; and H5N1 and HIV/AIDS governance, 81–82; and HADR governance, 158; and migration governance, 126–27. *See also* non-state actors

clean energy, 109, 179

climate change, 7, 39–40, 43, 85, 90–91, 96–97, 172–73, 224

Climate Change and Nuclear Energy, report, 173

Clinton, Bill, 59

Colombo Process, 137

COMMIT. *See* Coordinated Mekong Ministerial Initiative against Trafficking

communicable diseases. *See* infectious diseases

community-based organizations, 44

conflict resolution, 43

Consortium of Non-Traditional Security Studies in Asia, 44

Consultative Council on Overseas Filipino Workers, 127

containment, 5, 7, 24

Coordinated Mekong Ministerial Initiative Against Trafficking (COMMIT), 123, 124–25

corporate actors, 30–31, 232; transnational corporations, 41–42. *See also* private sector

Corporate Citizen Foundation (CCF), 162

Corporate Information Transparency Index, 109

corporate social responsibility, 32, 110, 129

Council for Security and Cooperation in the Asia Pacific (CSCAP), 24, 40, 46–47; Nuclear Energy Experts Group, 189–90

cross-border migration, 116

CSCAP. *See* Council for Security and Cooperation in the Asia Pacific

Dean, Michael, 216

Declaration of ASEAN Concord I, 151

Declaration of the 8th East Asia Summit on Food Security, 213

Declaration on Avian Influenza Prevention, Control and Response, 77

Declaration on the Conduct of Parties in the South China Sea, 18

Declaration on the Protection and Promotion of the Rights of Migrant Workers, 40, 123–24

DELSA. *See* Disaster Emergency Logistics System for ASEAN

development assistance for health, 75–76

Dirty Bankers (Greenpeace report), 106

Disaster Emergency Logistics System for ASEAN (DELSA), 149

disaster management, 143, 148, 153, 161, 232; recovery, 153, 160, 163; rehabilitation, 163; relief, 9, 24, 142, 143, 228, 234. *See also* humanitarian assistance and disaster relief (HADR)

disaster risk reduction, 148, 157

Djibouti, 202

domestic governance, 17

drugs, 19, 82, 132

Earth Summit. *See* UN Conference on Environment and Development

East Asia, 1; constructed region, 2–3; economic prospects, 1; geographical footprint, 2; multilateralism, 7; security outlook, 2, 4

East Asia Emergency Rice Reserve, 213

East Asia Summit, 2, 42, 63, 77, 187, 220

Economic Research Institute for ASEAN and East Asia, 213

economic security, 113, 121

ECPAT. *See* End Child Prostitution, Child Pornography and Trafficking of Children for Sexual Purposes

Emergency Center for Transboundary Animal Diseases, 75

emerging infectious diseases, 66–67

End Child Prostitution, Child Pornography and Trafficking of Children for Sexual Purposes (ECPAT), 44

environment: role of powerful functional actors, 97; securitization of, 89, 91

environmental security: and climate change, 90; definition, 88–89; and human security, 90–91; issues and challenges, 85–86, 92; stability and interstate relations, 95

environmental security governance: actors in, 97–98; in China, 109–11; defining a security referent, 95; local groups, 41, 107–8; and state actors, 98, 101. *See also* haze

environmental sustainability, 96, 97

epistemic communities: definition, 33; and HADR governance, 164–65; and policymaking, 34, 43; as research communities and institutes, 80; and security governance, 39, 64

equitable development, 54

Euro-Atlantic region, 27

European Union, 10, 27, 153, 188

faith-based organizations, 37, 38–39; definition, 33; and HADR, 49; and the security sector, 36. *See also* governors (security); Muhammadiyah; non-state actors

family reunification, 115, 134

FAO. *See* Food and Agriculture Organization

financial crisis, 3, 9, 14, 16, 201
Finland, 183
Finnemore, Martha, 4, 12
Food and Agriculture Organization
   (FAO), 73, 75, 196, 200, 211; FAO
   Food Price Index, 202
food security: challenges, 196–97;
   definition, 196, 204; securitization
   of, 197–203; and state actors, 219–20
food security governance: agenda,
   213–14; non-state actors, 211–13;
   regional frameworks, 203–11; state
   actors, 203–4
forced labor, 118, 122, 132
forced migration, 116–21. See also
   migration: irregular migration
Foreign NGO Management Law, 30
Forest Stewardship Council (FSC),
   107
Forrest, Andrew, 130
fossil fuel, 172–74, 174; uranium, 174
France, 183
Friends of Nature, 110
FSC. See Forest Stewardship Council
Fukushima Daiichi nuclear accident,
   171, 179–80, 181–84
Fukushima Nuclear Accident
   Independent Investigation
   Commission, 180
functional actors, 37, 97
Furuoka, Fumitaka, 103

Gavi. See Global Alliance for Vaccines
   and Immunization
Geospatial Information Agency,
   Indonesia (BIG), 104
gender, 32, 41, 119, 138
GF-TAD. See Global Framework for
   Progressive Control of
   Transboundary Animal Diseases
Ghana, 216

Global Alliance for Vaccines and
   Immunization (Gavi), 79
Global Framework for Progressive
   Control of Transboundary Animal
   Diseases (GF-TAD), 75
Global Fund to Fight AIDS,
   Tuberculosis and Malaria, 29, 79
global governance, 17, 18, 218;
   definition, 16
Global Influenza Surveillance and
   Response System, 64
Global Outbreak Alert and Response
   Network, 64
global warming, 9, 34, 89
globalization, 14, 31, 56
Goh Chok Tong, 62
Gore, Al, 59
governance, 4–5, 8, 17; definition, 15–16;
   enforcement, 18; institutional
   frameworks, 3; "state-plus" processes,
   220; state-led governance, 47;
   transnational regulation, 31, 32;
   versus government, 15
government, 15–16, 26
governmental agencies, 17, 37. See also
   state actors
governors (security), 4; consent,
   legitimacy, and sources of authority,
   38–39; definition, 12;
   intergovernmental networks and
   actors, 75; non-state actors and
   networks, 79–82; securitizing actors,
   37, 63–64
Grameen Bank, 30
grassroots organizations, 35, 39. See also
   non-state actors
Greater Mekong Subregion, 78, 99, 124,
   213
greenhouse gas, 172, 173, 174
Greenpeace, 30, 39, 97, 105–6, 179, 231
Guinea, 14

Haas, Peter, 24

Haass, Richard, 218

HADR. *See* humanitarian assistance and disaster relief

Hänggi, Heiner, 35, 36

haze, in Southeast Asia, 94, 98

haze governance: ASEAN level, 99–102; non-state actors, 105–11; state level, 103–5

haze monitoring system, 102

health: cooperation in Southeast Asia, 74; diplomacy, 80; expenditure, 65, 66; as a fundamental human right, 53–54; as integral part of human security, 54; universal health coverage, 61

health, securitization of, 58: HIV/AIDS, 58–59; infectious diseases, 63; SARS, 61–63

Health Action International Asia-Pacific, 81

Health Effects Institute, 93

health governance, 52; capacity, 73; definition, 61; and human security, 53–54; limitations, 73; at national level, 71; origins in East Asia, 52–53; at regional level, 73; and surveillance, 67

health insecurity: coordination and cooperation among different actors, 65–66; impact on East Asia, 59–60; lessons from the SARS outbreak, 71

health security, 57; and governance, 65; prioritization of, 61; and risk communications, 67; security governors, 75–82

HelpAge International, 158

Hewlett Packard Enterprise, 163

Highly Pathogenic Avian Influenza Task Force, 76

HIV/AIDS, 56–57, 60, 61; antiretroviral therapy, 69; dynamics in East Asia, 59; financial impact on East and Southeast Asian states, 56; governance of, 69; origins, 58

HSBC, 106

Human Development Report, 21

human resettlement, 54, 135

human rights abuses, 116, 170

Human Rights Watch, 133

human security: components of, 13; concept of, 21–22; and the environment, 90, 96; and food security, 198–99; framework, 21, 54; and HADR, 141; and health security, 53–54, 80; and migration, 121–22; non-state actors, 81; norm diffusion in East Asia, 225; and nuclear safety, 181

human trafficking: anti–human, 129; antitrafficking regimes, 125; criminalization of, 125–26, 225; definition and types of, 118; drug, 23, 122; in East Asia, 120

humanitarian actor, 135, 164, 231, 234

humanitarian aid, 140, 169

humanitarian assistance and disaster relief (HADR): emergency response, 147; government actors, 150–54; the HADR agenda, 142; issues and challenges, 165–68; regional mechanics in HADR governance, 146–50

humanitarian crises, 14, 111, 167, 169, 195

Hussein, Zeid Ra'ad al-, 139

Hyogo Framework for Action, 147, 226, 264

IAEA. *See* International Atomic Energy Agency

ICRC. *See* International Committee of the Red Cross

ILO. *See* International Labour Office

India, 2, 56, 137, 141, 201, 207

indigenous communities, 108

Indonesia, 1, 23, 56, 69, 86, 137, 176, 183; Aceh, 41, 135, 160; Batam, 47, 176; and H5N1 health crisis, 73; Kalimantan, 94; Riau, 95; and Rohingya refugees, 135; Sumatra, 94; transboundary haze and air pollution, 94–95, 99–101, 104

inequality, 31, 235

infectious diseases: Ebola, 14, 19–20, 24, 61; H1N1, swine flu, 55, 61, 66; H5N1, bird flu, 55, 60, 228; H7N9, avian influenza A, 73; malaria, 56, 61, 77; Middle East respiratory syndrome (MERS), 60; Nipah virus, 66; West Nile virus, 55. *See also* HIV/AIDS; severe acute respiratory syndrome (SARS); Zika virus

Institute of Defense and Strategic Studies, 36. *See also* Centre for Non-Traditional Security Studies

Institute of Public and Environmental Affairs, China, 110

intergovernmental organizations, *20*, 22, 63, 97, 226

Intergovernmental Panel on Climate Change, 198

Inter-Ministry Committee on Food Security, Singapore, 212

International Atomic Energy Agency (IAEA), 173, 176, 183, 186

International Campaign to Ban Landmines, 37

International Committee of the Red Cross (ICRC), 139, 147, 158

International Conference on Asian Food Security, 212

International Convention on the Protection of the Rights of All

Migrant Workers and Members of Their Families, 123

International Federation of Red Cross and Red Crescent Societies, 158

International Food Policy Research Institute, 216

International Health Regulations, 64

International Labour Office (ILO), 118

International Nuclear Security Education Network, 193

International Organization for Migration (IOM), 38, 115

Iraq, 202

Japan, 1, 2, 5, 13, 141, 153, 175, 193; trilateral cooperation with China and South Korea, 75–76, 103

Japan Atomic Energy Agency, 192

Japan Atomic Energy Commission, 192

Japan International Cooperation Agency, 73

Jordan, 202

Kalla, Jusuf, 95

Kan, Naoto, 144

Keohane, Robert, 6

Korea Nuclear Association for International Cooperation, 192

Korean peninsula, 4, 6, 93

Kranji Countryside Association, 216–17

labor migration, 115–16, 121, 134

Laos, 1, 69, 78, 79, 131, 158; the Hmong, 135

Latin America, 57

Le Luong Minh, H. E., 157

Lebanon, 202

liberal-institutionalism, 6–7

Liberia, 14
Lynas controversy, 184

Ma Ying-jeou, 181
MacArthur Foundation, 34
Makati Medical Center Foundation, 163
Malaysia, 1, 14, 46, 56, 69, 77, 127, 170, 176, 183; and Rohingya refugees, 131–36; and transboundary haze, 94, 98
Malaysian Physicians for Peace and Social Responsibility, 179
malnutrition, 21, 201, 216
marine ecosystems, 85
maritime disputes, 5, 43, 46
Maritime Environmental Protection Working Group, 46
market-based actors. *See* corporate actors
market regulation, 98
mass atrocity crimes, 3
Médecins Sans Frontières, 19, 33
media, 63; role in human trafficking, 130–31
Mekong Basin Disease Surveillance Project, 78
Mekong Delta, 86
Mekong Migration Network, 40
Mercy Malaysia, 158
Mercy Relief, 164, 233
Mexico City, 216
Meybatyan, Silva, 179
Middle East, 137, 202
Migrant Forum in Asia, 40
migrant workers. *See* labor migration
Migrant Workers and Overseas Filipinos Act, 41
Migrante International, 127
Migration Crisis Operational Framework, 137

migration: challenges, issues, and trends, 113–14, 125–26; definition, 115; irregular migration, 115, 116–17, 121–22, 134; mainstreaming migration into frameworks, 137; migrant protection, 137; mixed migration, 113, 117, 122; refugees in Southeast Asia, 119–21; regular migration, 115–16; securitization of, 121–23; threats in East Asia, 117–20
migration governance: challenges of, 113–14, 135–36; criminalization approach, 126; emerging issues, 137; non-state actors, 126–28; private sector, 129–30; protection approach, 116, 126–27, 128; role of the media, 130–31
migration regimes, 122–23; gaps and challenges in, 125–26
military-to-military coordination, 154, 230
Ministry of Environmental Protection, China, 109
Ministry of Health, China, 71
Ministry of Science and Technology, China, 71
modern slavery, 118, *119*, 120, 121, 130, 131
Muhammadiyah, 44, 49, 81, 233; and HADR, 160; role in combating avian influenza, 82
multilateralism, 7
multitrack processes, 42–45. *See also* Track 1; Track 1.5; Track 2; Track 3
Myanmar, 1, 56, 69, 131, 141, 153, 158; the Kachins, Shans, and Chins, 121; Mandalay, 149; Rakhine, 139; and Rohingya refugees, 131–32

NADI. *See* Network of ASEAN Defense and Security Institutions

Nansen Conference, 169
National Disaster Risk Reduction and
    Management Council, 31
National Nuclear Energy
    Agency of Indonesia (BATAN),
    176
National Secretariat for Social Action,
    159, 161
natural disasters: Cyclone Nargis, 141,
    146, 153, 222; Great East Japan
    Earthquake, 10, 141, 144; Indian
    Ocean tsunami, 10, 41, 141, 228;
    Mount Merapi volcanic eruption, 49;
    Nepal earthquake, 23, 232, 234;
    Sichuan earthquake, 23, 141, 229;
    Typhoon Bopha, 149; Typhoon
    Haiyan, 14, 21, 49, 146, 150
Nazeer, Nazia, 103
Nepal, 56, 128, 137
Network of ASEAN Defense and
    Security Institutions (NADI), 43,
    46–47, 156, 230
New Zealand, 2, 75, 155, 193
Nike, 37
noncombat operations, 234
noncommunicable diseases, 60, 61, 81
noninterference, 18, 136, 186
non-state actor, 26; definition and
    features, 28–31; legitimacy and
    authority, 27; in policy networks, 30;
    as security governors, 23–24, 39–42;
    types of, 30–35
non-traditional security (NTS), 13–15;
    definition, 13; framework, 96
non-traditional security (NTS)
    governance: definition, 18; in East
    Asia, 42–44; frameworks, 219,
    227–29; military actors, 233–34;
    non-state actors, 227, 230–32,
    223–24; process, 18–20; security
    actors, 20; in Southeast Asia, 221;

state actors, 26, 226–27;
    technological innovation, impact of,
    235
non-traditional security (NTS) threats,
    4–5; challenges and complexities,
    examples of, 14; future disruptors,
    234–35; impact and framing of,
    221–22; and international system, 220
North America, 1, 10
North Atlantic Treaty Organization
    (NATO), 27
North Korea, 2, 121, 191; North Korean
    regime, 4, 6
Northeast Asia, 1, 3, 42, 52, 192, 229;
    and air pollution, 103
NTS. See non-traditional security
NTS-Asia Consortium, 13, 164
NTS Centre. See Centre for Non-
    Traditional Security Studies
nuclear education, 194
nuclear energy governance, 171–72;
    concerns and challenges, 171,
    182–84; crisis management, disaster
    preparedness and response, 177, 185,
    195; effective coordination among
    multiple actors, 171; energy security,
    173; national legislative and
    regulatory frameworks, 185–86;
    non-state actors in Southeast Asia
    and beyond, 188–91; nuclear safety
    culture and human security, 184–85;
    state actors, 186–88; stakeholder
    engagement and participation, 171
nuclear energy: advantages of, 173–74;
    and energy security, 172;
    securitization of, 177–81; in
    Southeast Asia, 175–77, and state
    actors, 186–87
nuclear proliferation, 6, 220
nuclear safety, 24, 172, 181–83, 195;
    definition, 185

OCHA. *See* Office for the Coordination of Humanitarian Affairs

OECD. *See* Organization for Economic Cooperation and Development

Ong Keng Yong, 40, 144, 157

Organization for Economic Cooperation and Development (OECD), 93

Osa, Yukie, 159

Oslo Guidelines, 167

Ottawa Treaty, 37

Our Common Future (Brundtland Report), 89

Oxfam, 19, 158

Pakistan, 121, 137

pandemics, 5, 7, 23, 54, 60, 63, 219, 229

Paris Agreement, 10, 173

Participatory Disease Surveillance and Response project, 73

Peatland Restoration Agency, 104

PEPFAR. *See* President's Emergency Plan for AIDS Relief

Philippine Disaster Resilience Foundation, 162, 163

Philippine Migrants Rights Watch, 126

Philippine Migration Research Network, 126

Philippines, 1, 21, 41, 86, 126, 132, 137, 141, 234; Bataan Nuclear Power Plant, 176; Marawi, 169

Pitsuwan, Surin, 37, 44, 144

policy communities, 13, 222

policy network, definition of, 31

political security, 13, 52, 88

pollution, transboundary, 30, 98, 111, 229. *See also* air pollution

post-Cold War era, 8, 16, 22, 26, 85

poverty reduction, 38

President's Emergency Plan for AIDS Relief (PEPFAR), U.S., 59, 73

preventive diplomacy, 46

private actors. *See* non-state actors

private sector, 20, 35, 138; engagement with, 129–30; and food security, 216, 217; and HADR, 233; role in disaster management, 160–63

private security companies, military, 27, 32, 36, 39

protection (norm), 123–24, 127–28, 131, 132–34

public actors. *See* state actors

public health emergencies, 5, 10, 42, 55

Pulih Foundation, 41

quarantine, 15, 57, 64, 71, 224

Radanar Ayar Rural Development Association, 82

radiation exposure, 177–78, 184, 188

Radiation Monitoring and Emergency Response, project, 188

#REACHPhilippines, 161

realism, 6–7

receiving countries, 116, 122, 126, 222. *See also* migration

Refugee Convention. *See* UN Convention Relating to the Status of Refugees

refugees, 119–21; protection of, 133, 136, 137; refoulement, 136. *See also* migration governance; Rohingya refugee crisis

Regional Framework for Control and Eradication of Highly Pathogenic Avian Influenza, 76

Regional Haze Action Plan, 99

resilience, 143, 147, 164, 224, 235

Responsibility to Protect, 12, 19, 21, 37–38, 226, 241

Responsibility to Protect, The (report), 34

Rhodes, R. A. W., 235

Rice, Susan, 90
Rice Bowl Index, 212
Rockefeller Foundation, 33, 78
Rohingya refugee crisis, 131–34, 139–40
Roundtable on Sustainable Palm Oil
   (RSPO), 108, 231
RSIS. See S. Rajaratnam School of
   International Studies
RSPO. See Roundtable on Sustainable
   Palm Oil
Russia, 2, 171, 177

S. Rajaratnam School of International
   Studies (RSIS). See Centre for
   Non-Traditional Security Studies
Safer Future: Global Public Health Security
   in the 21st Century, A (World Health
   Report), 55
SAPA. See Solidarity for Asian People's
   Advocacy
SARS. See severe acute respiratory
   syndrome
Save the Children International, 30, 33,
   160
Scale Up, 107–8
SEARCA. See Southeast Asian Regional
   Center for Graduate Study and
   Research in Agriculture
Second Murdoch Commission, 207,
   213–14
securitization: definition of, 12; and
   NTS governance, 18–19, 39
securitizing actor, 37, 63–64, 179
securitizing audience, 246
security, definition of, 240
security actors, 7, 16, 20; definition, 4.
   See also governors (security);
   non-state actors; state actors; state
   security actors
security architecture, 17, 233; failure
   of, 26

Security Council Resolution 1308, 59
security governance: definition of, 27,
   96; dynamics of, 5; 45; in Europe, 27;
   key security concerns in Asia, 27–28;
   trends influencing the current state
   of, 8–9; unilateral actions and
   policies, 17, 229
security-related sector, 36
security sector reform, 22–23
security sector, 35–36
Sell, Susan, 4
Sendai Framework for Disaster Risk
   Reduction, 157
sending countries, 116, 126. See also
   migration
Senegal, 216
severe acute respiratory syndrome
   (SARS): and global health
   governance, 64; securitization of,
   61–63
sexual exploitation, 118, 120, 122
sexual violence, 120
Sheeran, Josette, 196
Shinawatra, Thaksin, 62
Sierra Leone, 14
Singapore, 1, 56, 63, 94, 99, 182, 193,
   201, 206; and transboundary haze,
   104, 112; and water security, 13;
   workers' rights and protection, 127;
   and Zika virus, 71
Singapore Civil Defence Force, 164
Snidal, Duncan, 31
social movements, 17, 20, 33, 34, 44
social protection, 79, 123–24, 203
Solidaritas Perempuan (Women's
   Solidarity) and Migrant Care,
   127
Solidarity for Asian People's Advocacy
   (SAPA), 48–49, 148–49
Somalia, 121
South China Sea, 2, 182

South Korea, 1, 2, 5, 93, 171, 175; and air pollution, 93; MERS, 56; trilateral cooperation with China and Japan, 75–76, 103

Southeast Asia Tobacco Control Alliance, 81

Southeast Asian Ministers of Education Organization, 80

Southeast Asian Regional Center for Graduate Study and Research in Agriculture (SEARCA), 212–13

sovereignty, 12–13, 21, 27, 30, 229, 233; and state actors, 38

Special ASEAN Summit on SARS, 62

Special Meeting on Irregular Migration in the Indian Ocean, 134

Sri Lanka, 121, 141

state actor: and multilevel governance, 17; role of, 22–23; and sovereign authority, 38; state security actors, 16–17, 22–23

state-centricity, 7, 11, 16, 21, 23, 25, 42, 221

state consent, 153, 166, 225, 229, 245

state legitimacy, 9, 202

State of the Environment Report, 92

state sovereignty, 226. See also Westphalian sovereignty

statelessness, 117

Strategic Plan of Action on Food Security in the ASEAN Region, 205–11, 210

sub-Saharan Africa, 118

Sustainable Development Goals, 86

Sweden, 183

Swing, William Lacy, 134

Syria, 21, 121

Taiwan, 181; Lungmen Nuclear Power Plant controversy, 181

Task Force on ASEAN Migrant Workers, 40

Temasek, 38

Tenaganita, 127, 133

TEPCO. See Tokyo Electric Power Company

territorial disputes, 2, 17, 219

terrorism, 2, 3, 7, 122

Thailand, 1, 23, 56, 63, 69, 131–32, 141, 201; the Karens, 121

Tokyo Electric Power Company (TEPCO), 180

Track 1, 43, 45, 189; definition of, 42

Track 1.5, 191, 192, 195; definition of, 43

Track 2, 45–47, 156, 188–91; definition of, 43

Track 3: and civil society actors, 43–44; definition of, 43

traditional security, 21, 22, 27, 39, 96

trafficking in persons, 118. See also human trafficking

Transboundary Haze Pollution Act, 104, 112

transit country, 115, 118, 136. See also migration

transnationality, as prominent feature of NTS issues, 14

transparency, 107, 159, 182, 230, 232

tropical diseases, 84

tropical medicine network, 80

Tunisia, 202

Tunisian Revolution, 202

Turnbull, Malcolm, 129

Ukraine, 177

UN Charter, 59

UN Conference on Environment and Development, 89

UN Conference on the Human Environment, 89

UN Convention Relating to the Status of Refugees, 132
UN Economic and Social Commission for Asia and the Pacific, 147
UN General Assembly, 3, 19, 139
UN Global Compact framework, 30
UN Guiding Principles on Internal Displacement, 169
UN Human Development Report, 90
UN Millennium Development Goals, 54, 97
UN Office for Disaster Risk Reduction, 156
UN Office for the Coordination of Humanitarian Affairs (OCHA), 141, 228
UN Office on Drugs and Crime, 125
UNDP. *See* United Nations Development Programme
UNEP. *See* United Nations Environment Programme
UNHCR. *See* United Nations High Commissioner for Refugees
United Filipinos, 41
United Kingdom, 19, 90, 166
United Nations Development Programme (UNDP), 21
United Nations Environment Programme (UNEP), 97, 257
United Nations High Commissioner for Refugees (UNHCR), 117
United States, 2, 5, 6, 59
urbanization, 54, 92, 197, 198, 214, *215*. *See also* agriculture

Vietnam, 1, 56, 63, 78; Hanoi, 216; and HIV/AIDS, 59; the Montagnards, 135
vulnerable communities, 114, 139, 152, 170, 222, and ASEAN, 169; and NGOs, 233

Walk Free Foundation, 130
Wen Jiabao, 62
West Africa, 24
Westphalian sovereignty, 50, 241. *See also* state sovereignty
WFP. *See* World Food Programme
WHO. *See* World Health Organization
Widodo, Joko, 129
Wolfers, Arnold, 12
World Agricultural Forum, 216
World Bank, 57, 79, 95
World Food Program (WTP), 147
World Health Organization (WHO), 19, 23, 54, 64, 75, 226; role in securitizing SARS, 61
World Humanitarian Summit, 168
World Order 2.0, 218
World Summit Meeting, 3
World Wide Fund for Nature (WWF), 30, 97, 105, 106–7, 108

Yao Wenlong, 144
Yergin, Daniel, 172
Yudhoyono, Susilo Bambang, 145

Zika virus, 57, 71
zoonoses, 57, 67